Networked Communities:
Strategies for
Digital Collaboration

Sylvie Albert
Laurentian University, Canada

Don Flournoy
Ohio University, USA

Rolland LeBrasseur
Laurentian University, Canada

 **INFORMATION SCIENCE REFERENCE**

Hershey · New York

Director of Editorial Content:	Kristin Klinger
Director of Production:	Jennifer Neidig
Managing Editor:	Jamie Snavely
Assistant Managing Editor:	Carole Coulson
Typesetter:	Jennifer Neidig
Cover Design:	Lisa Tosheff
Printed at:	Yurchak Printing Inc.

Published in the United States of America by
Information Science Reference (an imprint of IGI Global)
701 E. Chocolate Avenue, Suite 200
Hershey PA 17033
Tel: 717-533-8845
Fax: 717-533-8661
E-mail: cust@igi-global.com
Web site: http://www.igi-global.com/reference

and in the United Kingdom by
Information Science Reference (an imprint of IGI Global)
3 Henrietta Street
Covent Garden
London WC2E 8LU
Tel: 44 20 7240 0856
Fax: 44 20 7379 0609
Web site: http://www.eurospanbookstore.com

Library of Congress Cataloging-in-Publication Data

Networked communities : strategies for digital collaboration / Sylvie Albert, Don Flournoy, and Rolland LeBrasseur, editors.

   p. cm.

 Includes bibliographical references and index.

 Summary: "This book provides an understanding of best practices in building sustainable collaboration in intelligent community development"--Provided by publisher.

 ISBN 978-1-59904-771-3 (hardcover) -- ISBN 978-1-59904-773-7 (ebook)

 1. Information society. 2. Community leadership--Technological innovations. 3. Communication in politics. 4. Community development--Technological innovations. 5. Communication in economic development. 6. Computer networks--Social aspects. I. Albert, Sylvie. II. Flournoy, Don M. III. LeBrasseur, Rolland.

 HM851.N4764 2009

 307.1'402854678091724--dc22

2008030777

British Cataloguing in Publication Data
A Cataloguing in Publication record for this book is available from the British Library.

All work contributed to this book is original material. The views expressed in this book are those of the authors, but not necessarily of the publisher.

Table of Contents

Preface

PURPOSE OF THIS BOOK

Networked Communities: Strategies for Digital Collaboration focuses on communities that have—or want to have—digital broadband capability and are eager to make maximum use of that capability for their citizens. The stakes include increased economic development, organisational performance and improving quality of life. As communities undergo rapid change in the 21st century, their residents and workers are looking for ways to assure more positive outcomes. The authors provide success stories of community transformation that include elements of hope, and offer a framework for more active and informed development. Many communities are today connecting their local businesses and institutions into global broadband networks. This book suggests ways individuals, groups and organisations can contribute to the sustainability and well being of their communities while meeting their own needs.

The debate about the "how" and the "why" of networking communities has extended over many decades. In the late 1970s and early 1980s, there was much discussion in the United Nations and other international forums about a New World Information and Communications Order (NWICO) in which opportunities for easy exchange of information between and among all societies, both rich and poor, could be more equitably distributed using modern information and communication technologies. Under the auspices of UNESCO, Sean MacBride headed a multi-nation commission to consider recent developments in media and telecommunications in terms of their impact on national sovereignty, cultural identity and access to information. After a three-year study, MacBride and the commission released a much-discussed report through UNESCO Publishing (1980) entitled *Many Voices, One World*. It called for policy and structural solutions for democratizing communication flow and correcting imbalances in news coverage around the world. This debate helped to articulate and legitimize the idea of the basic human right to communicate.

In those early years, national governments were pressured to take action. The assumption was that only government could effect the kinds of changes needed to give all people a voice. Only governments had the authority to create infrastructure or had access to the resources that could make it possible for citizens to speak for themselves. In the new millennium, the New World Information and Communications Order debate is very much in evidence, but it now takes place under the conceptual umbrella of the Information Society, and more recently, the Network Society. A different set of assumptions has emerged about how to create a level playing field. National governments are still involved in this process, but more often as minor players. The locus of attention has shifted to non-governmental organisations, corporations and civil society. The focus of the renewed NWICO debate is on regions and communities and those multi-sector interest groups that embrace change at the community level. Today, greatest attention is given to the transformational power of the broadband Internet and the millions of new information and communication applications that are making change inevitable in local and global policy, infrastructure and practise.

This book is about communities making a conscious effort to ensure that they are not left behind in the new digital age, that they are positioned to join other "networked communities" in a new era of prosperity. Otherwise known as "wired communities", "smart communities", or "broadband communities", these geographic units can range in size from small to very large. For example, Pirai in Brazil has a population of 23,000, Evora in Portugal has 57,000, Waterloo in Canada has 115,000, whereas Taipei in Taiwan is approaching 3 million. The common denominator is that these communities have taken steps to make intelligent use of information and communication technologies (ICTs).

These communities have also broadcasted their accomplishments via the annual conferences of the Intelligent Community Forum (ICF), which take place in New York City. As consultants to the ICF, the authors have come to see the value in sharing their stories more broadly. In this book, the reader will learn how these and similar towns, cities and regions have reached a stage of digital development sufficient to be identified as an intelligent or "networked community".

INTENDED AUDIENCE OF THIS BOOK

The target readership of this book includes community leaders and stakeholders who are pondering the following question: "How can we achieve smart growth, promote green development, assure digital inclusion, build more transparent government, stimulate innovation, generate jobs, educate and retain talent, and provide a future for our community over the long term?" This book provides an outline of an answer by discussing how learning about and becoming a networked community lead to a positive response to that question.

Our intended readership consists of individuals who value collective action today to assure the future well being of the communities in which they live and work. Users of this material can come from the public, private or not-for-profit sectors; they can be elected or un-elected, paid or unpaid, and can represent any walk of life. The main focus is on elected officials, such as mayors, county commissioners and township trustees, and will include civil servants, such as directors of planning and economic development. That being said, just as important are the interested representatives of local business enterprises, the chairs of local non-profit organisations and institutions of health and education, libraries and museums, and the academic community.

An underlying assumption of this book is that there are people in every community who care enough to inform themselves—either out of fear of impending disasters or promise of better futures—about opportunities for community renewal, and will be willing to collaborate with others to work for the common good. The authors believe that these people are in search of a unique vision of what their community can become in the future. Whether they are elected or self-appointed, these people are the stewards of the community; they are willing to spend time and energy doing something that is very difficult but could have major benefits for future generations.

While community leaders are the primary audience, the content of this book should also appeal to members of academia who are interested in what practitioners are doing to ensure their success. Because communities are complex social entities, many fields of study have a stake in understanding them, notably public management and administration, telecommunications and media, and social studies. The authors selectively draw on the scholarly literature, aiming for a balance between practical examples and stories of community efforts and accomplishments, and research and theory that help to explain the stories that are told.

The authors have shared their understanding of the digital challenges that 21st century communities are facing. Meeting these digital challenges inevitably involves investing in broadband capability, training new types of workers and developing applications that meet a new set of community needs and expectations. This book describes the contexts that have set selected communities on this path, the specific strategies they pursued and the outcomes they experienced.

The community leaders that are targeted are more likely to act on, rather than react to, challenges. They are likely to be guided by an intimate knowledge of the conditions of their communities, to spend time analyzing problems, talking and consulting with others, and looking beyond for models that might be adapted to local needs and ways. A change management framework introduced in this book will help community leaders understand how digital community transformation takes place and how they can be more effective in bringing it about. These leaders can positively influence community development. This book can assist them in developing an appropriate mindset, a vision of the networked community and a specific set of strategies that will best serve their local interest.

Best Practise for Community Leaders

Think tanks and theoreticians have pointed to the global changes leading to knowledge-based economies and networked societies. Much less attention has been given to how these changes have influenced community structures and people at the local level. These futurists would likely be surprised to learn about the self-selected communities operating in networks that have quietly introduced a new dimension to the 1980s New World and Information Order.

On their own initiative, without waiting for definitive international government solutions, sometimes without the infrastructure support of transnational telecommunications corporations, communities have exercised their human right to communicate using the broadband Internet. The Internet allows them to get more of their needs met via the local-global applications of e-business, e-government, e-learning, e-health and practically e-everything else. The age of "many voices, one world" has arrived without fanfare.

This book attempts to put into perspective two sources of understanding: the conceptual and the practical. There is an academic literature from which the authors draw historical perspective, thoughtful analysis and contextual insights. There is also an experimental lab and idea incubator that is putting theory and historical judgment to the "test of reality". Elements of best practise have emerged out of the struggles of communities searching for a sustainable future, asserting their will to innovate, grow and change.

One of the key academic contributions of this book is to re-work a change management framework that can be used by community practitioners. This is a theoretical approach proposed by Professor Andrew Pettigrew, currently dean of the Faculty of Management at the University of Bath, England. This framework was the cornerstone of the prolific Centre for Strategic Management and Change, situated at the University of Warwick, of which Professor Pettigrew was the director. For a decade, Professor Pettigrew led major studies on the private and public sectors. The framework is simple and flexible, and helps to achieve clarity of mind when studying such complex and dynamic social phenomena as exist in local communities. The framework is described in Chapter 1.

The examples of best practise in this book are taken primarily from the applications submitted for the ICF Intelligent Community Award of the Year. Some background information on the ICF, a non-profit think tank and promoter of the broadband economy in local communities throughout the world, will help the reader to appreciate the value of these applications. The ICF aims to:

- Identify and explain the emergence of the broadband economy and its impact at the local level

- Research and share best practises by communities in adapting to the changing economic environment and positioning their citizens and businesses to prosper

- Celebrate the achievements of communities that have overcome challenges to claim a place in the economy of the 21st century (www.intelligentcommunity. org)

Through its activities and award programs, ICF creates a network of leaders in broadband applications at the community level. The Intelligent Community Forum was founded in 2003 by the board of directors of the World Teleport Association (WTA), an international trade association of teleports and related providers of broadband satellite services around the world. The original intention of the forum was to better integrate telecommunication facilities within communities as a means of supporting economic development and business opportunities via satellite.

The first true "intelligent communities event", which linked the emerging telecommunications revolution and the fledgling Internet to economic development, was held in Toronto, Canada, in 1995. This event, called *Smart95*, was developed by Toronto City official and ICF co-founder John Jung. For the first time, the telecommunications industry and the world of urban planners, political policy makers and economic development officials gathered under one roof to examine the impact of telecommunications on communities and economies.

In 2002-2003, Louis Zacharilla and Robert Bell joined Jung in establishing the Intelligent Community Forum with offices at the New York Information Technology Center in Lower Manhattan. ICF held its first "Building the Broadband Economy" conference in 2004.

The Intelligent Community of the Year is selected in the final stage of a 10-month award process that begins with selection of the Smart 21 Communities in November of the prior year. Each participating community must demonstrate, by completing a structured application form, that its strategy has produced measurable positive results. This form requires the responding community to give both qualitative and quantitative information on a number of topics, including its overall strategy; key people and organisations involved; the planning and collaboration involved; the connectivity and applications achieved; the digital users and knowledge workforce; job creation; digital involvement or democracy; and the marketing and economic development undertaken. While these applications are self-promoting, their contents are verified by knowledgeable members of the ICF and their extensive professional networks.

Guiding Methodology

The authors have been active participants in ICF activities since shortly after its founding. In recent years, the authors have served as correspondents, advisors and jurists in all stages of the community nomination and selection process. While this book is not a product of ICF, the conference venue provides a foundation for the synthesis of practical and academic knowledge that reflects both past and future trends. By sharing more broadly the stories and accomplishments of achieving communities, others will be able to better position themselves for future success. By means of *Networked Communities: Strategies of Digital Collaboration*, community leaders now have a way of envisioning what their communities might become and use this information to aid in their transformation.

Pettigrew's change management framework, which the authors have adapted, assumes it is possible for leaders of a given community to learn from the experiences of other communities. The authors have aimed for a better understanding of what happens when communities are networked. They have avoided any attempt to predict their development in a deterministic fashion. Community members transform their own communities according to their own priorities. The outcomes are often tentative, depending on circumstances. Because propositions about networked communities are not yet well developed, the authors allowed key concepts to emerge as they worked through the ICF archives, the published literature, the interviews and the conversations held with community leaders over the years.

The ICF communities constitute a purposive sample that we have used to illustrate important aspects of becoming a networked community. Triangulation was used in that the archival records were tested and one community compared to another over time, against the knowledge and experience of the authors. Coherence was sought through author discussions and sharing the scholarly literature of our diverse academic fields. In considering past and future trends, we sought a thread of continuity, in keeping with the importance of the global context with the New World Information and Communications Order extending into the 21st century, and the local context through the change management framework as applied to the purposes and dynamics of local communities.

The authors gave attention to the top seven communities of 2005-2008 because the documentation is considered of good quality and of sufficient detail. The ICF cases have the limitations of self-promotion as each community attempts to present a persuasive argument for becoming the winner of the award. On the other hand, the independent panels that ICF uses to assess applications help to validate the documentation provided by each community. Whereas Professor Pettigrew recommends comprehensive cases as the appropriate data collection for investigating change management, the authors are of the opinion that the stories contained in the ICF files serve our purpose. Those files, and the in-person presentations and discussions at the annual conferences, were often supplemented and confirmed by interview material and telephone calls. The authors placed no constraint on themselves in bringing in relevant cases from the outside. In the end, our approach has been to take what is best of each community story with the aim of presenting "best practises" in digital community development.

With this book in hand, community leaders and stakeholders, guided by the experiences of networked communities, will more easily create a transformational vision for their own communities. The authors wish and hope for this outcome.

Exhibit A. Overview model

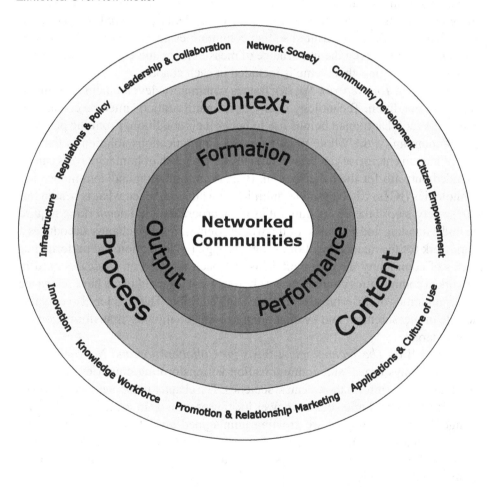

OVERVIEW OF THE CHAPTERS

This book is composed of eleven chapters that give guidance to local leaders whose ambition is to position their communities squarely within the Network Society. The Network Society is both a theoretical construct and an emerging reality in which communities use digital technologies and networks to create opportunities at the local level. The guidance given and the experience shared in this book relate to the transformational changes already being demonstrated in model communities resulting from advanced computing and telecommunication systems, regulation and public policy reform, and a new generation of knowledge workers who are creating applications and innovations of unprecedented variety and power. Community case studies and examples are used to illustrate the ways transformational leaders are emerging, citizens are being empowered, projects are being promoted and marketed, and outcomes are being measured so that communities are better able to compete, grow and prosper. Given the importance of measurement and evaluation for effective change strategies, this theme is included in each chapter.

Chapter I on *The Network Society* frames community development in terms of the human condition. Technology in any of its manifestations must be considered merely the tool that human beings use to better their condition. From the perspective of community, the whole point of a telecommunications solution is that the pace of human enterprise can be accelerated and the reach of human players can be extended outward for the benefit of all. Because information and communication technologies (ICTs) can be used to diminish as well as enhance what is best in human society, steps taken by communities to incorporate digital networking require the understanding and vigilance of the whole community. The chapter introduces a framework for the management of change through the formation and performance phases of community development. This approach is based on strategies used in networked communities around the world, strategies that are likely to have relevance for communities of differing size, culture and condition. The chapter also explains the role of measurement and evaluation in keeping community transformation efforts on target.

Chapter II on *The Technological Basis for Collaboration and Networking* describes the ways broadband communication is transforming countries as well as communities into information-centric societies. The chapter illustrates how telecommunications technologies that empower local users can spur social and economic change. Such technologies are creating unimagined opportunities at individual, organisational and collective levels of community and are shaping their futures. Also noted are the adverse and dysfunctional effects that can accompany these technological changes.

In Chapter III on *Regulation and Policy Reforms*, some of the ways that governments are fostering—but can also be hindering—the development of networked communities are described. Since both public and private sector participation is needed to create the networked community, local, state, and national governments should understand that they must be full partners if economic prosperity and a higher quality of life are to be achieved. Although openness brought about by easy connectivity to the global Internet can sometimes be painful, as in dealing with unacceptable influences and content, some level of participation and cooperation is required for communities to participate in the Network Society.

Chapter IV on *Knowledge Workforce* provides the work-related context for the networked community. Both locally and globally, the cutting edge of the labour market includes jobs that require proficiency in the management and use of broadband networks and their related applications. Individuals with digital skills, training and experience will be much needed participants in the radical restructuring of work and life that takes place in networked communities. Under the right circumstances, such ICT-enabled personnel will be a key asset in making significant contributions to the development of these communities. A skill supply strategy ensures that IT skills are available when needed to support community development.

Chapter V on *Creating Applications and a Culture of Use* discusses actual case studies of communities using broadband communication networks to produce jobs, stimulate their local and regional economies and reposition for a more positive future. The interconnected technologies enable local citizens to collaborate with others to do things they would never have thought of before, including taking political action and developing new products and services. The international examples illustrate the ways the Internet has created global communities of interest that reach beyond national boundaries, allowing local entrepreneurs to search out new business prospects, permitting residents to go to school online, and encouraging users to participate in decision-making and join with others as stewards of their societies. Participating in the virtual marketplace and in the new global workforce has led to the creation of many next-generation applications.

Chapter VI on *Innovation—Creating Ideas* makes the point that, in the ideal networked community, innovation is a shared value. When communities think seriously about their futures, they come to accept change as inevitable and look to all citizens as potential contributors. A favourable environment for innovation does not happen automatically; it has to be created repeatedly. Positive factors include promoting incremental successes, resource sharing and tackling directly the sources of community resistance. Developing a culture of innovation is possible wherever education is encouraged, work and learning are integrated and made meaningful, and experimentation and risk are encouraged.

Chapter VII on *Strategies for Community Development* identifies the patterns of action that networked communities are employing to transform themselves. The authors have found that a culture of familiarity and daily use must emerge before a community can make maximum use of the broadband capabilities available. Adaptation to digital practise is a complex process that takes time. The strategies that seem to work best are those adopted by local players pooling local resources while reaching outside for global partners and input. In the Network Society, collaborators can come from almost anywhere in the world. Thus, a community with imagination and initiative has the means to create its own opportunities when it has taken the time to evaluate its strengths and devise plans to take advantage of its core capabilities.

In Chapter VIII titled *Citizen Empowerment and Participation,* the authors note how linking computers and telecommunications has led to the democratization of production, enabling ordinary citizens to market and distribute their own created products and services. The Internet has greatly stimulated the supply of goods and services globally, thereby increasing demand for local products. The broadband Internet has made it much easier for community members go online to form social and business partnerships to accomplish things they couldn't have imagined before. Thus, those who know how to do this can get more of their needs met, faster, more effectively. Local people become part of a larger workforce. Unfortunately, digital exclusion and limited access persist, keeping many citizens of the world from fully participating.

In Chapter IX on *Leadership and Collaboration,* community transformation is described as a process that involves vision and consensus building, goal setting, shared leadership and broad implementation. Community organisations, businesses, government agencies and the general public are all necessary participants for rebuilding communities. Those strategies that seem to work best involve shared leadership, in which the entire community collaborates to manage change. No one pattern of leadership applies to all communities. Working in teams is seen as an effective way of pooling talent and effort to implement networked community goals.

Chapter X on *Promotion and Relationship Marketing* describes how networked communities effectively promote and market themselves. Quality of community living depends on the quality of non-commercial as well as commercial relationships, relationships among individuals, organisations and government bodies. The authors find that global alliances increasingly enter into the mix of partnerships. Promoting and marketing a community require both transactional and relationship marketing, but the latter is the better framework for building sustainable communities. Through long-term relationships, personal and community investment take place.

In Chapter XI, *Conclusion,* the authors highlight the key points addressed in the book and share important insights. The core messages of the preceding ten chapters are summarized to help the readers digest the entire content of the book. Community leaders are left with the task of crafting strategies to transform their own towns, cities and regions into networked communities.

Dr. Sylvie Albert
Faculty of Management, Laurentian University
President, Planned Approach Inc.

Don Flournoy
Professor, School of Telecommunications, Ohio University

Rolland LeBrasseur
Professor, Faculty of Management, Laurentian University

August 2008

Chapter I
The Network Society

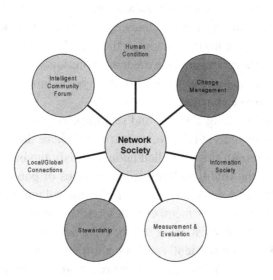

"In this early 21st century we are at the crossroads of the development of the network society.... The human potential embedded in new communication and technologies, in networking, in the new forms of social organization and cultural invention, is truly extraordinary." Manuel Castells (2006, p. 20)

Overview: This book emphasizes the centrality of the human condition—those things that make individuals and communities uniquely human—in our vision of the networked community. It also emphasizes that, to achieve their goals, communities must pay attention to the measurement and evaluation of multiple dimensions. The topics covered in Chapter I include:

*   The nature of the Network Society;
*   Communities on the front line of the Network Society;
*   The change management framework that guides each chapter of this book;
*   The Intelligent Communities Forum (ICF) and its participating institutions;
*   Evaluation and measurement as a strategy—measuring with purpose.

THE NETWORK SOCIETY AND THE HUMAN CONDITION

Key Concept: *The Network Society is a reality, but its effects are felt unevenly across the world. Each community is challenged to adapt so that its members can benefit from global membership in the network community.*

The classic conundrum of "the human condition" has been on the minds of the three authors throughout the writing of this book. The human condition refers to the tension that exists between who we are and who we could become, the ongoing struggle between human needs and human aspirations.

Basic individual needs include sustenance, activity, companionship and the enjoyment of leisure; these needs encourage the individual to seek stability and routines. In contrast, aspirations involve dreams, invention and exploration, which stimulate the individual to go beyond the current physical limits of his or her existence, to perpetually make changes.

These two forces—seeking stability and seeking change—are also present in the communities where individuals live collectively, where they work, play, rest and worship. Such communities are called upon to satisfy the basic needs of their members by offering the traditional municipal services of good roads and sidewalks, drinking water and sewage services, traffic control and police protection. To satisfy the aspirations of their members, these same communities are expected to offer increasingly more sophisticated services like daycare, training and education, challenging jobs, entertainment, and opportunities for self-expression. These individual and communal tensions are forever present and are part of a successful adaptation to the social and physical environment.

The arrival of the Network Society, in which everyone is connected to everyone else, puts stress on the human condition in multiple ways. For example, the easy formation and dissolution of virtual communities of individuals and groups connected electronically is inherently disruptive to a local community in which continuity is important. While this innovation in human communication easily erases the barriers of time and distance, and encourages both individuals and communities to imagine new visions of what is humanly attainable, it can also lead to situations that are socially undesirable. Our fascination with technology and its promotion as life enhancing can lead us to neglect dealing with the everyday world in which we live.

Human needs remind us that we are corporal and social in nature; we need to sleep, eat and drink, but we also need to play, laugh and dream. Information and knowledge can help us attain some—though not all—of these aspirations by extending the scope of social and economic exchange. Communication technologies can clearly connect us to larger networks of relationships, but two important questions arise. How can our communities ensure that the potential benefits of connectivity are within reach of our diverse membership, so we can each choose for ourselves which projects we want to undertake? How can our communities tap the creative and innovative potential of our people and organisations so we have more control over the directions we want to pursue?

Manuel Castells, a prolific writer and respected authority on digital developments, has defined the Network Society as a social structure based on networks operated by information and communication technologies (ICTs). These ICTs generate, process and distribute information on the basis of the knowledge accumulated in the nodes of the networks (Castells, 2006, p. 7). Nodes are points of intersection in the lines of communication that constitute the networks, and these networks evolve by adding or removing nodes to help attain the goals of the network participants. Castells argues that networks do not represent a new form of social organisation, but with the assistance of ICTs, participants can now undertake and coordinate large projects that previously could only be done by large vertical organisations with a strong central authority (p. 4). In essence, the Network Society is an advanced social structure making use of ICTs to gain greater openness, adaptability and flexibility for itself. Despite Castells' optimistic view of the Network Society, he encouraged policy makers to reflect before acting: "…the key question is how to proceed to maximize the changes for fulfilling the collective and individual projects that express social needs and values under the new structural conditions" (p. 16).

In previous works, Castells (1996, 1997, 1998) summarized and systematized much of the past and current thought on the Network Society. He concluded that ICTs have produced a Network Society in which organisations and individuals are beneficiaries of the electronic networks in that such networks help to develop and disseminate knowledge and information, and stimulate innovation. Mobilising knowledge and information has become more important than mobilising physical resources. Castells warns, however, that these changes are accompanied by growing wealth disparities, social fragmentation and dislocation.

An important component of the Network Society is the knowledge-based economy in which knowledge and other intangible assets have become the most important productive factor (Mandeville, 2005). Intangible assets include intellectual property, human and social capital, information economics, brand names, customer databases, core competencies, and business relationships. In modern communal society, such assets have to be managed. David Rooney and colleagues remind us that knowledge management involves more than information systems and processes: "There are much deeper and more fundamental social, cultural and communication processes that condition knowledge creation and use, and that predispose groups to different levels and kinds of outcomes in quality of life, learning, creativity and innovation" "(Rooney, Hearn & Ninan, 2005, p. 1). Some of the dangers that Castells has identified come from simplistic use of technology that over-emphasizes the technical aspects and under-emphasizes the human dimension.

Castells and followers have tended to view global forces as dominant, with nation states and regional bodies serving as powerful players through their legislative and regulatory powers and public sectors (Castells & Cardoso, 2006). Our own perspective is that the ultimate decisions concerning how networked communities evolve will be tied not just to technology and economy, but also to social well being and basic community values. In focusing on the importance of physical community to the human condition, our book brings the investigation of the Network Society to the community level.

The community level is where the effects of the Network Society are most readily seen. In using modern technologies to improve their political, economic and social standing, communities play out the scenario Castells describes. Communities as diverse as the town of Evora, a UNESCO heritage site in rural Portugal, and Mitaka, a suburb of Tokyo that is home to 75% of the world's anime cartoon production, can be observed literally transforming themselves using broadband telecommunications and community-specific ICT applications. Ideas linked to the digital revolution and the presumed power of digital networking are driving discussions in communities across multiple societies about how they too might obtain social and economic benefits from the new ICTs, while ensuring that there is a minimal negative effect on the human qualities that they hold dear.

Ursula Franklin, a respected Canadian physicist with an active interest in community issues, speaks of "the real world of technology" through which individuals, families and communities are able to appreciate a better quality of life (Franklin, 1999). In the real world, technology, including ICTs, can enhance quality of life or make life more difficult. Enlightened citizens and community leaders are urged to pay attention to the introduction of new technology to ensure that it benefits real people going about their daily lives.

LIVING IN THE NETWORK SOCIETY

Basic to all human societies is the presumption that they are location-based. While individuals and groups can move from place to place, they can be in only one place at a time. What the telecommunications industry has done is free human society to move about in virtual space, to be present—and to have its presence felt—in other places without actually being physically present. Using electronic communications, human societies can reach beyond physical space for their information, for their education, for their commerce, for their very identities. In very important ways, the advent of telecommunications is tantamount to liberation for it implies a freedom of virtual movement that may also be an essential condition of freedom of thought and expression.

In human history, the constraints of time and speed on society became competitiveness factors that influenced the success and failure of individual and collective enterprise. Information and communication technologies now allow the human community to reach into the past for archival knowledge and to reach into the future to make plans for what has not yet happened. Communication networks, along with the ICT tools of modern societies, are the outward expressions of society's aspirations to learn about others, to engage in trade and to collaborate at a distance. Such technologies save time, which can also mean saving money, improving efficiency and finding time to do other things, like joining with colleagues in community-building.

The implementation of modern communications networks and the availability of more sophisticated user terminals have also greatly extended our senses of sight and hearing; what we can see and listen to in any given day using the electronic media has multiplied many times over. The public response to iPods and iPhones and YouTube and Google Earth suggests the extent to which these tools are useful to us. Online services such as those offered by Amazon.com, MapQuest and Netflix allow the affluent, the knowledgeable and the skilled among us to search out our special preferences for reading and viewing and listening and to download them directly to where we are. Not everyone is in a position to participate, but the reason those services have emerged is that they respond to a basic human desire for convenience and immediate gratification.

In the news business, reporting on events that happened a month or a minute ago, in near and distant locations, can now be brought directly to our computers and handheld devices with no greater effort to the user than holding a mouse and touching a button. In competition with established providers, ordinary citizens in communities all over the world are sharing their own video versions of the news by posting their footage on the Internet. Today, it is not unusual for user-generated music and videos to attract more attention than the latest releases of the record labels and movie studios. Even the audio and video programming of non-profit organisations, government agencies and politicians running for office has a greater chance of reaching targeted audiences, a reality of considerable interest to community leaders.

Human beings characteristically want to be in touch with friends and family, maintaining e-mail and cell phone contact with those abroad as well as those right in the neighbourhood, at school or at the office. The modern-thinking societies of succeeding eras have developed telegraph, telephone, radio, television, cable, wireless, satellite, and the Internet to add immediacy, quantity, complexity, reach—and the factor of human presence—to the capabilities of communications instruments.

Such inclinations and innovations spill over into businesses and communities, so that marketers can sell to people they have never met, and community managers can seek advice from colleagues in places they have never been. To some degree, using these tools and learning from the interaction influences the openness of the marketer and the community manager to new ideas. Not surprisingly, these same tools when used by citizens can help them envision the future they would desire for their own communities and can assist them in linking up with others to make that future a reality.

The history of humankind demonstrates that technology is best understood in its social context and as part of humanity's search for meaning. This is an idea extensively developed by the technology historian Lewis Mumford (1967, 1970). People use ICTs for specific reasons, like "sharing the moment", when young people walking down the street chat with their friends on their mobile phones, or like "being the expert presenters" by using PowerPoint and short audio or video clips to impress their audiences. Technology is created for specific societal reasons, like "North America's love affair with the car" that involves gadgets like GPS (Global Positioning System) using the services of a satellite when a good paper map and a brain would do just as well. Arnold (2007) argued that technology provides new frames of reference. A community network may do more than fill some of the gaps between the needs and desires of its members; it may change their views on the needs themselves and how best to satisfy them. Given that people will use new technologies in a variety of ways, some predictable and others not, it behooves community leaders to pause and reflect. Under what conditions does technology become a positive force in a community? How does a community encourage these conditions while avoiding the negatives that technology can bring?

COMMUNITY WISDOM

The networks within a community will incorporate specific technologies and applications that are considered useful, but communities may give little thought to the effect that networks will have on peoples' everyday lives. In this spirit, Ursula Franklin (1999) identified three types of technology:

- Prescriptive—technology that simplifies tasks and mandates user compliance. Most of the technology in the workplace and everyday life oblige the user to work more efficiently in a standardized manner.
- Holistic—technology that is user-centered and allows the user to complete whole tasks.
- Redemptive—technology that minimizes damage or crisis

If digital networks and technologies are to be acquired and used for community transformation, time and effort must be given to serious reflection before decisions are made about infrastructure and applications. In practise, this means that community leaders must draw not only on "best practises" but on the wisdom that is grounded in their day-to-day experience, cooperative activity and traditions based on values that enhance peoples' lives (McKenna, 2005). Adapting a list offered by Ursula Franklin, we offer the following questions for reflection:

- Does the network promote sustainability for the community?
- Does it promote accessibility for all members of the community?
- Does it promote real dialogue or reciprocity?
- Does it promote benefits for all members of the community?
- Does it favour people over machines?
- Does the new ICT create costs that are avoidable or unmanageable?
- Is conservation favoured over waste?
- Is the reversible favoured over the irreversible?
- Does the network support creativity and innovation?

Sunderland, UK, is a positive illustration of a community that has demonstrated how transformation is possible using digital networks and community cooperation. Sunderland is the largest city in the northeast of England. According to the Intelligent Community Forum, "Sunderland has quite literally risen from the ashes of the Industrial Age to create a globally competitive city prospering in the Broadband Economy. This transformation was due to neither luck nor location, but to visionary leadership, good planning and unrelenting commitment." It reduced unemployment from 22% of the working population to 4% by moving from a shipbuilding and coal industrial base to a knowledge economy based on "telematics", the union of telecommunications and computers (Archives of the ICF, 2006).

Similarly, the U.S. city of Spokane, Washington, once a railroad town reliant on natural resources, has become the "terabyte triangle", with a downtown that has the largest density of broadband capability in the country consisting of fiber optic, xDSL and cable modem services. "Public-sector investment included Spokane's Educational Metropolitan Area Network, a gigabit Ethernet connection to all classrooms in more than 53 schools and colleges; an Inland Northwest Community Access Network that offers Internet access, training and social service resources to the economically disadvantaged; and a state-funded rural fiber network deployed by Inland Northwest Health Services connecting Spokane's health care community with the region" (Archives of the ICF, 2004).

In Tianjin, China, a major push on broadband connectivity was accompanied by rapid networked user growth, from 20,000 to 2.7 million Internet users in two years. Tianjin is an industrial and port city of 11 million people in northern China near the capital of Beijing. According to the Intelligent Community Forum, "the municipal government set out a strategy for broadband deployment in its 10th five-year plan. Collaborating with telecom carriers, cable TV companies and equipment manufacturers, the city has deployed 19,000 km (11,800 miles) of optical fiber providing the backbone for a broadband wireless network that blankets the entire city" (Archives of the ICF, 2005).

The above examples demonstrate why community leaders must craft a response to the Network Society, finding solutions that are appropriate to the local economic and social circumstances. In doing so, they can better serve their local population, including individuals, groups and organisations, in terms of their needs, wants and aspirations.

DEFINING NETWORKED COMMUNITIES

Key Concept: *Networked communities have a favoured position in the Network Society. Whether they are called "digital" or "intelligent" or "networked", these communities are making a conscious effort to understand and engage in a world that is increasingly connected.*

The networked community cannot be precisely defined. Communities differ; there is no one solution, no prescription or packaged answer that will serve all communities looking to restore health, re-invent themselves and better serve their members. In general, the idea is to work smarter using high-speed telecommunications infrastructures and clever software to achieve social and economic development goals. The terms "wired community", "broadband community", "smart community", "digital community", "intelligent community", and "community network" are today often used interchangeably. The common element is that communities can now be interconnected, internally and externally, both electronically and socially, and that community leaders can now think seriously about things they could never have done before. In this book, the networked community has a physical presence in space and time, and people live there on a daily basis, but all their members are virtually connected to everyone else. In the 21st century, the common assumption is that the social and economic well being of communities is very much tied to networking.

The Canadian Federal Government via its Industry Canada (2002b) Web site observes that "smart communities" result when local leaders and stakeholders form alliances and partnerships to come up with innovative ways to extract new economic and social value from electronic networks and the public Internet. The Canadian definition can be matched with definitions provided by several authors who use such terms as smart community network, virtual community and community informatics. All agree that such community initiatives include the design and implementation of interconnecting networks and applications capable of advancing community objectives faster with greater social participation. User-centered technologies and community-building applications are characteristic of networked communities.

The term "community informatics" suggests ways information and communication technologies are used to help communities achieve their social, economic, political and cultural goals (Keenan & Trotter, 1999). Fundamental to success is public access to shared telecommunication networks. Without universal access, the processes of meaningful civic education and engagement are greatly hindered. Access to technological networks is considered key to public involvement in decision-making, since these networks are ready sources of information. Effective community informatics depend upon a) the physical infrastructure made available to individuals and organisations, b) the content and applications made available on their networks, and c) the ability of citizens to use the technology and the information.

A "virtual community" refers to the ability of Internet users to complete tasks in an online environment, eliminating some of the traditional time and distance barriers and helping to unite people of common interest who are physically separated (Malhotra, Gosain & Hars, 1997). This term applies to communities of relationship or transaction or fantasy that go on within any established or emerging community of like-minded people. The same conceptual and contractual agreements that occur in the physical world occur in the virtual world, and have similar power over economic and social development within the local communities in which people operate in that domain.

An "intelligent community" is described as one "that views communications bandwidth as the new essential utility, as vital to economic growth and public welfare as clean water and dependable electricity" (ICF, 2007). The term "intelligent" refers to the broadband facilities those societies have put into place that open up new collaborative opportunities for addressing social problems, achieving business growth, improving education and enhancing quality of life. "Where communities once raced to build seaports, rail depots, airports and highways to attract businesses and create jobs, many now view broadband communications and information technology as the new keys to prosperity." As the digital economy develops, many local communities are recognizing that global connectivity through telecommunications allows them to identify their unique assets and leverage their strengths. Intelligent communities focus on local users of telecom networks not just as customers and consumers but as producers and creators of content, products and services.

A "digital community" is the expression used by the company Intel (2007). The Digital Communities Consortium is a partnership of such technology developers and vendors as Intel, Cisco, Dell, IBM, SAP, British Telecom, Civitium, Earthlink,

Panasonic, and Pronto Networks who work with 16 pilot cities in the Americas, Europe and Asia Pacific. Participating cities include Cleveland, Ohio; Mangaratiba, Brazil; Dusseldorf, Germany; Gyor, Hungary; Jerusalem, Israel; Principality of Monaco; Osaka, Japan; Taipei, Taiwan; and Westminster, UK. The Intel Consortium provides the following definition: a digital community is a connected community that combines broadband communications infrastructure and innovative services to meet the needs of governments, businesses, their employees and citizens. In a digital community, broadband technologies enable high-speed communication from virtually every corner of the community, and wireless, Internet-enabled tablet PCs and handheld devices enable field staff on the move—from meter readers to home health nurses to emergency response teams—to communicate with the office and access mission critical information (Intel, 2007, p. 2).

Blakely (2001, p. 140) posited that "smart communities will prepare for the global century by internationalizing their human social capital. . . these communities will be in a better position to develop and control knowledge. . . and forge a new, glob-ally based economic development system". Hence, Blakely identified economic development as a central driver among networked communities.

The economic and social benefits of broadband networks can be wide-ranging. One of the Government of Canada's several conferences (2004) focusing on build-ing the next century economy concluded that intelligent communities using smart infrastructure will serve as the backbone of Canada's e-economy. The stated goal has been to encourage investment, strengthen research, enhance commercialization and ensure that all Canadians have access to the latest information and commu-nication technologies and know how to use them. Access to high-speed network infrastructure was identified as an underlying requirement for building smart/intel-ligent communities.

A "community network" is defined as a publicly controlled network that serves the community. It has four basic components: a telecommunication infrastructure with broadband capability, applications or content; devices (such as computers, cellular telephones, iPods and BlackBerries); and users. The development of a community telecommunication network typically occurs through a governing board representing the needs of the users, which is supported by a small management structure (e.g. executive committee and network manager). Such networks rely on information and communication technologies (ICTs) that allow the community to create and process content, import and export information, promote innovation and overcome many of the constraints on work that involve time and distance. Opportunities for economic and social development are often contingent on attracting many users and creating a culture of "digital" use. To be successful, the network must fulfill user needs and be attentive to their requirements, which may include a method of training and education, a fair price, and access to computers and the Internet.

A community network will have users at the individual, organisational and community levels of human activity and endeavour. Individuals or end-users will access the network to communicate with friends, play games, acquire information, obtain training, and occasionally will generate new products and services. Once the network is established, collaboration manifests itself primarily in the virtual communities that are created for specific purposes such as civic participation and expert discussion. Organisations are often stakeholders and connect to the network for a wide variety of purposes (Waits, 2000). Even though they are intermediate users, they often drive the development of the network (Williams, Stewart & Slack, 2005). These organisations are the channels through which collective innovation is exercised and community change takes place (De la Mothe, 2004). At the community level, these individuals and organisations create collective demand and use of the network, and determine its sustainability. The challenge is to create a culture of "digital" use that is integrated into the broader culture shared by community members.

There is a substantial body of academic literature on networks that investigates the potential advantages they give to organisations and communities, and the conditions necessary for the advantages to be captured. Networked communities strive to integrate previously separated organisations into a common network where they can more easily share resources, do business and develop strategies for using their communities' resources more efficiently (Beale, 2000). Public policies dealing with ambitious or complex issues, like community sustainability, are better addressed with networked structures that allow for pooling and mobilising resources from both private and public sectors. Since collaboration is the central process that allows for these communal endeavours, the on-going challenge becomes that of creating, enhancing and sustaining this collaboration. (Bradford, 2003; Ebers, 2002).

TECHNOLOGY AND THE HUMAN CONDITION

Key Concept: *Under the stewardship of its leaders and stakeholders, the networked community serves the whole community. Respect for the goals, choices and freedom of expression of individuals, groups and organisations is a sound foundation for a networked community. Collaboration is a key element in this process.*

Table 1 outlines the core concepts (goals, choices and freedom) that constitute the basic background of human endeavour. Goal-setting and goal-directed behaviour are fundamental to intelligent beings who reach out to the future with their aspirations. In doing so, they make choices about their use of technology, reflecting their general attitude to technological change. In addition to exercising choice

Table 1. Human dimension of new technology at the individual, organisational and community levels

Core Concept	Individuals	Organisations	Communities
Goals	• Sharing in the good life • Contributing to others	• Sharing in its success • Gainful employment and career	• Sustainability • Stewardship
Choice	• New technology is a personal decision • Exercising choice requires a commitment of time and effort	• Employee involvement in the choice and use of new technology • Socio-technical fit	• New technology is a collective decision • Each community has a distinct context that must be respected
Freedom of expression	• Sharing of ideas • Expressing creativity	• An environment that encourages personal and organisational innovation	• An environment that supports freedom of expression, and values creativity and innovation

and focusing their efforts through goals, individuals have creative potential that expresses itself in a variety of ways when the surrounding structures are welcoming. At the collective levels of organisation and community, these core concepts are manifested as the local culture.

Goals. To enhance the human condition, the members of a community require common goals that are focused on sustainability. ICTs can be introduced and configured so as to give citizens both short-term and long-term benefits that outweigh the costs and minimize any negative impacts. The benefits and costs are related to the good life, and the key to achieving a high quality of communal life is the exercise of stewardship.

According to Peter Block (1993), stewardship is defined as holding something in trust for another, and doing so by pursuing service instead of self-interest. Stewardship gives people choice over how to serve their customers, their fellow citizens and their communities. Stewardship is the willingness to be accountable for the well being of an organisation or community by operating in service to, rather than in control of, those around them. In so doing, we build the capacity of the next generation to govern effectively.

Block states that stewardship stands at the intersection of spirit, community and the marketplace. Stewardship is practical and commercially beneficial at the same time in that it respects individuals and welcomes their exercise of choice and involvement. With the advent of the Network Society, broadband capability can be viewed as an essential service and a platform for helping the community develop.

Organisational success is defined by its stakeholders. When employees and managers as well as the rest of the community are considered stakeholders, organisational success takes on a broader view than simply economic performance as measured by growth in sales and profits (private sector) or service delivery performance as measured by the number of clients served within a given budget (public sector). Contributions to the economic and social health of the community become important goals. Such organisations control many human and technical resources that can be shared with the community to address issues of mutual importance that affect the local quality of life.

Stewardship is accompanied by a governance system based on partnership, which establishes a strong sense of ownership and responsibility for the outcomes that individuals experience in all stations of life. Stewardship empowers individuals and brings accountability into each act of governance, while partnership balances responsibility. From the perspective of commercial transactions, Block concludes that the practise of stewardship requires putting information, resources and power into the hands of those people closest to making a product, designing a product or service and contacting a customer. However, involving employees and citizens requires organisational changes in policies, processes and structure (Block, 1993).

Organisational goals of profit maximization and efficiency can produce mixed results. On the positive side, no serious observer would fail to notice the significant increases in material wealth and comfort that the profit motive and private enterprise have delivered in the last hundred years. However, employing technology for greater profit or efficiency can also harm the public good. Too many profit-oriented organisations produce tremendous amounts of pollution, about which they are unconcerned unless there is regulation and enforcement. At the individual level, the telephone has greatly expanded our ability to communicate over distances but efficient routing can make communication difficult. Try contacting any large organization, and you are faced with automation that offers you limited choices ("Press 3 for the list of names") that may not cover the purpose of your call and obliges you to listen to several choices before you are given the opportunity to speak to another person.

Worse is when the enquirer is never given person-to-person contact. This application can actually become counterproductive to communication.

Choice. When individuals use new technology, there is a process called appropriation that makes the technology one's own (Du Gay, Hall, Janes, Mackay & Negus, 1997). Users make choices around the selection and local deployment of the technological components, and create meaning and sense of the technology. Appropriation has both a technical and cultural side. In this spirit, Robin Williams and colleagues in their book *Social Learning in Technological Innovation* (2005) observed that user appropriation has two distinct but inter-related processes: innofusion (users adjust and innovate to improve the usefulness of the technology) and domestication (users adapt the use of the technology to integrate it meaningfully in their activities). When both processes are fully engaged, the community may be said to have a "digital" culture that sustains the network.

Goals are meaningful when people freely choose them. Individuals can decide what level of technological literacy they want to achieve and what technology they are prepared to use or avoid. However, this freedom is meaningful only when they invest the time and effort in exploring and assessing the technology issue. Many are they who drift away from exercising choice because of competing commitments or because of an attitude of compliance.

Traditionally, technology goals relating to community networks have not been chosen, but are imposed implicitly by expert authority, usually with the blessing of government. Individuals and communities were expected to comply with the type and use of technology without questioning the underlying assumptions that typically relate to goals of efficiency, productivity and competitiveness. Technological progress is presented as inevitable and best left to the experts. This view of the world has little room for social justice and collective decision-making or politics.

The issue of compliance is equally present in organisations, especially when technology is viewed as inevitable and the domain of experts. These experts frequently suffer from specialization and technology bias. For example, an engineer is more likely to favour automation because the involvement of people is less predictable. An information and control system designer similarly minimizes the human element because of a fascination with technology products and capability. When a broad spectrum of employees and managers is involved in the choice and use of technology, the end product is more likely to support the individual user.

Freedom of Expression. When individuals have freedom of expression, some of them will express new ideas and create artifacts for their personal satisfaction. Some of these personal outcomes will attract interest from others with entrepreneurial spirit and lead to innovations. Collaboration between the creator and the innovator gives rise to commercial products. A similar process is at work in organisations when employees are encouraged to think outside of their defined role and share their ideas for improvements in products, services and work processes. Porth, McCall and Bausch (1999) believe that the model of a "learning organisation" is one that allows the human spirit to flourish so that creativity and innovation are possible. The learning organisation emphasizes employee growth, collaboration and a sense of community.

Mandeville (2005) argues that organisational networks are complex and self-organizing. Knowledge and innovation evolve through social interaction and communication, and the appropriate role for the manager is to create contexts for self-organisation by setting visions and goals, ensuring ICT infrastructure and encouraging mutual trust.

A community is a complex organisation because it contains within it many organisations, both public and private, as well as a population that has settled there. Some families have resided there for several generations. Despite this complexity, a community may be said to have a culture with core values. Some communities value freedom of expression and its consequences, creativity and innovation.

DEVELOPMENT OF NETWORKED COMMUNITIES

Professor Andrew Pettigrew has developed a framework for change management that is useful in understanding how networked communities may be developed (1987, 1992). Pettigrew argues that events are best studied in their setting, where there is an interaction between actors and events and their environment. The framework includes three interacting components: the content of change (WHAT), the context of change (WHY) and the process of change (HOW). An investigation of the interplay of these three components reveals the patterns of change and can lead to a better understanding of the phenomenon studied (See Figure 1). In relation to community digital transformation, the phenomenon that we are trying to understand is the social dynamics involved. At the heart of the concept of community, we find people who work hard to realize their collective aspirations. Thus, the framework guiding this book reflects a focus on collaboration as the key process in community development.

Briefly, the content of change includes community goals and digital projects that change over time. Telecommunication networks operate within and share physical community space. Community leaders and their stakeholders generally recognise

Figure 1. Framework for change management

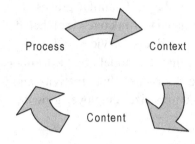

Process   Context

Content

the economic and social development potential within these networks and, over time, establish goals to make this potential a reality.

The context of change is composed of an outer and inner context that can encourage change or hamper it. The outer context is the global environment and the inner context is the community itself. These contexts can change and become either more or less favourable over time. The outer context includes both global (ex., globalization and technological evolution) and regional, national or regional dynamics (ex., central government assistance programs and services). Within the inner context, there exists a local context that includes the community's infra-structure, history, culture and economy. Changes within the global environment can provoke changes in a specific community, but the pace of change may differ because of particular features operating in the latter. For example, in Canada the federal government funded a limited number of pilot studies examining the concept of the "smart community", but only some communities were ready to participate in the project. In some cases, changes at the community level may influence the outer context; for example, local firms supported by the local university create leading computer products and applications that are launched through joint ventures with local venture capital. The new products and applications may be marketed world-wide, making competing products available in global markets less attractive, thus modifying the outer context.

Change consists of the patterns of actions and reactions of the participants and interested parties, with collaboration serving as the key process of community development. Both academics (Tan, 1999; Agres, Edberg & Igbaria, 1998) and government officials (Industry Canada, 2002a, 2002b) agree that the extensive col-laboration efforts that go on within networked communities give them an advantage for achieving their economic development objectives. Community networks can promote information dissemination, discussion and joint activity by connecting neighbours, using telecommunications infrastructure to create new opportunities, and empowering residents, institutions and regions.

DEVELOPMENT PHASES

Building on the change management framework, Albert and LeBrasseur (2007) described how network development takes place in two phases, noting that these are interactive in nature (see Figure 2). In Phase 1, the formation of the networked community is marked by the emergence of a leader, a board of directors or another coordinating mechanism, often in response to environmental pressures. These pressures may occur as a result of globalization and the need to remain competitive with communities in other regions. Context issues, which are influencing factors, may develop as a result of downsizing or the lack of local medical practitioners, departure of youth in search of more promising workplaces and the need to position the region as a tourist destination (Albert, 2003). Community champions emerge when a need is present.

Phase 2—network performance—involves the concrete objectives and steps taken by the board or coordinating committee in charge of the change process to achieve specific community goals. Larger communities tend to have less pressure in the development of infrastructure but need to resolve more complex economic and social issues. Smaller communities tend to need collaborators to help address their challenges, particularly when they include infrastructure problems. In this second phase, a culture and structure of cooperation will develop that gives meaning and coherence to the projects undertaken. Some communities take a permissive, hands-off approach, allowing the private sector groups and individual citizens to come up with plans and take the initiative. Others start with the vision for community transformation, which may include recommendations for an improved telecommunication infrastructure or network.

Phase 1 depends highly on leadership dynamics whereas Phase 2 depends more on management strategies. These two phases are interdependent over time in that formation sets the stage for performance, and performance impacts the board and

Figure 2. Development phases of a networked community

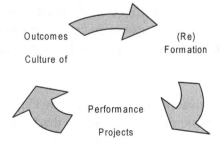

Outcomes Culture of

(Re) Formation

Performance Projects

leadership dynamics. Positive outcomes at the performance phase can consolidate the strategies undertaken and give momentum to projects being pursued; negative outcomes can challenge the community leadership and initiate a re-formation phase. This recursive process was demonstrated in the feedback loop illustrated by Arino and de la Torre (1998) in their study of joint ventures.

DEVELOPMENT CHALLENGES

Key Concept: *Digital networks present challenges to the whole community membership. Unless these challenges are met, the community is unlikely to secure those benefits that will contribute to its sustainability.*

Digital networks can present a different set of challenges for individuals, for organisations and for the community as a whole. When these challenges are being met for its separate constituencies, it can be assumed that the community is obtaining those benefits needed to sustain itself over time.

Challenges for Individual Users. Information technology and community networks challenge the individual because they call into question existing ideas and routines, and add a supplementary layer of knowledge and skill requirements. Being open to change means making an effort to understand and use the network. It is no surprise that the younger generation uses the Internet more than the older generation for social contact and is likely to push for faster Internet connections and systems for content creation in the home (Bernier & Laflamme, 2005). Older adults are more likely to be introduced to ICT changes in the workplace. Age aside, the Internet provides the local-global link through which knowledge and expertise from around the world can be channelled to community members (Stevenson, 2002). Creative individuals can exchange expertise and come up with innovations (e.g., open source development), and are motivated by reputation and recognition to broadcast via the Web site (Fischer, Scharff & Ye, 2004). To generate ideas, group support systems that ensure anonymity appear more effective (Pissarra & Jesuino, 2005). In general, the individual must learn to assess the trustworthiness of the Internet information sources (May, 2002) and assume risks when making transactions online. Similarly, participating in virtual communities and discussion forums challenges the individual to change roles from spectator to contributor and social change agent.

Challenges for Organisational Users. Since key individuals likely were involved in the network formation stage to ensure that the design of the systems would support expected transactions and activities, organisations that are stakeholders in the community network need to share their "network vision" with their board members, managers, employees and organisational partners within their supply chains and customer/client networks. At the performance stage, each organisation is challenged to mobilise its ICTs, skill base and network use, and do so in dialogue and coordination with their organisational networks. Internally, this means empowering employees and lower levels of management through information systems and decision-making authority. Externally, this refers to the network of relations and the integration of the organisational and community networks. Failure to have extensive collaboration diminishes the benefits that the community network can deliver to stakeholders. Knowledge sharing and knowledge management are useful frameworks for channelling this collaboration (Van den Hooff, Ridder & Aukema, 2004). In addition, involvement can include intra-preneurship and joint ventures supported by collaborative groupware (McKnight & Bontis, 2002). The organisation can also reach out to innovators and entrepreneurs in the community who view the network as their business platform, and initiate partnerships. The above array of activities pushes leaders and senior managers to adopt an organisational model that incorporates trust and, again, promotes collaboration.

Challenges for the Community. As the community network is fully implemented, a stewardship vision is required that extends inclusiveness to all segments of the local population, imagines a broad culture of use and provides for economic development with a digital component. Community leaders must have concrete programs to diminish access barriers such as network connectivity at a reasonable cost (or at no cost for public terminals) and access to training and education. Adoption of the network will vary across socio-economic dimensions, and programs are needed that are adapted to specific groups such as youth, seniors, and the non-profit and small business sectors. Developing and implementing these programs can take place as collaborative projects among community stakeholders. An innovation culture (Martins & Terblanche, 2003) linked to the network can be encouraged.

A culture of "digital" use has already emerged in many communities; the Internet and its many activities are being integrated into everyday routines of social communication, work and play (Wellman, Haase, Witte & Hampton, 2001). In contrast, civic participation has had less success. The evidence indicates that Internet use reinforces civic participation and makes it more sophisticated, but does not increase the levels of activity (Uslaner, 2004; Shah, 2002). Others continue to be optimistic; for example, Pigg (2001) has argued that networks can be designed to enhance civic participation, but so far these designs have failed to incorporate the nature of participation. The designs typically focus on customer services and support instead of the sharing of information, ideas and knowledge to influence civic decisions. With a customer focus, the civic authorities may increase the satisfaction of its citizenry, whereas a participation focus obliges the authorities to share decision-making powers and accept more uncertainty in the process and outcomes.

INTELLIGENT COMMUNITY FORUM

Key Concept: *We can learn from the experience of communities around the world that are striving to become networked communities. These communities are inventing strategies and tactics that could be applied and modified in other communities.*

Tony Stevenson (2002) explored five scenarios for future communities, three of them reactive in nature and the other two fully engaged with technological change: the virtual community and the viable community. The now popularized virtual community is located in cyber-space where people share a common interest and seem unconcerned with ordinary life. On the other hand, the viable community makes local-global links to create synergies by sharing resources and ideas in a global network society. The local community is both real and virtual at the same time. The viable community closely resembles the model of the networked or "intelligent" community put forward by the Intelligent Communities Forum (ICF), an organisation with which the authors have an affiliation.

Both the digital revolution and the industrial revolution highlighted the importance of technology as a tool for individual and collective pursuits. History has shown that technology can enhance or diminish individuals and their communities. Each revolution has had its activists and champions who are guided and motivated by a modern vision. The ICF has emerged as a champion of the digital revolution. This non-profit think tank operates from the premise that intelligently designed and managed networked communities are possible. Intelligent communities deliberately incorporate new technology linked to broadband capability to improve the quality of life of its citizens and to satisfy the demanding requirements of stewardship and sustainability. Because all communities are not alike, each community has to exercise its will to make informed and prudent decisions that will meet its current and future needs. And since each community faces its own distinct challenge because of its unique history, culture and economy, becoming a networked community will normally take place within a dialogue of collective survival and economic prosperity.

Community leaders who are motivated to meet the "digital" challenges at the individual, organisational and communal levels convene on a yearly basis in New

York City for the ICF annual conference. Through its activities and award programs, ICF creates a network of leaders in the broadband applications at the community level. ICF collects information on networked communities and has gladly shared it with the authors. This information is the primary empirical basis of this book.

"Building the Broadband Economy" is the theme of the 2009 ICF Annual Conference & Awards event produced in association with the Institute for Technology & Enterprise at Polytechnic University. The awards conference is an international meeting place and idea exchange for local government officials and their private-sector partners in telecom, IT, finance, real estate, and consulting. It is described as a unique opportunity to learn how the world's most innovative communities have made the broadband economy work for them, sometimes against great odds. It offers a global perspective on the best ways to create broadband infrastructure, attract knowledge workers, foster innovation and implement e-government programs that contribute to economic growth and bridge the digital divide.

The Intelligent Community of the Year is selected in the final stage of a 10-month award process that begins with selection of the Smart 21 Communities in November of the prior year. Selection of the Intelligent Community of the Year is based on research by the company Evalueserve and an international panel of experts. The community must demonstrate that its strategy has produced measurable results in one or more of the following areas:

- Attracting new business to the community or stimulating their formation
- New job creation
- Creating training programs to equip citizens with knowledge-worker skills
- New technology infrastructure investment, whether of "hard" assets, services or software
- Improvements in the delivery of government and public services such as education, administration, law enforcement or citizen participation
- Innovation in business processes and government procedures
- Ensuring access to broadband and IT resources for low-income and at-risk populations.

The ICF believes that ICTs can make a significant contribution to the social and economic development of a community. It emphasizes the essential presence of the traditional community in everyone's life, a physical place where we live and work. At the same time, ICF believes that there is some urgency for communities to fully engage with the emerging Network Society. Those communities who seek to implement the full potential of ICTs, it is argued, become networked communities that are sustainable for the foreseeable future. Communities that fail to engage run the risk of losing jobs and citizens as people and organisations move to communities offering more opportunities. The role of ICF as a champion of communities is demonstrated principally in the annual Intelligent Community of the Year Award. Through this coveted award, ICF promotes and showcases community success stories in the media. The 2008 award had the theme of sustainability and focused on both quality of life and economic prosperity of a community. Through ICF and their award participants, the authors have access to the completed applications and accompanying documents that each participating community submits for the award of Intelligent Community of the Year.

Since networked communities from around the world participate in ICF to share their accomplishments and learn what others are doing, this forum provides an excellent opportunity to identify community best practises and outstanding issues. Following the advice of Kyro (2004), best practise, otherwise known as benchmarking, is more fruitful when the content (what) and the process (how) of the subject are measured. We understand that copying the strategies of existing communities is of limited value in the fast changing environment of the Network Society. However, understanding the phenomenon of networking within a community and its environment, and its contribution to the sustainability of the community is the valued outcome. Best practise is assumed to be context specific, and that users and suppliers of advanced technology have different views on implementing and using the network and its applications (Swan, Newell & Robertson, 1999). By reflecting on the communities participating in the ICF, we hope to call attention to the network learning and success patterns that will enable other communities to transform themselves, according to their own vision, into networked communities.

A community transformation process can be facilitated through measurement and evaluation of quality indicators. The creation and management of an evaluation system ensure that the community becomes aware of its progress and the obstacles that can impede it. Full awareness of the outcomes of the community's development (see Figure 2) can align the corrective efforts of community leaders and stakeholders.

EVALUATION IMPERATIVE

Key Concept: *Although measuring the progress and accomplishments of technology-based projects can be difficult at the local level, a measurement system must be devised that can report progress to all stakeholders and can attract and retain collaborators.*

John Eger (1997), the founder of the World Foundation for Smart Communities in San Diego, California, identified several areas in the evaluation of smart community programs where community support was critical to success. Key indicators include citizen participation, the way people feel about their community, and the possible effects that technology may have on the way people play. However, key indicators are only part of an effective and ongoing evaluation program, which serves several purposes:

- Identify and test assumptions;
- Assess progress toward goals and identify any needed course corrections;
- Document progress for funding agencies and sponsors;
- Communicate results to community stakeholders; and
- Learn what works and what doesn't.

Technology-oriented projects share a common weakness—they make assumptions about how the technology can be used to accomplish a goal, address a need or solve a problem. Williams and Williams (2007) lamented that ICT-related investment does not always deliver value and could create unexpected problems. With new technology, there is little or no previous experience or evidence to justify the assumptions of adoption and effectiveness. The Industry Canada experience demonstrated that the best time to address this weakness and transform the networked community into a learning community is at the beginning of the project, by designing and implementing a robust, ongoing evaluation program (Industry Canada, 2003). This evaluation program serves as a continuous monitoring and feedback mechanism for assessing progress toward goals and objectives.

Sustainability is often quoted as a major reason for evaluation. However, definitions of sustainability often imply maintaining the status quo (Voinov & Farley, 2007), whereas networked communities tend to experience continuous growth and change as a result of innovation. A community may want to maintain some systems while shortening the life span of others to make room for new creative ways of delivering services. Voinov and Farley (2008) characterize this type of "renewal" as readjustment and adaptation (p. 207). Noted below is the Industry Canada (2003) approach to carrying out evaluation in its smart community program:

- *Establish the community baseline* (the current state of the community) and identify data that can be tracked for comparative purposes (before and after).
- *Identify key community indicators* through the needs assessment and strategic planning process, *and set goals and objectives* in terms that define certain measurable outcomes for these key indicators.
- *Create an evaluation plan* to define what data will be collected how and when, to describe the analyses that will be carried out on the data, and to identify

external events that can also have an impact on the indicators. Communities must be careful not to fall into "analysis-paralysis" or data collection for its own sake.

- *Collect data on key community indicators.* Efforts toward devising methods for collecting data automatically or making collection easier through Web portal counts and automated response systems should be considered.
- *Monitor external events* that may also have an impact on the indicators. Changes to the strategy may be suggested by external indicators.
- *Analyze data and report* at prescribed intervals according to the evaluation plan. Stakeholders will be looking for regular assessments. Use the information in public relations outlets to obtain more buy-in from existing and new stakeholders.

Measurement is one of the networked community activities requiring a high level of collaboration. The numerous projects or initiatives in a networked community environment will require planning to benchmark the current state of affairs and to establish the right measurement of success. Each activity will likely require data collection from several sources or collaborators. For example, a portal project may collect broad data on the number of clients that enter the site. However, since a portal is a collection of the communities' Web pages, information and other links, each agency contributing to the site will have differing opinions on successful measurement of site use. Some will want to see product sales numbers; others will want to know how much time users stay on the site and learn what it has to offer. Consequently, contributors will need to identify their evaluation or measurement requirements and help to construct the systems to obtain the necessary data to measure success (Albert, 2006).

Measurement is important to retaining and attracting collaborators. Some participants have strong personal commitments to the work at hand and are willing to "stick it out" no matter what happens. Other network collaborators have boards, government programs and investors insisting on a cost-benefit analysis of participation. At some point, the networked community initiative will need to discuss social as well as economic impact and should be ready to demonstrate the "before and after" effects of the project. Government support is usually contingent on program evaluation.

Although qualitative data is sometimes accepted, there is an increasing requirement for quantitative analysis that involves repeated benchmarking and measurement of progress. Most organisations, whether private or public, must report the outcomes of all resource allocations. The lack of an evaluation system that can measure outcome could signal misuse of funds to decision-makers and make long-term involvement of partners difficult. As a result, networked communities must plan from the onset what its stakeholders will need in terms of measurement, and how the measurement process will be implemented.

Arthur Thompson and colleagues, writing in *Crafting and Executing Strategy*, note that the vision, objectives, strategy and approaches of communities are never final. Managing the networked community initiative is an ongoing process and requires adjustments along the way. Evaluation allows communities to analyze decision points that may signal a necessary change in the strategy or execution methods. When communities encounter disruptive change in their environment, they need to re-assess their position (Thompson, Strickland & Gamble, 2006).

MEASUREMENT SYSTEMS

O'Donnell and Henriksen (2002) performed research on the social impact of ICT and stressed the importance of a humanist perspective, rather than a technological or market-oriented assessment. From a socio-technical and systems perspective, a blended approach is preferable; the ICF archives support this alternative in that the successful communities described undertake broad impact assessment. These communities understand that collaborators in ICT networked communities need to show results by identifying the impact on the bottom line (often through cost-benefit or return on investment calculations), and by tackling the "barriers to emancipation" (Hirschheim & Klein, 1994, p. 109) and the social constraints stemming from lack of access, knowledge, fear and affordability.

Key Concept: *Measurement is expensive; networked communities must carefully decide what processes to measure that will add value. Critical success factors include the ability to develop a plan, assign resources, and ensure consistency, validity and reliability in the data being collected, while developing a baseline using acceptable dimensions that can be benchmarked.*

The typical measurement systems look for growth in the number of jobs, capital expenditures and return on investment (ROI). In a community development setting, there are other measures needed, such as the social return on investment. Stephen Cummings' (2006) formula (SROI: x dollars in; x + y dollars out, where y is the social impact measured in dollars and/or quality of life) is being utilized by some projects in Ontario, Canada. This formula attempts to depart from a purely technical or market-oriented approach to evaluation by measuring cost avoidance (such as fewer visits to the hospital, retention of economic activity, fewer social ills including vagrancy). Some of these measurements are purely qualitative, but are needed and represent an important facet of evaluating "real" impact (Voinov

& Farley, 2007). Qualitative measurements also allow for capturing more complex conceptual levels, a requirement for studying networked communities.

Social measurements are less quantifiable, because they include direct as well as indirect benefits, such as non-quantifiable or quality-oriented outcomes. The authors observe that social impact and belief in a vision are sometimes difficult concepts to sell to funding agencies even when they are key to future innovation and change. Nevertheless, some aspects may be quantifiable, and increasingly governments are recognizing their significance. In a 2006 book on change and innovation, Westley, Zimmerman and Quinn-Patton argued that when most foundations and government funding agencies consider only proposals with clear, specific and measurable outcomes, these projects ignore important community values: "Such an approach is appropriate when problems are well understood and solutions are known. But for the complex problems that social innovators address, an equally innovative approach is required" (p. 47). These researchers are of the opinion that funders should be looking "to support people, not projects". The networked community will more likely demonstrate its value to its residents and stakeholders if it has a robust evaluation plan—one that includes social as well as economic measurement.

A sound evaluation plan requires thinking about what needs to be measured from the beginning of the project. A successful project depends on formally as-signing the responsibility for setting up and maintaining an evaluation program (Industry Canada, 2003). It also requires assigning a budget. Another option is evaluation by an independent agency or separate organisation, but this could be expensive, especially if several indicators are utilized.

Because information is costly, we need to ensure that the collection of data will be reliable, valid and consistent. Consistency among internal organisations and between communities can allow the community to benchmark. Benchmarking is a tool for learning whereby companies (or communities) compare themselves on performing key activities so that new strategies can be developed and implemented to improve institutional effectiveness (Thompson et al, 2006; Johnson & Misic, 1999). Within a sector, measurement may be difficult when the stakeholders are using varying measurement scales, protocols or descriptions. The evaluation process is rendered more difficult—even invalid—when these same measure-ments are expected to be used across sectors, across geographical areas and are challenged by differing timeframes (some organisations may be measuring based on different budget years, or have different baselines or timelines).

The solution is to find indicators and measurements that are compatible with one another—measuring apples to apples—and thus ensuring reliability. Using mutually acceptable dimensions and common systems is easier when communities have collaborated in their development. Other communities and researchers across the world have developed evaluation systems. They can be replicated or amended to suit the requirements of networks in other environments.

A return-on-investment calculation will be more difficult to do when social return on investment includes intangible or indirect benefits, variable timeframes, various government involvements, difficulties in partnership tracking protocols, and variable social targets of multiple agencies. Benchmarking, as an alternative, allows communities to understand and learn from best practices. For example, a local Web site or Internet portal can be compared with others to measure functionality and features that have been used elsewhere for other purposes. This comparison may help the network to maintain a competitive edge (Johnson & Misic, 1999).

Cost considerations aside, measurement needs to be as comprehensive as possible to give a convincing indication of success. Measuring the number of visits to a Web page does not give a good measure of the performance quality of the page, or its functionality. Contrast this one dimensional approach to that proposed by Madu and Madu (2002); they provided a list of 15 dimensions for measuring e-quality stemming from studies on products and services, and extended these concepts to define the dimensions needed in an ICT environment. The dimensions are performance, features, structure, aesthetics, reliability, storage capability, serviceability, security and system integrity, trust, responsiveness, product/service differentiation and customization, Web store policies, reputation, assurance, and empathy. Madu and Madu argued that the tremendous growth in e-commerce applications and greater dependence by consumers and businesses on virtual networks necessitated the inclusion of key factors that lead to customer satisfaction and competitiveness. The field of measurement is evolving, and networked community leaders are advised to follow its development and incorporate some of the proposed dimensions and procedures into their evaluation plans.

CONCLUSION

There is wide consensus that the global Network Society is a reality and that a growing number of communities are making efforts to become fully connected and active members. Those communities that have made the most progress, the networked communities, have a favoured position in the Network Society; they are likely to reap the potential social and economic benefits that flow from their global connectivity. That being said, preparing a sound foundation for a networked community depends upon the right people doing the right things at the right time. The authors argue that community leaders should adopt a stewardship approach in which the networked community serves the whole community. Respect for the goals, choices and freedom of expression of individuals, groups and organisations acts as a lever that taps into the dynamism and creativity of these community members. The stewardship approach recognises the conundrum of the "human condition" in which satisfying needs and aspirations are equally important. This approach presents some challenges for leaders and stakeholders, but it also can create pride and loyalty while building commitment, enthusiasm and momentum in their communities.

With its growing archive of networks and body of experience, the Intelligent Community Forum offers significant support to those who wish to learn from communities striving to become networked. The examples presented in this book are drawn from those inventing their own strategies and using tactics that could offer promise as examples for others. This book builds upon the ICF knowledge base and process by interpreting what has been learned and by considering how that knowledge might be replicated in different contexts.

By sharing the stories and accomplishments of these "intelligent" communities, and others around the world, within a change management framework, the authors hope to give aspiring communities some encouragement and direction in crafting their own versions of the networked community adapted to local conditions. Certainly, their efforts can be more effective when guided by a measurement and evaluation system—an important tool that allows community stakeholders to deepen their understanding of the changes taking place and keep them on target. For pragmatic reasons, communities must learn to measure output. This is key to attracting and maintaining collaborators, meeting community and investor expectations and promoting innovation and building creative local-global linkages.

Since evaluation is tied to promotion and recruitment, measurement must be planned at the onset of projects and begin with a baseline from which future evaluations can be carried out. Benchmarking against networks in other communities can provide valuable information, adding to the list of opportunities to advertise strengths and successes. Conversely, the setting of proper benchmarks can allow the local community to change its course when needed to overcome weaknesses and gain momentum.

In their quest to evaluate their network development, communities must be careful not to over or under measure. Evaluation is difficult and costly. Therefore, careful consideration of the right tools and processes should lead to better measurement systems and allow community collaborators to celebrate progress and successes. Understanding the nature of the outcomes is important for the sustainability and the long-term health of the network. A baseline of indicators may serve as guidance for many years. Given the importance of measurement for effective action, each of the following chapters addresses this topic.

REFERENCES

Albert, S. (2006). *Intelligent international portal measurement: Tools and examples.* Retrieved March 12, 2006, from the Regional Networks for Ontario Web site: http://www.rno.on.ca

Albert, S. (2003). *Smart communities: Defining factors and the influence of team membership on their development.* DBA Thesis, Nova Southeastern University.

Albert, S. & LeBrasseur, R. (2007). Collaboration challenges in community telecommunication networks. *International Journal of Technology and Human Interaction, 3*(2), 13-33.

Agres, C., Edberg, D. & Igbaria, M. (1998). Transformation to virtual societies: Forces and issues. *The Information Society, 14*(2), 71-82.

Archives of the ICF – Intelligent Communities Forum (2006). *Sunderland, England – Nomination submitted for the Intelligent Community of the Year Award.* New York.

Archives of the ICF – Intelligent Communities Forum (2005). *Tianjin, China – Nomination submitted for the Intelligent Community of the Year Award.* New York.

Archives of the ICF – Intelligent Communities Forum (2004). *Spokane, USA – Nomination submitted for the Intelligent Community of the Year Award.* New York.

Arino, A. & de la Torre, J. (1998). Learning from failure: Towards an evolutionary model of collaborative ventures. *Organizational Science, 9*(3), 306-325.

Arnold, M. (2007). The concept of community and the character of networks. *The Journal of Community Informatics, 3*(2). Retrieved April 15, 2008, from http://ci-journal.net/index.php/ciej/article/view/327/315

Beale, T. (2000). Requirements for a regional information infrastructure for sustainable communities: The case for community informatics. In M. Gurstein (Ed.), *Community informatics: Enabling communities with information and communications technologies* (pp. 52-80). Hershey PA: Idea Group Publishing.

Bell, R. (2001). *Benchmarking the Intelligent Community – A comparison study of regional communities.* The Intelligent Communities Forum of World Teleport Association.

Bernier, C., & Laflamme, S. (2005). Uses of the Internet according to type and age: A double differentiation. [Usages d'Internet selon le genre et l'age: une double différenciation] *The Canadian Review of Sociology and Anthropology/La Revue Canadienne De Sociologie Et d'Anthropologie, 42*(3), 301-323.

Blakely, E. (2001). Competitive advantage for the 21st-century city. *APA Journal,* *67*(2), 133-141.

Block, P. (1993). *Stewardship: Choosing service over self-interest.* San Francisco: Berrett-Koehler Publishers.

Bradford, R. (2003). Public-private partnerships? Shifting paradigms of economic governance in Ontario. *Canadian Journal of Political Sciences, 36*(5), 1005-1033.

Cam, C. H. (2004). A conceptual framework for socio-techno-centric approach to sustainable development. *International Journal of Technology Management and Sustainable Development, 1*(1), 59-66.

Castells, M. (1998). *End of millennium, Vol. 3 of the information age: Economy, society and culture.* Oxford: Blackwell.

Castells, M. (2006). The network society: From knowledge to policy. In M. Castells and G. Cardoso (Eds.), *The network society: From knowledge to policy.* Washington DC: Johns Hopkins Center for Transatlantic Relations.

Castells, M. (1997). *The power of identity, Vol. 2 of the information age: Economy, society and culture.* Oxford: Blackwell.

Castells, M. (1996). *The rise of the Network Society, Vol. 1 of the information age: Economy, society and culture.* Oxford: Blackwell.

Castells, M. and Cardoso, G. (Eds.) (2006), *The network society: From knowledge to policy.* Washington DC: Johns Hopkins Center for Transatlantic Relations.

Caves, R. (2001). E-commerce and information technology: Information technologies, economic development, and smart communities: Is there a relationship? *Economic Development Review, 17*(3), 6-13.

De la Mothe, J. (2004). The institutional governance of technology, society, and innovation. *Technology in Society, 26,* 523-536.

Du Gay, P., Hall, S., Janes, L., Mackay, H. & Negus, K. (1997). *Doing cultural studies: The story of the Sony Walkman.* London and New Delhi: Sage.

Ebers, M. (2002). *The formation of inter-organizational networks.* Oxford UK: Oxford University Press.

Eger, J. (1997). *Smart communities implementation guide. Section I: Implementing the smart community—evaluation program.* Retrieved November 28, 2007, from http://www.smartcommunities.org/guide/html/i__evaluation.html

Ferguson, D. *Be careful what you measure—It might get done.* Retrieved November 7, 2007, from the Pelicam Web site: http://www.pelicam.com/media_centre/be_careful_what_you_measure.php

Fischer, G., Scharff, E. & Ye, Y. (2004). In M. Huysman & V. Wulf. *Social capital and information technology* (chap. 14). Cambridge MA and London: MIT Press.

Franklin, U. (1999). *The real world of technology.* Toronto: House of Anansi Press Ltd.

Government of Canada. (2004). National conference on the e-economy. Retrieved November 5, 2007, from http://www.e-economy.ca

Hirschheim, R. & Klein, H. K. (1994). Realizing emancipatory principles in information systems development: the case for ETHICS. *MIS Quarterly, 18*(1), 83-109.

Huxham, C., & Vangen, S. (2000). Ambiguity, complexity and dynamics in the membership of collaboration. *Human Relations, 53*(6), 771-805.

ICF – Intelligent Communities Forum (2007). Retrieved October 15, 2007, from the Intelligent Community Forum Web site: www.intelligentcommunity.org

Industry Canada (2003). *Guide for creating a smart community.* Retrieved November 28, 2007, from http://198.103.246.211/documents/project_e.asp

Industry Canada. (2002a, April 4). *Fostering innovation and use.* Retrieved July 30, 2002, from http://broadband.gc.ca/Broadband-document/english/chapter5.htm

Industry Canada. (2002b, April 4). *Smart communities broadband.* Retrieved July 12, 2002, from http://smartcommunities.ic.gc.ca/index_e.asp

Intel (2007). Intel digital communities initiative will help maximize wireless capabilities worldwide. Retrieved September 26, 2007, from www.intel.com/technology/magazine/

Johnson, K. L., & Misic, M. M. (1999). Benchmarking: A tool for Web site evaluation and improvement. *Internet Research, 9*(5), 383-392.

Jordana, J.; Fernandez, X. & Sancho, D. (2005). Which Internet policy? Assessing regional initiatives in Spain. *The Information Society, 21*, 341-351.

Jungmittag, A., & Welfens, P. J. (2006). *Telecommunication dynamics, output, and employment.* Bonn, Germany: Institute for the Study of Labor.

Kavanaugh, A. (1999, September). *The impact of computer networking on community: A social network analysis approach.* Paper presented at the Telecommunication Policy Research Conference, Blacksburg, Virginia. Re-

trieved November 7, 2007, from http://www.ntia.doc.gov/top/research/reports/
tprc.userstudy.kavanaugh.pdf

Keenan, T. & Trotter, D. (1999). The changing role of community networks in providing citizen access to the Internet. *Internet Research: Electronic Networking Applications and Policy, 9*(2), 100-108.

De Koning J. & Gerderblom, A. (2006). ICT and older workers: no unwrinkled relationship. *International Journal of Manpower, 27*(5), 467-490.

Kyro, P. (2004). Benchmarking as an action research process. *Benchmarking, 11*(1), 52-73.

Madu, C. N., & Madu, A. (2002). Dimensions of e-quality. *International Journal of Quality & Reliability Management, 19*(2/3), 246-258.

Malhotra, A., Gosain, S. & Hars, A. (1997). Evolution of a virtual community: Understanding design issues through a longitudinal study. In K. Kumar & J. I. DeGross (Eds.). *Proceedings of the 18th international conference on information systems* (pp. 59-73). Atlanta GA: Association for Information Systems.

Mandeville, T. (2005). Collaboration and the network form of organisation in the new knowledge-based economy. In D. Rooney, G. Hearn, & A. Ninan, (Eds.), *Handbook on the knowledge economy* (chap. 13). Northampton MA: Edward Elgar.

Martins, E. & Terblanche, F. (2003). Building organisational culture that stimulates creativity and innovation. *European Journal of Innovation Management, 6*(1), 64-74.

May, C. (2002). *The information society: A sceptical view.* Cambridge UK: Polity Press.

McKenna, B. (2005). Wisdom, ethics and the postmodern organisation. In D. Rooney, G. Hearn & A. Ninan (Eds.), *Handbook on the knowledge economy* (chap. 3). Northampton MA: Edward Elgar.

McKnight, B. & Bontis, N. (2002). E-improvisation: Collaborative groupware technology expands the reach and effectiveness of organisational improvisation. *Knowledge and Process Management, 9*(4), 219-227.

Mumford, L. (1967). *The myth of the machine: Technics and human development.* New York: Harcourt Brace Jovanovich.

Mumford, L. (1970). *The myth of the machine: The Pentagon of power.* New York: Harcourt Brace Jovanovich.

O'Donnell, D. & Henriksen, L. B. (2002). Philosophical foundations for a critical evaluation of the social impact of ICT. *Journal of Information Technology, 17,* 89-99.

Pigg, K. (2001). Applications of community informatics for building community and enhancing civic society. *Information, Communication & Society, 4*(4), 507-527.

Pettigrew, A. (1992). The character and significance of strategy process research. *Strategic Management Journal, 13,* 5-16.

Pettigrew, A. (1987). Context and action in the transformation of the firm. *Journal of Management Studies, 24*(6), 649-670.

Pissarra, J. & Jesuino, J. (2005). Idea generation through computer-mediated communication: The effects of anonymity. *Journal of Management Psychology, 20*(3/4), 275-291.

Porth, S., McCall, J. & Bausch, T. (1999). Spiritual themes of the learning organization. *Journal of Organizational Change Management, 12*(3), 211-220.

Rooney, D., Hearn, G. & Ninan, A. (2005). Knowledge: Concepts, policy, implementation. In D. Rooney, G. Hearn, and A. Ninan (Eds.), *Handbook on the knowledge economy* (Chap. 1). Northampton MA: Edward Elgar.

Shah, D. (2002). Nonrecursive models of Internet use and community engagement: Questioning whether time spent online erodes social capital. *Journalism & Mass Communication Quarterly, 79*(4), 964-987.

Simon, S. (2004). Systemic evaluation methodology: the emergence of social learning from environmental ICT prototypes. *Systemic Practice and Action Research, 17*(5), 471-496.

Stevenson, T. (2002). Communities of tomorrow. *Futures, 34*(8), 735-744.

Swan, J., Newell, S. & Robertson, M. (1999). The illusion of "best practise" in information systems for operations management. *European Journal of Information Systems, 8,* 284-293.

Tan, M. (1999). Creating the digital economy: Strategies and perspectives from Singapore. *International Journal of Electronic Commerce, 3*(3), 105-22.

Thompson, A. A., Strickland, A. J. & Gamble, J .E. (2006). *Crafting & executing strategy* (15th ed.). New York: McGraw-Hill Irwin.

Uslaner, E. M. (2004). Trust, civic engagement, and the Internet. *Political Communication, 21*(2), 223-242.

Van den Hooff, B., de Ridder, J. & Aukema, E. (2004). Exploring the eagerness to share knowledge: The role of social capital and ICT in knowledge sharing. In M. Huysman & V. Wulf. (Eds.), *Social capital and information technology* (chap. 7). Cambridge MA and London: MIT Press.

Voinov, A. & Farley, J. (2007). Reconciling sustainability, systems theory and discounting. *Ecological Economics, 63*(1), 104-113.

Von Oetinger, B. (2005). From idea to innovation: Making creativity real. *The Journal of Business Strategy, 25*(5), 35-41.

Waits, M. (2000). The added value of the industry cluster approach to economic analysis, strategy development, and service delivery. *Economic Development Quarterly, 14*(1), 35-50.

Wellman, B., Haase, A. Q., Witte, J. & Hampton, K. (2001). Does the Internet increase, decrease, or supplement social capital? Social networks, participation, and community commitment. *American Behavioral Scientist, 45*(3), 436-455.

Westley, F., Zimmerman, B. & Quinn-Patton, M. (2006). *Getting to maybe: How the world is changed*. East Mississauga, Ontario, Canada: Random House Canada.

Williams, R., Stewart, J. & Slack, R. (2005). *Social learning in technological innovation: Experimenting with information communication technologies*. Cheltenham UK and Northampton MA: Edward Elgar.

Williams, M. & Williams, J. (2007). A change management approach to evaluating ICT investment initiatives. *Journal of Enterprise Information Management, 20*(1), 32-50.

Chapter II
The Technological
Basis of Networking

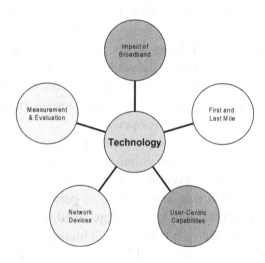

"Broadband is playing a crucial role in transforming countries into Information Societies." (International Telecommunications Union, 2006)

Overview: This chapter pursues the following themes:

* The extent to which telecommunications technology can serve as a platform for economic and social change;
* The role that broadband communication can play in community collaboration and networking;
* The specific technologies (networks and terminal devices) and their relative advantages and limitations;
* The community applications that offer greater user access and user control;

- The adverse and dysfunctional effects that can accompany technological change;
- Some ideas about measuring and evaluating outcomes.

COMMUNITY TECHNOLOGIES

Key Concept: *Access to technology not only shapes what communities can now do; technology shapes what communities can now dream about doing.*

Among the classic studies of sociological literature are those that have researched what happens when roads and highways are built connecting remote populations to the outside world. Roads not only brought a succession of strangers into these formerly isolated communities; they brought strange new ideas that sometimes threatened traditional ways of doing things. And those roads also became the principal means by which the rest of the world learned about and exercised influence over those communities. In today's society, roads are not the only avenues for exchanges; the "information highway" and its progeny the Internet have become essential channels for community development.

Prior to the Internet, information and communication technologies were already reshaping societies. Godwin C. Chu, Alfian, and Wilbur Schramm conducted in the 1980s a now-classic study about the effects on isolated Indonesian communities when satellite television was introduced to all parts of that vast island nation (1985). On the occasion of the launch of its Palapa satellite in 1976, the government of Indonesia declared its intention to develop all human and natural resources of the country. According to Marwah Daud Ibrahim, who wrote a dissertation about the satellite decision, "this could only be done if all the people and all parts of the country could be reached by direct means of transportation and telecommunications. For this reason, Indonesia devoted a great amount of its development budget improving and developing the country's highways, rural roads, waterways, pioneer seaports, pioneer airports, and telecommunications system" (Ibrahim, 2005).

The telecommunications infrastructure—more specifically the Palapa communications satellite—was viewed as a very important instrument for introducing via radio and television the national language "Bahasa Indonesia" to a country with more than 250 local languages and dialects. The government also hoped satellite coverage of the country would help with rural development, encourage family planning, and improve public health and education.

At the time Chu et al. (1985) were writing, modernization theory was in vogue among social science researchers. This theory assumed that technology and social change were in more direct relationship than is thought to be true today. That is, it was assumed that new technologies could cause, even force, particular changes to be brought about in a deterministic way. These particular researchers were interested in the effects of the new domestic satellite communication system but were careful not to assume any particular socio-cultural impact. Indeed, they found that it was the economic and socio-cultural backgrounds of the villages and regions studied, in this case quite different cultures, traditions and practises that most strongly influenced acceptance and use of information provided.

Rather than the new technologies being the determining factors, what was of greater immediate consequence was the role played by local opinion leaders. The local leaders were observed to be intensively and regularly using the provided media. Their innovative and progressive attitudes and practises seemed to come more directly from those technological innovations, so in the Indonesian villages there was perceived to be a kind of "two-step flow of information". The information was passed on and interpreted by the opinion leaders, which motivated the villagers to know more—to study and adopt technical and later cultural innovations. Technology was not a "neutral element" that could be divorced from the social, cultural and political life of the community.

There is ample research that addresses the impact on communities once they are connected to telecommunications technologies. One important realisation is that there are both positive as well as adverse effects. Some dysfunctional effects appear to be inevitable, since there are downsides to any change in the established order. But if communities are really like living organisms that must grow and change or die, which is the presumption of this book, the people who live and work in those communities must take some risk. That is what the Indonesian leaders of the time decided to do in spite of domestic and international criticism about risk, priorities and cost (The Role, 2005).

Although the nature and direction of social change cannot be anticipated and precisely predicted, it can be assumed that some modification to the established order does occur when information begins to flow more freely and citizens figure out for themselves what they can do with what they learn. With better communication tools, government officials are better able to consult with their constituents, local businesses are more accessible to their customers and citizens get more of their needs met more quickly. These are the results when users have access to the tools that give them choices. Whether or not the cost of the technology was worth it or the decision to install the enabling infrastructures was wise may be debated. The reality is that communities, like individuals, who have the opportunity to do so will use information and communication technologies to realise their dreams, whatever they are.

The digital networks of the 21st century have made two-way communication across oceans and continents just about as easy as communicating across town.

Along with greater ease and speed of communication has come the realisation that remote work and distant collaboration are also possible, even among those who have never met face to face. Business people, city managers, medical doctors and academics will use the new technologies to reach out to do things with others that they could not have imagined before.

Collaborative publishing presents itself as an interesting example. This book on networked communities was written by authors residing at Laurentian University in Canada and Ohio University in the United States under the guidance of a publishing team in Pennsylvania. To do the research, the authors made liberal use of the search engines of international information providers Google, Yahoo and Microsoft to find and download information from all over the world. They also searched the academic databases of university libraries to see what researchers around the globe were discovering about the Network Society and networked communities. The e-mail technology gave the team near-instant access to one another for sharing drafts and giving encouragement. Without the supporting telecommunications infrastructure in place, this project may never have been undertaken. Certainly the research, the drafting and editing, and the collaborative effort to prepare the manuscript for publication would have taken a lot longer.

The research literature on the traffic patterns of communities wired for broadband communications—the so-called "intelligent" or "smart" communities—suggests that surprising new forms of communication and collaboration are taking place all over the world. Examples of such developments will be found in every chapter of this book, since they are used to illustrate the transformational power of networking.

Once the technologies for bi-directional, high-speed communication are made available, and users are free to make calls and go online whenever they like, several benefits emerge: 1) geography and physical distances are no longer perceived to be the barriers they once were in conducting work at a distance; 2) virtual communication, e.g., using the tools of the Internet as an alternative to face-to-face interaction, is accepted as an everyday activity for almost everyone; 3) learning and teaching automatically become an organic part of living and working in communities, since every day there is something new to learn, and users are called upon to teach each other; 4) individuals feel more empowered to speak for themselves and have more opportunities to express their opinions and share what they know, and 5) small enterprises flourish and creative works find unexpected audiences.

By extending information highways into all regions, the richness and functionality of the digital networks are multiplied again and again, and transactional communication and relationship building are no longer enjoyed only by the elites who reside in urban communities in the more developed areas of the world.

To be truthful, this build-out is far from complete, but it is under way almost everywhere: in remote communities, in urban slums, in refugee camps, even in outer space. While the often-stated goal is to stimulate economic and social development, the implicit goal and ultimate impact is that all citizens everywhere will be linked for direct and personal communication. What inevitably happens with the installation of telecommunications infrastructure is that a few more barriers to the free flow of information collapse. Those who never had access to cameras and microphones, word processors and video editors, and broadband channels for content distribution will perhaps, for the first time, find the means for asserting their presence and making their aspirations known. By these methods, a larger and larger percentage of the world's population can learn about one another and, more significantly, can learn from one another. With the development of "open source" technologies and as the ubiquitous interconnected networks begin to level the playing field, more citizens in more communities can now contemplate doing things that were never in their most distant thoughts.

What changes in Estonia when the citizens of Estonia can develop their own Web sites in the Estonian language, in the Philippines when the Philippino people can build their own Tagalog Internet, and in Mongolia when Mongolians can communicate on the Internet in their own script? What happens to people's knowledge and understanding of the cultures of others when all these languages and scripts are machine translatable in near real-time? The answer is, the changes are unpredictable, often surprising and certainly not all bad.

Consider the example of an Arabic-language Internet service that provides search access to Arabic Web sites. A search engine is a service for finding information based on words or phrases Internet users type into their computers. One of the problems facing Arabic speakers seeking to make use of the Internet is that 70% of the material on the Internet is in English. According to *Muslim Tech Digest*, 65% of Arab Internet users do not read English (Hammond, 2006). There are two implications in this example. One is that, on an international level, it will be very difficult to develop a "culture of use" around the Internet when all languages are not represented. It also suggests that we are creating a "have-not" society if we do not.

A plan to launch an Arabic language search engine, called Sawafi, similar to the one called Baidu launched in 2006 for the Chinese language, was announced by a Saudi-German joint venture company operating from the Gulf Arab business hub of Dubai. The Sawafi (in translation, Sandstorm) goal was to see that the number of Arabic Internet users grew from 24 million in 2005 to 43 million in 2008, or at least to help make that growth possible. Hermann Havermann, an official of the company, was quoted as saying, "There is not enough Arabic content available on the Internet. But there's no motivation to put more Arabic content on the Internet as long as you don't have a system to find the content" (Hammond, 2006, p. 3).

The challenges involved in processing Arabic-language script and developing a working Arabic Internet search engine are considerable. To be successful, such an engine will be expected to develop the algorithms for increasingly more advanced searches using visual content analysis and personalization, including searches for individualized Web sites and the streaming of audio and video on demand. And beyond the technological challenges, managing what will be acceptable content in terms of text and images on behalf of the diverse Arab-speaking communities of the world will be no small concern.

Even so, with some 280 million Arabic speakers in the Middle East and North Africa, and large expatriate communities residing elsewhere, the potential of this technology to give voice to these communities is also great.

In summary, many community leaders and stakeholders around the world have recognised the potential of information and communication technologies, and soon all of them will do so. Given that the Network Society is gaining momentum and becoming more sophisticated, regions and countries should ensure that their local communities can connect to the Internet with broadband speeds.

Key Concept: *Access to broadband communication technologies changes the way government, business, health, education and individual enterprises operate, and can think about operating in the future.*

Broadband is a term having to do with the quantity and quality of information that can be exchanged over distance using one or more telecommunications channels. But broadband has taken on more than just a technical definition. It is an economic and business strategy and social goal yet to be fully achieved, a way of expressing corporate and public aspirations for a more perfect society based on people's ability to get more of what they want, faster. Today the phrase has become a symbol of empowerment for nations as well as communities and individual users (Flournoy, 2004).

The industry sectors responsible for bringing the broadband information highways into our communities are those we know as telephone, cable, wireless, satellite, radio, television and utility companies, and we know that they are dependent for their very existence on the local, regional and national customers who pay for these services.

In advanced information societies, competition and an explosion of products and services emanating from the telecommunication industries, aided by government deregulation and healthy risk capital, has led to such a proliferation of choices today that communities are often in a quandary to know which of the promised solutions are worthy of investment. Indeed, some municipalities have decided that, to get their real needs met, they will be better off overbuilding the established carriers, creating their own high-speed networks and making their own deals with vendors.

The telecom tool bag grows bigger every day. Some of the more prominent solutions available are identified in the public media as xDSL, fiber optics, digital cable, mobile and fixed wireless, mobile and fixed satellite, digital radio and TV, and broadband powerline (BPL). The applications being spawned carry names like IPTV, VoIP, Gaming, VOD, HDTV, 3G/4G Cellular, Podcasting, digital audio radio, and IP over satellite. To keep up with all these options is frustrating for everyone. Even so, being somewhat knowledgeable is important because somewhere among these technologies and applications could be the keys to helping communities and their citizens realise their dreams.

The New Partnership for Africa's Development (NEPAD) is an initiative by African leaders to extricate their countries from the malaise of underdevelopment and to see that they are not left behind in the information age. The e-Schools initiative is a NEPAD project to link African teachers and school children to the global Internet. The goal is to have some 600,000 African schools equipped and connected by 2015 using IP-Satellite technologies. What that means, in brief, is that PCs and computer labs will be linked via a two-way connection to the World Wide Web, including special Web sites being prepared for this purpose, by way of fixed satellite connections installed in local affiliated schools.

Because they are capable of covering an entire hemisphere, yet focus intense spot beams on a local area, modern satellites are well suited to providing high-speed Internet and related interactive services to underserved regions. The e-Schools pilot project was launched in July 2005 with satellite provider INMARSAT and network/software vendors Cisco Systems, Hewlett-Packard, Microsoft and Oracle agreeing to install the interconnecting equipment at their own cost and provide teacher training to insure effective use at approximately 20 pioneering school systems.

NEPAD was the recipient of a 2005 "Visionary of the Year" award from the Intelligent Community Forum at its awards ceremony in New York City. ICF cited the organisation's commitment to developing the capabilities of satellite technology to connect African schools to the global information infrastructure. "The scope and intention of NEPAD's plan, the degree of success they have had to date in generating both financial support and private sector collaboration, as well as their understanding that satellite communication is key to broadband access in more and more areas of the world," led ICF's Awards Committee to recognise NEPAD (ICF, 2005).

In March 2007, Egypt was the sixth country and the first in North Africa to launch the NEPAD e-Schools infrastructure after Uganda, Ghana, Lesotho, Kenya and Rwanda. The Al-Haddain Secondary School in El Behaira Governate served as the demonstration site. The project is a joint venture of the Egyptian Government, the HP and Oracle Consortia and the NEPAD e-Africa Commission, focusing on "end-to-end ICT solutions…to providing content, learning material and the establishment of health points at schools," using satellites to connect those sites to the Internet. In a *Business in Africa* news story, a student at Habiba School was quoted as saying, "We now have a very good chemistry teacher who teaches us from Cairo via the Internet. As he teaches, we see him and what he is teaching on a big screen. It is like we are with him in the classroom in our village. Chemistry is now very interesting to learn. I now want to become a doctor and save lives" (Country leads, 2007).

It is not surprising to learn that the more developed countries of the world are pushing hard to attain full broadband connection for their citizens. What is surprising is the fast pace of broadband developments in some developing countries. In either case, however, connectivity will be the key to progress on the road to development.

Key Concept: *Information and communications infrastructure is one of the important benchmarks in determining a community's competitiveness and level of prosperity. For economic and social development to be felt by individuals and groups, the infrastructure by which citizens can actively participate must be present.*

The International Telecommunications Union, an agency of the United Nations, has sought over several years to measure the impact of information and communication technologies on social and economic development. In 2006, it released the eighth edition of its "ICT Development Report" that looked at progress made in some 180 countries worldwide.

Quoting from this report, the ITU researchers found that "Access to information and communication technologies continues to grow at high speed, and the digital divide—in terms of mobile subscribers, fixed telephone lines and Internet users—keeps getting smaller. ITU statistics show that by the end of 2004, the telecommunication industry had experienced continuous growth, as well as rapid progress in policy and technology development, resulting in an increasingly competitive and networked world.

"Both the number of mobile subscribers and the number of Internet users more than doubled in just four years," the researchers wrote. "By end 2004, the world had over 840 million Internet users, which means that on average 13% of the world's population was online…..Our statistics show that within four years, from 2000 to 2004, the gap separating the developing and the developed countries has been shrinking in terms of mobile subscribers, fixed telephone lines and Internet users" (International Telecommunications, 2006, p. 1).

The report goes on to say, "At the same time, the world continues to be separated by major differences and disparities in terms of ICT levels…..Europe has almost 15 times the Internet penetration of Africa, where less than two out of 100 people use the Internet. Internet penetration also remains below world average in the Arab

States, where less than six out of 100 people are online" (International Telecommunications, 2006, p. 2).

In a 2005 United Nations Development Programme paper entitled "Community-based Networks and Innovative Technologies: New Models to Serve and Empower the Poor", Radhika Lal, of the Bureau for Development Policy, wrote, "If...deployment of ICT is to take place in the service of the MDGs (Millennium Development Goals regarding Universal Access) and poverty reduction, it must ensure that the *last inch* and *local level* are addressed with the same degree of importance as the macro and national levels. Without this, local communities will be unable to catalyze development activities, and their voices will be less likely to be heard in the distant places where policies are made. In this task, the role of community networks and community-owned infrastructure remains vital" (Siochrú & Girard, 2005, p. 6).

What is called for, says the UNDP paper, is "a participatory community development approach to the hard-nosed business of network and service development." Such an approach would include "community-driven enterprises, creating the structures within which individuals can be rewarded for their entrepreneurial and creative talents in solidarity with the community as a whole.....Active participation and community ownership are generally regarded in development practise as essential ingredients in sustainable actions to address poverty" (Siochrú & Girard, 2005, p. 17).

For the poorest of communities, the free market model does not work. Other solutions must be sought from within the community. The UNDP says "the new wave of wireless and related technologies, deployed and implemented through a cooperative or community-driven approach to community resource mobilisation may unleash significant potential for building networks outwards from community resources and needs, instead of waiting for the commercial equation to tip in favour of attracting external telecom operators." The cooperative rural telephone movement in the U.S. that extended telephony into all of rural America is cited as an example. More recent examples include the innovative cooperatives of Argentina, Peru, India and Poland that have brought advanced ICT services to areas presumed to be unprofitable to commercial interests (Siochrú & Girard, 2005).

An interesting phenomenon can be observed when communities and regions are sufficiently well organised to know that they have a need for advanced information and communication structures, and set out to build out their own; it becomes much easier to attract commercial partners.

The necessities of trade and profit-making bring with them a certain implicit predisposition: that some level of infrastructure, interconnecting devices and access to applications has to be in place for people to buy and sell things. Thus, community partnerships involving commercial, private and public sector institutions tend to spring up to make sure that local people can participate in the marketplace. With the development of markets can come—though not guaranteed—other opportunities that relate to increased choices, productivity, entrepreneurial activity and creative expression. It is assumed that these developments can also raise a community's level of competitiveness and prosperity.

Of the republics of the former Soviet Union, it is very likely that the Baltic state of Estonia has made the greatest progress in building the infrastructure to aid in the establishment of a new civil society. That infrastructure is the "public Internet" the country has installed to insure that a user-friendly communication system is within reach of every citizen in every part of Estonia.

Estonia emerged from behind the Iron Curtain in 1991. In 1995, Toomas Hendrik Ilves, Estonian Ambassador to the U.S. and Canada who later became president of the country, advanced the idea of connecting all schools to the Internet as a development goal. The government supported this plan. By 1999, all schools had been provided with PCs and Internet connections. During this time, a national campaign to build an information society in Estonia was advanced, called "Tiger Leap." Commercial banks introduced e-banking, newspapers made themselves available online, and computers on mobile platforms were taken outside the capital Tallinn to introduce ICTs to the rural population (Archives of the ICF, 2008).

A backbone network for data communications linking all municipalities outside Tallinn was in place by 2004, and by 2007 wireless WiMax nodes operating in excess of 1 Mbps were fixed to those lines. With 90% broadband wireless connectivity anywhere within the country and with public access to local and central government databases, as well as the other public and private online services that had been created to ride on this network, the concepts of electronic transparency and citizen participation took on new meaning for Estonians.

The level of trust in the new broadband Internet was such that some 82% of the population in 2007 was filling out its income tax forms online, and the central government was collecting local as well as state taxes online, distributing those funds in a timely way back to municipalities, says Ivar Tallo, the principal author of Tallinn, Estonia's application for ICF 2007 Community of the Year. In building its information society there was no single mover, no large donor, or centralised coercive action, he said. The government never created a comprehensive plan to achieve it, as Malaysia had done. "People in government did not feel they could very well predict the future. Instead, the Estonian Parliament passed a resolution on Basic Principles of Information Society in 1997 that asserted the development priorities, action principles and the framework for government action" (Tallo, personal communication, 2007).

"Government ideology," said Tallo, "was to give a free hand to all economic activities and not to do things that the private sector was happy to do itself." Rather, "the government took an active role providing leadership in issues that the private sector was not interested in or that rightfully belonged to the government." He gave the examples of creating a Public Key Infrastructure and e-Government development.

Within the Estonian application was a comparison of its level of development with the two other Baltic states, Latvia and Lithuania. It said that comparing the experience of the three independent states shows "conclusively that neither size, location nor recent history can explain the success of Estonia in building a vibrant information society. The explanatory variable should be something else and its seems the only logical explanation is the political leadership and public support" (Estonia, ICF, 2007, p. 3-4).

The Estonia example demonstrates that, within a period of ten years, a country can join and become an active participant of the Network Society. While ten years may appear to be a long time for leaders eager to help their local communities, the development period may shrink if they use Estonia and other success stories as examples of best practise.

TECHNOLOGICAL CHOICES

Key Concept: *The number and type of broadband communication platforms are growing, but not all provide the same advantages.*

Having a broadband digital network means there can be almost any type of imaginable communication and content coming in from multiple directions. The deliverables will arrive in greater quantities and in noticeably better quality. The outflow will match it. The most suitable channels for distribution can be chosen to increase the appreciation of the art and entertainment programme, the power of the sales message, and the personal presence in an intimate communication. Not that this ideal situation exists everywhere, it is just that the technology permits it. What is different from the old days is that we can think about and plan for the day when our communities and their telecommunications infrastructures work better than they presently do.

We can observe that in the more populated areas, especially in affluent neighborhoods, residents have more choices, largely because competition exists but also because citizens have lobbied for greater access. In some of these locations, cable will be the dominant provider of video, high-speed data and local and long distance telephony; and in other places, the dominant carrier will be a satellite or telephone company. In many instances, these services are accessible on proprietary networks using proprietary technologies; on rare occasions, one can find that the networks and attached consumer electronics devices have been rendered compatible, or at least easily interconnected.

Fixed and mobile wireless and Internet service provider networks will grow more numerous, and utility companies will have also entered the competition in offering the voice, video and data services that consumers want. The common future-oriented format of all these communication systems is that they will inevitably operate in a language that is digital and, because of this, will all eventually be open and interconnected for user downloading and sharing of whatever has been or can be converted into digital data. The great advantage of having Internet access, no matter the carrier, is that it is the most inclusive communications technology available, at least for the moment.

For those who can afford it, the user-community has never been in a better position to take advantage of these new information highways. The quandary of deciding what systems to purchase exists for communities just as it does for individuals and families. With so many options out there—some more appropriate than others, some becoming obsolete earlier than others, some appealing to high-end users and others that could be made to reach a larger population—communities are often at a loss as to how to proceed without expert (and product neutral) advice.

The five basic options available and the nature of the solutions they provide are noted below:

- xDSL Platforms
- Fiber Optic Platforms
- Cable Platforms
- Wireless Platforms
- Satellite Platforms.

xDSL Platforms: Voice-grade modems transmitting data at 56/64 Kbps over common telephone lines were faster than the old 14.4 Kbps modems. But they seem slow indeed compared to the megabit (1.5 Mbps or faster) modems connecting users to the new broadband cable, wireless and satellite installations now providing services in the local telephone loop.

Bandwidth limitations of voice-band copper are not necessarily the fault of the line. The slowdown comes principally from the low frequency ranges used in transmission and from filters placed on the line by the central telephone switching office to ensure clean, prompt connections of voice services over many miles. By shrinking the length of the local loop (the distance between the subscriber and an access node that is connected to the central office), telecom engineers learned that data rates over existing twisted pair telephone lines can be boosted to 1.5 Mbps and higher, which is the basis of what is called "digital subscriber line" (DSL).

Digitized copper, popularly clustered under the name xDSL (an acronym commonly used to encompass any and all of the various formats in which telephone copper is conditioned for digital transmission), is the way the majority of residences and small businesses in the world are connected to the Internet. Although cable still predominates in North America, DSL is much stronger in the rest of the world. (World, 2008).

Distance is a major consideration among the several varieties of DSL. By installing access nodes closer to the user, creating subscriber loops of approximately three miles (18,000 feet more or less), the telephone companies have found they can substantially upgrade line capacity and reduce signal attenuation and loss of power while increasing the number of premises served. However, the fact that DSL cannot under normal operating conditions reach more than three miles beyond the central office is a serious problem for Internet users who live out of town.

When the predominant application of local users is Internet access, for those who live within those three miles, data rates of 1.5 Mbps per subscriber terminal downstream will likely be more than sufficient. When the application is live television, requiring data rates of 8 Mbps or more, the distance will need to be much less, about 4,500 feet. When the application is full-HDTV, which can require line speeds as high as 19.4 Mbps, the loop may accommodate only those customers within a fifth of a mile, 1,000 or so feet. These are applications that will work best in heavily populated neighbourhoods and apartment complexes.

The city of Seoul, South Korea, is home to 10 million people, about a quarter of the population of the country. Most urban Koreans live in high-rise apartments, enjoying some of the fastest Internet speeds and lowest access costs in the world. The prime reason is that the government invested some $24 billion in building a national high-speed backbone network and invited competitor networks to wire homes and businesses. In South Korea, the large number of apartment buildings makes it relatively simple for a telecommunications company to draw a fiber line to the basement and then provide VDSL (very high speed digital subscriber line) to individual spaces. VDSL can offer as much as 50 to 100 megabits of service over short copper lines, so the DSL technology is well suited to buildings and apartment complexes of high population densities.

Why would Korean families need such speeds? According to CNetNews.com, Internet gaming has been a key driver in broadband demand in South Korea. "Online gaming is a massive cultural phenomenon, with three TV channels dedicated to the subject and good players attaining the fame of American sports stars.....A book series teaches English through the game StarCraft, and the country's president has served as the honorary chairman of the World Cyber Games organisation" (Borland & Kanbellos, 2004, pp. 1-3). Citizens can expect to find high definition television shows online. Students can study for the national examinations that determine college admission and future careers. The DSL medium has the capacity and ease of connectivity to give families living in apartment buildings in Korea some of the fastest access in the world.

Fiber Optic Platforms: Fiber optic networks can be a lot faster and more efficient than networks consisting of copper cables. With fiber in the local loop, a single fiberglass strand has the potential to transmit 1 Gigabit per second or more of information. Such capacity allows a 10-strand fiber cable to deliver 500 HDTV programs at once, or its equivalent in data.

On all-optic networks, that same fiber strand can be subdivided by wavelength, extending services all the way to the desktop or living room, making possible a 100 Mbps wavelength of light per customer.

Optical communication replaces electricity with laser light as the medium of transmission, and substituting for the copper wires are hair-thin glass fibers. A fiber optic transmitter encodes computer data, human voices, text, graphic images and motion pictures into modulated light waves. At the other end of the fiber path a photo detector picks up the light and transforms the optical information back into electrical energy.

Among optical fiber's biggest advantages is its ability to carry far more information in a given time over far greater distances than any currently available medium. Fewer signal regenerating amplifiers are needed. Whereas copper requires frequent local boosting to strengthen the signal, long distance optical amplifiers are commonly separated 60 to 100 miles apart along the line. Submarine transoceanic cables are now being laid without a single amplifier covering a stretch of 3,000 miles or more.

Workers go online to access content from distant Web sites. Virtual private networks keep mobile employees connected to their offices. Large multimedia files are exchanged at a distance. Conferences bridge distant sites using real-time audio and video streaming. All these applications consume greater bandwidth and require more sophisticated computer processing. Fast and reliable execution of such applications demands larger backbone capacities and friendlier end-user interfaces with better security.

Fiber optic lines can support basic telecommunications, such as voice, data and video to consumers, or more advanced ICT-centric business services in such areas as entertainment production and distribution, automobile manufacturing, construction engineering and healthcare. The fiber optic lines that Korea Telecom has pulled into the residential apartment complexes of Seoul to enable high speed Internet via DSL lines and interactive cable TV services via digitized coaxial cable are the same high-speed trunk lines that support inter-industry collaboration throughout the country.

According to Jon-Lok Yoon, chief technology officer of Korea Telecom, the goal of KT's 2.0 core infrastructure is "the development of smart technologies that can be used to provide intelligent, context-aware, real-life-like, customizable services" that give added value and meet customers' future lifestyle needs. Korea Telecom has been busy acquiring a mix of technologies thought to be promising in this regard, and has found partners to help in enabling these developments. His list included "RFID/USN, Human Computer Interface, Virtual Reality, Utility/Grid Computing, Mobile Broadband, and Nano Bio Information Technology" (Yoon, 2007, pp. 10-12)

The purpose and function of telcos, according to Yoon, is changing from providing communication pipes to providing total telecommunications solutions and adding new value to what travels over those lines. Citing KT's transition from phase 1.0 to phase 2.0, telcos have "expanded into new business areas such as broadcasting, content, culture, information system solutions, and computing power." Korea Telecom no longer sees itself as just a telecommunications carrier. Rather, KT is a key collaborator with industries, universities and research institutes. In development and in implementation, the applications technologies that KT will be helping bring to market are all, directly or indirectly, dependent on the ready availability of fiber optic communications.

Cable Platforms: As with dial-up and DSL telephony systems, cable TV operators use special modems to connect their customers to the Internet. The cable modem is an on-premise device allowing computers to be connected into the same broadband cable that feeds the TV set.

In North America, the total number of DSL and fiber line installations were expected to catch up with the number of cable modems installed by cable companies in 2008, but this hasn't happened. Cable broadband service is now available to more than 93% of all those U.S. households able to access cable TV service. The telcos have been aggressive in rolling out their type of broadband but cable modem services have been holding their own in terms of consumer adoption (Associated Press, 2008).

In addition to being the first platform to converge different applications— e.g., television, Internet, and telephone service, digital modems connected to upgraded HFC (hybrid fiber/coaxial copper) networks have opened up a host of new applications, including cable interactive programme guides, multi-user gaming, video on demand, IP-telephony, videoconferencing, and electronic commerce as well as faster connections to the Internet. The cable modems are also expected to give content providers more direct access to users for purposes of data mining, advertising and marketing.

The advantage of cable modem over telco dial-up in addressing the Internet is that the service is always up-and-running. The "always on" connection operates something like a business local area network (LAN) in which a number of computers are linked and run constantly. Perpetual connectivity takes away some of the cost concerns customers have about maintaining an open line for videoconferences, live instruction, online gaming or any activity that keeps them on the Internet longer. Although pricing is a variable, demands on cable network resources have increased, with cable capacity filling almost as quickly as additional capacity has been made available.

Some cable operators are copying the telco strategy by installing fiber direct to the home to keep up with consumer demand for increased bandwidth. But cable companies have also looked to advances in digital data compression to improve the performance of existing coaxial copper lines. Digital compression algorithms have increased by a factor of 10 the quantities of data that telecom networks, both wireline and wireless, are able to carry, and these technologies are said to be still in their infancy. What digitization has done for cable is to double or quadruple the number of TV programs they can cast down the line, with capacity left over for variable data rate return signals traveling outward from the home.

The greater number of residential applications involving two-way data flow will be asymmetric and asynchronous. For the tele-worker doing work from home, occasional rather than continuous uploading of files will be the norm. Managing the unequal flow of information traveling up and down the line is one of the technical challenges that cable modems are designed to solve in those cable systems originally designed to be one-way broadcast services.

In the 1980s, Ichikawa, Japan, established a cable TV company to provide a multi-channel TV service that offered an alternative to the commercial broadcast stations. In 2000, with demand for broadband Internet service growing, the Ichikawa Cable Network introduced a cable modem high speed data service whose prices were lower than those offered by NTT, the incumbent telephone company. By 2005, broadband subscribers on the cable network exceeded 46% of the city's population, compared with a national average of 39%.

The Chiba University of Commerce (CUC), located in Ichikawa, partnered with the local government and Cable Network to create distance education programs to be delivered over the Internet via cable. The city started training classes for residents and citizen groups on topics related to information and communication technology, providing instruction to some 30,000 people. An e-government project called 350+5 made many Ichikawa government services accessible online. Internet-access kiosks were installed at public locations throughout the city, including 600 convenience stores. Its e-Net programme allowed citizens to report crimes through mobile phones and PCs, and distribute weather and disaster information. The city was chosen by the Japanese Ministry of Education and Culture to undertake a model project connecting the public to schools and libraries to further open up resources to citizens (Archives of the ICF, 2006, pp. 10-11).

As the Ichikawa example illustrates, when permitted to do so and demand is evident, cable TV networks have tended to evolve into more than one-way broadcast pipes for video. In this case, the cable network has become the broadband carrier of whatever content and services the community decides it needs and can manage to provide.

Wireless Platforms: The goal of the next generation of voice and data wireless providers, and one of their greatest challenges, is to emulate the higher delivery rates of broadcast and wireless cable stations while incorporating the ease of access, interactivity and portability of cell phones.

Looking back, it is hard to imagine that in 1988 mobile telephones were considered a non-essential expense for businesses and purely luxury items for the general public. Twenty years later, when the world's population had grown to 6 billion, there were about 1 billion fixed telephone lines but at least 2 billion cell phones in the world, with wireless telephones doubling the number of land line phones. The growth rate of wireless is so rapid there are those who expect the number of wireless phones to be 3 billion before the end of the decade, having gone through several generations of upgrades. Analog phones were the first generation; digital phones were the second generation. The second generation of cell phones that used digital processing were quickly adopted because of their increased capabilities, wider signal reach, lower cost and greater convenience in voice communication. Now, wireless providers are coming out with even more advanced phone systems, the third and fourth generation, featuring wireless e-mail, Web browsing and virtual private network access, as well as mobile conferencing, electronic shopping and multimedia content-sharing.

More often than not, the successful delivery of wireless telephony services is dependent on highly capable public networks using copper and fiber as the principal basis for connectivity and distant carriage. The local and long distance voice networks, which have been serving customers for more than a century, are known to be reliable, low in cost and easy to use. These same networks can also handle packet-switched data traffic but with less efficiency. The merging of wireless voice and wireless data on common networks is an engineering feat of some complexity requiring time, effort and expense, and it is one of the big challenges facing Internet service providers who have to accommodate to both wireline and wireless communication.

Voice traffic and data traffic are each growing, and they are each becoming commodity businesses. Global voice communication has been doubling every five years; in recent times, Internet traffic has doubled every year. The volume of router-based Internet traffic surpassed circuit-switched traffic on distance carrier lines at the turn of the millennium. What has made this transition easier is the move to telecom networks based on open protocols, in this case Voice-over Internet Protocol (VoIP), which some prognosticators are predicting will eventually lead to "turning off" the public switched telephone network in most regions of the world.

Digital wireless networks offer substantially increased network capacity, lower operating costs and opportunities to provide greatly enhanced data transmissions. Compared to traditional landline networks, the relative speed and economy in installing wireless systems, the ease of use, portability and lower cost for consumers have made wireless an attractive option for communities as well as nations scrambling to expand and modernize their telecommunications infrastructures.

The big breakthroughs in wireless these days are in interactive multimedia, in both fixed and mobile wireless. The most widely talked about broadband wireless technologies thought to signify the appearance of fourth-generation networks go by the names WiFi and WiMax.

WiFi is the popular identifier given a wireless networking technology whose technical standard (IEEE 802.11) has been set by the Institute for Electrical and Electronics Engineers. This is a limited range but high capacity radio technology that allows users to transmit and receive data over distances of a few hundred feet. Today, WiFi "hotspots" appear in many airports, hotels, libraries and educational institutions where citizens with laptop PCs can log onto the Internet and check their e-mails as they move about, and several varieties of WiFi are being installed in homes and home offices as wireless routers for voice, video and data.

Bell and Nortel Networks were contracted to make WiFi technology available throughout the community of Chapleau, Canada. The installation was found to be technically difficult, with a number of obstructions to service, and they had some difficulties with user knowledge. In the end, the price was right but the community received an offer for DSL, which was easier on the user and more reliable. Chapleau took down its city-wide WiFi network.

The city of Tallin, Estonia, had a more positive experience. Mobile phone penetration in the country was in 2008 in excess of 95%, and wireless Internet access in all open public areas was free. All citizens carry a national ID Card that mobile users can use to access their bank accounts, vote online, pay their taxes, pay their parking tickets and access the school records of their children. The city hosts and maintains some 366 WiFi nodes that provide coverage everywhere for broadband Internet access. According to City Manager Toomas Sepp, cities in Belgium, Slovakia, Slovenia and Ukraine have visited Tallinn with the idea of establishing a similar model (Sepp, 2008).

WiMax is a more recent standard (IEEE 802.16) that can provide broadband wireless access up to 30 miles using fixed stations and 10 or fewer miles for mobile applications. Depending on how the base stations are configured, this technology is designed to deliver 15 megabits per second of capacity or more, which is sufficient to send and receive multimedia content and communications, and sustain such heavy content usage as multiplayer gaming in metropolitan, suburban or rural areas.

The WiMax infrastructure has been deployed in more than 60 cities of India using an unlicenced 5 gigahertz frequency band. In locations where the in-place infrastructure for data communications is thin or nonexistent, the wide area broadband wireless solutions are very attractive, since wireless tends to be the cheaper solution, in part because it is easier to build out. Wires and wireline networks do have their limitations. Copper can rust, causing more rapid deterioration in damp climates. Also, since the market for recycled copper is great, people are now more likely to steal it.

"WiMax offers the best answer to last-mile broadband connectivity in a country like India", says Stanford University Professor Arogyaswami Paulraj. The delivery of low cost WiMax enabling devices to non-urban consumers is a priority in India because of the low population densities in rural areas and the low paying capacity of users there that keeps them perpetually out of the loop. Because of the great need and the willing cooperation of such international providers as Aperto Networks, Motorola and Intel, Pulraj believes that India may be getting a jump on the rest of the world in the development of mobile WiMax products and developing markets for them (Singh, 2006).

Satellite Platforms: Even in the ascendant days of high-capacity fiber optics, space-based satellites continue to be major carriers of international voice, video and data communications. This is due to their in-place infrastructure, their ubiquitous global reach and their suitability for distribution everywhere. Both fiber optic and satellite are interactive media, but fiber optic technologies operate in a point-to-point configuration, while satellites are point-to-multipoint connectors to content. As such, satellites represent indispensable information networks for most nations. They are the principal means by which broadcast radio and TV network signals are relayed to affiliated stations, programming is delivered to cable headends and news is reported from distant sites. Satellites connect hospitals, hotel chains, banks, automobile dealerships, brokerage firms, military installations, and educational institutions into private data networks. Those same private data networks are today connecting home offices and individual users.

An aggressive rollout of wide area fiber optic networks in the 1990s left point-to-point connections in place between major cities and almost all countries, often in excess of need. That over-capacity presented an economic challenge to satellite providers relying on information trunking as their principal line of business. Satellite operators have been forced to rethink where they fit into the data distribution market and are now using more of their space capacity for niche services and value-added applications, especially for point-to-multipoint audio and video services that end users cannot get any other way as conveniently, cheaply or reliably.

It is not surprising that satellite technologies now figure prominently in the strategies of urban and rural planners to better manage their communities and to empower their citizens. The ready availability of maps created from remote sensing satellite imagery and the precision location services provided by geo-positioning satellites are seen as invaluable services. Today, such satellites are networking agencies and individuals into virtual work teams, even when those teams are widely dispersed.

What do modern satellites have to offer communities today? What are their special assets in terms of easier connectivity, interoperability, broadband delivery and user-control?

Satellites are best known for their wide signal coverage and everywhere access to popular programming. Good examples include direct to home entertainment, sports backhaul from the local stadium and distance teaching packages for remote schools and home schoolers. Satellites are well suited to broadcasting data files and providing on-demand two-way linkages among the remote offices of business or government. Satellite-based interactive data services essential to business are now being marketed to both urban and rural residential customers. Among the most attractive applications of data communications via satellite are the broadband Internet services.

Though the public is generally less aware of it, satellite technologies have evolved in ways that are very similar to computer technologies. In the beginning, their terminals were big, expensive and very complex to operate. Just as the computer technologies devolved from the mainframe, to the PC, to the laptop and hand-held devices, satellite terminals also began appearing in the home, in the car and in the field. Today, individual users can address satellites directly using mobile phones and phone-like devices. Internet service is made available almost everywhere and such services are "always on", awaiting the user's command. Since satellites now figure prominently in the timely and economical delivery of voice, data and video, their providers are making sure that space-based technologies and software are interoperable with terrestrial networks. This is especially true for Internet links that cross wireless and wireline platforms.

As satellites are purveyors of both telecommunication and media services, they are frequently the community partners of local telephony, cable TV, wireless and broadcast companies. In some instances, the satellite is their competitor and, in niche situations, satellites provide the only services available. The example below illustrates how the satellite can be used to link local communities and their partners in ways that no other provider can do.

Brazil is a such a huge country, with such diverse geography, that it is hard to imagine that broadband Internet might ever be rolled out to a majority of its 180 million population via a terrestrial telecommunications infrastructure. But the Gilat Satellite Networks Company of Israel was able to put into place Brazil's first consumer "always on" broadband Internet service using VSAT technology that reached from south to north and east to west, providing coverage to all parts of the country. In the satellite world, data communications is referred to as VSAT communication, named after the very small aperture satellite earth stations and the interconnecting satellite infrastructure that business and government offices, banks, retail outlets, hospitals and schools use for moving information around locally and globally. What Gilat Satellite Networks did was make data communications for businesses available to the population at large.

"With the power, reach and convenience of satellite technology, the service offers broadband Internet access to residential and small office/home office (SOHO) users across Brazil. This is especially good news for Brazilians without access to any other broadband connectivity solutions", wrote Barry Spielman of Gilat (Spielman, 2004). The satellite company's Brazil service supported multi-PC connectivity in residences and in small businesses, providing the hardware and the installation services needed on the ground.

Another example is from Kyrgyzstan, a landlocked country in Central Asia that was a republic of the former Soviet Union. According to Kyrgyz journalist Aida Aidakyeva writing in the *Online Journal of Space Communication*, NATO provided a grant in 2002 to establish the Virtual Silk Highway, a satellite network that would facilitate teaching, research and academic exchanges in the region. The name of the project referred to the ancient Silk Road that was not only a trade route connecting Asia and Europe but also an all-important road for the transfer of information and knowledge between major regions of the world.

The principal contribution of the Silk project was to provide a satellite channel for high-speed access to the Internet for academic societies and institutions of Central Asian and the Caucasus countries with the hope of reducing the digital divide between these lesser developed countries and those of Europe. The configuration consisted of locating satellite dishes and network equipment in participating institutions, a central distribution point (hub) in Western Europe, the contract with a satellite vendor, and an Internet access provider. In 2004, Afghanistan was also added to the group of eight former Soviet Union countries connected to the Silk Highway (Aidakyeva, 2007).

Among other applications, the satellite service in Kyrgzstan was used to import instruction from the outside. According to Beishenbek Ukuev, director of the

Institute of New Information Technologies, distance education was a solution to several problems in Kyrgyzstan. He thought more young people from rural areas who traditionally left home after high school to study in the capital Bishkek or abroad would be convinced to stay. The country would be less likely to lose its educated specialists when its students have an opportunity to integrate into the world's intellectual community while being in Kyrgyzstan, he said.

In summary, local leaders now have several options to choose from as the single or multiple technology platforms and networks of their communities, with each platform having distinct advantages and disadvantages:

- xDSL Platforms: easy to implement where fixed telephone lines exist and offering fast transmission speeds, but has line provisioning problems and distance limitations;
- Fiber Optic Platforms: fastest transmission speeds and greatest capacity, but dependent on the investments of major telecom carriers;
- Cable Platforms: fast transmission speeds, but limited in range and dependent upon the investments of cable television companies;
- Fixed Wireless Platforms: fast transmission speeds and some portability but limited in range;
- Mobile Wireless Platforms: high mobility but limited capacity and coverage; and
- Satellite Platforms: fast transmission speeds with limited capacity but wide coverage.

Having chosen one of these platforms, the others can be used to satisfy specific needs. The overall configuration of platforms of course should fit the local community requirements.

Key Concept: *Handy network-connected devices are doing more, faster and more economically for end users than ever before.*

Around the globe, microprocessor, consumer electronics, transmission and software businesses compete to make ICT technologies more capable, accessible and convenient to use. From the consumer's perspective, this trend represents a huge leap forward for personal enjoyment and professional productivity.

New digital audio and video editing software installed in laptops and personal computers is doing for personal media production, editing and distribution what the computer-based word processors and e-mail did for writing and publishing. With a digital camcorder and iDVD mastering system in a PC costing less than $5,000, home, school and small business users can render their self-made productions virtually indistinguishable from professionally crafted ones. It takes no leap of imagination to realise that with a broadband connection to the Internet and streaming software, home producers can now be broadcasters with a global reach.

As a glance at the popular video-sharing sites MySpace.com and YouTube.com will quickly demonstrate, media companies are making room for user-generated productions. Some of these video presentations attract such viewer numbers, they strike fear and envy among the most powerful television networks on the air. It was perhaps not surprising to see the MySpace and YouTube startups being quickly acquired by the media giant News Corp. and by the popular search engine-turned media purveyor Google. Amateur fare is now being courted by big media. Just as amateurs have their own news blogs and TV production facilities, they can also generate huge followings by creating an attractive presence on the Internet.

Within a decade there will be literally millions of new computing and communications devices interconnected to high-speed access lines from homes and offices that will be capable of capturing, storing and exchanging broadband video and data in multiple formats. When telecommunication lines are bi-directional, users can go in search of what they need to know, linking to people across vast geographic and cultural boundaries. Although the argument is not entirely convincing, there are those who hypothesize that such emerging technologies are allowing a new kind of participatory democracy by raising the public standard of living, stimulating general awareness and involvement, and allowing the easy sharing of creative expression.

The old model of mass media traveling one-way from content provider to a broadly targeted audience is clearly changing, at least among media consumers in the technologically-advanced nations. The reasons are multiple, but the main one is the greatly changed mindset and behavioural patterns of media audiences connected to the Internet who have the tools to be media producers as well as media consumers. The old broadcast model hasn't gone away, but the public has now seized the opportunity to share the content it has created. Consumers are using their laptops to go on the Web in search of quite personalized information and entertainment, accessing it whenever they want, almost wherever they are. And they are feeding into the Internet news events they have covered, music they have produced, photos they have captured, articles and reviews they have written.

"The infrastructure for delivering media content—the Internet—is fast becoming ubiquitous," writes the *Economist*. "Ordinary people are creating their own blogs, wikis and podcasts, because it costs almost nothing to do so. Most of them do not care how large their 'audience' is. Some choose to keep it small and intimate; a tiny number become stars—one-man and one-woman news organisations in their own right. Since the audience is made up of people who are themselves sounding off, new media are more of a hub-bub than a homily" (Talking, 2006, p. 14).

It is not hard to find examples of ordinary citizens sharing with their families and friends the digital products they have produced. It is also not hard to find citizens using the tools of new media collaboration to seek help with their personal creations, production assistance, promotions and marketing and even sales transactions. If these examples represent trends in our communities, which we believe they do, we can expect to see government officials, business employees, school teachers, health workers and other professionals learning how to take off-the-shelf consumer devices to accomplish the not-so-ordinary tasks that will improve the quality of their work.

COMMUNITY NETWORKING

Key Concept: *The networking of digital devices and broadband systems allows the local community to transform itself by reaching out to potential markets and collaborators.*

While information and communication technologies cannot guarantee the competitiveness and ultimate viability of any community, appropriate technologies can increase productivity, offer greater convenience and lower operating costs. In addition, everywhere connectivity can greatly contribute to the mix of factors affecting a community's ability to innovate and provide needed services.

Today, the Internet and its World Wide Web are inextricably woven into the fabric of global commerce, communication, education, health, entertainment, transportation, and manufacturing. Fortunately, the trend is to increase the speed and capacity of these structures and make them more readily attainable and manageable for all citizens. Today, it is widely assumed that any community, any company, any entrepreneur not online runs the risk of being left behind. This understanding is not universal, but the message is out there to be considered by large cities and small hamlets, by colleges and corporations, and by individual users.

From a technological perspective, the key is digital processing. The basic communication components in the local telecom loop, the physical linkages between local providers and their customers, are undergoing radical restructuring. This holds true not just for telephone companies but also for cable, broadcast, terrestrial wireless and satellite operators. These transformations are all grounded in an urgency to convert their physical plant to digital and to make all their networks Internet Protocol-compliant.

The networks on which Internet messages are conveyed around the world today include the faster, more sophisticated Ethernets and token rings of the private data networks as well as the slower public switched telephone systems. Efforts are now being made to provide a better bridge between the domains of voice and video switching and IP-data, integrating routers and switchers, and merging their support software. To achieve faster delivery, some companies are trying specific updates to Internet protocols, such as IPv6 (version 6) and multi-protocol label switching (MPLS). By these means, distance carriers are adding voice to the data-transport side of their networks, perhaps to eventually eliminate circuit-switching altogether.

In the local loop, exchange carriers and their competitors are facing similar problems in deciding which are the most efficient and economical ways to make broadband services available to their customers.

The creation of virtual private networks (VPNs) has proven to be a great boon to communication management within government offices and other community organisations. With the VPN innovation, access to city or corporate networks can be extended not just to on-site employees but also to employees on the road, to tele-commuters, to partner companies, to suppliers and to customers and clients. These virtual private networks will normally be accessed through the public switched telephone networks since the PSTN is globally available and comparatively economical in cost, but specially provisioned IP networks are now also used.

The VPN is a way to give direct and priority access to those outside the corporate LAN without those communities or companies having to bear all of the leased line and dial-in costs of remote access connectivity. Remote users can be treated as if they were on the computer systems of the home office, and the computer server can keep up with the number and demographics of visitors who enter the system. As a firewall, the VPN provides the security (encryption, authentication and access control) needed to protect sensitive internal information. When the VPN rides on broadband fiber and satellite, whatever heavy data transactions are possible back at the office are also possible from remote locations, with security assured.

The Internet has today become the default wide area network to most corporate LANs and the front door to many government offices. Without regard to size, complexity or even capitalization, private and public organisations can now have their own personal global net whereby remote parties with authorization can gain immediate access. Once there, visitors will encounter Web sites that are custom made; they will be able to conduct site searches that speed up locating, uploading and downloading information, and get responses to their inquiries and their orders filled. In earlier times, most of these transactions would not have happened because they would have required an appearance in person.

In the aftermath of the "bursting of the Internet bubble" that occurred just at the beginning of the 21st century, there was much talk about the over-optimistic investment that had produced a glut in global fiber capacity. If such a glut existed, it is now quickly disappearing. Why? Uncountable new applications are being created at the far edges of these networks. The prospects of the telecom providers now look rosier than ever. With more efficient data transport, end-users are finding ways to create and manage entirely new products and services. Local communities now see that they need broadband networks to support the more robust end-to-end, person-to-person, organisation-to-organisation, and community-to-community transactions they envision. And the reverse is also true: communities can now take on previously unimagined projects and programs because the technology permits it.

Like new roads and highways, new technologies and technological networks alter people's perceptions of what is possible. For all practical purposes, it makes no difference to collaborating scientists whether, in sharing their work, their research papers are sent to Internet addresses on the other side of the planet or only across campus. Such transactions take almost no time and very little expense. With e-mail and file-sharing connections, local area networks blend into global area networks in an instant.

Long-haul satellite service providers offer programmers the means to bypass the over-crowded Internet by delivering content directly to edge locations almost anywhere in the world. Network services providers have built strong businesses linking the super-high data speeds of Internet carriers to the low bandwidth processing and limited storage equipment of ISPs. Billions of dollars have been spent installing high-performance data centres and optical networking infrastructures closer to where the ultimate users are, just to make needed information a click away.

New classes of applications are being stored in physical space closer to users and being exchanged via interconnected telco, cable, wireless and satellite networks. Community-based centres are becoming the local hubs for e-commerce, teleconferencing, video on demand, streaming audio/video, gaming, digital photography, Web hosting, and tiered Internet access. Having offices at home, hosting businesses and providing non-profit services locally that give the inquiring public on-demand access to specialised libraries, unique schools, bookstores, shopping malls, arcades, race tracks, banks, stock brokers and auction houses are now possible for consumers who never before thought of themselves as creators, producers, marketers and sellers (Flournoy, 2004, pp. 12-16).

Ashland, Oregon, is one of the first communities in the U.S. to establish a broadband telecommunications system run by the municipality. Ashland is a geographically isolated community of about 10,000 households located on the west coast about half way between San Francisco, California, and Portland, Oregon. Until recently, Ashland was a community mainly known as a tourist destination. In 1997, wishing to diversify its economy, the town funded installation of a fiber optic network that by 2002 reached 95% of all addresses with digital cable and high speed Internet services.

"Since the broadband infrastructure was built, the net number of active business licences in Ashland has increased by 571. That's better than a 30% increase", Information Technology Director Joseph Franell reported in an interview. "Testimonials are commonplace from business owners who are now doing business nationally and globally because of the Internet access," he said (Franell, 2007).

The local Chamber of Commerce leverages the Internet to provide targeted marketing and informational videos to people who are considering relocating their businesses there. Franell also describes a project in which a local group of high tech businesses teamed up to launch a new community Web and TV channel, called AshlandTV 20. With the Ashland Fiber Network in place, local viewers can choose to get their information and entertainment through the Web, while others can take advantage of advanced Web-based features over their traditional TV-based entertainment systems.

"AshlandTV 20 is exactly the type of technology we've hoped to enable with AFN, and it's great to see it becoming a reality," said Franell, who also serves as the director of Ashland's Fiber Network. "One of the most exciting aspects of the new channel is that users will be able to submit their own videos to the Web site www.ashlandtv20.com for broadcast, offering a local service similar to the popular YouTube service."

Franell also give a retail example and a health care example to illustrate profitable high-tech businesses bringing national/international attention to Ashland. Dream-Sacks Inc. is a local Web business selling silk travel sheets, bamboo fiber clothing, Chinese furniture and corporate gifts of silk. Online, Plexis Health Care Systems provides software for the administration of such healthcare benefits as medical, dental and vision claim processing. Each of these businesses is dependent on the fast Internet access of the AFN and is growing exponentially. Plexis is planning on a significant physical expansion of its facilities in Ashland, he said.

"It is particularly satisfying and validating to see these types of businesses flourishing here in Southern Oregon. From the standpoint of the business owners, it is their ability to live and do business in a small town in the mountains that is so important. The Internet has dramatically changed the model for locating a business. In the past, business owners had to locate in large commercial centres, in big cities. Today, they can choose their business sites based on quality of life for them and their employees. This is the benefit of broadband infrastructure deployment in small communities" (Franell, 2007).

The case of Ashland illustrates that a local community can best serve its interests when it deliberately chooses a technology platform to meet community goals.

Key Concept: *Technology and networking often come with downsides, and discovering how to maximize advantages without causing harm can be a challenge.*

In thinking about the Internet, it is helpful to keep in mind that less than 20% of the world's population has regular access to a telecommunications network on which the Internet can be accessed. While there could be as many as 3 billion cell phones in use in the world today, only a small fraction of those phones can be used to access the Internet, and cell phone usage is very unevenly distributed. It is probable that as many as two thirds of the 6.2 billion people on Earth have never sent or received an e-mail.

Even in the most connected of societies, there is worry about a troublesome gap between those who have access to Internet technologies and those who do not. The rapid build-out of Internet infrastructures in certain places has not diminished our concern about its absence in other places. There is increased Internet access at work, home, school, the library and local cafes for some people, but not all. The number and types of digital databases now available on the World Wide Web is a great boost for those who can get to them. These are good but not sufficient steps. While the literature supports the general hypothesis that the Internet has emerged as a social force for good like no other medium, there are parents and community groups and even governments that long for the days when our societies were less well connected. And the rest have no basis for an informed opinion because they have no chance to be connected.

Digital divide issues are political as well as social. Politicians tend to back high tech initiatives that they think might help to grow the economies of the communities they represent, and could reduce unemployment and serve as a stimulant for better education. Sometimes it works out that way; often it does not. This book focuses principally on success stories, but there are also dashed hopes. Although Internet investment euphoria was credited for a notable and growing inequality of income, many of the wealthy benefactors of the dot-com bubble were also taken down in the bankruptcies and layoffs that occurred in the fallout; some (not many) went to jail for fraudulent business practises.

No one doubts that the Internet will be present in the long run, or that vigilance will be needed to protect citizens against intrusion. Internet advertising, marketing and selling should not degenerate into spam, and content owners need to protect their intellectual property from piracy while keeping the Internet open and innovative. Evil can happen on the Internet. Children can be hurt; racism can be inflamed. Since anyone with a computer is free to publish almost anything they like, there is the risk that objectionable material will appear on the Internet—or that individuals will be defamed or defrauded, personal privacy invaded, copyrights ignored and junk mail abundant in e-mail boxes.

As the digital economy expands throughout the world, the changes will disrupt the way people live and work. Whether those changes will on-balance be more positive or negative cannot be precisely foreseen. What can be assumed in a competitive world is that failure from not trying will be a harder lesson on all participants than failure from not getting it entirely right; the latter allows a community to learn from its mistakes and try again.

Whatever infrastructure is put in place will require a continuous process of review, leading to updates, revisions and reassigning resources according to community priorities. When early decisions do not work out, the successful strategy will be to assess the situation, learn from those errors of judgement and get to work implementing alternative plans.

Key Concept: *Measuring and evaluating the desired outcomes of investments in facilities and infrastructure will be key to determining which technology becomes part of the solutions sought.*

Technical infrastructure represents perhaps the most easily quantified component of measurement within networked communities. The broad measures of the percentages of homes and businesses with access to broadband, and the number of public access points within the city or region are frequently used indicators. Sustainability of the network is a more complex matter to measure. For example, assessment of the potential for adding more users to the network and meeting public need for even speedier networks, devices and services requires constituency research. Making a decision to interconnect wireline and wireless services, so that city services can be transported into the mobile domain, may require only a determination of the technical viability of upgrading, but will likely also involve such issues as sustainability of revenues, finding partners to share costs and covering maintenance.

We know that innovation is often intricately linked to the success of infrastructure as a promoter of economic development in the community and region. In an assessment of the growth of information and communication technology in the U.S. and in EU countries, Jungmittag and Welfens (2006) found a direct correlation between telecommunication density and economic output. These researchers recommended that communities and regions measure the specific uses being made of Internet technologies and applications as a measure of economic growth. Since the relative cost of telecommunication services can determine usage and, as an extension, impact innovation and creative expression, communities are advised to keep up-to-date records.

Table 1 provides an overview of potential measures for infrastructure sectors, as well as the types of demonstrations and evaluation approaches that may be considered.

Table 1. Assessment of telecommunications infrastructure

Technology issues to be evaluated	Possible approaches to measurement
Digital Subscriber Line (DSL) and Fiber Optics	Improved competitive position due to high-speed exchanges of information between businesses
Hybrid Coaxial/Fiber and Cable Modems	Increased productivity and user satisfaction due to faster access from home
Digital Wireless Networks WiFi and WiMax	Anywhere access to e-mail and audio and video entertainment due to broadband coverage
Satellite Video and Data Networks	Lower operating costs and convenience due to ease and speed of access
Digital Television and High Definition TV	Enhanced advertising due to high impact visuals and recording capabilities
Broadband Internet and On-Demand Streaming	Freedom of expression within civil society due to user-friendly equipment and software

CONCLUSION

Manuel Castells, author of *The Rise of the Network Society*, more than a decade ago was pointing out some of the ways that information and communication technologies were leading us to a new kind of global community. He defined the Network Society as an advanced social structure making use of ICTs to gain greater openness, adaptability and flexibility for itself. Organisations and individuals benefit from the electronic networks, he said, in that these networks deliver information and communication support in the development of knowledge, which can spur innovation and change (Castells, 1996).

Taking Castells a step further, the authors conclude that the Network Society and the New World Information and Communication Order—a working concept of UNESCO in the late 1970s and early 1980s that inspired debate on the Information Society—go hand-in-hand in the new millennium. We believe that it will not be sovereign governments that will be the drivers of democratization and everywhere access to information around the world. Rather, it will be the "networked communities", working person-with-person in public and private partnerships within and beyond national borders using the tools of digital collaboration, that will be on the front line of social expression, innovation and change.

The Internet has become the agent of societal transformation, both locally and globally. What is now clear is that, as the new Network Society evolves, not just nations become linked, but communities, groups and individuals within those nations are linked one with the other. Borders are no longer conceptual and physical constraints to people getting what they want.

Looking back, the telecom networks will be seen by future generations as one of the fundamental developments of human history, perhaps as important as the invention of the printing press or the gas combustion engine. Networks and networking are important not just because they put human beings in touch with one another, but also because they greatly reduce the constraints of time and distance and go a long way toward automating work. As the technologies of telecommunication become more accessible, more capable and more affordable, familiarity, acceptance and use tends to go up. This is what happens in modern communities when the tools of digital collaboration are available and citizens can put their heads together to think about how to best use local resources in creating a healthier, safer and more productive environment for everybody.

Some communities are of course better positioned than others to take advantage of information and communication technologies as an asset. And because of adverse economic conditions and social strife, some communities and countries will be left far behind. Not all communities will choose to take the same approach—even if they could—nor should they. The strategies outlined in this book are aimed at bringing broadband digital networks into the very core of communities where they will be used by local people as platforms for the unique types of social and economic development they have chosen.

The assumption is that, when combined in the right context, physical and interpersonal networks can be the basis for empowering individuals and communities to effect those changes they give highest priority. In other words, becoming a networked community requires a transformation. The process will inevitably be difficult, but we believe that local community leaders who work together to move in this direction will find their communities energized, and improvements in "the human condition" will also be realized.

REFERENCES

Aidakyeva, A. (2007). Distance education projects in Kyrgyzstan. *The Online Journal of Space Communication.* Issue No. 11. *www.spacejournal.org.*

Archives of the ICF – The Intelligent Communities Forum (2008). *Tallinn, Estonia – Nomination submitted for the Intelligent Community of the Year Award.* New York.

Archives of the ICF – The Intelligent Communities Forum (2007). *Ichikawa, Japan – Nomination submitted for the Intelligent Community of the Year Award.* New York.

Associated Press. (2008). *Cable modems winning over DSL.* Retrieved May 16, 2008, from www.time.com.

Borland, J., & Kanbellos, M. (2004). South Korea leads the way. *Digital Agenda Broadband. cNetNews.com*, 1-3.

Brown, K. (2006). Telecos rev up broadband adds. *Multichannel News*, 32.

Castells, M. (1996). *The rise of the Network Society, Vol. 1 of the information age: Economy, society and culture.* Oxford: Blackwell.

Chu, G. C., Alfian & Schramm, W. (1985). *Satellite television comes to Indonesian villages: A study of social impact.* Jakarta & Honolulu: Leknas/LIPI and East-West Centre.

Country leads the way with Nepad E-Schools. (2007, March 13). *Business in Africa.* Retrieved July 20, 2007, from www.allAfrica.com

Flournoy, D. (2004). *The broadband millennium: Communication technologies and markets.* Chicago: International Engineering Consortium.

Franell, J. (2007). *Private interview with the director of the Ashland, Oregon, Fiber Network.*

Hammond, A. (2006). New search engine could boost Arab Internet usage. *Muslim Tech Digest.* Retrieved August 15, 2007, from http://muslim-tech.blogspot.com/2006/05/is-sawafi-google-killer.html

Ibrahim, M. D. (2005). Planning and development of Indonesia's domestic communications satellite system PALAPA. *Online Journal of Space Communication.* Issue No.8. *www.spacejournal.org.* Ph.D. Dissertation completed at the American University, Washington D.C. in 1989.

ICF – Intelligent Community Forum (2005). *ICF announces recipients of 2005 Awards.* Retrieved July 7, 2007 from www.intelligentcommunity.org

International Telecommunications Union. (2006). *World Telecommunication/ICT development report 2006: Measuring ICT for social and economic development* (8th ed.). Geneva: International Telecommunications Union.

Sepp, T. (2008). *Personal interview with the author,* at the 2008 Building the Broadband Economy conference, Intelligent Community Forum, New York City.

Singh, S. (2006, September). India connects to wireless Internet. *IEEE Spectrum*, 20.

Siochrú, S., & Girard, B. (2005). *Community-based networks and innovative technologies:* New models to serve and empower the poor. Geneva: United Nations Development Programme.

Spielman, B. (2004, Fall). Gilat delivers broadband to Brazil. *The Online Journal of Space Communication.* Issue No.7. Retrieved August 12, 2007, from *www. spacejournal.org*

Talking to yourself. (2006, April). *The Economist, 14.*

The role of satellites in Indonesian national development. (2005, Fall). *Online Journal of Space Communication.* Issue No.8. Retrieved August 12, 2007, from *www.spacejournal.org*

World Broadband Information Service. (2008). Retrieved May 16, 2008, from www. informa.com.au/

Yoon, J. (2007, January). Telco 2.0: A new role and business model. *IEEE Communications Magazine*, 10-12.

Chapter III
Regulation and Policy Reforms

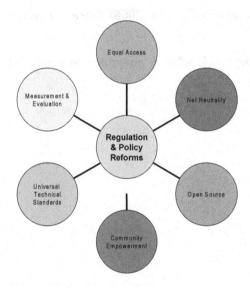

"The government managed to create a situation whereby to use and be associated with ICTs was fashionable across the population, not only among the young people. This broad-based support allowed the topic of information society building to be above usual party political fights" (Estonia, Archives of the ICF, 2007, p. 8).

Overview: This chapter examines the following ideas on regulation and public policy:

- Information societies are enabled by regulations and public policies that support open communications;
- Government, business and public sector collaboration is key to establishing policies that lead to economic and social development;

- Open source applications, products and collaborative culture are accelerated by adopting universal technical standards;
- To be sustained, accessibility to the Internet and keeping it free and open requires some vigilance;
- Ways must be devised to assess the local impact of policy and regulations and to provide next steps.

THE FREE FLOW OF KNOWLEDGE

Key Concept: *The fate of nations, communities and their enterprises are intertwined. For corporations to be competitive and for communities to be value-adding societies, national governments and associated agencies must cooperate to ensure that ICT infrastructure is enabled by regulations and public policies that support open communication.*

In Jared Diamond's book, *Guns, Germs and Steel: The Fates of Human Societies* (1999), the author explores the question of why it was that 62 soldiers from Europe mounted on horses with the aid of 106 foot soldiers conquered the Inca Empire, rather than the other way around. Diamond's take is that the Spanish had ships and the Incas did not. Also, invader Francisco Pizarro had prior knowledge of the Incas because the Spanish had been to the New World, while no Inca had ever been to Europe.

Unlike the Incas, the Spaniards had writing, which made documentation and communication easier. Pizarro was an informed military man in a literate society; thus he knew about the successful strategies of Cortez, who had earlier conquered the Aztec Empire. Literacy, information, communication and such advanced technologies as ships, horses and gunpowder gave Pizarro a conqueror's advantage.

Diamond argues that lesser developed societies are not less competitive because their populations are intellectually inferior or less capable. For reasons of geography, resources, cultural heritage, political structures, and perhaps medicine, those societies simply have not had the same opportunities as their more developed counterparts. Under different circumstances, the Inca King Atahuallpa with 80,000 troops might indeed have been the conquerors of Spain.

Diamond raises one of the central questions of world economics: why are countries like the United States and Switzerland so rich, while other countries like Paraguay and Mali are so poor? Why is it that the per-capita gross national products (GNP) of the world's richest countries are more than 100 times those of the poorest countries? According to Diamond:

This is not just a challenging theoretical question giving employment to economics professors, but also one with important policy implications. If we could identify the answers, then poor countries could concentrate on changing the things that keep them poor and on adopting the things that make other countries rich.

Obviously, part of the answer depends on differences in human institutions. The clearest evidence for this view comes from pairs of countries that divide essentially the same environment but have different institutions, with different per-capita GNPs. Four flagrant examples are the comparisons of South Korea with North Korea, the former West Germany with the former East Germany, the Dominican Republic with Haiti, and Israel with its Arab neighbors. Among the many "good institutions" often invoked to explain the greater wealth of the first-named country of each of these pairs are effective rule of law, enforcement of contracts, protection of private property rights, lack of corruption, low frequency of assassinations, openness to trade and the flow of capital, incentives for investment, and so on (Diamond, p. 438).

"Good institutions" are one of the reasons for the differences in wealth among nations. He notes that many economists believe that good institutions make the most important contribution to national wealth. Effective governments, agencies and foundations build their policies, foreign aid and loans on this foundation. Similarly, the development of good institutions in poor countries is propagated for sustainable wealth creation. However, Diamond notes:

But there is increasing recognition that this good-institution view is incomplete— not wrong, but incomplete—and that other important factors need addressing if poor countries are to become rich. This recognition has its own policy implications. One cannot just introduce good institutions to poor countries like Paraguay and Mali and expect those countries to adopt the institutions and achieve the per-capita GNPs of the United States and Switzerland.

Good institutions are not a random variable that could have popped up anywhere around the globe, in Denmark or in Somalia, with equal probability. Instead it seems to me that, in the past, good institutions always arose because of a long chain of historical connections from ultimate causes rooted in geography to the proximate dependent variables of the institutions. We must understand that chain if we hope, now, to produce good institutions quickly in countries lacking them (Diamond, p. 439).

Competitiveness of Nations is an economic theory that serves as an analytical framework. It considers the facts and policies that shape the ability of nations to build and sustain environments that promote value creation for their enterprises and prosperity for their people.

Among the 10 "Golden Rules of Competitiveness" advanced by the World Competitiveness Center (WCC), five relate to the contributions governments can make. The first one is to "Create a stable and predictable legislative environment". Number three is to "Invest in traditional and technological infrastructure". Number six is to "Focus on quality, speed and transparency in government and administration". Number nine is to "Invest heavily in education, especially at the secondary level, and in the life-long training of the labor force". Number 10 is to "Balance economies of proximity and globality to ensure substantial wealth creation, while preserving the value systems that citizens desire" (Garelli, 2006, pp. 1-12).

The World Competitiveness Center studies the interaction of four competitiveness factors that it believes define a country's national environment: economic performance, government efficiency, business efficiency and infrastructure. In the competitiveness of nations, as with the competitiveness of corporations, communities, families and individuals, not everything rests on strategy, finance and structure. There are "less rational" factors. Included in modern definitions of competitiveness is the notion that the economic consequences of non-economic issues, such as education, sciences, political stability and value systems, also hold power.

The WCC uses education as an example of national policy that affects all sectors. "Education policy can be viewed as an expense in a nation's budget. However, education policy also increases the general level of literacy. It raises the skills and competencies available throughout the economy. Education policy also influences and even shapes the value system of a country.....Enterprises bear the consequences of education policies. They can only compete if they can rely on a pool of talents. In addition, they also have to be attractive to such talents" (p. 1).

Another important idea is that "Frontiers between nations are losing importance: ideas, values and practises move freely from one nation to the other. Inside enterprises, boundaries (the so-called 'silos') are under attack. They are dismantled to ensure a free flow of knowledge." Companies—and by extension communities—can no longer ignore the demands for ethics and environment protection from the younger generation. If they do, these new talents will simply go elsewhere (p. 1).

In 2006, Harvard University's Institute for Strategy and Competitiveness released its Business Competitiveness Index, part of the Global Competitiveness Report prepared in cooperation with the World Economic Forum. The Index ranks nations by their microeconomic competitiveness, identifies competitive strengths and weaknesses in terms of business environment and company operations and strategies, and assesses the sustainability of current levels of prosperity as measured by per capita GDP (Harvard Business School, 2006).

The Index also analyzes the contextual factors of each country surveyed, focusing on the impact of political stability, location and natural resource wealth. Such factors help to explain why the prosperity of nations can deviate from the level predicted by their competitiveness. China was used as an example. The 2006 Index found that "the Chinese economy has faltered, falling to the middle of the pack at number 64. China (down nine ranks from last year) continues a downward trend that started in 2002....This year's decline was driven especially by high levels of corruption, weaker assessment of buyer sophistication, and concerns about labor relations. China also suffers from weak property rights, poor board governance, low quality of management education, and poor access to loans. Overall, it is clear that euphoria about China is moderating as the realities of its competitiveness become more apparent."

According to the Index, India faired better with a ranking of 27. India won praise for "recording the highest rate of 'dynamism' in improving its competitiveness among low-income countries". The report focused on improvements in business environment and the sophistication of its companies (pp. 1-2).

None of these reports addresses the competitiveness of communities directly, nor do they seek to assess the direct impact of good government on community health. However, the Diamond essay and the national competitiveness reports are useful for thinking about why and how one community might have a competitive advantage over another, including the alternating facilitating and restraining roles that governments and public policy may play in that process. What are the reasons that some communities realise wealth by seizing opportunities while others remain afflicted by poverty, lack of education and public malaise?

Estonia is a country worth considering in our search for answers. Here is a state with only 1.38 million citizens, that only emerged from behind the Iron Curtain of the Soviet Union in 1991, yet is now a full member nation of the European Union. Estonia's economic growth rate exceeded 5% annually for the last decade. In 2006, the country was ranked number 25 in the country competitiveness index of the World Economic Forum. The United Nations Human Development index of 2005 put Estonia in the 38th position, and Transparency International awarded Estonia 27th place, the highest among countries of Central and Eastern Europe, in an index that measures freedom from corruption (www.ega.ee & www.riso.ee).

Although intuitively it would seem that Estonia should still be at a great disadvantage, having been a republic of the former Soviet Union for many years, it is not. What has made the difference? How was such a remarkable transformation possible? Estonia's competitiveness and human development indicators make it an interesting case study for testing Diamond's premise of "a long chain of historical connections from ultimate causes rooted in geography to the proximate dependent variables of (the country's) institutions". To pursue this thought, the authors interviewed Ivar Tallo, head of the eGovernance Academy of Estonia, an organisation that spends much of its time promoting the use of ICT and helping to build an information society not just in Estonia but in other countries of Central and Eastern Europe. Tallo said about Estonia,

> We are not a very wealthy country and despite that fact we have succeeded in building an information society here. As a crude measure we could use Internet penetration, which is about 60% now. There are countries where it is higher like yours, or in Scandinavia. Estonia is comparable to Germany or France but these countries have a GDP per person four to five times that of Estonia.

> The story gets more interesting as we compare what people are doing on the Internet. With e-business applications, Estonia has a usage rate comparable to the UK. And when it comes to e-government services, we would be at the very top. This year [2006] 82% of those who had to fill out a Personal Income Tax Declaration form did it online.

> I would argue that we are the only country in the world with a functioning e-government infrastructure. Yes, we have a lot of problems and we speak of those too, but we have in place government information systems that are interconnected and are safely accessible over the Internet as a result of the fact that our adult population now have electronic ID cards and there is a functioning public key infrastructure. These allow us to use sophisticated e-services. Last year, we became the first country in the world to have nationwide local elections where people could cast their vote over the Internet (Tallo, 2006).

In comparing development of the Baltic nations of Estonia, Latvia and Lithuania, Tallo noted that neither the size of the community nor the geographic location or socio-political experience of the population would explain Estonia's success in building a vibrant information society. Latvia and Lithuania were of similar size and location and shared a similar 50-year history, but their rate of development in moving toward an information society was two to three times slower. He thought the only logical explanation was the difference in political leadership and public support for an information society in Estonia.

Like other historically disadvantaged societies under consideration by Jared Diamond, Estonia was greatly shaped by its subjection to the former USSR. Its application to the Intelligent Community Forum's ICF Community of the Year Award in 2007 cites some of the challenges Estonia had to overcome to find a new identity and a more workable political and economic system.

Regaining its independence in 1991 after the break-up of the USSR, Estonia was busy restoring its statehood, passing the constitution, creating state institutions and stabilizing the economy. Russian troops were finally withdrawn in September 1994 but the Estonian people quickly discovered that freedom alone does not bring investment and prosperity. During the debate on the future of the country, decision makers understood that Estonia could not remedy 50 years of socialist mismanagement with one short miracle effort. It would be a long development process.

To jumpstart the economy, a number of radical steps were implemented. First, to stop the hyperinflation, the Estonian currency Kroon was introduced in 1992 and pegged to the German mark, followed by radical privatisation. The tax system introduced a flat rate income tax of 26%. Enterprise income tax was abolished and a law was passed that required a balanced state budget.

During the economic reconstruction, it became clear that economic measures alone were not sufficient. There was a need for modernisation of the entire society. The explosive growth in personal computer and World Wide Web use in the Western world provided the idea of an information society as a goal of development. Then Estonian ambassador to the U.S. and Canada (and recently elected President of Estonia) Toomas Hendrik Ilves publicized the idea of connecting all schools to the Internet in 1995. Estonian President Lennart Meri supported this, and the government created a plan called "Tiger Leap" to provide all schools with PCs and Internet connections between 1996-1999.

"Tiger Leap" became much more than simply an educational modernisation project. Everybody knew somebody who went to school and came back home with the message that something quite different was happening. There was a wide publicity campaign about building an information society. Different initiatives with the prename "Tiger" came into being, e.g., "Tiger Tours" in conjunction with an NGO [non-governmental organisation] in which computers on mobile platforms were taken outside Tallinn to introduce ICTs to the rural population. Banks talked about their "Tiger Leap" while introducing e-banking; newly emerging newspapers immediately made themselves available on-line; and so on. (Archives of the ICF, 2007)

The ICF Award Application addressed the difficulty of Estonia's decision to focus on ICT development. Many had argued persuasively that as a matter of first priority school roofs should be repaired and windows replaced. If there was still money remaining, teachers' salaries that were pegged at US$100 per month at the time should be increased. The strongest counter-argument was that the whole population, especially the new generation, would need to learn the new information technology skills so they could compete in the modern economy. Moving forward to build the infrastructure and provide public access proved to be one of the country's biggest challenges.

Because of the population's low purchasing power and the potential expense of ICT adoption, there was general agreement that there should be support for public access. The first public access point was opened with the help of the United Nations Development Programme (UNDP) in the National Library in Tallinn. Soon after, the Open Estonia Foundation [Soros Foundation] started a programme inviting enthusiasts to create public access points all over Estonia. In 2000, a private foundation Look@World was created with the help of telecoms, banks and computer companies, and they also created public access points.

In 2000, the Estonian Parliament passed the Public Information Act. It stipulated that all public libraries in the country would need to provide public access. Today, there are 730 Public Access points across Estonia (www.regio.delfi.ee/ipunktid). Their importance has somewhat receded, however, since the purchasing power of the population has risen. With the widespread use of Wi-Fi people are able to use the Internet free of charge from pubs, hotels and city squares. In 2003, two big companies owning gas station chains throughout Estonia put Wi-Fi in all stations with free customer use, practically completing the coverage of Estonia with convenient access to the Internet from everywhere.

The Look@World Foundation commissioned a study in 2001 to better understand the need for the further information society development in Estonia and found that the major barrier for wider Internet use by the population was not the lack of access but the lack of motivation. In response, the foundation created and executed an education programme to educate 100,000 people (about 10% of the adult population!) in basic computer and Internet use. Public authorities in Tallinn and elsewhere provided rooms (computer classes at schools after hours, Public Internet Access points and so on), with programme financing coming from the private sector (Archives of the ICF, 2007).

Estonia needed a better communications infrastructure. Since it had few natural resources producing revenues, it became necessary to create an attractive investment climate to draw modern know-how and finances from abroad. The country approached this challenge carefully. The main telecom operator Eesti Telefon had been privatised to Finnish Sonera and Swedish Telia with government involved as a minority shareholder. The new Eesti Telecom received a 10-year concession agreement in return for a promise to provide regular landline connections to all Estonian households within five years. Mobile operators appeared when the government granted three GSM licences, contrary to the prevailing thought that the market was too small for three operators. The ensuing competition drove down the prices, and by 2003 many people were giving up their fixed landlines, using cable for Internet and GSM as a primary phone. Data traffic was left out in Telecom's concession agreement, which ensured a high level of competition between ISPs providing Internet service on the various platforms (ICF Archives, 2007).

In summary, the fates of nations and their communities hinge on open communications and the free flow of knowledge—essential characteristics of network societies. Competitiveness is a factor, but so are the economic consequences of such non-economic issues as education, sciences, political stability and value systems. All of these factors require articulation in public policy with supportive legislation.

PUBLIC AND PRIVATE COOPERATION

Key Concept: *Responsive government with broad private and public sector participation appears to be the essential ingredient for producing goods and services that will give citizens a rising and sustainable standard of living.*

Estonians were not happy about exchanging one centralised authoritarian government for another, as they had seen happen among numerous other republics of the former Soviet Union. In this newly independent Baltic state, distrust of centralised government posed some interesting challenges for elected representatives and public officials. However, this distrust actually hastened the adoption of more open information systems.

Memories of the former totalitarian regime led to support for dismantling the omnipotent central administration, leaving public authorities with only those tasks that could not be privatised or contracted out. The prevalent ideology supported a lean and efficient state. Rapid deployment of information and communication technologies provided a way to achieve that goal. At the same time, the need to keep public sector employment levels low gave an additional impetus for the development of the ICT industry.

Because the previous socio-political order had been delegitimised, the legacy systems—both technological and procedural—could be easily abandoned. Moving away from totalitarianism also meant moving away from strong centres of power, which made it more difficult to achieve any concerted action. Decisions had to be based on example rather than coercion. This allowed for the ICT initiatives in the government to develop in a decentralised way. Estonia, therefore, did not experience those expensive failures that characterised the development of e-government in many places (Archives of the ICF, 2007).

Estonia's development as a networked community was not just the result of government action taken on behalf of its citizens; it was a concerted effort by players at all levels of the society. In its ICF application, the authors noted, "Despite popular agreement to build an information society in Estonia, the government never created a comprehensive plan to achieve it." The leadership that supported the development had the momentum, but there was never an attempt to dictate its direction. Instead, the Estonian Parliament passed a resolution on Basic Principles of Information Society in 1997 that stated the development priorities, action principles and the framework for government action. The ICF applicants wrote:

> First, government ideology was to give a free hand to all economic activities and not to do things that the private sector was happy to do itself. Also, the government did not develop in-house competence for software development but acted as a "smart purchaser" and procured the necessary assistance from the private sector.

> Second, the government took an active role providing leadership in issues that the private sector was not interested in (like creating a Public Key Infrastructure) or that rightfully belonged to the government (e-Government development).

> Third, the government created an advisory body in the form of an Informatics Council where representatives of state, business, academia and non-profit sectors informed each other of major developments in the planning stage, so that other sectors could fashion their projects accordingly and not duplicate unnecessarily.

> Fourth, the government provided the necessary legal framework but because of this forum for exchange of ideas, it did not over-regulate. Rather, it reacted to requests. A good example was the creation of the Digital Signature Act. Although Estonian banks began using electronic banking in 1997, only in 2000, when the use of electronic banking had become massive and third parties started to provide their services together with e-banking, did Estonia enact a law recognising those transactions as legitimate.

> Fifth, the government created a framework for its own actions that can be characterised as "project based development". It meant that every year the government approved the e-development plan for the next two years with financial commitments to approved projects. (In the post-socialist transformation there is something that political scientists call "Implementation Gap". That means a lot of nice plans are never implemented.) With this mechanism, the Estonian government avoided some of those problems in the long-term development of its information society.

Sixth, the document prioritized two broad areas of action for the public sector. These were Education and e-Government development (ICF Archives, 2007).

The strategy that Estonia followed was characterised in the ICF Application as one of "interested support." The framers of this document conclude there was "no single mover, no large donor or centralised coercive action." There was an initial push to advance the concept of a future based on the use of information and communication technologies that was accepted and taken up by the people. "The government managed to create a situation whereby to use and be associated with ICTs was fashionable across the population, not only among the young people" (ICF Archives, 2007). This broad-based support allowed the topic of information society building to be above usual party political fights.

Today, Estonians can celebrate the fact that their country is the birthplace of such Internet tigers as Skype, Kazaa and Hotmail. As of 2002, all public laws and regulations are now published in digital form and may be searched electronically. Access to government documents is aided by the fact that broadband wireless is universally available in every corner of the country, and it is free.

In summary, the Estonians did not know in advance which path they would take to free themselves from their past. They chose to rely heavily on their own resourcefulness, involving all sectors of their national community in building a new, more open, productive and creative society.

SUPPORTIVE POLICIES AND REGULATIONS

Key Concept: *Radical regulatory reform and the establishment of information and communication policies that favour a more open society allow nations and their communities to avoid a stalemate in their goal to progress economically.*

In seeking to implement the broadband networks that will connect communities and resources, business and policy reforms are often a prerequisite to taking those first steps. As Rahul Tongia asserts in his article, "Connectivity in Emerging Regions", "Availability and affordability remain important issues, but these depend not only on technology choices, but also business and regulatory models" (Tongia, 2007, p. 97).

Ghana and China have had some success in bringing about regulatory changes to help their communities acquire the connectivity needed to stimulate business and trade, provide easier access to government offices and deliver vital services related to health and education. In some cases, government agencies themselves have been the principal drivers for change; in other cases, the impetus has come from commercial sectors and non-governmental organisations. In the case of Ghana, representatives at the community level have maintained a constant dialogue with government offices to effect change. In the case of China, almost all changes have been from the top down.

Satellite infrastructure is the ICT example used. As data applications have come of age, so have the satellite networks being used in Ghana and China to connect towns and villages to governmental and business centres. The rationale for satellite use has to do with satellite's availability and reach, the widely dispersed areas this broadband technology can cover, and the advanced interactive technologies that now make on-demand data connections via satellite more robust, flexible and comparatively economical.

One of the workhorse technologies for local access using satellite is the very small aperture terminal, basically a two-way dish receiver/transmitter identified in the trade literature as the VSAT. Having been used for years to complement terrestrial business networks, VSAT technologies have now caught on in education, health, government services and residential applications for the delivery of interactive video, Internet and multimedia services. Internet access and distribution services today produce major revenues for the global satellite industry.

The International Telecommunications Union, the United Nations agency located in Geneva, publishes "Network Readiness", "Digital Access" and "Digital Opportunity" indicators. On the premise that access to ICTs is a prerequisite for an inclusive information society, the ITU has commissioned studies that seek to measure on a country-by-country basis the ability of individuals to access and use information and communication technologies given such limiting factors as affordability, knowledge and infrastructure (*World Information*, 2006, pp. 8-18).

The ITU's *World Information Society Report 2006* introduces the Digital Opportunity Index (DOI) as a tool for policy-makers and regulators to track progress and gain greater insight into ICT trends and policies within each country. It uses the DOI to evaluate the major forces driving the growth of the Information Society; it also shows how the DOI can yield real insights into policies and their impact in the areas of regional development, urban/rural divide and gender analysis (*World Information*, 2006).

Ghana. Access to information and communication technologies is an endemic problem for many communities in the Republic of Ghana, as well as other countries in Africa. At the end of 2005, in a nation of 20 million people, only about 3 million Ghanaians had regular access to a telephone line. Access to the Internet was largely limited to the cities, especially the capital city of Accra.

In Ghana, the only Internet access was via the telephone companies' dial-up modem services. In the early 1990s, there was a shift towards greater use of satellite communication technologies in business and government sectors, bypassing the public switched telephone networks. Satellite earth stations and connecting equipment were installed by private and state entities, and several Internet Service Providers (ISPs) emerged to meet the growing demand for voice, data and video services.

Although Ghana privatised its telecommunications services and made an effort to attract both domestic and foreign investors to participate in the delivery of competitive communications businesses, the onerous licensing and fee structures established by Ghana's regulatory National Communications Authority made doing profitable business difficult.

Kwasi Boateng, a Ph.D. student at Ohio University and now an instructor at the University of Arkansas, wrote his dissertation on the regulatory struggles of ISPs and cyber cafes of Ghana, whose business plans were to use VSAT satellite networks to connect to the World Wide Web, thus avoiding the local telephone networks. These satellite-based businesses were, however, unable to bypass the charges levied by the telecommunication authorities. According to Boateng, the government was charging "roughly $10,000 to $12,000 in the first year to obtain a licence and then there would be an annual site fee of about $4,000." These fees were to be paid on top of the cost of the VSAT equipment, installation and bandwidth. A narrowband link for a rural community communications centre required equipment costing between $5,000 and $10,000 and then there were service charges of approximately $500 per month (Boateng, 2006).

The VSAT operators in Ghana petitioned the Ministry of Communications for relief on the government imposed costs, asking that the office differentiate between the big, medium and small size operators. Their proposal was that the government, when possible, should provide tax and other incentives to those entities and individuals willing to commit resources to bringing new media and communication services to the country, which everyone seemed to agree was much needed (Boateng, 2004).

VSAT operators were also limited by law to the delivery of data services, which in Ghana was interpreted to mean non-voice services. This was a problem because Voice-over Internet Protocol (VoIP) was very quickly perceived as an attractive added service for Internet users, especially those looking for ways to reduce the highly inflated cost of local and long distance telephone calling. In a country with such a limited telecommunications infrastructure, ISPs and satellite providers saw the application as a way to greatly increase telephone access throughout the country, and it could mean a much-needed source of new revenue for commercial providers.

The impediment in Ghana, and in almost every other developing nation, was that telephony services were still big income producers for the country. Although the national telephone network reached only about one-sixth of the population, regulators were reluctant to allow the legacy telephone lines to be by-passed to reach the rest of the society. Satellite service providers made the counter argument that they should be part of the national solution. Satellite services could help expand the penetration of the terrestrial telephone lines. This was important as the former telecommunications monopoly Ghana Telecom, and its new competitor Westel, were already charged with the task of making the Internet more widely available in the country.

As of 2007, 165 Internet service providers had been authorised by the National Communications Authority with 29 of these operational at that time. The NCA had also authorised 175 VSAT data operators and 57 of these were operational (Summary, 2006). These improvements can be attributed largely to a radically revised national telecommunications policy. According to the Ghana National Communications Authority, the new policies aim to promote:

- Universal access for all communities and population groups in Ghana to telephone, Internet, and multimedia services by the year 2010;
- National penetration of universal telecommunications services to reach 25% of the population, including at least 10% in rural areas, by the year 2010;
- Connection of all schools, medical clinics, government offices and public and community broadcasting stations to advanced telecommunications services;
- Fully open, private and competitive markets for all telecommunications services;
- Streamlined, efficient, and effective regulation of the telecommunications industry on a fully transparent, technologically neutral, and competitively balanced basis.

The Vision and Objectives statement of Ghana's Ministry of Communications acknowledges in its ICT policy of 2005, "the need to integrate Ghana with the new emerging economic order wherein information and knowledge are fundamental to achieving competitiveness, investment, development of human capacity and improved governance, leading to wealth creation and national prosperity, through the appropriate use of information and communication technologies in an entrepreneurial, open, participating and facilitating environment". The statement affirmed that "development of the national telecommunications infrastructure, and promotion of an open, competitive, and innovative telecommunications industry throughout

Ghana, is a vital priority for achieving these goals" (Ministry of Communication, 2004, p. 6).

China. When China joined the World Trade Organization (WTO) in December 2001, major changes were made in China's regulatory system. Becoming "a most favoured nation" in the WTO required that China treat its affiliated trading partners in ways that were equal to the best treatment given to that country by WTO member countries.

The WTO also expected China's regulatory system to be more transparent. This meant the country must publish all internal regulations relating to trade in services. China was obliged to ensure that its monopoly service supplier activities were consistent with the General Agreement on Trade in Services (GATS). Further, China was required to have a mechanism for dispute resolution to ensure administrative review and appeal procedures when disagreements arose about market access or national treatment.

It is important to note that China's strategy in joining the WTO was not to privatise its telecommunications industries, as had been the case in Ghana and many other developing countries. Rather, the word that it used was "to liberalize", meaning to open up an industry by encouraging non-government participation in the industry, and to expand the number of participants or competitors in an established market without necessarily selling out to private businesses. Normally, privatisation refers to the direct transfer of ownership and control to private firms or individuals.

China was also expected to have a policy and an administrative mechanism to deal with antitrust issues to prevent major suppliers from engaging in anti-competitive practises. China was obliged to have an independent regulator to ensure that telecommunications regulatory authorities were separate from, and not accountable to, any supplier of basic telecommunications services. Also, China was to ensure fair and non-discriminatory allocation and use of limited telecommunications resources, such as bandwidth, frequencies and rights of way.

In discussing "offshoring" in his book *The World Is Flat*, Thomas Friedman takes up the impact of WTO membership on China. He describes the rapid opening of business networks that allowed China to more easily enter into manufacturing relationships with Western corporations. Such collaboration provided auto parts, electronics, toy and shoe manufacturers with access to low cost labor and China with transfer of western technology and modern business practises, as well as unparalleled revenue streams. The effect on China's economy and the many success stories illustrating China's ability to compete under the new WTO rules suggested that China had made big leaps in transforming itself from a communist to a capitalist society.

Friedman offers a word of caution. He writes that even if China implemented all the WTO reforms, "it will soon be reaching a point where its ambitions for economic growth will require more political reform. China will never root out corruption without a free press and active civil society institutions. It can never really become efficient without a more codified rule of law. It will never be able to deal with the inevitable downturns in its economy without an open political system that allows people to vent their grievances. To put it another way, China will never be truly flat until it gets over that huge speed bump called 'political reform'" (Friedman, 2006, p. 149).

Even though Tianjin (China) is an example of a Chinese community that made it into the Top Seven in the ICF Intelligent Community of the Year Awards (in 2005 and in 2006), it cannot be assumed that local or national government in China operates as an open institution. China is still a highly centralised society; the Communist Party still reigns supreme. Putting agenda items on the ballot for public vote is not the way national decisions are made in China.

Friedman interviewed Pat Powers who headed the U.S.-China Business Council office in Beijing during the WTO accession. According to Powers, had the Chinese government put World Trade Organisation membership to a popular vote, "it never would have passed". A key reason that China's leadership sought WTO membership was to use it as a club to force China's bureaucracy to modernise and to dismantle internal regulatory walls and pockets for arbitrary decision-making. China's leadership "knew that China had to integrate globally and that many of their existing institutions would simply not change and reform, and so they used the WTO as leverage against their own bureaucracy" (Friedman, 2006, p. 149).

There is no question China is making major progress in building ICT infrastructure nationwide and is using it to strengthen its social institutions. The country began to open up its telecommunications market in 1999 when China Telecom was divested of some of its assets, resulting in the creation of four companies, each responsible for a different sector. The entities were China Mobile, China Unicom, China Satellite and China Telecom. As a follow up, the Ministry of Information Industry (MII) adopted the following operational policies to ensure its telecommunications industry would meet national expectations:

- Full competition in the domain of value-added telecommunication and information services;
- Ordered competition in the domain of satellite and wireless mobile telecommunication services; and
- Limited competition in the domain of basic telephony services (Xiongjian & Jing, 2001).

According to the "2005 e-readiness rankings" of the Economist Intelligence Unit, China was ranked 55th of 65 countries examined, with an e-readiness score of 3.85 on a scale of 10. It ranked 12th of 16 countries considered in the Asia-Pacific region. But the Economist reporters also noted that China surpassed Japan to attain 2nd place worldwide—after the U.S.—in broadband lines installed, with broadband adoption growing at about 8% per month (2005 e-Readiness, 2005, pp. 14-15).

The Economist Intelligence Unit publishes e-readiness rankings of the world's largest economies based on their ability to promote and support digital business and information and communications technology (ICT) services. "A country's e-readiness is essentially a measure of its e-business environment, a collection of factors that indicate how amenable a market is to Internet-based opportunities." The magazine takes the position that "digital business is at its heart business, and that for digital transactions to be widely adopted and efficient, they have to thrive in a holistically supportive environment." The Economist rankings use quantitative and qualitative criteria to measure social, political, economic and technological development. The criteria include broadband connectivity and access, Internet security, penetration of public-access wireless "hotspots," ICT spending, and education (2005 e-Readiness, p. 1).

Establishment of a domestic satellite-based public communication network has helped China's internal communications, especially in linking to remote areas. Following admission to the WTO, China rapidly developed its VSAT telecommunication services. By 2004, there were in China more than 30 domestic VSAT communication service providers and 15,000 small station users, including more than 6,000 two-way users. Specialised communication networks were established by such departments as finance, meteorology, transportation, oil, water resources, civil aviation, power, public health, education, and the media, with more than 10,000 VSAT systems covering the whole of China (Country commerce, 2007).

Distance learning is a priority application and VSAT is the workhorse technology. According to Tom Wang, CTO of China Education Television, "China is a large country with imbalanced economy and education. To make high quality educational resources flow to non-developed areas, satellite distance education is needed to play an important "role in modernization" (Wang, 2007).

Since China opened its VSAT educational TV broadcasting services, millions of people have received technical, secondary school, college and continuing education through it. Although exact numbers are not known, it is possible that China has more distance-learners enrolled than the rest of the world combined. And in China an additional broadband multimedia transmission network has been established on the country's direct broadcasting satellite (DBS) platform to provide broadcast education services directly to homes and schools in remote areas.

According to Wang, China's Ministry of Education, Ministry of Finance and the National Development and Reform Commission have launched jointly a massive experimental distance education project for primary and junior secondary schools in the countryside. First establishing experimental units seeking breakthroughs in important districts and then progressing step by step, this programme seeks to solve some of the problems related to a shortage of teachers and low quality schooling at the lower grade levels.

By November 2005, this programme had established 141,724 satellite reception stations, 96,607 disc play units, 291,631 sets of devices for disc teaching and 25,389 computer classrooms, covering 29 provinces and districts, benefiting 50 million primary and junior secondary pupils. Wang says this project, which will give rural students access to teaching resources and information technologies closer to those received by their counterparts in cities, is ultimately intended to lay a favourable foundation for an information society in China (Wang, 2007, p. 3).

In summary, regulatory reforms and policy articulation in many cases can have a ripple effect throughout the society. Ghana and China illustrate two very different approaches in rolling out infrastructure and making communication services available to the whole population.

United States: In the U.S., the heart of free market liberalism, public-initiated implementation of broadband solutions was complicated by government constraints on competition. The examples to follow demonstrate the extent to which the lobbying of the big telecommunications and cable operators made implementing metropolitan broadband networks difficult—and in some cases illegal—for such cities as Philadelphia, Boston, Spokane and San Francisco. The time frame being discussed is 2004 to 2008.

The communities mentioned chose to bypass their incumbent telecom carriers in favor of implementing their own citywide broadband networks. In each of these cases, the interconnecting technology to be installed was the high-speed wireless service called Wi-Fi, which required attaching Internet routers on streetlights throughout the city. The cities were motivated by the attractiveness of the technology and the opportunity to make broadband available more quickly for the delivery of city services. This network would also connect all non-government institutions, businesses and citizens, and offer these services at subsidized rates to low-income residents.

In 2004, the city of Philadelphia released its plan to build the nation's largest municipal Wi-Fi network, spanning 135 square miles (350 square kilometers), serving 1.5 million people. (Somerset-Ward, 2005). The $10 million project was intended to encourage economic growth and help poor residents gain access to the Internet with a broadband service priced at an estimated $15-20 per month.

At that time, according to the city's chief information officer Dianah Neff, about 60% of Philadelphia's neighborhoods didn't have access to any broadband service (Lawson, 2004).

This municipal broadband initiative, and others like it around the country, was actively opposed by the United States Telecom Association, representing such companies as Verizon, AT&T, Bell South, CenturyTel and NTT, using the argument of unfair competition. In the states of Florida, Pennsylvania, Texas and Virginia, legislators aligned with the telcos successfully argued that the municipalities should not be allowed to use taxpayer monies to unfairly compete with private companies, and passed laws restricting, placing conditions upon or prohibiting municipalities from offering broadband services.

In opposing the Pennsylvania Wi-Fi bill, the sympathetic state legislators had argued that the incumbent telco and cable companies, principally Verizon and Comcast, had "fallen short" on their promises to build a more up-to-date network over the past 10 years, which had contributed to the lack of broadband availability (Lawson, 2004, p. 2). The telcos and the cable companies, on the other hand, pointed to the billions of dollars they had spent to build new digital networks and argued that public bureaucrats didn't know the first thing about installing and operating such systems.

This issue became a state rather than a federal concern because municipalities in the U.S. are under the authority of state governments. State governments were, therefore, free to determine whether it is permissible for a municipality to offer broadband services. The city stakeholders received only verbal encouragement from the national government.

In the case of Philadelphia, the telcos and cable companies had a chance to say "I told you so". In 2008, the city announced that its ailing service provider EarthLink was shutting the system down and removing its wireless routers from the city's streetlights. EarthLink is an Atlanta-based carrier operating similar services in several states, most of them losing money. Earthlink had financed, built and operated the Wi-Fi network at no cost to Philadelphia's taxpayers, sharing revenues with the non-profit Wireless Philadelphia set up to provide subsidized services to low-income residents. There were delays in rolling out the network and, by 2008, it was able to reach only about 5,000 residential and business subscribers. The number of customers under the subsidized plan was fewer than 1,000 (Lawson, 2008).

The Wi-Fi technology also did not live up to its early promise. The high-speed wireless service was difficult to deploy and often unreliable. Line of sight interference from buildings and leaves on trees and rain attenuation often disrupted the signal. Dependable reception required more routers than initially predicted, which raised the cost of constructing the network. In the city of Seattle, Washington, chief technology officer Bill Schrier saw some of Wi-Fi's shortcomings when an early broadband wireless network was installed there in 2005:

> First of all, if you put up a Wi-Fi point, it will work outdoors, but the radio waves don't go through walls. If you put the Wi-Fi point down low, it reaches to the back of restaurants and buildings, but you don't get a wide coverage. If you put the Wi-Fi points up high, you get a broader footprint, but you don't get the interior coverage you want (Harris, 2008, p. 4).

Schrier also found that users were monopolizing bandwidth by participating in Internet gaming, sending spam and attempting to hack the system. On a shared network, speed slows down as usage goes up.

Chicago was one of the cities affected by EarthLink's change of direction. EarthLink scrapped its Wi-Fi plans after the city was unwilling to commit to becoming an anchor tenant on the EarthLink network. The former CIO of Chicago, Chris O'Brien, said that cities shouldn't be daunted by the recent failures of wireless systems; it just means more research is required. He believes there is compelling interest for local government to roll out free wireless in the community because it can contribute to an increased quality of life for residents. "Our cities are far behind international cities as far as broadband [is concerned], and this is a matter that has to be addressed" (Harris, 2008, p. 9).

The U.S. is an example of a country that has gone to great lengths to let capital markets decide when and where broadband services are made available. If broadband policy exists in America, it will more likely be developed at the local or regional level, and not at the national level. In this circumstance, towns, cities and regions have no choice but to determine their own priorities and strategies for broadband services. Given the lack of national support and the financial and technical challenges involved, these local communities should continue to stimulate public-private partnerships.

SETTING STANDARDS

Key Concept: *The development and adoption of technical standards for delivering information around the world are one of the great achievements of the network society. E-readiness depends on such standards.*

The Internet holds a powerful influence because it has been adopted globally as the electronic network of choice for home users as well as business and other social institutions. The technology persists in its relentless penetration into even the most remote of societies. One of the reasons for the unprecedented diffusion and adoption rate of Internet products and services is that they are based on an information processing and distribution format that has been accepted as a universal standard. A big constraint on the international exchange of information was overcome with the adoption of TCP/IP (transmission control protocol/Internet protocol). This standard emerged from a government lab of a single country but its success is due to the fact that it has been embraced and sustained as a global public utility.

One of the operational definitions of "networked communities" is that they are wired for digital two-way communications. The most common platform on which these digital exchanges take place today is the Internet and its software application, the World Wide Web. In effect, a networked community is a community where the Internet has been adopted and is made widely accessible, and citizens of every age and socio-economic level are trained to use it. "Broadband communities" are those where Internet services are available at speeds fast enough to provide citizens with real time voice, video and data communications on demand.

Communities are still trying to figure out what the Internet can do for them and what good things can do with it. Almost always the products and services of the Internet are compared to what people have known before, and frequently those products and services come up short. Internet telephony isn't as good as regular telephone service. Video over the Internet doesn't match the quality of regular TV. E-mail is mostly spam. Nevertheless, the Internet continues to surprise us in the ways it has made itself useful— even indispensable.

Quality of service on the early Internet was not a big issue, since few knew what to expect and were only learning what this new kind of electronic network could do. When NSFnet was transferred from the supervision of the U.S. National Science Foundation to commercial service in 1992, the prime objective and the great achievement of early TCP/IP standards setting was ensuring that computer files got to their destination. Gaining a modicum of predictability and consistency with data traveling over dial-up telephone networks was considered a major engineering feat, which it was. "Best effort" was all that anyone could count on, with success determined by whether the transmissions were received or not, and little more than that (Flournoy, 2004, pp. 364-365).

Achieving higher transport efficiencies and increasing the volume of delivery while maintaining predictable and consistent behaviour in a packet-based environment was not—and is not—easy to do. The challenge wasn't just that IP-technologies had to be developed from scratch, but that the public-switched telephone system was an inhospitable transport infrastructure that had to be accommodated. As it has turned out, multiple incompatible infrastructures, namely telephone, cable, wireless, broadcast, satellite, and power line systems, had to be reconditioned for the Internet to reach everybody and work effectively.

Since few understand this, the general public perceives the Internet to be too slow. Actually, the Internet may be fast but end-users are comparing the time it takes to click on a Web site and see good video pictures streaming across their computer screens with the time its takes for the picture to come up on the home TV set. With a black-box mentality and an inordinate faith in the cleverness of engineers, the community of Internet users generally expects guaranteed levels of performance. Users want faster, more reliable Internet service, and they would prefer that it be made available wherever they are, whenever they want.

The Internet Engineering Taskforce (IETF) has worked to improve Internet performance (www.ietf.org). One successful approach has been to segment Internet traffic so that certain types of transmissions are given preferential treatment. Unlike broadcasting, there is a direct relationship between the number of subscribers and the total amount of bandwidth available for use on the Internet. On publicly shared media, such as cable and wireless media, Internet subscribers behaving as "bandwidth hogs" can consume all the available network resources, or significantly slow the download and upload speeds of other users operating on the same shared platform.

Where bandwidth is constrained, the IETF strategy has been to differentiate classes of data service that can be given higher-precedence at the expense of those of lower-precedence. Just as e-mail—which can be managed intermittently—places fewer demands on the network than streaming media that must play continuously in near real-time, it is a matter for service providers to work out with clients what is a fair allocation of bandwidth per user, per class of service.

Another strategy is to develop better bandwidth management tools to ensure users have access to the applications they need when networks get congested. Streaming media helps Web pages appear more life-like, interactive, and appealing, and the number of these pages is growing daily. But for the majority of Web users, acquisition of dense data streams is not yet an option. The problem is not with the end-user software or the server sending the data, but insufficient network capacity to handle transmitted packets of such magnitude.

Such approaches as Fast TCP and by-pass alternatives like Internet2 may help to speed up the Internet. Fast TCP is a method developed at the California Institute of Technology for improving the tracking of transmitted packets and acknowledging arrival. Using this approach, a movie downloaded from a video server via the Internet could arrive in a matter of seconds. The Internet2 is a parallel Internet that allows universities and research centres to get off the public-switched telephone networks, thus avoiding the traffic jams that are more common on the popularly used networks.

Interoperability among the various telephone, cable, terrestrial wireless and satellite networks is an event eagerly awaited among consumers and is advocated by planners of the smart communities of the future.

One of the services in greatest need of equipment and software interoperability is the mobile Internet. The portable Internet is an emerging application that is so splintered into competing offerings that neither customers nor businesses know when to enter the market and how to make informed purchase decisions. *IEEE Communications* notes the following organisations, in addition to the Internet Engineering Taskforce (IETF), that are participating in shaping the next-generation wireless networks that connect users to the Internet:

- Wi-Fi Forum
- WiMax Forum
- Third Generation Partnership Project (3GPP and 3GPP2)
- Institute for Electrical and Electronics Engineering (IEEE)
- Open Mobile Alliance (OMA)
- Unlicenced Mobile Access (UMA)
- Fixed Mobile Wireless Convergence Forum

Each of these advocacy organisations consists of "interest groups" hoping to develop specifications for infrastructure and access. What will emerge will be the architectures, protocols and standards for applications made possible by the wireless Internet, including VoIP, messaging, movie downloads, peer-to-peer file sharing, conferencing, and multiplayer gaming (Mohan, 2006, pp. 64-65).

The public may wish government bodies to enter the fray to standardize this process, but the reality is that few governments have the expertise or the willingness to take on the task. Instead, such standardization bodies as the IEEE and the IETF have risen to the occasion, working to find an appropriate Internet-based architecture capable of seamlessly delivering services to end-devices over disparate wireless and wireline networks, and supporting all types of end-user devices. Although achieving workable standards is often a slow, deliberative process, it seems that partnerships involving both public and private sectors work best.

AVOIDING PROPRIETARY TECHNOLOGIES AND SOFTWARE

Key Concept: *The development of universal technical standards has accelerated development of open source applications, open source products and even open source culture.*

The term "open source" refers most commonly to the source code of software made publicly available with few or no intellectual property restrictions. Since software represents the basic instructions for digital networking, making the source code more widely available is thought by some to be the fastest, most efficient means to stimulate innovation and entrepreneurship in bringing new products and services to the market, through either incremental individual effort or collaboration.

According to the Linux Information Project, open source software's source code is freely available for anyone to inspect and study, possibly to modify and improve. A common example is software for computer operating systems and application programmes whose code is written in one of the thousands of programming languages available. "Most open source software is also free software. Free software is software for which everyone has the right not only to inspect and study the source code but also to use it for any desired purpose without monetary or other restrictions. These other purposes include making as many copies as desired, installing on as many computers as desired, modifying (including extending) in any desired way, and redistributing in its original or modified form" (Open Source Definition, 2007).

In 2006, the European Union (EU) commissioned a study on the "Economic Impact of Open Source Software on Innovation and the Competitiveness of the Information and Communication Technologies (ICT) Sector". UNU-Merit of the Netherlands prepared the final report, concluding that the information economy represented approximately 10% of the EU's GDP and accounted for more than half of its economic growth. The report noted that "Software is one of the key elements driving ICT's role in the economy, and the structure, competitiveness and performance of the ICT industry has the potential to be strongly affected by FLOSS (Free/Libre/Open Source Software)" (Ghosh, 2006, pp. 2-12).

FLOSS, in this case, referred to open source software that is freely available and free of charge. Some of the highlights of the Executive Summary's multiple conclusions and recommendations were:

- FLOSS applications are first, second or third-rung products in terms of market share in several markets, including Web servers, server operating systems, desktop operating systems, Web browsers, databases, e-mail, and other ICT infrastructure systems. FLOSS market share is higher in Europe than in the U.S. for operating systems and PCs, followed by Asia. These market shares have seen considerable growth in the past five years.
- Defined broadly, FLOSS-related services could reach a 32% share of all IT services by 2010, and the FLOSS-related share of the economy could reach 4% of European GDP by 2010. FLOSS directly supports the 29% share of software developed in-house in the EU (43% in the U.S.), and provides the natural model for software development for the secondary software sector.
- FLOSS potentially saves industry more than 36% in software R&D investment that can result in increased profits or be more usefully spent in further innovation.

- Increased FLOSS use may provide a way for Europe to compensate for a low GDP share of ICT investment relative to the U.S. A growth and innovation simulation model shows that increasing the FLOSS share of software investment from 20% to 40% would lead to a 0.1% increase in annual EU GDP growth excluding benefits within the ICT industry itself— i.e., more than Euro 10 billion annually.
- FLOSS provides opportunities in Europe for new businesses, a greater role in the wider information society and a business model that suits European SMEs; FLOSS in Europe is threatened by increasing moves in some policy circles to support regulation entrenching previous business models for creative industries at the cost of allowing for new businesses and new business models.
- Policy strategies focus mainly on correcting current policies and practises that implicitly or explicitly favour proprietary software—for example, discouraging public R&D funding and public software procurement that is currently often anti-competitive; not penalising the open source software in innovation and R&D incentives; encouraging partnerships between large firms, SMEs and the FLOSS community; avoiding lifelong vendor lock-in in educational systems by teaching students skills, not specific applications; and encouraging participation in FLOSS-like communities. (Ghosh, pp. 9-12).

As a principal driver of convergence within computer and telecommunications systems, the Internet is responsible for much of the momentum toward open source software. When first introduced, PCs using specialised chips ran proprietary software, while the legacy phone systems of telecom companies had their own chips running their own brand of software. When the Internet came along and proved capable of linking any kind of computer to any other kind of digital platform, consumers got the idea that this was an operating system that ought to be available free to everybody for whatever use, wherever they were. It was perhaps from this point that the community began to think, and eventually argue, that the Internet is such a necessary service, it must be treated like a public utility.

A good illustration of the benefits of innovation, competition and public empowerment has been the development of an alternative Web browser using an open source strategy. FireFox 2 in 2006 won the CNET and *PC Magazine* Editors' Choice awards in 2006 and the *PC World* 100 Best Products and Webware 100 Winner awards in 2007. In its announcement, Webware wrote:

> Firefox is a free, multiplatform browser. Its popularity is second only to Microsoft's Internet Explorer among Web browsers, but unlike IE, it has open-source code. The result has been an avid development community, filled with people eager to squash bugs and create new functionality. Firefox

also has the option to create and use extensions that can add new features or services right on top of the user experience. These add-ons have gotten so popular that Firefox creator Mozilla has created its own directory for users to search and sort through them. The latest release of Firefox has integrated some of these extensions, and Mozilla will continue to do so in future developments (Needleman, 2007).

The Firefox project was a spin-off of Netscape's Mozilla Web browser that merged when Netscape, losing the browser competition to Microsoft's Internet Explorer, decided in 1998 to release its underlying code to the open source community. Blake Ross, a 15-year-old high school student, working with Netscape engineer Dave Hyatt, stripped the Mozilla browser down to "bare essentials" with the idea of making a "leaner but more flexible browser for the masses" (Kushner, 2006, p. 29). The result was contagious. Thousands of coders shared the code online and collaborated to build applications on a free and public browser that has been downloaded by an estimated 200 million people worldwide.

In a blog appearing on www.mozilla.org, Mozilla Foundation Chair Mitchell Baker explains why Firefox is not a "for profit" business. He wrote, "Firefox is not the creation of a 'company' or a set of employees. Firefox is created by a public process as a public asset. Participants are correct to feel that Firefox belongs to them. They are correct legally, since the Mozilla Foundation's assets are legally dedicated to the public benefit. They are correct practically because Firefox could not exist without the community; the two are completely intertwined.....A people-centered Internet needs some way for people to interact with the Internet that isn't all about making money for some company and its shareholders" (Baker, 2007, p. 1).

From the Web site, the "Mozilla Manifesto" explains that "The Mozilla project is a global community of people who believe that openness, innovation and opportunity are key to the continued health of the Internet. We have worked together since 1998 to ensure that the Internet is developed in a way that benefits everyone. We are best known for creating the Mozilla Firefox Web browser. The Mozilla project uses a community-based approach to create world-class open source software and to develop new types of collaborative activities. We create communities of people involved in making the Internet experience better for all of us."

The not-for-profit Mozilla corporation operates from a set of "Principles":

1. The Internet is an integral part of modern life—a key component in education, communication, collaboration, business, entertainment, and society as a whole.
2. The Internet is a global public resource that must remain open and accessible.

3.   The Internet should enrich the lives of individual human beings.
4.   Individuals' security on the Internet is fundamental and cannot be treated as optional.
5.   Individuals must have the ability to shape their own experiences on the Internet.
6.   The effectiveness of the Internet as a public resource depends upon interoperability (protocols, data formats, content), innovation and decentralised participation worldwide.
7.   Free and open source software promotes the development of the Internet as a public resource.
8.   Transparent community-based processes promote participation, accountability, and trust.
9.   Commercial involvement in the development of the Internet brings many benefits; a balance between commercial goals and public benefit is critical.
10.   Magnifying the public benefit aspects of the Internet is an important goal, worthy of time, attention and commitment. (*The Mozilla Manifesto*, 2007)

Even Microsoft has accepted some of the basic principles of open source when it comes to the Internet. In 2006, the company released its "Microsoft Open Specification Promise", a document affirming that Microsoft would not sue anyone who created software based on Web services technologies, a set of communication protocols designed by Microsoft and other vendors. Jason Matusow, Microsoft's director of standards affairs, explained that Microsoft spends more than $6 billion a year on research and development and remains committed to generating intellectual property. But, he said, the company has chosen a "spectrum approach" to it "which ranges from traditional IP licensing to more permissive usage terms that mimic open-source practises" (LaMonica, 2006, p. 1).

In summary, growing public expectations of the Internet have led to global commitments and many practises aimed at keeping it open as an all-society resource. This idea is guided by the belief that open technologies are not only the most efficient means to stimulate innovation and entrepreneurship, they are key to achieving a more sustainable future for communities and nations in which public participation, accountability and trust are valued.

NET NEUTRALITY

Key Concept: *The openness of the Internet is a facilitating factor in its rapid adoption worldwide, but this desirable condition means that it is perpetually under attack and is often in need of protectors.*

Public policy as well as corporate practise is very much in flux when it comes to cyberspace law and regulation. As one of the most powerful instruments of creative destruction in the new digital age, the Internet has emerged as a lawyer's Mecca. Opportunities are almost endless for legal litigation, legislation, court findings, arbitration, and negotiation—the result of Internet threats to the status quo in almost every sector of media and communications.

The public occasionally explodes over such issues as invasion of privacy, intrusive advertising, insecure commercial transactions, indecent content, and threats to children on the Internet, and Internet providers understand those concerns are ignored at their own peril. As a whole, however, Internet players have been very clear on the matter of government intervention. At least among Western countries, most Internet champions want it left alone. The content rights holders, the service providers, and the equipment manufacturers all have been asking for time and space to prove that the market can solve whatever problems arise without government intervention.

With few exceptions, the Western governments have done just that. In the U.S., the Congress, the Federal Communications Commission, the Federal Trade Commission, the Securities and Exchange Commission, and the Federal courts have exercised great restraint in tampering with the way the Internet is evolving. On both the Republican and Democratic sides of the legislative aisle, elected representatives regularly state their preference for letting the technology and the market develop unfettered, intervening only when absolutely necessary to aid public access, protect intellectual property and public safety, and sometimes to insure competition and innovation.

One contentious exception is over "net neutrality." In this case, U.S. government officials are under pressure to intervene to insure equal and open public access to the Internet. They are being asked to shut down monopolizing practises on the part of telecommunications providers who argue that they should be free to exercise operational control over the Internet because they own the pipes that convey it. The concern is that those who own the networks will take advantage of their ability to establish differential pricing for slower (narrowband) and faster (broadband) lanes on the Internet, thus creating an artificial system of public access based not on ability to get online but on ability to pay. At the same time, the controllers of Internet access, principally the telco and cable ISPs, will be able to charge higher rates to such companies as Amazon.com and eBay for faster access to their customers, creating a tiered system of content providers, also based on ability to pay (Kennard, 2006).

Google CEO Eric Schmidt has explained what is at stake from the perspective of the content providers: "Network neutrality is the principle that Internet users should be in control of what content they view and what applications they use on the Internet. The Internet has operated according to this neutrality principle since its earliest days. Indeed, it is this neutrality that has allowed many companies, including Google, to launch, grow and innovate" (Schmidt, 2007, p. 1).

Google (and other advocates for an open Internet) have argued in the U.S. Congress that government should act to place limits on telephone and cable carriers, who threaten to charge both consumers and content providers higher rates for access to their broadband infrastructure. That is, by setting up toll-booths on the Internet, these carriers force both consumers and content providers to pay extra to use the same information highways that such countries as Estonia, Japan and Korea provide for free. Rather than broadband access being managed as an essential universal service, as are public utilities like water, electricity and the public highways, the Internet will be segmented into differentiated services for which premium prices must be paid by those who use the faster lanes. The effect, these advocates argue, could be to suppress innovation while creating an elite class of users.

The plans of U.S. telephone companies Verizon and AT&T, cable operators Comcast and Time Warner, and other last mile service providers owning the distribution networks are facing a fire storm of protest from those who want to see fast Internet services available to all "as a matter of public policy". Critics are complaining that the promises of telcos and cable operators to lay broadband infrastructures in exchange for tax credits and a relaxed regulatory environment have not been met. Free market principles, they argue, especially in the less populated and less affluent communities of the U.S., have failed to deliver on equal access expectations, resulting in the U.S. falling behind its competitor nations in broadband penetration. Critics fear a move to charge differential prices would push the nation even further away from the prospect of universal service. On their side, the carriers counter-argue that their shareholders are the ones footing the bill in building the broadband infrastructure and that they deserve to be rewarded for their efforts.

North Dakota Senator Byron Dorgan expressed the worries of many concerned legislators when he articulated the following three reservations: that the network operators might get the idea they could control who should gain access to the Internet, that they could control what devices users could connect to the Internet, and that they could put additional requirements, such as demanding that users sign up for TV service or phone service, as a condition of access. Dorgan said,

> The success of the Internet has been its openness and the ability of anyone anywhere in this country to go on the Internet and reach the world.....If the big interests who control the pipes become gatekeepers who erect tolls, it will have a significant impact on the Internet as we know it (Bylund, 2007).

Google and Yahoo took the sides of the general public and the dot.com content providers who could be disadvantaged by tiered Internet access. In an open communication to Google users with copies to Internet regulators, the CEO wrote:

Today the Internet is an information highway where anybody—no matter how large or small, how traditional or unconventional—has equal access. But the phone and cable monopolies, who control almost all Internet access, want the power to choose who gets access to high-speed lanes and whose content gets seen first and fastest. They want to build a two-tiered system and block the on-ramps for those who can't pay.

In our view, the broadband companies should not be permitted to use their market power to discriminate against competing applications or content. Just as telephone companies are not permitted to tell consumers who they can call or what they can say, broadband carriers should not be allowed to use their market power to control activity online. Today, the neutrality of the Internet is at stake as the broadband carriers want Congress's permission to determine what gets to you first and fastest. Put simply, this would fundamentally alter the openness of the Internet (Schmidt, 2007, p. 1).

Schmidt quoted Tim Berners-Lee, inventor of the World Wide Web, who said, "The neutral communications medium is essential to our society. It is the basis of a fair competitive market economy. It is the basis of democracy, by which a community should decide what to do. It is the basis of science, by which humankind should decide what is true. Let us protect the neutrality of the net" (Schmidt, 2007, p. 1).

This conflict is not a recent confrontation between the carriers, content and service providers, consumers and consumer advocates. For more than a decade these factions have been publicly debating over the control and the mission of the Internet. These debates are continuing and the result remains uncertain.

MEASURING CHANGES IN PUBLIC POLICY

Key Concept: *Although measuring the impact of policy and regulations in the context of local communities can be difficult, ways must be devised for reporting progress to stakeholders and for preparing next steps.*

Every community exists within a regulated environment. Each has both inherited and self-imposed policies, rules and expectations. Rules are artifacts of culture but can also be the result of some political process. Thus, some rules are clear and explicit, while others are more open and ambiguous. Community rules are needed for a stable and predictable living and work environment, but have to be modified from time to time to meet the changing needs and expectations of community members. This is the context for evaluation.

At some point, ICTs have stood at the gates of every community and asked permission to enter. In cases where they have been invited in, they are more often than not considered an essential part of community culture necessary for its institutions to function. Because telecommunications and the accompanying digital culture disrupt established ways of operation, they require justification. This is the link between evaluation and public policy reform.

Table 1 suggests some of the typical public policy matters of interest to communities embracing information and communication technologies. These public policy

Table 1. Public policy assessment

Policy issues to be evaluated	Possible approaches to measurement
Community broadband as a public utility	Calculate economic and social costs of having broadband installed, or not
Universal connectivity throughout the community	Quantify the numbers of connected households, businesses, government and non-government offices and public access points
A fair and competitive market	Conduct a longitudinal study of the local business economy in terms of competitive services provided and monopoly protections in place
Open access and Internet neutrality	Assess whether government intervention is needed to keep the broadband Internet open to providers and end-users
Interoperability among networks and equipment	Locate points of access denial and public frustration due to lack of connectivity between and among provider equipment and networks
Protections for creative products, inventions and intellectual property	Identify and measure abuses of copyright leading to loss of revenues and control
Protections against hackers and data security losses	Collect and analyze case studies of computer attacks and data theft
Avoidance of intrusive advertising, spam and viruses	Subscribe to Internet services that monitor, account for and give users control over unwanted content and provide advance warnings of threats to their systems
Legal controls over indecent content and threats against children	Join with other communities in identifying the specific abuses and their sources with the idea of pressuring governing agencies to take action

points are of concern to communities, but they may or may not have legislative or other regulatory remedies.

CONCLUSION

In the United Nations report on *Community-based Networks and Innovative Technologies: New Models to Serve and Empower the Poor*, Siochrú and Girard (2005) observe that regulatory obstacles to new technologies and players have often been the major barrier to progress in many areas of ICT development. That being said, there exists a recent openness to new solutions such as Voice over IP and wireless protocols. They argue that:

> The reality of ICT environments and needs, of vested interests and investment possibilities, varies hugely. But principles such as technology neutrality, "open access" to backbone infrastructure, and a "public good" rationale in certain ICT network components are beginning to be heard.….A layered approach to network development, each with potentially a different set of regulatory and ownership possibilities, is emerging. Alongside private or public ownership, partnerships, local authorities, SMEs, and indeed communities are seen as having a role to play (p. 11).

Public policy reforms and establishing supportive regulations will perhaps never be sufficient to make poor countries competitive with wealthy countries, but good policies can remove barriers. Legislation and enforcement can provide guidance and encouragement. The example of the Republic of Ghana is illustrative. After long deliberation on the matter of whether and how to join the Network Society, the Ghana Ministry of Communications declared that "the appropriate use of information and communication technologies in an entrepreneurial, open, participating and facilitating environment" was one of the things it could do to insure that the country would achieve "competitiveness, investment, development of human capacity and improved governance, leading to wealth creation and national prosperity". As a matter of national priority, Ghana made a conscious and public effort to "integrate with the new emerging economic order" (National Telecommunications, 2005, p. 6).

The success of nations and their enterprises often hinges on the policy positions they take in defining progress and future development. However, for policies to produce results, local agencies and operators at the community level have to embrace and implement the vision. Responsive government with both public and private sector participation appears to be the only way create and sustain a better standard of living.

The UNDP report suggests a number of steps that might help to create a regulatory climate favourable to local network deployment in poor countries.

1. Technology neutral licences, so that services use the most effective and cheapest available;
2. Flexibility should be allowed in licence award and conditions;
3. Licence exempt spectrum for wireless use should be free of costs and administrative burdens;
4. Interconnection pricing should be favourably set, including "asymmetric" pricing;
5. Universal service funds should be accessible to develop community-owned networks, including at the application and content level;
6. An "open access" policy for connections to the national backbone could be promoted that would also recognise the development benefits and higher conventional costs of services in rural areas; and
7. Local regulations could be developed to ensure that service and application initiatives embody significant elements of community ownership and control (Siochrú & Girard, 2005, p. 13).

As for *Networked Communities*, it is the authors' judgement that such steps are worthy of consideration everywhere.

REFERENCES

2005 e-readiness rankings. (2005). *Economist Intelligence Unit in co-operation with the IBM Institute for Business Value.* Retrieved November 15, 2007, from www.eiu.com.

Archives of the ICF – The Intelligent Communities Forum. (2007). *Taillin, Estonia – Nomination submitted for the Intelligent Community of the Year Award.* New York.

Baker, M. (2007). *Firefox is a public asset.* Retrieved August 9, 2007, from http://blog.mozilla.com/blog/2007/08/09/firefox-is-a-public-asset/

Boateng, K. (2004). Satellite communications in Ghana: Challenges and prospects. *Online Journal of Space Communication* Issue No. 7. Retrieved October 12, 2007, from http://satjournal.tcom.ohiou.edu/issue7/ov_africa.html

Boateng, K. (2006). Bringing new media to Ghanians: The political economy of Internet deployment. *Dissertation Abstracts International, 67*(01). (UMI No. 3203331)

Bylund, A. (2007). Net neutrality rises again. *The Motley Fool.* Retrieved January 18, 2007, from http://www.fool.com/investing/general/2007/01/18/net-neutrality-rises-again.aspx

Country Commerce China (2007). *Economist Intelligence Unit.* Retrieved August 15, 2007, from www.eiu.com/un

Diamond, J. (1999). *Guns, germs, and steel: The fates of human societies.* New York: W. W. Norton & Company.

Flournoy, D. (2004). *The broadband millennium: Communication technologies and markets.* Chicago: International Engineering Consortium.

Friedman, T. L. (2006). *The world is flat: A brief history of the twenty-first century.* New York: Farrar, Straus & Giroux.

Garelli, S. (2006). Competitiveness of nations: The fundamentals. *IMO World Competitiveness Yearbook.*

Ghosh, R. A. (2006). Economic impact of open source software on innovation and the competitiveness of the information and communication technologies (ICT) sector. *UNU-Merit,* the Netherlands. Retrieved November 20, 2006, from http://ec.europa.eu/enterprise/ict/policy

Harris, C. (2008). Muni Wi-Fi projects struggle with technology and economic challenges. *Government technology: Digital communities.* Retrieved June 8, 2008, from www.gov.tech.com.

Harvard Business School (2006). *Professor Michael Porter ranks business competitiveness of nations.* (2006). Retrieved November 14, 2006, from http://www.hbs.edu/news/releases/111406_porter.html

King, R. (2006). *Open source takes on telecom,* Retrieved July 10, 2006, from http://www.businessweek.com/technology/content/jul2006/tc20060707_042679.htm

Kennard, W. E. (2006). *Spreading the broadband revolution.* Retrieved October 21, 2006, from http://www.nytimes.com/2006/10/21/opinion/21kennard.html

Kushner, D. (2006). The Firefox kid. *IEEE Spectrum, November,* 27-31.

LaMonica, M. (2006). Is open source getting to Microsoft? *CNET News.com.* Retrieved September 15, 2006, from http://www.news.com/Is-open-source-getting-to-Microsoft/2100-7344_3-6115914.html

Lawson, S. (2004). Law may snag Philadelphia Wi-Fi rollout. *IDG News Service: MacCentral.* Retrieved June 8, 2008, from Macworld.com: http://www.macworld.com/article/40973/2004/11/philadelphia.html

Lawson, S. (2008). EarthLink to remove Philadelphia Wi-Fi. *IDG News Service*. Retrieved June 10, 2008, from http://www.pcworld.com/businesscenter/article

Liang, X. & Zhang, J. (2001). A summary of telecommunications reform in China. *IEEE Communications Magazine, 39*(10), 35-37.

Ministry of Communications. Republic of Ghana. (2004). *National Telecommunications Policy*. Retrieved September 15, 2007, from http://www.moc.gov.gh/moc/PDFs/telecom_policy_final.pdf

Mohan, S. et al. (2006). Scaling the mobile Internet. *IEEE Communications Magazine, June,* 64-65.

The Mozilla Manifesto (2007) Retrieved August 16, 2007, from http://www.mozilla.org/about/mozilla-manifesto.html

Needleman, R. (2007). *Webware 100 winners announced!* Retrieved June 18, 2007, from http://www.webware.com/8301-1_109-9728770-2.html

Open source definition. (2007). *The Linux Information Project*. Retrieved January 3, 2007, from www.linfo.org/open_source.html

Schmidt, E. (2007). *A guide to net neutrality for Google users.* Retrieved January 20, 2007, from the Google Web site: http://www.google.com/help/netneutrality.html

Siochrú, S. O. & Girard, B. (2005). *Community-based networks and innovative technologies: New models to serve and empower the poor.* Geneva: United Nations Development Programme.

Somerset-Ward, R. (2005). *Broadband community networks: Building the digital commons.* Philadelphia, PA: Haas Charitable Trusts.

Summary of Operators and Service Providers (2006). *Regulatory Framework: Industry Statistics,* Ghana National Communications Authority. Retrieved April 26, 2007, from www.nca.org.gh

Tallo, I. (2006). *Interview with the Head of the eGovernance Academy of Estonia,* on December 1, 2006.

Tongia, R. (2007). Connectivity in emerging regions: The need for improved technology and business models. *IEEE Communications Magazine,* 96-103.

World Information Society Report (2006). Retrieved January 15, 2007, from the International Telecommunications Union Web site: http://www.itu.int/osg/spu/publications/worldinformationsociety/2006/report.html

Wang, T. (2007). Satellite distance education in China. *Online Journal of Space Communication*. Retrieved May 16, 2008, from http://satjournal.tcom.ohiou.edu/Issue11/wang.html.

Chapter IV
Knowledge Workforce

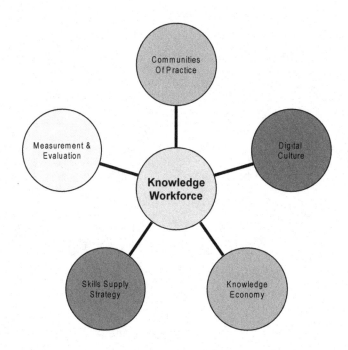

"R&D and education in the traditional sense are not enough for growth. Technology becomes more soft and increasingly depends on the cooperation between people in networks." Lambert Van der Laan (2005, p. 276)

Overview: This chapter focuses on knowledge workers—who they are and what they do, and the impact they have on organisations and communities in the Network Society. As technology-savvy individuals, they have the training to understand and apply telecommunications and electronic media at work, at home and in the community. Because of their ICT skills and potential contributions to innovation and productivity, knowledge workers constitute a critical labour market for networked communities. Training and education institutions can play an important role in ensuring the local supply of ICT skills. To illustrate these points, four networked communities are described:

- **Issy-les-Moulineaux, France.** This suburb of Paris has transformed itself into a preferred location for knowledge workers to live and work;
- **Mitaka, Japan**. Mitaka is a suburb of Tokyo offering exceptional quality of life to its knowledge workers;
- **Taipei, Taiwan.** This is a large city with a CyberCity Plan and an impressive labour force;
- **Waterloo, Ontario, Canada.** This university town has developed an international reputation based on public-private collaboration and entrepreneurship.

The chapter ends with suggestions for the measurement and evaluation of a community's knowledge workforce.

KNOWLEDGE ECONOMY AND ITS WORKERS

Key Concept: *Prosperity within the Network Society depends upon the knowledge-base economy and its knowledge workers who are both local and global in nature.*

Within the Network Society, the economy is driven by information and knowledge, which trigger rapid innovation in products and services for the markets of the world. The terms information and knowledge are often used interchangeably but they are not identical concepts (Steinnmuller, 2002). Computers process information and telecommunications provide ample mechanism for sharing information, but selecting and interpreting information requires knowledge and purpose. Information serves as the raw material that becomes the basis for acquiring knowledge, which comes about through experimentation and learning. Such trial and error learning can take place at the individual, group and organisational levels (Antonacopoulou & Papamichail, 2004; Mentzas & Apostolou, 2004). We live in a time that is frequently referred to as the Information Age, and certainly we individually and collectively have access to so much information that we sometimes feel inundated by it.

Data indigestion is often what happens when digital networks stream more information than can be processed and productively put to use. The successful communities of the future will not only have access to ICTs, interconnected infrastructure and vast streams of information; to grow and sustain themselves, they must also engage in creating new knowledge. They must focus not just on gathering information but also on solving problems, reducing costs and innovating with new products and services. This work will principally be done by people we think of as "knowledge workers".

Knowledge workers are critically important to the Network Society and its knowledge-based economy. Surrounded by rapid changes in technology and technological applications, today's organisations and communities both influence and are influenced by the talented people whose mastery of ICTs make work faster, easier and often less costly. Knowledge workers are at their best when allowed to exercise their initiative and creativity. In doing so, they contribute to organisational and community development, which sometimes results in the creation of small and large job-producing commercial enterprises.

Holding such titles as software developer, advertiser, consultant, researcher, manager, and educator, knowledge workers are present throughout developed economies but they tend to be concentrated in IT industries, universities, and research institutes (Matthiessen Schwarz & Find, 2006). They are comfortable with ICTs and view them as tools to increase their own productivity and that of others (Haag et al., 2006). Knowledge workers manage information—the data components from which knowledge is derived— and share the products of their creation with others through communication networks. They are the expanding group of thinkers in the Knowledge Age described by Charles Savage (1996) in *Fifth Generation Management*. Savage explains that wealth is based upon the ownership of knowledge and the ability to use that knowledge to create or improve goods and services. The added values to these products are improvements in cost, durability, suitability, timeliness of delivery, and security.

Statistics. Knowledge workers are predominant in the service sectors of the economy. Since 1995, the service sectors have offered the majority of employment within the industrialized countries, and those sectors continue to grow. A statistical report by the Organisation for Economic and Cooperative Development (OECD, 2007) documented that in 1995 the service sector represented 67.7% of civilian employment in the G7 countries and 64.5% in the 15 countries of the European Union. By 2005, these figures had increased to 73.7% and 69.8%, respectively. The U.S. is the country with the most extensive service sector, representing 78.6% of employment. As expected, the less industrialized countries have smaller service sectors. For example, the following countries have between 50% and 60% of their employment in the service sector: Czech Republic, Mexico, Poland, Portugal, and the Slovak Republic. Turkey trails the OECD survey with 48%. It is noteworthy that the service sector in Turkey rapidly expanded in the 10 years covered by the survey, from 33.9% to 48%. Statistics on communities are much harder to come by. Diversification has been a sustainability theme throughout the 1980s and 1990s, and we can expect communities of 50,000 inhabitants or larger in industrialized countries to have large service sectors. Focusing on large research institutes, Matthiessen et al. (2006) reported that these communities were located primarily in the large urban centres such as Tokyo and London, but an exception was the small community of Cambridge England.

The service sectors in towns and cities, as with other sectors, depend heavily on a growing talent pool of workers who are skilled in information management. These employees help local organisations and institutions achieve their goals using information. In practise, they use ICTs to process, create, manipulate, store, retrieve, and distribute data. Some of these knowledge-able individuals are self-employed and serve as consultants and entrepreneurs.

Knowledge workers in communities will use ICTs in a variety of patterns, combining such traditional approaches as face-to-face and phone communication with newer communication tools like e-mail, Web sites, online services and conferencing to fit their jobs and their personal styles. ICTs rarely entirely replace face-to-face communication, largely because human contact is so solidly anchored in what it means to be human. Rather, ICTs tend to serve the goal of extending human presence.

As far back as 1959, Peter Drucker, the management guru, foresaw the importance of the knowledge workers in his book *The Landmarks of Tomorrow*. In a 1999 *Atlantic Monthly* article, "Beyond the Information Revolution", Drucker equates leadership in the knowledge-based economy with a mind-set that welcomes innovation, values knowledge workers and creates an environment in which these workers can thrive. The term knowledge worker has somewhat fallen out of use, probably because industrialized countries have high levels of education and many occupations include knowledge use. Academic researchers have gravitated to such organisational terms as organisational learning and knowledge management. Nevertheless, Drucker's message has received much attention: teamwork and new personnel approaches are needed in the emerging knowledge economy. Linking competence to communication, the Australian Professor Richard Joseph agrees with Drucker that knowledge workers often know more than their managers on "what to do" and "how to do it". However, they thrive only when given rich communication channels (Joseph, 2005).

The academic Edward Steinmueller (2002) describes the knowledge-based economy as one that invests in knowledge to increase the productive capacity of capital goods, labour and natural resource inputs. This type of economy is based on ICT networks of knowledge workers who collectively create new knowledge in private and public laboratories and institutes, and use it to make organisations more productive. The knowledge economy is widely expected to create new industries and render existing ones more productive, as more communities of networks come online.

Steinmueller holds the view that the discipline of economics has been slow in recognizing the central role of collective knowledge creation and deployment, and is reluctant to use the language of organisational capability, learning and cognition. Traditional economics assumes that through the division of labour, workers become interchangeable. A new approach is needed that values knowledge workers and their collective efforts to create and deploy knowledge. In practise, ICTs and the products and services they spawn have become the model that an organisation adopts to become a "network organisation" in its pursuit of distinctive competence. The reasoning is that ICTs give the organisation greater flexibility through information and knowledge sharing, leading to new ways of controlling and organising work in space and time.

DIVERSITY OF NETWORKED COMMUNITIES

Key Concept. *Knowledge workers live and work within virtual as well as real communities. Because the Internet can erase many of the barriers of time and distance, knowledge workers can have both local and global collaborators and partners.*

According to Nicholas Ashford (2005), communities can meet the challenge of our technology-driven economy through technological, organisational and social innovation. Taking a systemic approach to innovation will help communities become more efficient and competitive, achieving greater social cohesion (challenging work and employment) and protecting the environment. Though Ashford does not mention knowledge workers explicitly, they are the ones who provide access to rich information and timely exchanges, thus fostering innovation.

Cities tend to be magnets for talent and the collective human engines of enterprise. One can observe the ways that large and small cities connected to the broadband Internet have been able to make quality-of-life changes that attract talent. One can also note that, while the Internet is made possible by the physical community, it requires a supportive culture to make effective use of that infrastructure—it takes training and an environment that nurtures freedom of expression and entrepreneurship to produce the products and services that modern cities require to compete. Knowledge workers seek out such communities as places to live and work. They participate in both the local and global "communities of practise" for a variety of social purposes (Lin & Lee, 2006; Johnson & Ambrose, 2006) and for accessing the flow of ideas for work (Matthiessen, Schwarz & Find, 2006). Locally, these communities of practise are a mix of face-to-face and online exchanges, whereas globally the online exchanges dominate. The following two illustrations describe one large and one small city, each having achieved the status of networked community and each possessing a highly educated workforce.

Taipei is a city with 2.6 million inhabitants (Archives of the ICF, 2006). Located in northern Taiwan off the eastern coast of Asia, Taipei is the country's government, business and cultural centre. The city is surrounded by satellite communities that form a cluster of manufacturing facilities that produce chips and motherboards for notebooks and other computers. With 27 colleges and universities and 10 research institutes, Taipei can claim a highly educated population, since close to 50% of the adult population holds a university bachelor's degree. Taipei has an extensive telecommunications infrastructure supporting some of the most advanced ICT applications in the world, with a broadband Internet usage rate of almost 80% of all households.

Waterloo, Ontario, Canada, has experienced exceptional economic growth. With about 100,000 inhabitants, the city has spawned world-class entrepreneurs in part because it has put effort into recruiting, educating and using its knowledge workers. The area around Waterloo, formerly a rural area, now has a combination of software, hardware, wireless, medical imaging, and radio technology enterprises. As region's economy has grown, it has attracted newcomers from all over Canada and the world. The region ranks third in Canada in net migration and is among the top five destinations for new immigrants to Canada (Archives of the ICF, 2007b).

Key Concept. *The suburbs of large cities can also be network communities. They benefit from their proximity to the metropolis and offer high quality of life for their knowledge workers.*

Not so long ago, the suburbs were seen as the most desirable locations for owning homes and raising families. Employees would commute into the city where good jobs were found. The suburbs generally had good schools and nice shops to serve their residential communities. With the growth of cities, the suburbs have often been transformed from a supportive role to that of independent communities having symbiotic relationships with the city. Traffic jams, high rents and increasing pollution have made the large city less desirable and the suburb even more so. The suburbs offer a quality of life and work that makes them attractive; their proximity to the city is seen as a plus because of the large markets and specialty services offered. The examples of Mitaka, Japan, and Issy-les-Moulineaux, France, illustrate the ways that suburbs become attractive places for knowledge workers.

Mitaka is a suburb of Tokyo, home to 173,000 people in its 16.5 sq km (6.8 sq miles) of space (Archives of the ICF, 2005). The city has attracted universities, corporate research offices and data centres drawn by Mitaka's proximity to Tokyo. JRC, a well known technology company, has its corporate headquarters there. The city developed a culture that prized technology and considered research and development highly important. In 1984, Mitaka became the first city in Japan to host a field test of fiber-to-the-home networking. In 1988, it served as a test bed for Japan's first integrated services digital network (ISDN) service and, in 1996, Musashin-Mitaka Cable Television became the first Internet Service Provider (ISP) in Japan to offer broadband at 10 Mbps.

According to Intelligent Community Forum files, Japan is a world leader in both broadband deployment—third in the world after South Korea and Canada—and broadband pricing, with some of the world's lowest subscription costs. Even more important is its tradition of strong citizen participation that equipped Mitaka to respond flexibly and energetically to the challenges of competing in a global economy. Mayor Keiko Kiyohara, came to office after decades as a technology educator and leader of citizen groups. As the city created development strategies, citizens collaborated in planning future services such as transportation and public services, land use, and communications.

In the late 1990s, Mitaka launched a "SOHO City Mitaka" programme to promote further development of the small office/home office businesses that were an important part of its economy. An organisation called the Mitaka Town Management Organisation (MTMO) was founded to create a SOHO incubator. Its seven facilities are home to 100 technology businesses. MTMO also provides business-matching programmes, venture investment and other financial services to encourage business start-up and growth. As of 2005, Mitaka was home to research and data centres for Dentsu, IBM Japan, SECOM and a variety of Japanese government agencies. There were a total of 61 educational institutions in the city employing 3,000 academics and researchers, and a group of universities was creating a new Mitaka Network University. The city of Mitaka holds the distinction of being the worldwide hub for production of "anime" cartoons, producing an estimated 75% of all anime seen around the globe

Another notable example is that of **Issy-les-Moulineaux,** a suburb of Paris, France (Archives of the ICF, 2007a). This small city of 61,800 people began its journey to become a networked community by building upon a small cluster of IT, telecommunications and R&D organisations attracted by its proximity to government agencies. Under the leadership of Mayor Andre Santini, the municipality launched a campaign to lure more technology companies into the area and make high-tech the backbone of the local economy. In January 1998, the French government ended the monopoly of France Telecom, and Issy seized the opportunity. The city negotiated deals with competitive carriers that led to the construction of new fiber networks. When the monopoly officially ended, the new carriers switched on service, and local companies were able to take immediate advantage of price competition.

By 2006, Issy's IT and communications infrastructure had undergone vast changes. Government, school, library and healthcare buildings were fully wired with broadband, and there was one PC for every 11 students in the primary schools. The multimedia City Council room began broadcasting deliberations via cable TV and the Web, and accepting citizen input in real time. A robust e-government portal provided online public procurement, online training, access to a "citizen relationship management" system called IRIS, and even online voting. An outsourcing contract allowed Issy to substantially reduce costs. The city invested in creating a cyber-kindergarten, public-access terminals, "cyber tearooms" that provided access and training to the elderly in a familiar and comforting environment, and video conferencing to connect parents with children away at holiday camps. The government consulted online with a representative Citizen Panel to gather opinions on local issues, and a "Participative Budget-Making Platform" enabled citizens to help the city in setting local investment priorities.

The city of Issy-les-Moulineaux ranked in the top 15 out of 110 French cities of more than 50,000 inhabitants for low operating costs, according to a 2005 survey. The population had grown 35% since 1990, swelling tax revenues without any increase in the government payroll. In 2007, 60% of the companies based in Issy-les-Moulineaux were in information and communications technology, including Cisco Systems Europe, France Telecom, Hewlett Packard, Orange Internet, Sybase, Canal+, Canal Satellite, Eurosport, France 5 and France 24. A partnership between the city and France Telecom's R&D facility has made Issy a test bed for such new applications as fiber-to-the-home, which was first deployed to a test group of 4,000 households. Business attraction and growth have been so robust that Issy-les-Moulineaux has more jobs than residents—a claim that few cities in the world can make. The city has no difficulty attracting knowledge workers because of its reputation for leading-edge ICT applications. Some knowledge workers choose to live in Issy to raise their families or enjoy the quality of life, while others prefer the bustle of Paris and commute to Issy for work.

CLUSTERS OF KNOWLEDGE WORKERS

Key Concept. *Developing a local market of knowledge workers can be accelerated where there is a concentration of IT-using organisations sharing information and creating knowledge.*

In specialized communities like science and technology parks, high-paying jobs tend to attract highly skilled technical and managerial personnel. Two communities with an abundance of IT facilities are Taipei, Taiwan, and Waterloo, Canada.

Nankang and Neihu are two well established technology parks in Taipei (Archives of the ICF, 2006). A content academy, software research and development centre, and semi-conductor academy have been established in the Nankang Software Park. The goal is to make Taipei a centre for integrated circuits design and R&D by providing high-tech facilities, professional service systems and management support services to increase the productivity of software workers. The park is described as a "human resource incubator". The Nankang Software Park's annual revenue in 2005 was about US$5.3 billion dollars. More than 200 companies were located inside the park, employing some 12,000 knowledge workers.

The Neihu Technology Park is a very different model. This park includes housing, culture and education, logistics, and wholesale and retail businesses, as well as manufacturing. It is equivalent to a small city offering a high quality of life. Created through a private-public collaboration, in 2006 this park contained more than 4,000 companies with 150,000 employees, and generated US $63.5 billion in revenue, representing a 35% growth compared to 2005. Many recognized companies like Compal, Liteon and BenQ have established their headquarters and R&D centres in the Neihu Park.

For its small size, it is surprising to observe that **Waterloo** has more than 150 research institutes in and around its boundaries (Archives of the ICF, 2007b). This high concentration of research activity illustrates why this area has such a strong domestic and international reputation as an advanced technology and knowledge leader. Three examples are the Perimeter Institute for Theoretical Physics, the Institute for Quantum Computing and the Centre for Wireless Communications.

> The Perimeter Institute was founded in the fall of 1999 to provide a place for Canadian and international researchers to work together on issues in overlapping sub-disciplines of theoretical physics. The institute was created with a substantial financial donation of $100 million by Mike Lazaridis, president and co-CEO of Research in Motion (RIM), the company that created the popular hand-held device called the BlackBerry. In addition to being a collaborative environment for scientific interaction, the institute has become a significant contributor to the cultural life of Waterloo. It is the site for concerts and public events, and has an active educational outreach programme in local schools and classrooms. Perimeter Institute enjoys the prestige of being in a peer group that includes research institutes at Princeton and Cambridge Universities.

The mission of the Institute for Quantum Computing, associated with the University of Waterloo, is to accelerate developments in the field of quantum computing and information processing, drawing on research and theory in relevant areas of science, mathematics and engineering. In practical terms, its goal is to harness the quantum world, the one we enter at the scale of atoms and molecules, to produce new technologies that will be key economic engines of the 21st century.

The Centre for Wireless Communications at the University of Waterloo conducts innovative research activities, educates tomorrow's engineering leaders and provides an environment that fosters teamwork and strategic collaboration in the areas of wireless technologies, systems and applications. Thrust areas include circuit design and lower power electronics, RF systems, communications, networks, and multimedia. This centre is funded by the provincial and federal governments, as well as by business.

In close association with the University of Waterloo, the above three institutes have created a community-oriented mechanism that ensures the supply of and demand for high-end knowledge workers in the city and region of Waterloo. Promising students and graduates are encouraged to build relationships with these institutes, obtain specialized on-the-job training, and over time contribute to their success by filling vacant or new positions. In addition, talented individuals from outside Waterloo are drawn by the sophistication of these institutes and the attractiveness of the city.

Key Concept: *When local communities do their labour market planning, they must concentrate on assessing their pool of knowledge workers and determine what can be done to attract and retain these knowledge workers.*

Although "technology worker", "information worker" and "knowledge worker" are often used interchangeably, we would like to point out some subtle differences. Knowledge workers are those who are skilled at transferring what they know about hardware, devices and processes in ways that lead to new applications and solutions. The work that they do is a creative act, not just a matter of data processing. It is principally through the human-technology interfaces—using modern computers and the multimedia Internet—that the work gets done, but these knowledge workers are always looking for ways to make tasks faster, and more efficient and productive. In networked communities, these creative acts involve managers, professionals, suppliers, consultants, trade associations, consumers, and government agencies who learn from one another. Since these networks are interconnected, extensive and flexible, they form communities of practise that pursue common goals, joint innovation, and adaptability over time.

Attracting, developing and retaining knowledge workers has become a challenge. Without an adequate supply of the right kind of personnel, productivity and competitive advantage in organisations and communities suffer. In terms of labour markets, which are usually described by occupations and their employment rates, the people who are in scarce supply are the professional, managerial, and IT skilled employees. With respect to ICTs, these individuals may be found in many occupations and at any level depending on the specific industry. For example, the multimedia industry includes game designers, graphic designers, Web programmers, animation producers, and Internet or intranet site developers.

Underlying any occupation are the skills that the employee needs to achieve the desired objectives and complete the required tasks. IT skills tend to fall into three distinctive groupings: technical, enabling and managerial skills. In the multimedia industry, examples of technical skills are graphic modeling, animation and composition. Enabling skills are broad skills needed across occupations, such as basic mathematics, keyboard use, and reading and writing. Managerial skills usually complement the technical skills; examples include marketing and distribution, project management and human resources management. While the labour market perspective gives an overview of a community's situation, the skills view is more useful for training and education institutions that prepare future knowledge workers. The skills perspective is also helpful for identifying the underlying requirements of a particular occupation or position, and identifying skills supply gaps.

The University of Queensland in Australia offers students and career-seekers the following multimedia job descriptions:

The work of multimedia developers can be described as the generation and manipulation of graphic images, animations, sound, music, text and video into consolidated multimedia programmes for entertainment, educational and instructional purposes.

Specialisation is common among multimedia developers, although most use a combination of the following skills at some stage:

(1) **Animation** is the design, drawing, layout and production of animation sequences that are incorporated into multimedia products.

(2) **Author-based programming** involves writing scripts or extensions in order to integrate a variety of images, text, animation, and/or sound before selecting and applying the desired programme structure to produce a multimedia end-product.

(3) Computer-based graphic design involves the use of computing technology and specialist software packages to manage production, interface and integration of various graphics and other mediums into the multimedia package design. The graphic designer's primary role is the design of art and copy layouts for multimedia products.

(4) Digital video-sound editing is the use of computer-based editing systems to prepare video sound for multimedia products. Under instruction from directors, editors manipulate sound effects in consultation other professional staff.

(5) Instructional design is used in developing multimedia applications for contexts including teaching, corporate training and information distribution. Instructional designers are used to target specific learning objectives and audiences through multimedia productions.

(6) Multimedia programming involves writing code to incorporate the range of audio-visual elements contained within a given multimedia package, and solving problems associated with conversion between different platforms. Multimedia programmers also specialise in such areas as video systems development or may work as programmers in other areas of information technology.

What Training Is Needed for Jobs in Multimedia Development?

Because multimedia development includes a wide array of different skills, combining art, music, education and many other areas with computing and information technology, there is no single background that could be considered the ideal pathway into multimedia. One will find that an increasing number of degrees in Communications or Computing are being designed specifically for multimedia, although other areas of expertise are also considered useful by employers of multimedia professionals (often depending on the type of production). For example, teachers or educators are often preferred by employers for instructional design, or people with backgrounds in visual art (with or without formal qualifications) may be preferred as graphic designers.

Having said this, it is of course important that anyone involved in multimedia development should have some familiarity with the technology involved. (Multimedia, 2007)

Local governments and community agencies can monitor their communities' labour markets to ensure sufficient numbers of people with the right skills to fill positions in the profit, not-for-profit, and governmental sectors of their economy. Skill shortages are of particular concern because they diminish the prospects for full employment and can negatively affect productivity. Vacant positions either remain unfilled or are filled with less skilled individuals. To avoid or contain skill short-ages, organisations develop strategies to attract and retain people with the desired skills. At the community level, such strategies often focus on local training and education opportunities to create supply, and on the quality of life to attract external candidates and retain local supply. Another strategy is the joint effort by public and private sectors to monitor and improve the supply and demand of knowledge workers. For example, business leaders can indicate weaknesses in the training and education system, and agency leaders can help to finance student internships and career placements in industry.

Key Concept. *Networked communities require a skill supply strategy for knowl-edge workers, one that meets the demands of their ICT-intensive organisations and maintains and improves their numerous telecommunication networks.*

Researchers of the knowledge economy have observed a shift from material products and processes to immaterial ones (Van der Laan, 2005). For example, data generation and handling using advanced information and communication technologies became key activities in the expansion of banking, stock trading, health services, entertainment, and education. Van der Laan believes that to benefit from the knowledge economy, a region must create a synergy among three kinds of knowledge capital: economic, social and cultural.

Economic capital refers to technology, R&D and education that creates added value. Social capital, otherwise known as relationship capital, involves communica-tion—and sometimes an element of persuasion—among groups and organisations. Cultural capital is the ability to give meaning to information and ideas by generat-ing, selecting and organising information. To operate effectively in networks with customers, suppliers, colleagues and managers, knowledge workers must have such skills as organisational sensing, expressive (verbal and written) communication, artistic expression, and service-oriented and persuasive skills. These soft skills complement the more traditional skills that are involved in producing and manag-ing material products and services.

In March 2008, the ICF named Scot Rourke, President of OneCommunity in Cleveland, Ohio as the Intelligent Community Visionary of the Year. Rourke was selected based on his groundbreaking work as a social entrepreneur in Northeast Ohio and his willingness to share lessons learned from ICT-based economic development with communities across the United States and around the world. The ICF explained that under Rourke's leadership, "OneCommunity forged partnerships with the region's telephone and cable carriers, under which the carriers donated unused fiber-optic circuits to OneCommunity and OneCommunity contracted for last-mile fiber and VPN services from the carriers. The result was an 'ultra-broadband' network connecting the major government, institutional and nonprofit users in the region. In recognition of OneCommunity's achievements, the Intelligent Community Forum named Cleveland as one of its Top Seven Intelligent Communities of the Year in 2006, and honored Northeast Ohio with a Top Seven ranking in 2008" (Archives of the IFC, 2008).

Scot Rourke is an example of a entrepreneur who uses all three types of knowledge capital in his work within the NE Ohio region: economic, social and cultural. Under his leadership, and with strong support from the co-founders, OneCommunity attracted a wealth of resources, including donated fiber and equipment to power this next-generation communications infrastructure. Partnerships with the region's telephone and cable carriers also were critical. As an experienced executive, capital raiser and investor, Mr. Rourke was able to make the case to carriers and technology providers that OneCommunity would build demand for bandwidth and related services by helping the public and nonprofit sectors identify and realize the benefits of advanced IT and telecom services. As a result, OneCommunity has attracted tens of millions of dollars, including in-kind donations from leading global technology businesses interested in taken part in this groundbreaking collaborative and innovative test bed.

The ICF noted that the OneCommunity network has expanded and will be connecting more than 1,500 schools, libraries, governments, hospitals and universities to each other via the broadband Internet. Subscribers receive high-speed telecommunications connections at a fixed cost, while schools are receiving many free services. OneCommunity's "OneClassroom" initiative, for example, captures content from the Cleveland Clinic, Cleveland Museum of Art, PBS and other sources for use in the classroom project. In 2006-07, the OneCommunity network hosted an 18-month program called Voices & Choices that engaged thousands of area leaders in Web-enabled "town meetings" in order to educate people about the challenges facing the regional economy and obtain their input. Voices & Choices led to a regional economic development plan called Advance Northeast Ohio, which focuses on business growth and attraction, talent development, inclusion and government collaboration for greater efficiency (Archives of the IFC, 2008).

As a nonprofit think tank that focuses on the creation of local prosperity and social inclusion in the "broadband economy," the ICF conducts research, hosts events, offers tours of Intelligent Communities, publishes newsletters and presents awards to help communities understand the opportunities and challenges of the broadband economy, and to promote best practices in economic and social development. Giving support and recognition to knowledge workers is an important part of the ICF mission.

SUPPLY OF KNOWLEDGE WORKERS

Key Concept. *Training and educational institutions are the cornerstone for the local supply of knowledge workers. To support the Network Society, communities must demonstrate openness to connectivity and willingness to change traditional educational practises.*

Modern communities provide educational systems that range from pre-school, elementary, high school, college and university, and can have a host of public and private institutes of learning and research. Educational institutions, which promote learning and prize intellectual capital, are important participants in the Network Society. However, educational systems are often challenged to incorporate ICTs, whose connectivity increases intellectual growth. This challenge is difficult because educational systems tend to be large, traditional, cash-strapped and given to incremental innovation at the best of times. Nicholas Ashford's (2005) challenge of triple innovation— technological, organisational and social—is illustrated in the following examples using the cities of Mitaka and Taipei.

Mitaka, Japan, developed a skills supply strategy focused on information and communication technologies that required new technology in educational settings, curriculum adaptations and measures to diminish the digital divide (Archives of the ICF, 2005):

> The Mitaka area is home to such universities as the International Christian University, Japan Lutheran College and Kyorin University, as well as the University of Electro-Communication and HOSEI University. There are a total of 61 educational institutions in the city, employing 3,000 academics and researchers. In addition, HOSEI and 13 other universities are now cooperating with the city to create a new institution, the Mitaka Network University, which will open in 2005. At the levels of primary and secondary public education, Mitaka is a leader in the development of the next generation of knowledge workers. As early as 1989, the city adopted a computer literacy training system for teachers and created a programme for applying ICT to the education of young people. The full scale ICT educational plan,

Chart 1.

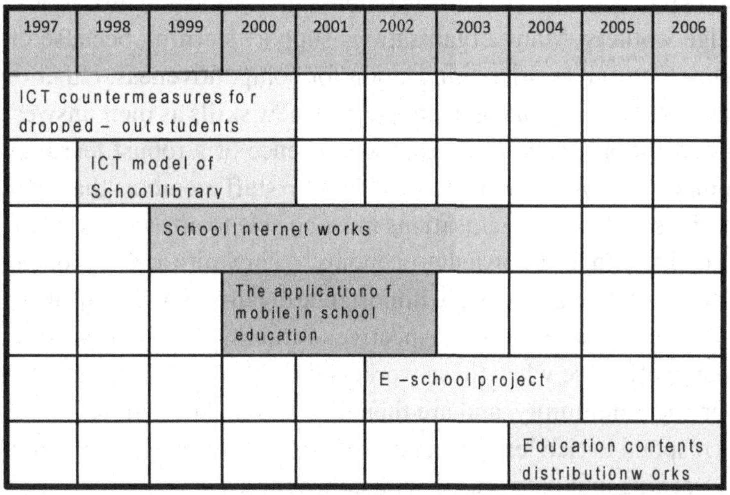

1997	1998	1999	2000	2001	2002	2003	2004	2005	2006
ICT countermeasures for dropped – out students									
	ICT model of School library								
		School Internet works							
			The application of mobile in school education						
					E –school project				
							Education contents distribution works		

known as the "Regional Information Systems Plan of Mitaka City", was published in 1996.

As of 1997, all public primary and secondary schools were interconnected via the cable TV system's optical network and have access to the Internet at broadband speeds. With the support of the Japanese government, the Mitaka school system is using this infrastructure to introduce a diverse range of educational programmes, as shown by the Chart 1.

The goal of these ICT applications in the education field is not to train computer or communications technicians but to make general education more effective using ICT. The school system seeks to create an educational environment where students learn willingly and positively. However, it is clear that strong ICT skills will be a requirement of the 21st Century workforce, and these programmes will ensure that Mitaka's students are well equipped to succeed. The Japanese Ministry of Education, Culture, Sports, Science and Technology plans the establishment of nationwide educational content based on the Mitaka programmes.

The Mitaka example demonstrates the importance of sustained skill investment and development over a decade to achieve institutional transformation. Building on the skill foundation created by the educational system, a community can consolidate and extend the learning space to encompass the various organisations that contain knowledge workers. Many organisations support learning because their industry is fast changing and requires innovation for competitiveness. Other organisations may rely more on recruitment of people with new skills as their answer to changing business conditions. In both cases, the existence of a robust learning network in the community helps them to attract and retain staff members that are well trained. Communities and their organisations must be able to attract and retain knowledge workers to thrive in the knowledge economy. Alan Smith and his colleague William Rupp (2002, 2004) emphasize the importance of nurturing the loyalty of knowledge workers. From a community perspective, attracting knowledge workers to work there is only effective when these workers develop attachment and loyalty to their employer and community, and are therefore retained over time. These knowledge workers respond to rich learning and communication because of their penchant for lifelong learning and networking with colleagues.

A choice illustration of a collaborative public-private strategy is that of Taipei (Archives of the ICF, 2006). The city government and interested representatives from the private sector work together to promote education and training programmes that meet the human resource needs of the region:

> The mayor's office is the driving force behind the CyberCity Plan for sustainable growth in Taipei. A key component is the collaboration between academics and professionals to shorten the time it takes to transform academic students into knowledge workers. Companies and colleges work together to develop long-term plans to carry out programmes, including incentives, overseas training, scholarships, innovation awards, and experience camps to incubate new talent. Thus, the effort to consolidate academic education and practical professional training accelerates the cultivation of knowledge workers and the formation of a knowledge workforce.

> City officials estimate some $3 billion dollars is earmarked to fund IT education in Taipei. IT education is widely taught in elementary schools, high schools and universities, as well as in incubator centres. The private sector has aggressively joined this effort to cultivate talent. For example, computer software vendor Microsoft selected Taipei as the world's first location for its Future School Programme and annually holds its professional career experience campaign there for college and university students. Networking gear supplier Cisco Systems also implemented its Network Academy in Taiwan, a programme to shorten the time needed to transform students into IT workplace employees.

In addition, Taipei City Government has set-up the Taipei e-University that addresses both academic theory and hands-on experience. This university has a professional certification system, which is widely recognized in Taiwan. There are 13 community universities with different operational models; most of these are sponsored by non-governmental organisations. These community universities provide educational and training opportunities for 60,000 citizens per year. As of 2006, 219,012 participants had taken courses in these community universities.

Taipei is targeting both the general and student populations, and its officials and agencies are working closely with employers. This skill supply strategy includes both the supply and demand for IT skills.

Key Concept: *Public-private collaboration can create an effective skills supply strategy for acquiring knowledge workers.*

Waterloo is an excellent example of a collaborative strategy (Archives of the ICF, 2007b). As of 2005, more than 18,000 workers were employed in 550 high-tech firms in the Waterloo region, which had the lowest unemployment rate (6.5%) among the cities in the province of Ontario. More than 50% of the area residents who were 15 years of age and over had pursued postsecondary education. These achievements were built upon multiple public-private collaborations that gave priority to the interests of the community:

Business in Waterloo has benefited greatly from the foundational research of local academicians. The value of information technology investments in the Waterloo region has doubled over the past four years. David Johnston, president of the University of Waterloo and a member of the Intelligent Waterloo Leadership Group, believes a unique spirit of collaboration is at work in Waterloo. "There is the spirit of taking talent and ideas from different spheres and different settings and putting them together for a common purpose, that common purpose being to grow the community better than any community I know". The spirit of collaboration, together with the community's strong emphasis on lifelong learning, has allowed the city of Waterloo to retain its innovators and attract the best and brightest from around the world.

The Communitech Technology Association, established in 1997 to support the technology clusters that began forming around Waterloo in the 1980s, serves high-technology companies and research institutes in diverse fields. Its membership now includes more than 450 technology companies.

Communitech's primary mission is to build capacity by being an active and effective driver on issues that are central to the region's technology sector. It advocates for Waterloo and the region as a world class centre of technical expertise.

Waterlootechjobs.com is a member-supported site managed by the Communitech Technology Association, created in partnership with the City of Waterloo, Canada's Technology Triangle Inc. and a private benefactor. The Web site encourages member companies, partners and sponsors to post locally available technology-related jobs. The technology jobs portal is now a key vehicle for attracting technology workers to the region. The site also seeks to make the region attractive to those outside the community, providing information and emphasis on the people, companies and lifestyle attributes of the region.

Communitech partners with technology companies, government and the community on talent recruitments, workforce development programmes and continuing education for technology workers. Communitech has become a hub for the technology community, an organisation through which people can meet, network and get advice through peer-to-peer networking, venture support services and a range of special events. The organisation also takes a leadership role in such community issues as transportation concerns and the availability of medical services. Both Communitech and CTT (Canada's Technology Triangle Inc.) contribute to a better quality of life by encouraging and attracting investment, growth and interest in Waterloo. Recently, Communitech was awarded $11 million from the provincial government to support entrepreneurship development. In 2005, Communitech and 50 area employers launched a high-profile recruitment drive to attract tech workers. Research in Motion (RIM) hired 1,200 people in 2004, with additional hires in 2005.

Waterloo's skill supply strategy echoes that of Taipei in that attention is played to both the supply and demand for IT skills. They differ in that Waterloo is a distributed model of governance whereas Taipei represents a centralized one. Choosing one of these models for inspiration should depend upon the local context and what is considered socially appropriate.

KNOWLEDGE WORKERS AND COMMUNITY PARTICIPATION

Key Concept: *Community decision-makers must learn to include knowledge workers in all of their processes. However, for a balanced view these leaders should rely more on their own understanding of the human condition to chart a course for their community.*

Knowledge workers help to set the ICT agenda for senior managers and leaders in organisations and communities. Their expertise makes them natural advisers for IT investment decisions. They have personal and organisational networks through which they keep up to date on technical changes and possibilities. Decisions about technology diffusion—the adoption of a particular technology or application—will be made at multiple levels, whether among community officials, corporate managers, non-profit agencies that have volunteer boards or individual employees with designated authority. All of these tend to rely on those most knowledgeable and skilled to give guidance and come up with tech usage strategies that work for the situation at hand.

Jonathan Allen (2000) reported that "communities of practise" define the technology problem and the appropriate solutions. In other words, knowledge workers are organised into virtual networks that have a particular point of view on what the future of ICT deployment and use should be, and try to persuade others that their viewpoint is the right one to guide investment decisions. Knowledge workers may enthusiastically explain the situation and propose their preferred solutions, but unless they are coached in community stewardship, they may ignore some of the community's needs and aspirations. Needless to say, once the investment is made, both knowledge workers and decision-makers are committed to the new ICT configuration and would be reluctant to reconsider their decision. From a community perspective, over-reliance on knowledge workers is a mistake. Broad community consultation should take place to avoid becoming captive to a particular group's preferred solution.

MEASUREMENT AND EVALUATION OF KNOWLEDGE WORKERS

Measures relating to the number of workers online and how they use their digital capability are useful for assessing the extent to which the Internet is being utilized. As for the creation of a local knowledge workforce, it can be monitored through the training and development activities offered by employers, colleges, universities and the person-to-person help performed by individual users. Eger (1997) identified a number of topics in education and training that he considered critical to the success of networked communities. These topics can be integrated into a measurement system that assesses the basic preparedness of knowledge workers:

- High school drop-out rates.
- Trade school graduations.
- Post-secondary education enrollment and completion levels.
- SAT scores.
- Modification of curricula to include technology.
- Level of public access to technology and telecommunications for educational purposes.
- Level of computer literacy and use (by population).
- Credit hour equivalencies.
- Youth involvement in community service.
- Adult literacy.
- Awareness of global community.
- Skill base of workers.
- Accessibility of self-instruction resources and ability to use them.

Table 1 provides some examples of measurements that may be taken to evaluate the success rate of knowledge development in networked communities. This

Table 1. Knowledge workers evaluation

Knowledge development to be evaluated	Possible approaches to measurement
Development of knowledge workers in post-secondary educational institutions	Number of IT-related training programs Percent of businesses participating Percent of citizens participating
	Number of college and university level IT-related programs
Demonstrations of competency by residents	Rate of change of IT knowledge levels
Flexible models for learning are made available	Number of college and university courses and degree programs available online Number of students registered Number of yearly graduates
Knowledge workers are present in the community	Skills inventories across major organizations IT use in small and medium-size organizations Inventories of communities of practice
	Number and types of tele-workers

evaluation can focus on the skill supply strategy of a community, in which case other measures may be proposed that are more closely tied to it.

CONCLUSION

This chapter has argued—using the examples of Waterloo, Canada, and Taipei, Taiwan—that becoming a networked community is possible for both small and large cities Similarly, a networked community can be realized in a suburb of a large city, as shown by Issy-les-Moulinaux, France, and Mitaka, Japan. Each of these examples demonstrates the importance of developing a local market of knowledge workers through partnerships among IT-using organisations and education sectors. These knowledge workers will be needed to drive ICT use and innovation and will be the principal keepers of the telecommunication networks found throughout the community. Attracting and sustaining sufficient numbers of knowledge workers of the right type calls for a strategy. Community leaders must pay attention to the potential sources of such workers. Networked community goals should be (1) to devise plans for meeting the current and future demand for knowledge workers within their ICT-intensive organisations and (2) to see that the numerous telecommunication networks present in the community are maintained. These two goals are interdependent.

The most likely source for such personnel will be the community's training and educational institutions. With the guidance of community leaders, these institutions can usually be persuaded to include a curriculum that covers the technical, enabling and managerial skills essential for ICT-intensive organisations. If they have not done so already, institutions can be assisted in establishing Internet connectivity, and modifying their educational practises to include Internet use. Furthermore, Internet use must be more than an add-on to existing curriculum and practises. It requires rethinking and redesign so that both the communication and content advantages of the Internet are used. When young individuals are shown that the Internet is important and can be instructive as well as fun, they are likely to express themselves, both socially and creatively, by way of networks. Leaders in both the public and private sectors can craft effective strategies that integrate the learning and work settings, and ensure the adequate supply of knowledge workers of all kinds. The effectiveness of these strategies can be monitored using a variety of training and education, and workplace measures.

Community leaders must understand that it will take time, effort, resources and effective strategies to realize the economic development opportunities inherent to the Network Society. A five-to-ten-year period is an appropriate time span, based on the illustrations that we have presented in this chapter. As community leaders reach out to potential partners and stakeholders to build the networked community, they must learn to include knowledge workers, who understand the issues and possibilities of the globally connected Internet. However, community leaders should ultimately rely on their own understanding of human potential to chart a course for their communities.

REFERENCES

Allen, Jonathan. (2000). Information systems as technological innovation. *Information, Technology & People, 13*(3), 210-221

Antonacopoulou, E. & Papamichail, K. N. (2004). Learning supported decision-making: ICTs as feedback systems. In G. Doukidis, N. Mylonopoupos & N. Pouloudi (Eds.). *Social and economic transformation in the digital era* (pp. 271-288). Hershey PA: Idea Group Publishing.

Archives of the ICF – Intelligent Community Forum (2008). *OneCommunity, Cleveland Ohio USA – Recognition of the Visionary of the Year Award.* New York.

Archives of the ICF – Intelligent Community Forum (2007a). *Issy-les-Moulineaux, France – Nomination submitted for the Intelligent Community of the Year Award.* New York.

Archives of the ICF – Intelligent Community Forum (2007b). *Waterloo, Canada – Nomination submitted for the Intelligent Community of the Year Award.* New York.

Archives of the ICF – Intelligent Community Forum (2006). *Taipei, Taiwan – Nomination submitted for the Intelligent Community of the Year Award.* New York.

Archives of the ICF – Intelligent Community Forum (2005). *Mitaka, Japan – Nomination submitted for the Intelligent Community of the Year Award.* New York.

Ashford, N. (2005). Pathways to sustainability: Evolution or revolution? In M. van Geenhuizen, D. Gibson & M. Heitor. *Regional development and conditions for innovation in the Network Society.* (pp. 35-59). West Lafayette IN: Purdue University Press.

Browning, L., Saetre, A., Stephens, K. & Sornes, J.-O. (2004). *Information & communication technology in action: Linking theory and narratives of practise.* Abstrakt forlag. Copenhagen, Denmark: Copenhagen Business School Press.

Drucker, P. (1999, October). Beyond the information revolution, *The Atlantic Monthly*, *284*(4), 47-57.

Drucker, P. (1959). *Landmarks of tomorrow*. New York: Harper & Row.

Haag, S., Cummings, M., McCubbrey, D., Pinsonneault, A. & Donovan, R. (2006). *Management information systems for the information age* (3rd Canadian Ed.). Whitby, Ontario, Canada: McGraw Hill Ryerson.

Johnson, G. & Ambrose, P. (2006). Neo-Tribes: The power and potential of online communities in health care. *Communications of the ACH*, 49(1), 107-113.

Joseph, R. (2005). The knowledge worker: A metaphor in search of a meaning? In D. Rooney, G. Hearn & A. Ninan. *Handbook on the knowledge economy*. (pp.) Cheltenham UK: Edward Elgar.

Lin, H.-F. & Lee, G.-G. (2006). Determinants of success for online communities: an empirical study. *Behaviour & Information Technology*, 26(6), 479-488.

Matthiessen, C., Schwarz, A. & Find, S. (2006). World cities of knowledge: research strength, networks and nodality. *Journal of Knowledge Management*, 10(5), 14-25.

Mentzas, G. & Apostolou, D. (2004). Leveraging knowledge assets in firms of the digital era. In G. Doukidis, N. Mylonopoupos & N. Pouloudi. *Social and economic transformation in the digital era*. (pp. 289-311). Hershey PA: Idea Group Publishing.

Multimedia. (2007). Retrieved October 14, 2007, from the University of Queensland Web site: http://www.uq.edu.au/careers/index.html?page=31372&pid=0

OECD. (2007). Organisation for economic and cooperative development. *OECD in Figures 2006-2007*. OECD Observer, 2006/Supplement 1, p. 32.

Savage, S. (1996). *Fifth generation management* (2nd ed.). Burlington MA: Butterworth-Heinemann.

Smith, A., & Rupp, W. (2002). Communication and loyalty among knowledge workers: A resource of the firm theory view. *Journal of Knowledge Management*, 6(3), 250-261.

Smith, A. & Rupp, W. (2004). Knowledge workers' perceptions of performance ratings. *Journal of Workplace Learning, 16*(3), 146-166.

Steinnmueller, W. E. (2002). Knowledge-based economies and information and communication technologies. *International Social Science Journal, 54*, 141-153

Van der Laan, L. (2005) Measuring and interpreting the knowledge economy of regions. In M. van Geenhuizen, D. Gibson & M. Heitor. *Regional development and conditions for innovation in the Network Society* (pp. 273-293). West Lafayette IN: Purdue University Press.

Chapter V
Creating Applications and a Culture of Use

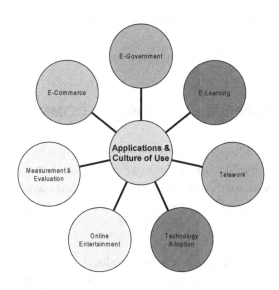

"This growing concern with urban sprawl, coupled with the nostalgic yearning which the 'new urbanism' movement represents, are evidence of sweeping changes in public attitude toward physical space....No technology in human history is having, or is likely to have, such tremendous influence on life and work and play, and in the transforming process, on our physical space, as the Internet." (Eger, 2007, p. 1)

Overview: Chapters I to IV have introduced the networked community and described its environment in terms of the Network Society, technology, telecommunication regulations and public policy, and the knowledge workforce. In this chapter, the focus shifts to the content specifics—the telecommunication and software applications found on the broadband networks. The usefulness of these applications can stimulate the creativity of users, leading to a continuum of use, otherwise known as a "culture of use". The difficulty in benchmarking innovative applications is that they change minute by minute; what is exciting today will probably be common tomorrow. Nevertheless, even established network applications should be considered because they represent innovations that might serve as springboards to next-generation production, making communities more distinctive, competitive, and creative. Several types of worldwide community innovations in applications are described here. This chapter will deal with:

- A description of applications and groupings of applications;
- An overview of sector-specific applications and some international examples;
- A discussion on technology adoption issues that should be considered in developing a culture of use;
- Measurement and evaluation approaches.

APPLICATIONS IN THE NETWORKED COMMUNITY

Key Concept: *Networked communities employ a growing variety of devices, software and sector-specific applications to improve their social and economic standing. Wider collaboration among community stakeholders can lead to the development of carefully targeted applications that will offer solutions to the real problems communities face.*

Applications relate to the user content, products and services that make useful the telecommunication infrastructures of networked communities. Applications are the reason people want to make maximum use of information and communication technologies, and why they expend effort acquiring new systems and devices, and learning how to use them. Access devices include IP telephones, desktop computers, cable modems, satellite receivers, i-Pods, BlackBerries, game players, and cell phones, to name a few. Most of them are different ways to interface with the Internet. Sector-specific applications include the programmes and projects that are delivered through those devices and infrastructure, such as e-health, e-learning, e-commerce, e-government services, and the digital content and online services that enrich entertainment, leisure and quality of life.

These applications will originate from within the community and from outside stakeholders by means of Web portals, search engines, virtual networks, service providers, innovators, newsgroups, chat rooms, file sharing, e-mail, and gaming platforms. Satisfied users will have access to high-capacity, on-demand, two-way communication via telephone lines, cable lines, or terrestrial or satellite wireless. When applications are made available and provide attractive personal and business services, users will want to use them on a regular basis, creating a culture of use. As the number and complexity of applications grow and demand increases, users will expect faster speeds, more efficient delivery of services, and more gadgets. Therefore, developing applications and encouraging public participation will also necessitate planning in infrastructure growth.

Innovation in devices leads to greater consumer adoption. For example, technological convergence allows the combination of such applications as data, video and voice services into one network, or into one device, including Internet TV and cellular telephones that are also providing Internet and iPod services. A growing number of these "all-in-one" technologies are being launched each year and are creating economies for consumers, improving ease of use and flexibility, and consequently attracting more users.

The diffusion of innovations from one sector to other sectors of a community can be encouraged through local structures. Bringing together multi-organisational and multi-sectoral partners can spur additional innovation, advance the adoption of new applications and provide an additional measure of sustainability. In the U.S., Cleveland, Ohio, is an example of a community that attempted to build applications that were appropriate and useful for its constituent institutions by promoting a collaborative environment.

> To make participating members aware of the wide variety of applications being created, and their potential uses, Cleveland developed a communication plan along with opportunities for consumer training and input. The city developed and hosted a computing environment that provided maintenance free, secure and fully managed public computing, along with dozens of open-sourced applications and shareware for schools, churches, libraries, community centres, government offices, train stations, and other public spaces.

> To further promote applications and collaboration, Ideastream was created in 2001 as a non-profit, public service multimedia organisation to deliver high quality public broadcast programming. It is now linked to the county libraries, the Convention and Visitor's Bureau, Cleveland Hopkins International Airport, Case Western Reserve University, and the Regional Transit Authority. For Cleveland these projects demonstrate how multi-sectoral and multi-organisational approaches to projects can work (Archives of the ICF, 2006a).

Culture of use is based on adoption patterns that are dependent on utility and ease of use (Venkatesh & Bala, 2008), and innovativeness of users and ease of access (Atkins & Jeffres, 1997). The broadband infrastructure must be available for citizens to easily buy-in and for innovators and entrepreneurs to offer applications and devices. Demonstrations of buy-in, or large adoption rates are usually an indicator of the presence of a culture of use. Fredericton, Canada, and Västerås, Sweden, are two examples where several service providers shared the same infrastructure in what is often called "open access networks" to encourage inter-networking among organisations in the community. This approach encouraged the development of applications and a culture of use at a faster rate than would normally occur without the intervention of networked community leaders. The result is that multiple applications and a vibrant culture of use make telecommunication infrastructures more sustainable.

Leaders in the City of Fredericton, New Brunswick, Canada, shared a vision to increase the connectivity and hence the productivity of their firms and citizens. The IT department of the city, the Economic Development staff and members of the Municipal Council deployed some 300 Wi-Fi wireless access points throughout the downtown and business corridors starting in 2003. They lit public facilities and retail malls and inventoried high traffic areas to deliver free Wi-Fi access nodes to these spots. The 22-kilometre ring allowed individuals to connect their computers to the broadband Internet free of charge. The Fred-eZone was started by connecting key organisations to the fiber ring and allowing the unused network capacity to service the Wi-Fi zone. The community's commitment to innovation has encouraged new private sector and government departments to locate in Fredericton, launching the city as a leading knowledge community (ICF, 2008b).

Another example is MalarNetCity, a broadband network that links every building in Västerås, Sweden, into a metropolitan area network for all kinds of digital communication. The network provides access to the Internet, and local traffic is swiftly routed around town. The project is said to be one of the most open access Municipality Area Networks in Europe. Built and operated by energy provider Mälarenergi's subsidiary company Mälarenergi Stadsnät, the network provides more than 50,000 Ethernet connections and reaches all parts of the city of Västerås, one of Sweden's 290 municipalities (Archives of the ICF, 2006f).

Among the customers of MalarNetCity are at least 7,000 residential villas that are connected with fiber to the home, all schools, hospitals and a majority of

Figure 1. Västerås, Sweden (2008)

the companies in Västerås. The goal is to have 90% of Västerås hooked up. What is characteristic of this municipality network is that several service providers compete on the same infrastructure, which is said to have led to better prices and quality. There are more than 25 service providers active in the network, including the two leading providers of TV content in the Nordic region, Viasat and Canal Digital; the leading telecommunications company in the Nordic and Baltic region, TeliaSonera, which also holds strong positions in mobile communications in Eurasia, Turkey and Russia; and Tele2, the second largest telecom provider after Telia. More than 62 services are being offered, including residential and business Internet access, TV, voice, Video on Demand, Games on Demand, home & office security, e-Learning, IP-telephony, and IP-TV. Among the services now available on the metropolitan network are nine different ISP-services for households and five different ones for companies that give users a range of Internet service speeds at differentiated pricing (Archives of the ICF, 2006f).

As faster, less costly and more user-friendly telecommunication technologies provide new ways to offer product and service opportunities, innovators think of new applications that the public might want but until now could not access. Each community must decide which application is most appropriate to its circumstances and find a fit between community needs and entrepreneurial energies, and available technologies and useful models being demonstrated world wide.

SECTOR-SPECIFIC APPLICATIONS

In her book *Smarten Up: Create a Smart Community*, Sylvie Albert (2003) notes several types of community projects for which new and improved network-based services and applications have been and are being created every day. There are three perspectives on applications: devices and applications, community activities and sector-specific initiatives. Sector-specific initiatives include tele-work and call centres, tele-medicine and tele-health, tele-education or e-learning, virtual libraries and museums, e-commerce, tele-entertainment, and e-government. To elaborate on the applications and community perspectives, the remainder of this chapter deals exclusively with the sector-specific initiatives that are present in networked communities. The following section reviews definitions of sector-specific applications and provides examples of work being performed internationally by networked communities, as well as other innovative projects that are using broadband networks to deliver content.

Tele-work and call centres. Tele-work includes working from home or a subsidiary office for an employer located in another region, running a home-based business selling goods and services, or working from home to supplement jobs done at a local office, using available information and communication technologies. Specialised skills, equipment and software are sometimes required but the advantages are apparent to almost everyone. Communities are happy since local talent doesn't have to leave to find meaningful employment, and workers tend to demonstrate increased job satisfaction.

Key Concept: *To attract new jobs with call centres, home-based Web centres and other related facilities, networked communities will look carefully at the capabilities of the local infrastructure to meet tele-working needs, market their human resources skills and develop new links with the organisations that are seeking these skills.*

Simply put, tele-working is moving the work to the workers, instead of the workers to work. With telecommunications, local people can work for companies or organisations located anywhere in the world either directly from their home or a central location where they may share office space with other tele-workers. Tele-working methods can be adopted by any person or group whose job allows them to communicate and share information digitally, use conferencing, engage in file sharing, exchange e-mail, or pick up the phone to keep in touch with employers and customers.

Fleming (2006a), a freelance writer who has followed the development of tele-work and online opportunities, noted that "The way we communicate today has little to do with where our office is located—millions start their own businesses right out of their homes. Even employers are seeing the benefits of having employees work from home." Some of these benefits include recruiting, employee retention, decreased office costs, productivity increases (10-30% on average), less absentee-ism, and an improved image of social responsibility by helping reduce pressures on the environment.

Work can be carried out wherever the appropriate skills are available at the optimum mix of costs and other factors. In some circumstances, recruitment costs can be reduced, as can the costs associated with high staff turnover and attrition, reducing the potential for corporate raiding. Staff can be on "standby time" from home at retainer rates and then paid at higher rates when needed for active work. Teams with the best skills and experience for a particular project can be brought together, regardless of geography and time zones, with a minimum need for extra travel.

Companies are now able to build new links not just with customers, but with employees in different parts of the country or around the world. Employees in different countries or regions are able to work together in teams on the same project. For example, teams of engineers and architects in India work on projects for international firms without ever leaving the comfort of their own offices. This situation encourages competition and allows businesses to compete internation-ally. Computers and communications are allowing companies to use networks of independent workers specialising in what they do best and outsourcing everything else to other suppliers. The information technology, professional services, finance and human resource department services are increasingly contracted out to work-ers who reside in other geographical areas. The fact that they can now be managed at a distance allows companies to concentrate on core capabilities, drawing on the skills of specialist groups when needed.

Technology workers have gained visibility and importance as they have become prime candidates for the tele-work environment. However, they are not the only likely candidates—almost 120,000 U.S. federal employees were identified as tele-working in a survey performed in 2005, with continuous growth in the popularity of the programme, and more than 70% of the federal government workforce designated as eligible for tele-work (United States Office of Personnel Management, 2007).

Tele-working lends credence to the development of a sound infrastructure. Some manufacturing companies see a benefit in allowing employees to monitor processes and equipment from home rather than coming to the plant each time an irregularity occurs during off times. This approach can save hours of overtime and travel, and improve the quality of life for workers who are on call for emergencies. According to Frances Cairncross (1997), who wrote *The Death of Distance*, foremost among the benefits of working from home or a remote office is greater job satisfaction and lower stress. It can be assumed that one result of universal computer connectivity is that employees in the future will increasingly work in smaller units or on their own. Companies will recruit the best skills, regardless of location, for better productivity, and new business opportunities will spring up for consulting and outsourcing to support this human resource strategy.

Call centres are often large buildings filled with people servicing an entire region, country or global market. Typically, call centres locate in places noted for less expensive labour as well as a suitable telecommunication infrastructure.

> Moncton, New Brunswick, Canada, became famous for welcoming larger call centres in the 1990s. Over time, employees were able to move from less lucrative sales-oriented outbound call centres to better paying jobs offered through centres that provided technical support services or inbound services (Larner, 2002).

Banks no longer need as many small branches when people can conduct more of their banking over the Internet and via telephone. Travel agencies no longer need as many people in local offices when customers can book vacations online. Such activities can be handled by a single call centre that can be located, in principle, in any city. Call centres offer customers the opportunity to obtain general or technical information and make purchases; they also offer companies greater outreach to more consumers.

Today, the new trend in call centre servicing is to decentralise the work, which means that the activity is centrally organised, but the place of work is distributed. This is possible when high speed infrastructure is made available not just to businesses but to citizens. Call centre operators can hire people to work from home, managing them from "virtual call centres" that are home-based. Web-integrated call centres have the potential to unlock online opportunities and revolutionize direct contact performance. They are ideally suited to handle help desk and sales order functions and do not necessarily require large inputs of labour.

Tele-medicine. These applications include exchanging health information via the Web or private networks, consulting by means of videoconferencing systems, sending digital patient data to specialists for an opinion, preparing assessments requiring remote diagnostic tools, and executing medical practices at a distance (American Telemedicine Association, 2007).

Various aspects of tele-health or tele-medicine are demonstrating their value. The report by Williams and Whittier (2007) on electronic health records argues that "EHRs can replace paper-based medical records, improve the quality of patient care and decrease medical errors. EHRs also support product innovations such as e-visits and online prescribing" (p. 26). Johnson and Ambrose (2006) relate that more than 30 million Americans participate in online health-related groups to fill a void in the health care system. The Internet and online health systems are providing a holistic way for users to evaluate and help solve their problems.

Key Concept: *The adaptation of medical services to digital processing and tele-communications delivery can be an effective and cost-efficient way to extend health services to underserviced and relatively inaccessible communities and regions.*

Basic health networks were established to educate the public on health issues, with the build-out of telecommunication infrastructure greatly improving information delivery. The more advanced health networks were an attempt to use ICTs to provide medical consultation and services online, creating tele-medicine or tele-health services. Hospitals can be linked to allow remote medical facilities to access professional medical services, thereby decreasing travel costs for users, medical practitioners and patients.

Another level of tele-medicine is being provided in the home through telemetry (remote sensing) equipment that allows users and their families to track problems and access professional opinion and guidance from home. Lately, more creative partnerships have been formed to link doctors with hospitals, and with associations of like-minded individuals and organisations. Virtual networks allow hospitals and health agencies to provide more information to the public and adopt more efficient business processes and practices. Databases can be exchanged among partners while preserving the security of patient information. Some staff functions can be shared and the savings re-invested in front-line services, better technologies and education leading to improved self-management.

Telecommunication technologies can assist in solving a variety of medical-related problems at a distance. The most common applications are remote medical diagnosis, patient monitoring and management and the transfer of medical information from one location to another. Some of the work currently carried out in hospitals can be done in doctor's offices or in people's homes. The promise of tele-medicine is not only to improve speed of delivery but to make healthcare more efficient while reducing costs. Cost-effective access to quality medical care is of particular concern to those in remote locations. When people cannot find or afford specialised care, telecommunications can sometimes create an acceptable alternative.

Some larger centres are exporting tele-medicine services, and numerous smaller communities are reaping the benefits. If both patients and physicians can decrease the amount of travel and time spent in hospitals, larger centres can realise some efficiencies of scale, and more remote communities can obtain improved healthcare for their residents. These opportunities are contingent on a favourable policy and financial environment for tele-health as it relates to patient information dissemination, the ability of physicians to bill for work performed online, the investment in support services, the collaborative environment, and the willing participation of physicians.

North Network is providing tele-health services in Ontario, Canada, through videoconferencing and remote diagnostic tools. North Network is part of the Ontario Telemedicine Network, funded by the provincial Ministry of Health. It has facilitated acceptance and new policies and directions for tele-health in the province and has grown to 360 urban and rural sites. The network was established to provide specialised services to more remote regions, starting with a handful of communities spread from Toronto to Northern Ontario who wanted to improve the quality and quantity of their medical service. For the pilot project, acquiring and paying for the telecommunications components, namely the technological devices and connectivity, was a hurdle. Beyond that was the additional challenge of securing a buy-in from health practitioners and finding a way for physicians to bill the government-subsidized health system that only allowed face-to-face consultations. Support systems were required at hospitals where most of the equipment was located, and the whole project had to be funded. With nearly 200 partners in Ontario, including academic health science centres, community hospitals, psychiatric hospitals, clinics, nursing stations, medical and nursing schools, professional organisations, Community Care Access Centres, Local Health Integration Networks (LHINs), long-term care homes, educational facilities, and public health, Ontario Telemedicine Network (OTN) membership provides access to the world's largest collaborative community of tele-medicine-enabled organisations, permitting participation in clinical, educational and administrative events. In 2005-06, more than 23,000 patients and 800 specialists and physicians used the network (*Telemedicine*, 2007).

Tele-medicine uses information and communication technologies to process and transfer medical information for diagnosis, therapy and education. Such information may include medical images, live two-way audio and video, patient medical records, output data from medical devices, and sound files. By transmitting a patient's medical file from a primary care provider to a specialist by linking the referring clinician and the specialist through video conferencing, the guesswork is taken out of many of these cases.

The growth of tele-medicine over the next decade is expected to transform medical care delivery throughout the world. Hub and spoke systems are now linking caregivers, facilities and patients into broader networks, greatly improving the reach and effectiveness of healthcare. The following are among the leading applications in remote medical delivery projects:

- Tele-radiology
- Psychiatry
- Emergency Medicine and Trauma Care
- Dermatology
- Cardiology
- Surgery: connecting with a colleague or mentor during an operation
- Pathology
- Medical education
- Patient monitoring (mostly at home)
- Innovative applications that are multi-sectoral such as distance-controlled robots to link long-term sick children with schools and correctional care

Tele-homecare of the aging population is an area of potential growth worldwide. To complement in-person, in-home patient care, the home monitoring industry has introduced equipment that allows medical care services to be provided online. A medical monitoring system allows subscribers to take readings from an onsite device and upload results via a phone line to a confidential database. Caregivers and medical personnel can access the information via a password-protected, secure Web interface and immediately view the effects of medications and track their performance. Thousands of individual patients now pay a small fee to have their diabetes, heart and lung conditions monitored each month by such services. Medical companies and practitioners review patient data. When the results indicate that a patient is at risk, the doctor, caregiver and patient communicate with one another via telephone, fax or e-mail.

Other preventative programmes make use of the Web, where patients enter their data online. Personalized health information responses are sent back from doctors and nurses. With the patient's permission, this information can be passed on to regular caregivers. The doctor's nurse can make regular contact with the patient by phone or e-mail. If a problem is detected, the monitoring nurse receives an automatic computer alert. The nurse then contacts the patient to discuss his or her condition. Online monitoring will also allow loved ones to monitor the health of an aging diabetic parent in another location without needing to call each day, easing worry and allowing families to participate in caring for their loved ones at a distance. A number of private sector companies market video surveillance packages that enable families to remain connected. Self-management is made easier with emergency devices worn on the body.

Communication is an important element of a successful tele-health initiative. When it comes to health, nothing creates more public fear and outcry than the prospect of a reduction in quality. Most people are likely to hear about technological innovations from their healthcare providers. For improved communications, medical institutions may need to promote use of these services to their doctors and staff. It is important to inform and enlist all local physicians into tele-health projects, not just physicians who are technology-friendly. Physicians sometimes see tele-health projects as competition or a waste of time. Therefore, the community must be armed with facts and arguments to secure their cooperation. A demonstration project eases the transition for local practitioners who may gain access to new patients in underserviced areas, learn from experts by attending patient-specialist online visits, link with other professionals online to discuss diagnostics, and attend conferences and education events without leaving their communities and offices.

Healthcare administration has its own telecommunication opportunities. Several health organisations may want to coordinate such functions as purchasing and document management, or link physician offices, laboratories and pharmacies. Ideally, all nurses will have laptops or handheld devices to help improve response time and information sharing between and among providers. Wireless devices will allow nurses to complete flow sheets, upload information to a secure central server, transfer and share client information, standard care plans and best practices, and improve the billing system.

Worldwide use of smart card applications has proven worldwide that the smart card allows patients to transport their health files from one health provider to another. The smart card can provide a full picture of the patient's record and reduce cost, time, and errors in delivering information from one provider to another. It can help management in its goal to diminish the paper-based records system.

Taipei (Taiwan) has integrated its healthcare resources by interconnecting 300 hospitals and clinics. Patient records, test results and medical scans are shared. The city has an epidemic and disease information and notification system. Using their digital ID cards, citizens can communicate electronically with their local healthcare providers to obtain information from their healthcare records (Archives of the ICF, 2006d).

Innovation in distance health delivery applications can include multi-sector initiatives. High definition video conferencing enables Cleveland Clinic doctors and clinicians to engage with Cleveland's children in the use of such healthcare technologies as diagnostic imaging. Some 68,000 students were involved in 2006 in a project spearheaded by the Cleveland Municipal School District, the Cleveland Clinic Foundation, and OneCleveland. The consortium offers the latest educational tools and training to the region's teachers, along with content and programming aimed at engaging, inspiring and preparing youth for highly skilled job opportunities like those available in the growing healthcare field. At the project's launch, Collinwood High School biology students first demonstrated its potential, engaging and interacting with Cleveland Clinic surgeons performing open-heart surgery relayed over the Internet via the OneCommunity high-speed network (Archives of the ICF, 2006a)

To maximize the long-term success of these tele-health applications and ensure that the needs of the large percentage of the underserved population are met, the authors encourage users to consider the impact on human resources. Not all things that could be done perhaps should be done. It may be that the number of health professionals is too few to extend services to meet the demand created by tele-health. Healthcare initiatives delivered at a distance will also need to take into consideration cultural issues that may make medical delivery difficult for certain patients and their families.

Key Concept: *Tele-education and e-learning can be cost-efficient ways to bring new services and diverse programmes to communities while creating a better quality of life for residents.*

Tele-education or e-learning. Attending online colleges or universities; receiving training programmes at home; connecting a community classroom to any number of educational institutions; attending a conference from home, a community centre or office while the trainer or conference is located in another region—all are examples of e-learning.

E-learning is an Internet application in education and training that is based on digital tools and content distributed in electronic format. Also called IP or online education or tele-education, its principal characteristics are individualization and interaction using such Internet-based delivery methods as the World Wide Web, Web browsers, search engines, virtual worlds, video conferencing, interactive TV, and e-mail communication. Dial-up telephone lines can handle audio conferences with e-mail delivery of attached documents, but it takes a symmetric broadband connection for video conferencing. The advantage of this application is that learners are given more in control over what they learn, when they learn, and how they learn.

Beottcher (2007), in "Ten core principles for designing effective learning environments", writes about the importance of learning as a social process, offering possibilities for collaboration with other learners, for interaction with the content and for guidance from teachers, trainers and tutors, many facilitated by technology. Multimedia makes learning more interesting by increasing the scope of presentation (Simon, 2004). Simon, in his article, "The emergence of social learning from environmental ICT prototypes", reinforces his views with a pithy quote from Europe's Information Society:

> These learner-centred approaches put the learners back in command, with a wealth of learning resources at their fingertips, customized to their individual needs. Teachers and trainers, however, continue to play a central role, using virtual and traditional face-to-face interactions with their students in a "blended" approach (2001).

Excellent examples are found in Europe, where e-learning has been studied as a science and where innovative new perspectives are being demonstrated. Among them is a mobile game-based learning environment—a research project begun in 2005 with funding from the European Community aimed at improving the effectiveness and efficiency of learning among young people using various game formats. Similarly, the Web site, entitled SecondLife.com, promotes a 3-D interactive gaming environment that allows people to re-live history, build models and alter decisions to learn outcomes. In the business programme of universities, many are using the Business Strategy Game, where more than 25,000 students worldwide compete in running a shoe manufacturing operation. The students make weekly decisions on plant location, human resource practices, marketing strategies and financial management in an attempt to win on various levels, including profit maximization. Gaming is increasing in popularity with instructors, who believe this teaching method can motivate students and assist in retaining and applying knowledge. It often allows online students to compare their capabilities against students in other parts of the world.

The physical context of school has changed, from a set of static buildings on a single campus, to satellite campuses and distance courses using new digital technologies demanding new literacies from students. Howard Rheingold, a prominent author on the uses people make of mobile and digital media, the ways these technologies have been deployed in online collaboration, and their impact on the lives of young people around the world, stated the following at a "vision of the Future" presentation he gave in Melbourne, Australia:

Education, media-literacy-wise, is happening now after school and on weekends and when the teacher isn't looking, in the SMS messages, MySpace pages, blog posts, podcasts, [and] videoblogs that technology-equipped digital natives exchange among themselves. Schools will remain places for parents to put their kids while they go to work, and for society to train a fresh supply of citizen-worker-consumers to be employed by the industries of their time. But the kind of questioning, collaborative, active, lateral rather than hierarchical pedagogy that participatory media both forces and enables is not the kind of change that takes place quickly or at all in public schools (Rheingold, 2007, pp. 2-3).

In a paper presented to the president of Ontario universities (Canada), Albert and Campbell (2007) reviewed the challenges of e-learning and the use of participatory technologies and methodologies in the classroom. Their research indicates that we are living in a chaotic technological environment whose impact can no longer be predicted. Students and workplaces have evolving requirements and expectations of the post-secondary educational system and many institutions are not prepared to deliver what is needed. In a similar vein, Prensky (2001) notes that the new Net Generation is both self-guided and in need of guidance in terms of their educational experience—the system lacks the skills to deal with this environment of continuous change.

Carneiro and Nascimbeni (2007) noted that e-learning is barely scratching the surface of what is possible: "There are at least as many e-learning options as the different learning sub-systems (school, higher education, vocational training, corporate professional development, adult learning, informal learning) and visions of the world that those in charge of promoting and designing e-learning systems had in mind." Indeed, e-learning is blooming, with more opportunities for people of all ages to take courses online. Colleges, universities and secondary schools are delivering increasingly sophisticated programmes to the home, as well as to the workplace, using video-conferencing technology, video streaming and Web-based programming, sometimes simultaneously. These lessons have interactivity built in, and some will employ intelligent agents to follow and guide the progress of students. Group projects are encouraged among students who may be located in more than one country, working in academic disciplines as diverse as archaeology and space engineering.

Distance delivery technologies enable these institutions to provide a wider array of courses and ways to monitor field experiences in remote locations while decreasing their long-term costs, providing more equitable access and reaching a wider audience. The delivery methods have also become more interpersonal, evolving from text-based correspondence to audio conferencing, to video conferencing and

Internet delivery. Today, most institutions attempt to provide hybrid solutions that marry flexibility, interactivity and social contact. The authors were involved in the following example:

> Like numerous other institutions, Laurentian University, Canada, offers graduate study as an online option. Their MBA programme allows students to complete each course within thirteen weeks in a Web-based environment. An international class is divided into groups that work on assignments each week through discussion boards and Web-enabled teleconferencing, while using textbooks, online research and instructional videos as additional tools. The professor is in touch daily with students online, and students are able to log on from any location with Internet access. There are neither travel constraints nor a need to complete course work according to a strict daily schedule. The multimedia classroom provides an environment with ample interaction with peers and the instructor.

In some communities, especially among those in the developing world, online learning is seen as a solution to the out-migration of youth toward larger centres. No technological solution will stop young people still wanting independence from their families; however, some cannot afford to leave and others are not ready. Some students face economic hardships that leave them no choice but to complete their degrees on a part-time basis, which often means study at a distance.

E-learning at the university level is not well coordinated as a service, nor is it available everywhere; the Internet offers global delivery but language restricts its use. Many courses are available, but there are only a modest number of programmes that allow students to complete a full degree. Web-integrated courses can be costly, which necessitates an investment mindset. Universities also tend to guard carefully their on-campus programmes, and older faculty members tend to favour the established ways of delivering education. As universities become increasingly wired, as demand increases and younger faculty are hired, there will be more interest in these new delivery methods. Thus, more e-learning is being made available. One of the recognised educational growth markets of the future may be older learners who need more education or refresher courses where they live and work.

From an infrastructure standpoint, colleges and universities have had a tremendous impact on developing a culture of use among young people. When classrooms, libraries and dorms are wired for 10-100 Mbps access speeds, students become addicted to the ready access and use these connections for lessons, music file exchange, instant messaging, toll-free phone calls, e-commerce, gaming, and digital movies. Students find it difficult, even unacceptable, to revert back to slower connections when they adopt broadband communications as a "quality of life" condition. This development is a lesson for communities looking to attract and retain young people. Although millions of households now have high-speed Internet connections, college students dominate high speed connectivity by about three to one, through their schools and college residences. School administrators note that students often base housing decisions on Ethernet availability, and incoming freshmen sometimes decide whether to attend a school based on high-speed access (*Los Angeles Times*, 2000).

Promoting oneself as a "wired" community becomes an important consideration when college graduates are being recruited. Young people tend to want to be in a place where digital is "spoken" and the broadband Internet is readily available. They will see living and working within a networked community as a key to their own personal and professional productivity as well as to their quality of life. E-learning applications can start early, with connectivity to research centres, health organisations, museums and schools in other countries—all with the objective of expanding the minds of our youth, and giving them an avenue for other ways of learning and using online resources. Community portals provide an opportunity to link online learning resources worldwide and allow users of all ages to engage in lifelong learning. Networked community leaders will find e-learning an important economic development engine that will open doors for many years to come.

Key Concept: *Electronic commerce can open doors for collaborating with others to create new business opportunities while providing more cost-efficient ways to deliver products and services.*

E-commerce. E-commerce includes doing business using a public or proprietary network that may be local or wide-area in coverage. Activities include booking a hotel room, exchanging inventory and financial data, purchasing items online and developing a site where consumers can shop, pay bills and obtain information. E-commerce refers to any electronic business transaction or the exchange of business information over a computer network. As a culture of use develops, more applications are offered online, striving to attract consumer dollars.

Sometimes called e-business or e-tailing (for online retail selling), e-commerce typically involves the use of electronic search engines, automated processing, shopping carts, a secure payment system, and e-mail to buy and sell goods and services. E-commerce offers the advantages of global reach, 24-hour-a-day availability, targeted searches, comparative pricing, personalization, and real-time transaction processing. Using the Internet for commercial transactions enables companies to be more efficient and flexible in their internal operations, to work more closely with their suppliers and to be more responsive to the needs and expectations of their customers. It also allows companies to select the best suppliers regardless of their geographic locations and to sell to a global market.

E-commerce has become a way of life: credit card authorizations, travel reservations, fund transfers and other electronic banking, retail point of sale terminals, and centralised payroll processing are all examples of e-commerce. Direct selling, mostly using the Internet, has grown more than 91% in the last 10 years with half of a million people around the world generating US$130 billion in revenues (Fleming, 2006b). Internet usage grew 225% between 2000 and 2007, according to Internet World Stats (Internet World, 2007). Annual B2B (business-to-business) e-commerce was a 4.5-trillion dollar business in 2005, doubling each year since 2003 and expected to continue its high growth rate (Budde, 2007). According to Goldman-Sachs, e-commerce was virtually a $0 business in 1990 (Goldman-Sachs, 2000).

E-commerce for the private sector essentially has two facets: business to consumer (B2C) transactions and business-to-business (B2B). B2C represents consumer-centred interactions related principally to retail services and products while B2B consists of exchanges between and among businesses related principally to the wholesale market. The term B2G or business to government is also used but it is essentially a consumer or business relationship. Another component of online commerce consists of transactions between consumers, also referred to as C2C.

The first phase of business to consumer (B2C) e-commerce was concerned with developing Web pages and providing basic information and services to consumers. New developments in e-commerce include the availability of videoconference services on the Internet site, such as "concierge" services, providing advice and answering consumer questions computer-face to computer-face. Virtual reality sites and the increase in the number of video components being made available online increase the demand for higher bandwidth on the consumer end. The majority of companies recognise that, in today's competitive world, a well designed site on the World Wide Web can be a valuable way to boost sales, enhance customer service and market to prospective customers. Some communities have provided citizens with resources to the private sector to create Web pages and improve their presence on the Web.

Every financial transaction at some point turns into an electronic process; the sooner it does, the more cost effective the transaction is. Automation saves the business person valuable time, allowing for an increased number of transactions and increased profits. E-mail has allowed companies to send documents and information at a fraction of the cost of conventional mailing. Making documents available for downloading on the Web has made consumer interactions with business more convenient for the user. Chambers of Commerce and other organisations have conducted training workshops and hired consultants to establish next-level approaches in e-commerce so that private sector firms can get maximum benefit from the online economy.

B2B e-commerce can take many forms. A practical example is the purchasing department of a company posting its requirements online that include an extended forecast of its possible future purchases. This approach enables potential suppliers who visit the Web site to make a bid, thereby creating an opportunity for competition that could result in lower prices. The Internet can, on the other hand, sometimes create other problems stemming from an over supply or over demand. Some employers have received hundreds or thousands of responses to an online request or offer. Caught unprepared, the organisation can be overwhelmed by the Web.

In conjunction with the increase of e-commerce use, the number of support services has grown. For example, the practice of using "digital wallets" (e-wallet) has been stepped up. An e-wallet is a portable personal profile that allows consumers to store their "ship to," "bill to" and credit card information in one secure place. Once this personal documentation is accomplished, the consumer will no longer have to re-enter this information at every site where he places orders—the digital wallet fills in the required information. Use of the digital wallet feature allows merchants to offer simple, quick shopping for their regular customers. It also enables predictive marketing to help target customers and serves as the basis for anonymous customer profiles with detailed demographic and behavioural information. Smart cards are an example of an e-wallet application; they allow citizens to charge on account, which provides such customer database management opportunities as monitoring and evaluating customer trends.

> The Taipei, Taiwan, Mass Rapid Transit EasyCard system has proven to be an innovative tool for electronic commerce in the public sector. The EasyCard is a multi-functional, value-added card that deducts payments automatically as it is used. EasyCard provides payment for mass transit, bus, taxi and parking fees, and can also be used at self-service libraries. Students and senior citizens receive discounts on EasyCard purchases. As of 2007, some 5.73 million cards had been issued, one of the highest distributions in the world. The Taipei government is now cooperating with such companies as BenQ, Panasonic and Swatch to create even more innovative products of this type, such as embedding an EasyCard chip in mobile handsets, MP3s and watches. We've also heard examples where smart cards were accepted by merchants throughout a community (Archives of the ICF, 2006d).

E-commerce can yield continuous benefits. It requires businesses to pay attention to world trends and react in ways that will safeguard their investment. It opens the door for providing services worldwide, for obtaining best pricing, for maintaining a competitive edge and for collaborating with other firms in cluster environments to create new opportunities. Networked community leaders can assist the e-commerce agenda by ensuring that training activities and mentoring are provided to community organisations; that networks are created to exchange information on best practices; and that discussions are held around clustering opportunities.

Key Concept: *Library and museum staff members have important skills to share in helping build and leverage the resources of communities. Access to good libraries and museums is among the attractive features of networked communities.*

Tele- or Virtual Libraries and Museums. The term "tele-libraries" refers to the ability of users to browse through local libraries—or any other interconnected library—whose holdings are accessible in the digital domain. Via the Internet, library users can now download books or articles, reserve and order materials, consult a professional librarian online, and select and download videos that are available for sharing via the library. The tele-museum is a similar online service by which students and art lovers worldwide can enter museums to browse, learn, communicate and perhaps purchase art and art supplies from virtual curators.

Digital libraries and museums make their holdings accessible online. Collecting, classifying, managing and studying information and objects of public importance, these institutions are creating vast computer databases that can be searched and downloaded in digital form. With high-speed digital processing linked to the broadband Internet, users have easier access to materials or collections housed in a single location. Also, institutions can transform, through digital promotions and effective marketing, their internal practices and communication with varied audiences into online exhibitions and public information programmes.

Curators and staff are typically important players in the networked community. They have access to, or can usually quickly find, information on a range of topics for a wide variety of stakeholders. Librarians and curators are often highly knowledgeable about communities, and they are service-oriented people accustomed to extending their professional help to schools and other groups within the community. Community leaders can greatly benefit from a librarian's cataloguing, archiving and search experience. In a similar way, museums can often teach real and virtual communities how to value and preserve important documents and resources.

Several international examples of digital libraries and museums follow:

The region of Halton, Ontario, Canada, used library staff extensively to plan their portal, especially around the integration of several databases, to ensure a sound structure from the onset and to encourage the development of a better system for metasearching among the databases of the many stakeholders contributing to the project.

The National Museums of Northern Ireland (2008) created the Digital Museum, a virtual museum and computerized inventory of all the collections held by the museum. The Digital Museum is a tool for managing the collections. The use of electronic and digital interpretation will enable the development of multi-media products. Knowledge, data, on-going and completed research will be published, aiding in the development of partnerships and consortia at all levels. It will project Northern Ireland's image to the world electronically.

The Tibetan and Himalayan Digital Library (2008) is an international community using Web-based technologies to integrate diverse knowledge about Tibet and the Himalayas for free access from around the world.

The New Zealand Digital Library at the University of Waikato (2008) consists of user-contributed collections on such topics as world environment, agricultural information, community development and health disasters. The Digital Library is also a research programme whose aim is to develop the underlying technology for making digital libraries available publicly so that others can use the technology to create their own collections.

The Digital Museum of Cornish Ceramics offers "examples of the work produced, the potters' marks and background information" on the historic ceramics made in Cornwall, UK (2008).

NEC Corporation developed one of the world's first network-based virtual libraries. Established in 1997 as the Universal Digital Library, it employed "walk-around" and "virtual agent" technologies to provide an advanced three-dimensional graphical interface that seeks to imitate browsing through a real library. Users look at the screen and the 3D effect makes them feel as if they are walking through it in real life. The virtual agent technology lets users interact with an animated virtual librarian to obtain such information as directions inside the library, or the location of a book (*NEC develops*, 1997).

Many countries have in place the Global Information Infrastructure (GII) and Fiber-to-the-home (FTTH) high-speed networks necessary to handle multimedia services. Digital libraries are among the developments expected to take full advantage of such a capacity. Many books have been digitized and more will become available online. Being able to carry several books in a chip the size of a quarter is very appealing for travelers and students. Libraries will play an important role in lending digital books once large files are easily transmittable between the library, publisher and user.

Museums are also active participants in the online environment, forming networks of specialists providing expertise to collaborating institutions worldwide. The Metropolitan Museum of Art (2008) in New York has often obtained international expertise in the valuation and assessment of art, which can reduce the number of errors in acquisition and restoration. The Museum has shared its own expertise online—Web innovations in museum programme management have yielded benefits for all stakeholders. The following example gives more evidence of the museum's digital role:

> Cleveland, Ohio, is a networked community that continually experiments in matching likely and unlikely partners. The schools provide online training programmes that link students to local museums. Students receive specialised lessons from such workers as curators, historians and restoration experts. School children are able to preview collections online and collaborate with the museums on various projects. Another Cleveland partnership has resulted in an international music and dance convention using new technology as a medium to interpret art. Those involved in this collaboration note that this project was quite outside the normal activities of a school board or a museum, but it created opportunities that added new economic, scholastic and cultural dimensions to community networking. The event was broadcast to remote audiences with the opportunity for the larger community to participate. Cleveland also uses an initiative called "Voices for Choices" to encourage conversations about the collective future of the community. Area residents are involved in making decisions and offering solutions. This effort lays the foundation for the kinds of synergistic innovation discussed in our chapter on innovation. (Archives of the ICF, 2006a)

Leaders need to involve libraries and museums when planning networked communities—to devise strategies for managing information, to identify known databases and to formulate strategies to preserve knowledge.

Key Concept: *The Broadband Internet has become a major entertainment destination, where millions of users are taking advantage of the opportunity to access games, video, software and music.*

Tele-Entertainment or E-Entertainment. Online entertainment refers to videos, music, games, or other forms of recreation and enjoyment derived from the Internet. E-entertainment consists of communication and media products and services designed to appeal to Internet users. This category also contains those same types of products and services—and entirely new genres of entertainment—that are being created by Internet users. Broadband Internet in the home has provided consumers with the opportunity to become producers and distributors of entertaining content that they have developed as home-based or business applications and are making available to the world.

This application encompasses any form of information and communication exchanged in digital format between users and providers that has a recreational, leisure or artistic purpose. Sometimes called digital media or new media, these computer products and services include digital text, graphics, audio, video, animation, and the compatible technologies of the World Wide Web that can be used to create, distribute and consume digital "content." E-entertainment is one of the most advanced of all electronic applications because demand and profitability. E-entertainment concepts are also being used extensively by businesses as marketing tools and by educational facilities to engage learners.

A number of communities and regions have made themselves unique by focusing on a particular recreational media. Examples are Mitaka, Japan, producing some 80% of all anime, and India's Bollywood films, a major competitor to the U.S.'s famous Hollywood. Other notable examples include:

In 2007, News Corporation reported that NBC Universal and News Corp were launching a video-rich Web site with thousands of hours of free full-length programming, representing premium content from at least a dozen networks and two major film studios. AOL, MSN, MySpace and Yahoo! were among the new site's initial distribution partners. Their users, who represented 96% of the monthly U.S. unique users on the Internet, were given access to the site's library of entertainment. The content is advertiser-supported and includes free long- and short-form video. This service is designed to compete with the popular YouTube, now owned by Google· that allows users to post and share their own video content on the Internet (News Corporation, 2007).

Another example of entertainment development is the Cinenet network, operated by the founders of Rising Sun Pictures in partnership with Australian broadband ISP and network provider, Internode. The infrastructure was initially established to enable Rising Sun Pictures and other South Australian production and post production facilities to effectively move large volumes of data between their facilities and clients around Australia and to and from major international markets. Cinenet is now being marketed independently to the film, television, traditional and new media industries that require large amounts of bandwidth. "This means it doesn't matter whether you're in Hollywood or Homebush; you can collaborate with people on different continents, in different time zones or across town, as if you were in the same building. And that's a big help for Australian companies who traditionally have had to battle with the misconception that we're just too far away to be considered a major production hub", says Cinenet's Managing Director Tony Clark. Cinenet is able to offer direct connection via fiber or dedicated microwave link at a range of speeds, typically either 10Mbps, 100Mbps or 1Gbps. The service differs from typical corporate data plans by offering fully asymmetrical bandwidth. In addition to secure broadband connectivity, using dedicated mail and file servers, Cinenet hosts multiple options for distance collaboration such as videoconferencing, voice-over IP, transfer of film rushes and scans as digital files, and specialised work tools like cine-Sync, software that allows simultaneous viewing and discussion of visual media in multiple locations (Cinenet, 2007).

The Internet has become a major entertainment provider, and millions of users are taking advantage of the opportunity to access games, video, software and music. In the future, the Internet platform will support highly sophisticated recreational interactions involving users in 3-D and virtual reality gaming, video streaming, two-way live audio and other bandwidth-hungry applications. The increasing popularity of such sites as Skype and YouTube, which offer opportunities for point-to-point networking, including video sharing, is a small demonstration of the demand for entertainment and social exchanges on the Internet.

Communities offering high-speed telecommunications services to their residents will be perceived as modern and innovative—and thus more attractive—to those citizens with the skills, the consumer technologies and the motivation to take advantage of them. The breadth of applications in entertainment is an expanding phenomenon requiring robust infrastructures. Informed citizens will not tolerate being excluded from the mainstream of these new applications, and community planners are wise to insure a good quality of communal life that includes access to opportunities for recreation, entertainment and social development. In some cases, communities will be able to feature entertainment production and distribution as an important export.

The City of Gangnam-gu, Seoul, South Korea, has deployed an iTV Digital Government channel, which it says is also the first broadcasting in real-time to district residents the information they need to know. It believes that by using digital television with capacity for interactivity, the channel can help bridge the information gap (digital divide) between generations and social strata, and it can contribute to public awareness and can ultimately nurture new IT growth engine industries (Archives of the ICF, 2007a).

Even the concept of television—television stations, programming, scheduling and audience—is changing. With thousands of providers offering thousands of channels on multiple distribution platforms, people now can receive the content they want, when they want, wherever they want. Not all people will have access, of course, but this is the goal in networked communities. Certainly the concept of broadcaster has changed. Any citizen with a modicum of skills and enabling technologies can cover the news or take an editorial position and make it available at any time. Local artists can now make movies, create animation, devise games, develop advertisements and humanitarian appeals for funds, and then post them on the Internet. The potential audiences for these creative products are in the millions. It can be assumed that people everywhere will be looking for television that suits their tastes and their sense of identity. The lesson is that local community-based providers will need access to computer processing power to create those products and the bandwidth to deliver them, and that community members will also need the capability to receive and use the services offered worldwide.

Services requiring interactivity will become especially popular, and they will require higher bandwidth. Interactive television games that allow groups of subscribers on different parts of the network to play against each other—the Canadian team against an Austrian team for example—have caught the public's imagination. Programmers are delivering high-immersion games in which players are displayed as video-rendered versions of themselves inside a computer-generated environment. Among the first commercial examples of this new immersion technology was "Video as Input". A computer equipped with special software interpreted signals from the video camera and tracked the player's image (the player's face is pasted on the action figure) (Marriott, 1999). Combined with high speed Internet, the technology was thought to have significant applications in education, health and business. Already, this technology is being used in hospitals to enable sick children to attend school. From his or her hospital room, the child controls a robot located in the classroom. The child's face is broadcast on the robot's face, and the child is able to see and hear what is going on in his/her classroom. He or she can also control the robot to raise a hand to ask a question, or turn the robot to focus on another area of the classroom.

Robotics technology is in its infancy. Lego's Mindstorm is a leader for home applications, allowing young people to learn about robotics with some entertaining options. The designers suggest that an electronic robot posted at the door of the child's bedroom can take a picture of any intruder and send that information to the child's cell phone. We have all heard of fridges calling their owners for replenishment and dishwashers calling for repair. Bill Gates forecasted a robot in every home (Gates, 2007) and encouraged colleges and universities to speed up programming in robotics technology while also addressing students to take up this growing field during his 2007 tour of post-secondary institutions. Growth in robotics will increasingly require good wireless and wireline telecommunication connectivity for such applications as information sharing and remote diagnostics, each of which will have a large role to play in the future of online entertainment.

Art and entertainment have often been thought of as a quality of life element in communities and seldom as an important economic generator. The networked community can make more efficient use of these important assets by linking them in multi-sectoral approaches that develop new content and new opportunities. Staff members within these organisations have important skills to help build a networked community. The increased use of media in all sectors can make libraries, museums, and entertainment groups a valuable tool to build attractive sites and programmes for users. Networked community leaders are advised to reach out to key players in this segment and engage them in identifying opportunities for growth, inventories of assets, and to link them with other business community leaders and e-commerce initiatives to promote cross-fertilization.

Key Concept: *Few applications will affect the general public more personally and continuously than e-government, which is the use of ICTs by governments to connect to and engage their citizens, and by citizens to connect to and engage in governance.*

E-government. E-government has to do with accessing a street map, getting a variance to a city code, filing a change of ownership, paying a parking ticket, downloading a birth certificate, getting a marriage license, completing a census form, voting for the office of county commissioner, and learning about government services online.

In numerous cities and regions, the Web portals of electronic government are the one-stop-shop gateways for inquiring citizens. Putting government services online is making exchanges with government offices easier, reducing the cost of delivering programmes and encouraging participation in decision-making. It also demonstrates the need for community infrastructure and citizen acquisition of the tools that make digital communication possible. Generally these services are seen as positive developments; they can, however, snowball, requiring constant updating, reorganisation, and improvements to meet the changing needs of users.

Behind the "public face" of the Web, Dundee, Scotland, developed a comprehensive approach to its digital relationship with citizens. It established a Citizen Account database system that captured data on citizens (with their permission) and used it to pre-fill online forms. Some of the data was amassed through issuance of the Dundee Discovery Card, which replaced 10 separate card-related services in the city, for everything from bus service and parking to social services. The Discovery Card was the first example in Scotland of a university (Abertay) and City Council sharing a single card for their different purposes. One of the outstanding benefits of the Discovery Card, in the eyes of the City Council, is that it eliminates the social stigma attached to social services cards for low-income residents. So popular has it become—with 44,000 cards issued, used by 87% of 12-to-18-year-olds for school meals and bus travel, and 85% of +60 year olds for leisure access and bus travel—that the Scottish Government decided to deploy a multi-application card for the whole country and asked Dundee to run the program (ICF, 2008a).

Governments play a large role in providing equitable access, delivering timely information and giving voice to residents. Telecommunication networks have proven to be an excellent infrastructure on which to deliver these requirements, and government portals are one of the potential applications. Community information presented on an Internet portal takes the form of Web pages that link to community offices and information. They allow citizens to more easily conduct research and business online. Local and regional governments are increasingly looking at information dissemination through such portals with a focus on providing a wider variety of information, links, GIS and knowledge management tools.

E-government services can include paying bills online, viewing a municipal council meeting video or voting online. Voting systems are springing up in many countries, for example, a site entitled "Jott the Vote", a free and politically nonpartisan service that allows anyone with a phone to send a jott e-mail message directly to a presidential campaign, allows voters all over the U.S. to easily and readily communicate with those candidates running for President (Haller, 2007). Participatory learning and action are being promoted increasingly with ICTs all over the world.

Users may want to superimpose information or conduct a meta-search. For example, a tourist may need to superimpose canoeing maps with walking trails and bed and breakfast locations to produce a self-made tool for a future vacation. Another user may wish to search for specific information, such as the quality of water in reports hosted by a government department, correlating this information with reports from other providers such as the Chamber of Commerce. Such portals may also be personalized for each user by storing information on preferences and history. To increase the level of sophistication of portals, information providers from throughout the community must participate, including library experts, security personnel, health officials, schools, community action agencies, and the city planner's office.

The Internet-based administration system of Gangnam-gu, Seoul, South Korea, hosts one of the world's most advanced systems of "Digital Government", allowing citizens to download documents, interact with government offices and receive communications of pressing concern. In 2006, the number of such electronic handlings via the Internet was approximately 6.45 million. The city's major service systems include a civil service provider kiosk; an Internet-based tax payment system; and, an Internet-based car registration system. Administrative services such as the Cyber Civil Defense drill, the Road Control system, broadcasting of the National Learning Ability Test and distribution of the e-Book programme are all carried out over the Internet. In 2004, Gangnam-gu in South Korea deployed an e-fingerprint recognition system to confirm identities in processing passport applications. As passport forgery crimes had increased from 867 in 2002 to 1,840 in 2003, measures to counter a passport illegal issuance were urgent. Forged passports were sold each year on the black market, mainly in China, causing massive problems. The city now keeps an e-record of the person's fingerprints when issuing a certificate for an applicant's personal seal, which was necessary because of the large floating population (Archives of the ICF, 2007a).

Issy-les-Moulineaux, France, a self-proclaimed "digital city" on the outskirts of Paris, is a city in which 89% of the population uses the Internet daily, compared to a French average of 56%. Issy's public administration Internet Web site IRIS is its "citizen relationship management" system providing easier and faster access to city services. IRIS is a "one-stop-shop" portal for public services. Using a database available to all municipal agents, IRIS centralises the information needed to answer many of the current questions asked by the citizenry. Multi-channel technology allows communication by different means: personal visit, downloading, mailing, e-mail, or telephone (Archives of the ICF, 2007b).

Tianjin, China, is the biggest coastal city and largest seaport in northern China. It functions as neighbouring Beijing's gateway to the sea, and is one of four Chinese municipalities under the direct jurisdiction of the central government. According to its self-report in the Intelligent Community Forum Competition, Tianjin participates in a national Identity Card System and Resident Registration System that controls internal travel and residency, which is the foundation for a demographic databank, an insurance management system, and a payment collection system. Since the card is now in the hands of the city's entire population, it has generated interest in a wider variety of applications. As of 2006, the city had implemented 600 e-government applications in such areas as public finance, taxation, city planning, housing, commerce, education, and justice. Proposed government policies are posted on the Web so that citizens can offer comments before the policy is implemented. More than 250 departments use the network for internal management. The broadband network also links the city's 210 hospitals and clinics, and an online payment system settles almost all healthcare charges. A Distance Tax Collection System allows taxpayers to check their accounts and make payments online, while a Port Information System expedites customs clearances for ships' cargos in Tianjin's port. The report says that cash transactions are gradually being replaced by three network-access cards—bank, bus and social security—that residents use to manage their financial and transportation needs (Archives of the ICF, 2006e).

The Eastserve Web portal in Manchester, England, is an IT-based solution deployed to help address community problems while strengthening social bonds. It offers a virtual police station with anonymous crime reporting, a home finder project for residents to find public housing, and a street reporting system. Included are a job search and employment service, resumé preparation assistance, interactive work/training systems, work placement listings, and free job advertising to local businesses and government agencies. Also hosted are 3D visualization videos of regenerated areas in partnership with a housing market renewal team. Manchester also linked up with banking institutions to help with low-cost computer purchases and provide Internet connectivity to low income residents (Archives of the ICF, 2006c).

Public safety was a concern for citizens of Ichikawa, Japan, a suburb of Tokyo. In 2005, the city began installing video cameras in public locations to help prevent crime. In the same year, the city launched the Ichikawa Safety e-Net programme that allowed citizens to report crimes and concerns through mobile phones and PCs. This service was implemented by the city in cooperation with neighbourhood associations. In addition—via its municipal cable company—Ichikawa broadcasts disaster warnings, climate information, earthquake information, tsunami information, and rain information in cooperation with the Japan Weather Association. This information also goes out to the registered e-mail addresses of mobile phones and PCs. Ichikawa's 360+5 e-government portal has put many public services online, making them accessible in text and video format through keyword searches by topic. The portal hosts a read aloud system for the blind and character magnification for those with limited eyesight. Videos and high-vision images of local archaeological and cultural assets are made available as part of its online museum collection. Internet-access kiosks have been made available in some 600 convenience stores. By 2005, the city had provided information and communication technology training to some 30,000 citizens (Archives of the ICF, 2006b).

E-government is perhaps one of the most quoted online applications with hundreds of projects worldwide, each adding its own flavour to meet the specific requirements of its geographical region. Networked community leaders have a unique opportunity to look at best practises in this sector and find ways to disseminate information, market programmes, promote concepts of stewardship and volunteerism, decrease social inequities, give people a voice, and resolve social problems.

DEVELOPING A CULTURE OF USE

Key Concept: *Understanding the psychology behind technology adoption guides the planners of community networks to provide the infrastructure and applications best suited to local needs.*

Planners will seek the broadest use possible to justify any public funds provided by government. Broader participation encourages more targeted applications and innovations that are community-generated, which will attract more users and increase the feeling of ownership. Positive momentum takes place when more users attract more suppliers, and more applications attract more users. Attracting ready-made users is easy; galvanizing a wider range of people to support the existence of ICT tools such as infrastructure, devices and applications is a challenge (Simon, 2004). As Agres et al. (1998, p. 71) have concluded, "Technology by itself does not ensure the coming of the virtual society; rather it is an enabler and shaper". Marketing and the media (radio, TV, magazine, and public spaces) can develop digital awareness and a culture of use.

Researchers have identified a number of important factors in the successful adoption of a technology or technological application (Carey, 1997):

- The technology and its applications must be affordable.
- The technology and applications must be located in areas of the home or business that will support access and use.
- The technology and applications must be desired, something people would like to use often or regularly.
- The application must be easy to use and require as little outside help as possible.
- The application must be fast and efficient and lead to improvements in productivity.

People embrace change slowly in response to a need. The ways people adopt new technologies and their applications will be influenced by culture, convenience, cost and availability. Involving users in acquiring and applying technology should shed light on their needs and their reservations, and help planners to avoid costly mistakes.

Most people, especially the older ones, have their preferred way of doing things and may be slow to consider alternatives. Younger people are more adaptable and, as far as technology adoption and use are concerned, can be a positive force in helping others obtain training, and attain skills and knowledge. The authors can point to the example of Ennis, Ireland, a smart community that included volunteerism in its school curriculum, encouraging young people to go into seniors' homes to help them set up their equipment and teach them about technology. This process accelerated acceptance of the technology in the community, and the effort led to other positive outcomes including more entrepreneurship and new relationships and understanding as a result of the interaction between youth and seniors (Industry Canada, 1999).

Age may be a concern with municipalities with a high proportion of older workers who find it difficult to make the transition to anything digital. Demonstrating the advantage of the new technology may convince them, but the technology still has to be of some practical use; it has to fit the individual's lifestyle and work within the physical environment of community, work and home. Researchers have proposed a number of theories and models to explain these behaviours. The task-technology fit model—based on fitting technology to the task, or analyzing need in order to provide adequate solutions—was discussed by Ziguars and Khazanchi (2008) in an effort to better understand collaboration online. Hsieh, Rai and Keil (2008) employed the theory of planned behaviour in an assessment of one of the ICF intelligent community award applicants, LaGrange. Using this model, they explained adoption by socio-economically disadvantaged groups in the community. The technology acceptance model (TAM) is perhaps the most quoted, used by such authors as Venkatesh and Bala (2008), who reported on the determinants of perceived usefulness and perceived ease of use toward adoption of technologies and use. These theories are relevant because they explain why people adopt technology and how to successfully introduce technologies.

The more effort it takes to master a technology or technological application, the slower and more limited will be its diffusion. The personal computer is already a deterrent because it is not always obvious to the uninitiated what must be done. Any project involving change will need to find ways to make information easy to acquire and use.

Home appliances are conveniently located to suit the users' lifestyle; the location of new digital technologies and their applications must be made as convenient. This provision further supports the concept of convergence, in which the information and communication functions of computers, telephones, radio and television are better integrated to make them easily accessible. Wireless connectivity and portable Internet access that make file exchanges between home and office easier illustrate the greater convenience that users can readily appreciate.

The Internet has flourished with declining costs. When community network projects are announced, some residents ask if there will be a subsidy toward the purchase of new computers and equipment. The community must find ways to ensure a greater rate of use throughout the community regardless of ability to pay. Therefore, access points are needed for those who cannot afford to purchase their own equipment and pay the monthly costs of connecting to an Internet service provider if the community wants to avoid creating technology ghettos. Also, training is needed. The successful use of IT requires a computer *and* information literacy skills. A sound plan for developing a networked community will include opportunities for open access and a related education programme.

Although telephone and cable companies may be looking for a magical solution prior to introducing services, they are more likely to experience a confluence of factors that will create demand. The question has to do with what applications, products and services consumers will need to manage such important matters as family, jobs, the market, medical services, and education. Having a mix of uses will attract demand, but there will rarely be one single "killer application".

This scenario was true for cable TV. When national cable programme distribution became easier via satellite, many new channels were created, and franchises were negotiated with individual communities. The majority of cable companies today offer more than video services. On their broadband networks they can provide voice and data and sometimes wireless as well. These factors came together to spur demand for a package of "triple play" offerings (cable TV, VoIP and broadband IP), making the cable companies less vulnerable to outside competition within the communities they serve. Historically, the major cable players have been slow to provide service to communities until the demand is evident and lucrative. Some metropolitan centres and many regions have reacted to the caution of cable and telecom players by pooling public resources to build out their own infrastructure or application projects.

New services require new equipment and this investment makes adoption more difficult. Not only will users need to adapt to new services; they will also need to change the way they use the media. Research suggests that technology adoption will follow several distinct steps that will change over time. Once the first step is done—reaching early adopters—the group introducing the technology should try to anticipate the future mix of users and what their technology needs will be. For example, the early adopters/first users may be attracted to the broadband Internet as a result of their roles as tele-workers from home. In this case, they will need good download speeds to receive documents from head offices, while uploading capabilities perhaps need not be as fast. The second generation of users may need the broadband Internet to provide training programmes to distant clients or course materials to students. In this case their activities may require higher upload speeds for sending larger documents. Here is the problem. In the conversion of their one-way cable TV lines into data carriers, the trend among cable operators has been to maintain only a few lines for upstream communications, since every line used for voice and data has meant one less for video. Such a configuration may be good for the cable company but not so good for home users.

In some cases, the acquisition of a single technology or medium may be linked to the purchase of other equipment and software. From a business perspective, the replacement cycle for existing media provides an opportunity to introduce new media. Implementation of a networked community project will increase demand for a host of other products and services, including computers, computer applications, security systems and upgraded telecommunications connections. The mere presence of upgraded technologies, software and connections will be sufficient to encourage some people to conform to a pattern of adoption and learning.

Technologies fail when they cannot be linked to a real consumer benefit. There are fads and cyclical patterns of adoption. Providing a real service that consumers will keep using ensures that the initial period of success is not followed by a sharp decline in its use. Some products are cyclical, popular for a time and then out-of-use for another period of time, then again popular through a new generation of equipment or service. This was true of game consoles which experienced peaks and dips in popularity. These cyclical patterns of adoption are not failures, but false starts.

Most users are not interested in the black box. They want to know what the box can do that meets a particular need they have. Marketing efforts must be geared to those needs and should avoid techno-language. People will adopt technologies because they have:

- A strong, unmet need in their lives, a need that can be met at an acceptable price, for example, the need to support work from home or to gain access to educational services);
- An insatiable appetite for some content or service, including gadget lovers who will pay a high price for the latest technology for accessing the Web, or people who can't get enough of movies.
- A need to avoid pain and disappointment, such as those who are experiencing pain as a result of slow Internet access, disappointment over an inadequate stock of popular movies in video-rental shops and poor customer service by existing broadband service providers.

Table 1. Applications and content evaluation

Indicators of efforts to develop innovative content	Demonstrations	Possible approaches to measurement
Useful and wide range of applications	Health sector initiatives	Percent of users affected and able to use the application
		Cost reductions or avoidance as a result of e-health initiatives
		Preventative nature of application or device and cost/benefit
	Education sector initiatives	Improvements in communication among parents, learners and instructors
		Improvements in students' grades
		Increased access for workers, parents at home, learners at a distance
	Business initiatives	Growth in clustering and alliances
		Demonstrations of economies of scope or scale
		Growth in knowledge management and dissemination systems
		Business-to-business relationships
		Business-to-consumer sales efforts
		Business-to-government sales and partnerships/collaborations
	Service sector	Number and variety of users in social, political and cultural programmes

continued on following page

Table 1. continued

Indicators of efforts to develop innovative content	Demonstrations	Possible approaches to measurement
Useful and wide range of applications	Health sector initiatives	Percent of users affected and able to use the application
		Cost reductions or avoidance as a result of e-health initiatives
		Preventative nature of application or device and cost/benefit
	Education sector initiatives	Improvements in communication among parents, learners and instructors
		Improvements in students' grades
		Increased access for workers, parents at home, learners at a distance
	Business initiatives	Growth in clustering and alliances
		Demonstrations of economies of scope or scale
		Growth in knowledge management and dissemination systems
		Business-to-business relationships

Creating a culture of use is not easy or automatic; it requires an effort from local leaders who understand the community's inherent uniqueness stemming from its specific history, geographical layout and political and economic experience. They appreciate the social conditions that exist within their community, but can also learn from international best practices. A community can develop its own recipe for success through assessment, self-education and cross-sector collaboration.

Key Concept: *Evaluation is one of the keys to success in knowing which applications should receive priority attention.*

EVALUATION OF APPLICATIONS AND CULTURE OF USE

The networked community encourages collaboration for application development in a wide range of sectors. Collaborators would include interested parties in health, education, government, business and other networks. There are many examples of content being developed collaboratively in all sectors of the economy. Evaluation tools need to focus on the extent of collaborative activity, the number of applications, consumer use, potential cost savings and revenue generated. Table 1 discusses some potential measurement indicators.

Criteria for networked community achievement are often based on the content and applications that are useful and attractive enough to draw citizens into a culture of use. The unique products and services generated may necessitate a wide variety of evaluation systems and the ability to categorize in order to reach conclusions. Approaches may include the use of surveys and data collection from Internet service providers, content developers and intelligent software systems that gather data on consumer use of ICT technologies.

Discussion on standardizing the criteria should be held early in the development of applications and content. For example, incompatible devices and processes in e-health applications could make it difficult for medical end-users to collaborate with those in other communities, thereby diminishing the value of the project. Both consumers and professionals experience this challenge when working with proprietary technologies. Standardization of access devices may make measurement easier, but requiring everyone to use the same equipment and software may also take away an important differentiation advantage.

CONCLUSION

Networked communities attempt to better manage their resources, create new wealth and improve quality for life of their citizens. Leaders of these communities are advised to investigate consumer needs and look at international as well as domestic best practices for ideas. Community planners and their counterparts in industry are also advised to take stock of the local knowledge resources and plan for the retention and growth of knowledge workers. These activities will allow them to strategize around applications that are likely to succeed, promoting quality of life and potential economic development.

Broadband communications and accessible applications are important factors. Applications can be imported, but those developed through partnerships with local stakeholders are more likely to increase their adoption and sustainability. Among the key items for consideration will be projects relating to tele-health, virtual learning, e-government and other information and communication projects that promote synergy among community organisations. Economic development opportunities also abound with tele-work, e-commerce, and e-entertainment strategies for creating new online content and services in all sectors of the economy.

Networked communities must encourage a culture of use and can do so by involving users in the planning and adoption of technologies and their applications.

This will often require new learning for everyone involved. Community leaders and stakeholders must also consider the long-term impact of ICT applications on the local telecommunication infrastructure and plan for their perpetual upgrade and modification.

Leadership in applications development will come from all sectors. Each application will have its own challenges and require its own set of skills. Decision-makers within and across sectors need to collaborate on issues of common concern. These issues may include upgrading infrastructure, avoiding duplication, sharing applications and promoting a culture of use.

REFERENCES

Agres, C., Edberg, D. & Igbaria, M. (1998). Transformation to virtual societies: Forces and issues. *Information Society, 14*(2), 71-82.

Albert, S. (2003). *Smarten up: Create a smart community.* Victoria, British Columbia, Canada: Farringtonmedia and Trafford Publishing.

Albert, S. & Campbell, B. (2007). The challenge of participatory technologies for teaching and learning at Ontario universities. *Council of Ontario Universities Colleague Paper Series.* Retrieved November 17, 2007, from http://www.cou. on.ca/_bin/publications/onlinePublications.cfm

Allan, B. & Lewis, D. (2006). Virtual learning communities as a vehicle for workforce development: A case study. *The Journal of Workplace Learning, 18*(6), 367-383.

American Telemedicine Association. (2007). *Telemedicine: A brief overview.* Retrieved January 15, 2008, from the American Telemedicine Association Web site: http://www.atmeda.org/news/library.htm

Archives of the ICF – The Intelligent Communities Forum. (2007a). Gangnam-Gu, Seoul, South Korea – *Nomination submitted for the Intelligent Community of the Year Award.* New York.

Archives of the ICF – The Intelligent Communities Forum. (2007b). Issy-les-Moulineaux, France – *Nomination submitted for the Intelligent Community of the Year Award.* New York.

Archives of the ICF – The Intelligent Communities Forum. (2006a). *Cleveland, Ohio, U.S. – Nomination submitted for the Intelligent Community of the Year Award.* New York.

Archives of the ICF – The Intelligent Communities Forum. (2006b). *Ichikawa, Japan – Nomination submitted for the Intelligent Community of the Year Award.* New York.

Archives of the ICF – The Intelligent Communities Forum. (2006c). *Manchester, UK – Nomination submitted for the Intelligent Community of the Year Award.* New York.

Archives of the ICF – The Intelligent Communities Forum. (2006d). *Taipei, Taiwan – Nomination submitted for the Intelligent Community of the Year Award.* New York.

Archives of the ICF – The Intelligent Communities Forum. (2006e). *Tianjin, China – Nomination submitted for the Intelligent Community of the Year Award.* New York.

Archives of the ICF – The Intelligent Communities Forum. (2006f). *Västerås, Sweden – Nomination submitted for the Intelligent Community of the Year Award.* New York.

Boettcher, J. V. (2007). Ten core principles for designing effective learning environments: Insights from brain research and pedagogical theory. *Innovate: Journal of Online Education, 3*(3). Retrieved April 10, 2008, from http://innovateonline.info/index.php?view=article&id=54&action=login

Budde, P. (2007). Global business users B2B market statistics. *Paul Budde Communications Pty Ltd.*, Retrieved May 8, 2008, from http://www.budde.com.au/

Cairncross, F. (1997). *The death of distance.* Boston: Harvard Business School Press.

Carey, J. (1997). *The first 100 feet for households: Consumer adoption patterns.* Retrieved May 8, 2008, from Harvard University Web site: http://ksgwww.harvard.edu/

Carneiro, R. & Nascimbeni, F. (2007). Observing the eLearning phenomenon. *eLearning Papers n° 4.* Retrieved September 18, 2007, from http://www.elearning-papers.eu/index.php?page=home

Cinenet. (2007). Retrieved September 18, 2007, from the Cinenet Web site: http://www.cine.net.au/?q=node/25

Cornwall, UK. (2008). *Digital Museum of Cornish Ceramics.* Retrieved May 8, 2008, from www.cornishceramics.com

Eger, J. M. (1999). *Smart growth and the urban future*. Retrieved November 5, 2007, from the Smart Communities Web site: http://www.smartcommunities. org/library_cities.htm

Europe's Information Society (2001). *The eLearning Action Plan: Designing tomorrow's education*. Retrieved January 7, 2008, from http://ec.europa. eu/information_society/eeurope/2005/all_about/elearning/index_en.htm#eLearni ng:%20People%20and%20Technology

Fleming, J. (2006a). *About DSN*. Retrieved October 17, 2007, from http://www. directsellingnews.com/aboutdsn.php

Fleming, J. (2006b). Unlocking your entrepreneurial spirit. *Your Business at Home Magazine, 1*(9), 8-14.

Gates, B. (2007). A robot in every home. *Scientific American, January*, 58-65. Retrieved May 8, 2008, from http://www.sciam.com/article.cfm?id=a-robot-in-every-home

Goldman-Sachs. (2000). *Technology: Internet-commerce, United States*, Global Equity Research.

Good, R. (2006). *Participatory Media and the Pedagogy of Civic Participation*. Retrieved January 6, 2008, from http://www.masternewmedia.org/news/2006/11/14/ participatory_media_and_the_pedagogy.htm

Haller, C. (2007). *Jott the Vote—Messages to presidential campaign via phone to text*. Retrieved December 5, 2007, from eParticipation Web site: http://jottthevote. com/

Hsieh, J. J.; Rai, A. & Keil, M. (2008). Understanding digital inequality: Comparing continued use behavioral models of the socio-economically advantaged and disadvantaged, *MIS Quarterly, 32*(1), 97-126.

Igbaria, M., Shayo, C., & Olfman, L. (1999). *On becoming virtual: the driving forces and arrangements*. Proceedings from the 1999 ACM SIGCPR conference on computer personnel research, New Orleans, LA, USA, 27-41. Retrieved November 15, 2007, from http://portal.acm.org/citation.cfm?id=299513.299610

ICF – The Intelligent Communities Forum (2008a). *Community profile of Dundee, UK*. Retrieved June 5, 2008 from www.intelligentcommunity.org (Click on Events/ Awards).

ICF – The Intelligent Communities Forum (2008b). *Community profile of Fredericton, N.B., Canada*. Retrieved June 5, 2008 from www.intelligentcommunity.org (Click on Events/Awards).

Industry Canada. (1999). *Smart international community profile: Ennis, Ireland.* Retrieved May 29, 2008, from http://198.103.246.211/profiles/ennis_e.asp

Internet world stats: Usage and population statistics (2007). Retrieved September 18, 2007, from http://www.Internetworldstats.com/stats.htm

John, G. J. & Ambrose, P. J. (2006). Neo-tribes: the power and potential of online communities in health care. *Communication of the ACM, 49*(1), 107-113.

Krebs, V. (1998). *Knowledge networks: Mapping and measuring knowledge creation, re-use, and flow.* Retrieved September 17, 2007, from http://www.orgnet.com/IHRIM.html

Larner, W. (2002). Calling capital: call centre strategies in New Brunswick and New Zealand. *Global Networks: A Journal of Transnational Affairs, 2*(2), 133-152.

Los Angeles Times. (2000, January 14). *Wired dorms gets students accustomed to high speed Internet.* Retrieved May 29, 2008, from CAnet-3-NEWS Web site: http://mail.canarie.ca/MLISTS/news/1396.html

Marriott, M. (1999, December 23). Through the looking glass, virtually; Immersive technology puts your image inside the game and may soon replace the mouse. *New York Times.* Retrieved November 19, 2007, from http://query.nytimes.com/gst/fullpage.html?res=9407E5D71739F930A15751C1A96F958260

Metropolitan Museum of Art. (2008). *Metropolitan Museum of Art.* Retrieved May 8, 2008, from http://www.metmuseum.org/

National Museums of Northern Ireland. (2008). *The Digital Museum.* Retrieved May 8, 2008, from http://www.magni.org.uk/future_developments/digital_museum

NEC develops the world's first virtual library (1997). Retrieved November 19, 2007, from NEC Web site: http://www.nec.co.jp/press/en/9701/0801.html

News Corporation. (2007). *NBC Universal And News Corp. announce deal with Internet leaders AOL, MSN, MySpace And Yahoo! to create a premium online video site with unprecedented reach.* Retrieved September 18, 2007, from News Corporation Web site: http://www.newscorp.com/news/news_329.html

Prensky, M. (2001). Digital natives, digital immigrants. *On the Horizon, 9*(5), 1-2.

Rheingold, H. (2007). *Vision of the Future—Howard Rheingold's Presentation.* Retrieved May 22, 2008, from http://www.educationau.edu.au/jahia/webdav/site/myjahiasite/shared/seminars/Rheingold_Melbourne_Speech.pdf

Shahin, K., Cogoi, C. & Sangiorgi, D. (2006). mGBL – mobile game-based learning: Perspectives and usage in learning and career guidance topics. *eLearning Papers n° 1.* Retrieved September 18, 2007, from http://www.elearningpapers.eu/index. php?page=home&vol=1

Simon, S. (2004). Systemic evaluation methodology: The emergence of social learning from environmental ICT prototypes. *Systemic Practice and Action Research, 17*(5), 471-496.

Tibetan & Himalayan Digital Library. (2008). Retrieved May 8, 2008, from http:// www.thdl.org

Telemedicine in Ontario. (2007). Retrieved November 20, 2007, from the Ontario Telemedicine Network: http://www.otn.ca/telemedicine.html

United States Office of Personnel Management. (2007). *Status of tele-work in the federal government: Report to Congress.* Retrieved September 18, 2007, from http://www.tele-work.gov/surveys/2006_TW20Report.pdf.

University of Waikato. (2008). *New Zealand Digital Library.* Retrieved May 8, 2008, from http://nzdl.sadl.uleth.ca/cgi-bin/library

Västerås Stadsportal. (2008). *MalarnetCity.* Retrieved May 22, 2008, from http:// malarnetcity.se/pages/City%2CHomeAndDisplayWindow

Venkatesh, V. & Bala, H. (2008). Technology Acceptance Model 3 and a Research Agenda on Interventions. *Decision Sciences, 39*(2), 273-315.

Williams, S. D. & Whittier, N. C. (2007). Competitive balance implications for hospitals of innovations in networked electronic health records. *Competitiveness Review, 17*(1/2), 26-36.

Ziguars, I. & Khazanchi, D. (2008). From profiles to patterns: A new view of task-technology fit. *Information Systems Management, 5*(1), 8-13.

Chapter VI
Innovation:
Creating Ideas

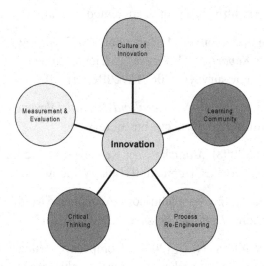

"The future belongs to organisations that learned to truly unleash the creative powers of self-organising project communities, knowledge networks, open source teams, and other new ways of work and learning, based on free associations of people who are passionate about what they do together. Communities of practise are in the centre of this widening innovation movement." (Pôr & van Bekkum, 2003, p. 3)

Overview: The global environment has become more turbulent, and innovations in telecommunication and information processing are both part of this turbulence and an adaptive response to it. How can telecommunication infrastructure enable the social and economic development of communities? With diminishing barriers in terms of price, speed and availability, how can individuals and groups in a community become innovators?

This chapter will discuss:

- The importance of innovation in an ICT-enabled world;
- A model of innovation for continuous and discontinuous change;
- The nature of innovation—describing the concepts of creativity and invention, and the source of innovation;
- The development of a local innovation culture;
- Evaluation of the innovation environment.

THE IMPORTANCE OF INNOVATION IN THE ICT WORLD

Key Concept: *Growth in the new economy is achieved through greater performance. Given that there will be increased competition, access to additional resources—especially knowledge-based resources—will be needed. New growth also intensifies the need for differentiation.*

According to Abraham and Knight (2001), many managers operate with an industrial economy mentality based on the rules of scarcity and diminishing returns. In continually worrying about the bottom line, companies and communities, even governments, can lose sight of the need for innovation. Trying to provide more products and services while decreasing costs often results in products and services being treated as commodities. Lack of innovation—and thus lack of differentiation—hampers growth and can eventually become the death-knell of many such organisations and communities.

Commercial and other community organisations spend considerable time establishing relationships that work, but Birkinshaw, Bessant and Delbridge (2007) point out the inflexibility of long-term relationships and value-chains. The authors conclude that long-established relationships can create obstacles to innovation, and they recommend forming new networks of relationships that can bring new insights, competencies and innovative possibilities (p. 69). In the new millennium, wired and "digitally networked communities" are creating new opportunities for themselves by promoting more open, community-based systems of innovation.

Writing in the *Wall Street Journal* more than a decade ago, R. T. King noted how the high-tech advantage was giving U.S. firms the global lead in computer networks:

> Networks have become the information factories that speed innovation and compress product cycles.... Like factory systems in the 1920s, networks will be the key to establishing leadership in many industries in the future.

Only by chaining together computers with instant access to vast databases, new market information, and the work of colleagues, have companies begun to reap the benefits of information factories. [The results have been] great increases in the metabolism of companies; the speed with which they can launch new products and businesses; the power to glean and react to information before competitors; the ability to cut costs... and the ability to eliminate the barriers of time and space with continual global communications (King, 1994).

King's comments highlight that globalization and accelerating technologies do not necessarily signify only bad news; they also allow corporations and communities to think innovatively about how to change processes, eliminate silos and increase knowledge creation for their own renewal. Chakravorti (2004), in describing the new network economy, has another point of view. He agrees that the networked market allows for the rapid diffusion of news, ideas, and in theory, innovations. However, the rate of change also erects formidable barriers to the rapid adoption of innovations (p. 60). His argument is based on institutions that tend to adopt similar technologies and become entrenched. Chakravorti presents the example of banks that wait to implement innovations until other competitors adopt them. In today's online market, there are too many opportunities for new competitors to substitute products. Smaller and faster operators can nip at profit margins with competitive offerings.

Innovation can and will make a real difference in creating sustainable and healthy communities, and ICTs are a vehicle for creatively meeting the needs of society and individual groups within it; new inventions can spur entire new industries. ICTs are often blamed for downsizing, but restructuring efforts are not always the result of ICTs. At least among corporations, they were occurring long before as a result of competitive pricing of good and the impact of poor management. Technology has played its role in reducing the need for some functions, but it has benefited regions that adopted an ICT strategy early and developed networks. These communities were able to increase productivity and avoid the downsizing trend. Hicks and Nivin (2000) have emphasized the commercial value of information flow:

[T]he better "wired" a regional economy, the greater its capacity to discover and develop commercial value in the information that flows to, through, and from it. This, in turn, can increase a region's capacity to incubate innovation, launch new enterprise and bring the results to markets at home and abroad more rapidly than competing regions (p. 119).

Strategic innovations that are planned and deliberately launched can help community stakeholders expand markets and redirect resources for improved efficiency. Failure to innovate in terms of both technology and culture can allow the best-intentioned government or private sector agency to deteriorate into an ineffective bureaucracy or worse. As government offices and corporate enterprises at all levels slowly move toward a networked world of more efficient service delivery, it becomes critical to understand the importance of IT innovation and the barriers that prevent it. Sometimes resistance to change, the established processes and the deeply rooted private interests, can't be overcome alone (Vander Veen, 2006); it requires a strong network of visionaries who are committed to a course of action.

Several forces are pushing communities toward greater reliance on digital networks. For example, Agres et al. (1998), Igbaria et al. (1999), and Tapscott and Williams (2008) have pointed to global economics, politics, the development of an enlightened population, technology, social and psychological factors, and organisational norms as the forces that move communities toward collaboration and transformation, which in turn can result in innovative problem solving. Communities are looking for new processes and products that can create a competitive or comparative advantage, which can sometimes be accomplished with the pooling of resources. The following are examples of courageous communities that have achieved a turnaround using ICT strategies:

Sunderland, UK, a former North Sea shipbuilding and coal-mining centre hard-hit by industrial decline, had an unemployment rate exceeding 30% in the 1980s, higher than in the Great Depression. They were in the top 10% of UK "distressed districts" with a low-skilled workforce and a heavy concentration of elderly and disabled workers. By 2003, the unemployment rate had dropped to 4% and the city was ranked as one of top five most competitive business locations in the UK. This was accomplished through community innovation, partnerships, and building synergy in the development of new ideas. (Archives of the ICF, 2007b)

Spokane, Washington, U.S., was built during the 19th century on natural resources (silver, timber) and geography (as a railroad hub). By the 1980s, it was an economic backwater compared to the Seattle region to the west. By 2003, it had turned its economy around and was home to the "Terrabyte Triangle"—a 30-block downtown region offering one of densest concentrations of broadband in the U.S. Despite its small size of 177,000 residents, it attracted $1 billion in private and public investment. Again and again, we see communities like Sunderland and Spokane managing a turnaround based on leadership that encourages change and innovation. (Archives of the ICF, 2004)

LaGrange, Georgia, U.S., a rural city of 26,000 located 60 miles southwest of Atlanta, lost much of its industrial base in the late 1980s as Raytheon and other manufacturers closed their plants. They were also bypassed by carriers for deployment of advanced telecommunication services. In 1998, the city became the operator of a 200-mile + fiber ring in alliance with a cable TV provider. By 2000, they launched their first free Internet and e-mail service on TV, and VoIP for voice service. They were able to generate over $1 million annually from service delivery and gained 5,000 new jobs due to their innovative telecommunication infrastructure. (Archives of the ICF, 2002)

William Eggers (2005), in his work on overcoming obstacles to technology-enabled transformation, underlines the lack of statewide leadership in the U.S. in developing the transformation needed in many communities. He is one of many who believe that transformation will be inevitable as a result of declining budgets and resources. The lesson is that communities must think strategically about how they can encourage innovation before conditions deteriorate. Community organisations tend to focus on "business as usual" and become entrenched, which can stifle innovation. Understanding that the system is naturally static is the first step to finding solutions to break down barriers to innovation, or as aptly put by Westley, Zimmerman and Quinn-Patton, "[T]he established organisations and institutions in any society absorb most of the resources, sometimes leaving little to innovation" (Westley et al., 2006, p. 95).

The challenge with innovation is to create a vision that can attract the attention of local stakeholders—one that generates a sense of urgency and demonstrates the reasons for collaboration. Historically, organisations have been very guarded with their innovations. More than 25% of respondents in a UK survey (Innovation, 2006) felt that they could rely on prior innovations. Almost 50% felt there was no need to innovate due to market conditions. Unfortunately, this type of thinking will leave many communities behind. Many organisations have not had the time, the resources or the imagination to keep up with current developments, and the changes suggested by the concept of "networked community" may seem overwhelming.

CHANGE AND INNOVATION

Innovation and change are closely related concepts. Abraham and Knight (2001) discussed three levels of change in the marketplace: gradual, continuous and discontinuous (represented in Figure 2 below as part of the explanation on transformational change in the technology arena). Gradual change can be planned using standard innovation processes to cut costs or upgrade existing systems. Continuous change requires ongoing benchmarking, reduction efforts and, at times, re-engineering.

Change is happening at a faster pace and, as a result, a nucleus of innovators is required to find new solutions to keep up with global changes. Many communities operate in a chaotic environment of continuous change and need to pay attention to their innovation processes to retain their economic position. Discontinuous change is non-linear and could have serious effects on communities by radically changing, at a moment's notice, the structure of industry and the economy. This transformation can and does happen to communities. The impact of globalization is extensive, and the rate of displacement can be enormous and immediate. The search is on for breakthroughs that lead to new products, services, processes, systems, and structures.

Communities can experience all three levels of change—gradual, continuous and discontinuous—and organisations can come together to find innovative solutions to deal with this change. Understanding the types and nature of change and mobilising the right players to work on solutions are critical to the health of communities. No one knows what the future will hold; however, networked communities work with, rather than resist, those changes. In these communities, innovation becomes part of the culture so that members are better prepared to deal with discontinuous change and perhaps stay ahead of the curve.

The rate of discontinuous change has accelerated over time as a result of the increased use of ICTs. As more international players seek markets, the effects of globalization on any given community are multiplied. Although ICTs have been linked to globalization in terms of enabling firms to compete internationally, the networked community can also be of local benefit by encouraging local/regional restructuring to take advantage of opportunities closer to home. The two phenomena of change and transformation are represented in Figure 1 below (adapted from a presentation by James Balsillie at the 2006 ICF New York conference).

Key Concept: *A community will face continuous or discontinuous change at different times. The former requires upgrading and reengineering, whereas the latter calls for transformation. Creating an innovation culture allows community stakeholders to plan for adaptation.*

James Balsillie, Co-CEO of Research in Motion (RIM), the producer of the BlackBerry, described the adoption of IT innovation as a process that leads many communities toward transformation over time. These communities and their organisations (private and public) will move from technology adoption to process

Figure 1. Change over time (adapted from James Balsillie, 2006)

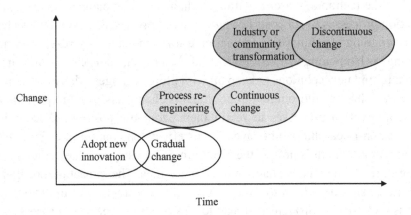

Figure 2. Innovation and change

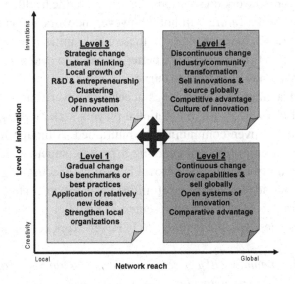

re-engineering to transformation, the reason being that adopting ICTs promotes new systems and processes that are more efficient or perceived as indispensable (or attractive) by users. These new ICT systems are more easily integrated internationally and can lead to new growth, but they also allow more competition. As competition increases, firms react by clustering, re-engineering and/or forming new patterns of business. Eventually, industries and communities move toward transformation to keep up, or to equip themselves for change.

The ability to lead the community in a transformation effort is possible only if its implementation is planned over time. Unplanned transformation can occur quickly or slowly but can inflict a lot of damage while it is occurring. Planned community transformation is a choice to prepare for the future. Though not based on a technology, its process for building a new culture of change, innovation and use opens up opportunities regarding technology. For example, communities can wait until a telecommunication company upgrades its broadband infrastructure or take steps to do it themselves to encourage earlier development. Communities can plan around the telecommunication infrastructure they adopt to attract jobs or match resident skills with the requirements of companies located far away. Communities can teach residents how to better use the Internet to create a culture of use. These multiple innovations can be continuous and synergistic.

Figure 2, proposed by the authors, provides a matrix for thinking about the various levels of innovation possible within networked communities and the level of change needed to fit into these various strategies.

At Level 1, communities are being creative and importing innovations from best practises or international benchmarks. These communities will undergo gradual change, strategically importing new products and processes to suit their needs. Implementing e-learning practises in schools is an example, where school boards or post-secondary organisations carefully plan the implementation of new practises. Networked communities at Level 1 will implement new ideas to strengthen local organisations and provide new services that will lead to job growth or retention and to improve quality of life for its citizens, and they are using the experience of others to carefully implement innovations.

At Level 2, the networked community may find some comparative advantages in producing some applications. For example, communities may find that they can extend the use of their e-learning or telemedicine applications or programmes to a wider region or a global community. The networked community is extending its reach beyond its own borders because it feels it has become specialised or has acquired some core competencies in an area.

At Level 3, innovation is being pushed to a higher level locally. Waterloo (Ontario, Canada) is an example of this type of innovation strategy. The networked community supports an environment for new inventions and patents, and will often focus on attracting researchers and firms that are focused on R&D. This is difficult since the competition for researchers is strong, but success comes when the community is able to encourage new forms of entrepreneurship, develop and support clusters, and promote open systems of innovation.

At Level 4, communities strive to push innovation into a global arena, which often means developing the economies of scale and the talent to become recognised as a centre of excellence in one or more industry or product. These communities are often in a state of discontinuous change or transformation as they attempt to compete on a global scale, and there are many larger communities in this situation. They need a culture of innovation because they must stay ahead of the curve and have at their fingertips a continuous stream of innovation.

The community may not have a choice in the level of change being cast upon it. Some communities will be subjected to discontinuous change and face an environment requiring a transformation effort.

THE NATURE OF INNOVATION

In *The Republic*, Plato wrote, "Necessity is the mother of invention". A need or problem encourages creative efforts to solve it. Indeed, there are many examples of communities or regions embarking on innovation strategies out of necessity, including intelligent or networked community development. Dire circumstances such as a primary industry failing or moving away are the kinds of motivators that will push communities to think actively and creatively. Some communities are able to plan ahead—to avoid the problems experienced by those who wait to have change forced upon them, to diversify their economy, or to promote growth and efficiency within.

Innovation is about new products, new systems and new business processes. Driven by mindset, innovations not need to be based on breakthroughs; they could be an application or an infrastructure new to the community.

An international group of companies (Microsoft among them) are providing an interesting example—they are planning to innovate around the cost of the laptop computer, with the hope that its price can be brought down to $100 so that it can be placed in the hands of more people around the world, with a particular focus on low-income populations (One Laptop, 2007). The plan is to distribute mostly in developing nations at the onset, but the ability to offer a reduced price will soon overflow to all countries and allow, among others, more young people to be equipped with computers in schools.

The One Laptop idea should exponentially speed up content development in years to come. It is an example of system innovation; the product already exists, and companies are working on reducing the cost of components so that more people can acquire it. With more people using ICTs, some economies of scale are possible, allowing for more investment, more growth and new demand for content and services. This is a synergistic process as one state of change promotes another.

Inventions are measured by the number of patents; innovation is measured in terms of application and is rooted in the individual and institutional resources invested (Hicks and Nivin, 2000). Measurement of innovation for networked communities is more than counting inventions; it is about looking at improvements in systems, tools and new applications using ICTs. People and organisations within communities use creativity to produce and apply new ideas in a specific context. Setting benchmarks and highlighting best practises are excellent ways to develop creativity within communities.

Creativity, according to Zhuang (1995), "requires the synthesis of new ideas and concepts by the radical restructuring and re-association of existing ones"—as Einstein did when his Theory of Relativity created a new way of looking at space and gravitation. Networked communities can innovate or be creative around telecommunication infrastructure and around opportunities to collaborate in the delivery of products and services by looking at product lines (video conference systems, iPods and portals), and finding new ways to apply these technologies. Opportunities in service innovation, process innovation, and cultural innovation are all possible at the community level (Meha, 2006). Such steps can be demonstrated in infrastructure, devices, applications, content, opportunities to various segments of the population, and skills and knowledge development.

But where does innovation come from? Innovation occurs in the course of various activities aimed at improving, expanding and creating ventures, whether in community or in business (Kodama, 2000). Because it is so fundamental to development, innovation should be (Gurstein, 2004).

Innovation performance depends to a large extent on how firms and organisations collaborate to share experiences and knowledge (Isaksen, 2001). At the community level, innovation is perhaps a little more complex to encourage, since it is a cumulative process with constant interactions among key players with different talents and skills (Carty, 1997). It appears that the best strategy is to begin by creating a social environment that encourages diversity, tolerance and pursuit of knowledge, which in turn will help to establish social networks and encourage individual and group-supported entrepreneurship. Innovation is fueled first by the energy, time and skills of people, then by the financial capital and leadership within organisations (Westley et al., 2006). Creating an innovation culture starts with social development and later builds economic development.

Key Concept: *Communities need to develop an innovation culture to survive and prosper in a turbulent global economy. Change and innovation, led by a network of visionaries, can support any transformation necessary.*

A culture of innovation, as described by Pôr and van Bekkum (2003) who write about knowledge economics, is achieved "when innovation occurs naturally, almost as a by-product of how people attend their work" (p. 9). Among the practises that leaders of networked communities should adopt to create a culture of innovation are a) meaningful dialogue that includes stories, experiences and ideas; b) a safe environment for open dialogue that encourages new ideas and allows for questioning and evaluation; and c) partnerships formed across boundaries and partners chosen carefully to build sustainable alliances. The concepts of collaboration and cross-functional communities of practise are important elements of building a culture of innovation.

An open environment for dialogue is one of the keys to success in creating a culture of innovation. Evidence of open dialogue can be evaluated through demonstrations of clustering, collaborations within and between industry groups, and the participation of a wider variety of community stakeholders in developing new ideas.

A collaborative innovation environment often occurs in clusters. According to Isaksen (2001), clusters are a "concentration of interdependent firms within the same or adjacent industrial sectors in a small geographic area" (p. 104). Clusters are an important element in promoting innovation because they allow member firms and organisations to learn from one another, share best practises, and when trust is established, innovate at the group level. Clusters combine like products or services to develop economies of scale and improve supply chain management. Discussions will be needed around intellectual property rights, "coopetition", strategic alliances and so forth, but once resolved, clusters can work together to investigate best practises within and without to replicate, improve and cross-fertilize. Clusters can be integrated vertically with subcontractors and other production capacities, and/or include horizontal cooperation among firms. In today's ICT environment, clusters can be developed locally, nationally and internationally, since one of the critical elements of clustering is the ability to more efficiently carry out business transactions, dialogue and communication (Rosenfeld, 1997).

Although it is important for networked communities to foster local clustering, they can also move toward "regional innovation networks" or "regional innovation systems". The first depends on partnership and collaboration among closely related institutions, and the second encourages partnerships or collaboration between a broader range of organisations. In writing about the building of regional innovation systems, Isaksen (2001) observed that:

> Complete regional innovation systems also involve co-operation among such firms and knowledge creating and diffusing organisations as universities, colleges, training organisations, R&D institutes, technology transfer agen-

cies, business associations, finance institutions, etc. These organisations house important know-how, train labour, provide financing, etc., that support regional innovation. Thus, regional innovation systems consist of a) firms of the region's main industrial clusters, including their support industries; b) "supporting" knowledge organisations; and c) interaction between these actors (p. 107).

Yet another step in the ladder of developing an innovation culture is to think beyond innovation systems to the development of a "learning region" where innovation becomes embedded in social and regional structures, and collaborators develop a planning process to achieve greater levels of innovation. In this case, "the actors in a region collaborate closely with each other on an institutional level in order to develop and implement regional innovation strategies" (Boekema et al., 2000). Learning regions must be created by a combination of collective political decisions and bottom-up local initiatives (Isaksen, 2001). The main driver for innovation is often the courage and energy of local stakeholders to seek to improve the regions in which they live and work, perhaps with the idea to also better the world. Dundee and Estonia are examples of the achievements possible in a structured collaborative innovation environment. They demonstrate the potential positive impact of community innovation and how the actions of one organization can affect another. They are also living laboratories showcasing how a holistic view of ICT development, one where several community players are paying attention to the provision and development of broadband access, citizen empowerment, knowledge workforce, and user needs, can make a real difference in creating innovations leading to new economic opportunities and quality of life:

> The Estonian government created a program called "Tiger Leap" to provide all schools with PCs and Internet connections starting in 1999. This simple idea was a spark that lit a wildfire of innovation. Banks in Tallinn talked about their own Tiger Leaps while introduce e-banking, and newspapers being published for the first time put out online editions. An NGO created a program that put computers into vehicles to introduce ICT to the rural population. Lack of purchasing power, however, posed a clear obstacle. In response, the National Library in Tallinn introduced the first public access Internet services with funding from UNDP. The Soros Foundation began a program that invited enthusiasts to create public Internet access points all over the country, and in 2000, a private foundation called Look@World, funded by telecom, banking and computer companies, spread public access Internet even farther. Government was a major partner in innovation. As part of Tiger Leap, the national government made wholesale purchases of

computers and persuaded banks to support leasing programs that included Internet access. It encouraged the Look@World foundation to provide computer literacy training to 100,000 adults. The government also introduced an electronic ID card and developed a data security system to support safe e-commerce. (ICF, 2008a)

Dundee in the United Kingdom operates 300 PCs with free Internet access at locations including 12 learning centers for adults, generating 15,000 user sessions per month. At least one free-access terminal is located within 2 miles of every household in the city. A network of 350 networked bus stops provides real-time travel information to digital signs and kiosks onsite as well as to mobile phones. A professor at the University of Abertay has founded ADD Knowledge in partnership with government agencies to deliver Scotland's first home-study program for over 400,000 primary school children using next-generation video game consoles. Meanwhile, local health services use text messaging to remind patients about appointments and medications, and Dundee is proposing to become a test bed for Scotland's Project XYZ, which aims to create a WiMax network across major cities (ICF, 2008b).

Key Concept: *Putting technology in the hands of more people will create new complex webs of relationships that can lead to new social and regional structures and networks that support innovation.*

Pôr and van Bekkum (2003) have suggested that creative ideas can come from a wide variety of sources. Communities need to perform an inventory of the community's current innovations, which should indicate each community's core capabilities. Identifying core capabilities may lead the community to discover opportunities for sharing innovations or applying concepts from one sector to another. This capacity and opportunity inventory includes:

- Identifying un-met needs;
- Using existing technology for new applications—how a technology, product or system used in one sector can be launched in another;
- Looking at what others are doing: peer-to-peer help in problem solving, reviewing best practises, sharing knowledge, upgrading knowledge through attendance at conferences and international events, and reviewing published papers and technological advances;
- Starting with organisations with the resources to innovate and bring in experts;

- Bringing lateral thinkers to the front and developing cross-sector approaches to innovation.

Whether it is a new technology or a new application of an existing technology that is tested on a new customer group, or a new way of delivering existing programmes to users, the purpose of community innovation is to meet needs. Meeting needs can be accomplished through training individuals in an existing technology, providing price incentives (employee purchase plans, free Internet access), easier technology access and availability (access centres, distribution of free reconstructed computers). Unmet needs often stem from a lack of financial, human and knowledge resources, so citizens must consider what needs are important. It may be that an infrastructure upgrade is necessary but the economics are not there for a single organisation to undertake the project. By continually evaluating needs, a community can promote an innovation culture that stimulates thinkers to come up with new ideas to solve problems. Therefore, communities need to reflect on how they can meet citizen needs. Noted below are some examples:

By launching broadband and using students to teach business new skills, a small town experienced a rebirth and was able to trace its success to changes made in a high school class with an information technology experiment, an example provided by Gillis and McLellan (1998). The results included several process improvements in local businesses using information technology and virtual services that changed the way business was done. It encouraged a transformation in other non-profit and public service sectors and allowed the small community to survive and prosper in an otherwise harsh economic environment.

In San Francisco, planning and getting buy-in from unconventional users helped the city create an environment that promoted equitable access with free Internet for all. This innovative approach changed the way the Internet was viewed by many. San Francisco had a large vagrant population, to which the city hoped to offer Internet-related skills to address a sensitive social issue. San Francisco, the nearest city to "Silicon Valley", one of the most prosperous regions of the world, is in constant need of human resources and developed a long-term plan for providing solutions to its social and human resource requirements. Citizens also thought that increased use of the Internet would promote and continue to improve the innovation environment already in the region (Concepts presented at the ICF Intelligent Community Award Conference, 2006).

The city of Windsor adopted the strategy of encouraging device use among a larger percentage of the population in western Ontario, Canada, developing new ways of using wireless devices and experimenting with new forms of infrastructure. Widely acclaimed as an innovator in using mobile devices and networks, the city negotiated a reduced price on BlackBerries for selected community members, especially those involved with school boards, post-secondary institutions, municipalities, hospitals, and a few larger private-sector companies. Windsor's initiative allowed these devices to be adopted for use throughout the region at a faster rate. People were encouraged to develop innovative business processes using the device. The region is, as a result, witnessing improved productivity in both business and non-profit sectors.

Piloting a new application, Bell Canada and Nortel Networks introduced a WiFi project covering an entire community in Northern Ontario, Canada. The technology had previously been used for hotspots—to service a single building or a small portion of a neighbourhood. Introducing the technology to cover an entire community was a new approach, both risky and costly. However, if the pilot project works, it could possibly give that community a competitive or comparative advantage.

In adapting technologies to fit its economic situation, Evora, Portugal, developed the MuTIC and Dream Shop innovations. These are broadband-equipped buses and trucks that serve as mobile learning systems for informatics support in remote community schools (Archives of the ICF, 2007a).

Leadership is another important component in identifying and meeting needs. It may be that a sector or an organisation is unaware of available opportunities, or aware but lacking a motivational leader to undertake them. Communities sometimes need to amass the knowledge and skills necessary to encourage the creativity needed for innovation.

New ideas and new applications come about sporadically even when the technology has been available for a long time. The Internet was not invented for the purpose it serves today, but innovators found more applications and made it an indispensable tool with multiple uses. Technology by itself does not generate innovation or new ideas, but creating human bridges between knowledge and ideas, and seeing things from an outside perspective can often result in creative solutions. Winston-Salem provided a good example of multi-sectoral approaches leading to creative solutions:

In 2004, Targacept, a biopharmaceutical company spun out from R.J. Reynolds, joined WinstonNet in a cooperative program to demonstrate state-of-the-art "grid computing" in local schools. WinstonNet is now exploring development of a supercomputing center to be housed at the Piedmont Triad Community Research Park, where Wake Forest is constructing a high-performance data center. This research park, anchored in Winston-Salem's historic downtown business district, will provide 5.7 million square feet (529,547 m²) of "green" commercial space for life science research on land donated to the city by R.J. Reynolds. It is being developed by another public-private partnership called Idealliance and is currently home to five buildings including the Biotechnology Research Facility of Wake Forest University Health Sciences. (ICF, 2008c)

The combination of a wider set of experiences obtained from within (local think tanks) and outside the community (external thinkers) can lead to new innovation. In writing about collective knowledge on communication and innovation, Antonelli (2000) noted:

> In a world where nobody can claim full control of all existing knowledge, each agent possesses diverse and yet complementary pieces of information and knowledge which are not only useful per se, that is in the dedicated activity in the course of which they have been implemented and elaborated, but also for broader and different uses (p. 537).

In other words, bringing together idea generators at the community level and calling in experts when necessary is an effective way to generate innovation for a particular project or an entire sector; this strategy is also likely to create opportunities in other areas. Chesbrough and Appleyard (2007) define this phenomenon as open innovation—models of innovation based on harnessing collective creativity. The Goldcorp example in Tapscott and Williams' book *Wikinomics* is illustrative:

> Goldcorp's leader demonstrated a creative way to utilize the power of international networks to resolve a complicated mining problem. The company issued a challenge to anyone who could help them find mining resources in a property they owned in Northern Ontario and were rewarded for their strategic thinking with great success. They used a collaborative and networked approach to problem solving, sometimes referred to as "open systems" of innovation (Tapscott & Williams, 2008).

The work of Fuller, Bartl, Ernst and Muhlbacher (2006) provide yet other examples of open innovation from Adidas, Audi, BMW, Siemens and Swaroski. These authors explain that more companies are expanding their network of innovators to yield higher results. There are risks in opening up one of the most strategic sectors of the firm—the innovation department—but there could be great benefits. Knowledge is built from information exchange among agents, and each piece of knowledge can help reduce dead ends and wasted resources, perhaps to build a foundation for new innovation and new economic opportunity. The exchange among owners of tacit knowledge of information is critical because such knowledge is difficult to codify and requires an environment of dialogue.

A collaborative environment is needed to develop a culture of innovation—one that includes public and private collaborators and, perhaps through open systems of innovation, seeks involvement from other people. The authors call this the Public/Private/People Collaborative or the 3 Ps of collaboration. We have found the strategic effort to bring community stakeholders together to be a critical component in successful networked communities as demonstrated by the example below:

Melbourne, Australia, developed within its Telstra Innovation Centre a series of innovation pods focused on incubating and commercializing new products and services. Groups of up to 10 to 12 specialists from Telstra's strategic partners, clients and institutions were brought together as think-tanks for 12 weeks, during which they rigorously developed and tested concepts with a view to achieving a marketable product or service. A number of projects have emanated from this group, including EmStream, a customized music solution tailored to the specific demographics and feel of the customer's premises. Blue Reef, another brainchild of the Telestra Innovation Centre, is a unique identity-enforced network security technology designed to allow organisations to securely open their networks to users and business partners. Schools are using the system to manage a student's access rights throughout the day, and more than 200 sites in the private sector and public schools are using the technology throughout Australia. This think-tank has generated products sold in 27 countries and in 10 languages. It has also initiated WebAlive, a programme that creates first-class Web sites for its clients that include powerful business management tools and some flexible online training (Archives of the ICF, 2005).

The authors have seen a number of examples where innovation has started with those agencies and enterprises that have the time, money, knowledge, tools, and technology to innovate. These projects seek and encourage partners both inside and outside the community with the resources to develop innovative applications.

Hospitals, school boards and micro-enterprises with few resources spend much of their time and energy making the best of what they have. They won't be spending much time dreaming for things they can never hope to purchase or achieve. However, a hospital, school board or micro-enterprise with highly innovative and energetic entrepreneurs, when properly supported, may have timely and relevant ideas about how technology and innovation can be applied in a networked community environment. These innovators can clear the path for others to follow.

Key Concept: *To become a networked community, organisations that have resources and the willpower can start the process, but it needs to be amplified by broader participation that leads to a culture of use and innovation in the entire community.*

Communities cannot work only with those who "have". We have discussed that communities cannot wait to satisfy all of the players; they should consider pilot projects and involve organisations with resources. However, at some point, communities will need to bring in other stakeholders who, for one reason or another, have not joined in the effort and are beginning to fall behind. Community organisations will not all be at the same level; encouraging innovation means educating decision-makers on what is possible and allow them to dream. Offering innovation in one or two schools while 10 others remain the same will not be well accepted by residents, since such actions could create a "have-not" environment. Yet, since partial development is better than no development at all and innovative applications are going to be developed according to the situation of each collaborator, the goal should be to involve as many stakeholders as possible in the long run to effect the sweeping changes needed. In fact, the networked community plays a role in educating all of its citizens and collaborators. Individual communities will never know from where new innovative ideas will come. A culture of use and innovation eventually requires participation by all.

Chapleau, Ontario, Canada, with a population of 2,700, has three school boards, one of which features a well supported information technology environment and plans to create a technology-intensive demonstration project. Introducing the intelligent community concept through an investment in an infrastructure demonstration project made by Bell Canada and Nortel Networks simply accelerated the plans of that school board in the community. They had spent the time dreaming and had many ideas for pilot projects to initiate change in the ways children were being educated. Identifying those collaborators who were ready, willing and able allowed the networked community to realise quick wins. Success breeds success. The ability to demonstrate action encouraged others to join.

Organisations with the time and money to dream, research, compare or implement projects are often found among colleges, universities, schools, research centres, large employers, or economic development organisations. If the ability to innovate is weak within these organisations, then a proper strategy would call for sending them to communities more advanced in the field, or to conferences to generate new ideas. Communities need to challenge local organisations to work on their behalf. The Department of Industry in the UK, in its report on innovation, identified the critical role that universities could play in process innovation, but reported little actual involvement by universities (Swann, 2002). In the age of digital networks, proximity to universities is not a necessary condition for development. Communities that see a need can seek out universities with special knowledge to help develop potential projects.

Edward deBono, recognised for his work on critical and lateral thinking, explained that working in a chaordic pattern (part chaos, part order), could lead to higher levels of innovation (deBono, 1988). The chaordic and lateral thinking approach pushes us to think outside the box and to look at approaches in several sectors. An example of this thinking can be found in *The Nature of Economies*, a book that describes how scientists are studying the workings of animals and plants for new innovation (Jacobs, 2000). Such industrious insects as the spider spin a strong web and, if their process could be replicated in an industrial setting, it could help revolutionize many industries. The point is that communities need to look at best practises in several sectors—sometimes beyond the normal thinking process—and find ways to apply these techniques to other sectors. If we want to increase the level of energy or output in the long run in networked communities, we need continuous innovation. We already know from science that, unless outside force is applied, the normal human response is the status quo—that silos specialising in specific functions tend to dominate.

Key Concept: *Communities need lateral thinkers to innovate and vertical thinkers to implement what they create. When lateral and vertical thinkers collaborate, the community benefits.*

Vertical thinkers take a reasoned view of their communities' situation and proceed logically to work toward solving problems, using probabilities and structured decision-making processes. According to deBono, this kind of thinking flows like a river along the most probable path. Lateral thinkers, on the other hand, explore different ways of looking at problems rather than accepting the most promising alternative; they will continue to seek innovative ways to turn problems into opportunities. As a result, networked communities need lateral thinkers to encourage an innovative environment, but they also need vertical thinkers to implement projects in an efficient and cost-effective manner.

MANAGING INNOVATION

The gap between developing and implementing creative ideas is one that most communities will need to bridge. Doing so includes removing impediments, but also distributing ideas throughout the community to prompt stakeholders into action. Organising community meetings to collect innovative ideas but not passing them on achieves nothing. Motivation requires understanding and excitement on the part of the doer. Therefore, vertical thinkers may need to meet the lateral thinkers to discuss details. Coming up with new ideas can be quite separate from implementing them since implementation requires technical know-how. Arriving at new ideas may come, for example, from looking at a video conference system being used in the health sector and figuring out how it can be used in the education sector. Technical knowledge is not sufficient to bring about new ideas, but entrepreneurs often need the network of technical specialists to implement an idea.

Another consideration is when and how often to launch innovations. Some communities feel more secure in working on fewer projects at any given time and want to minimize risks by using a traditional innovation process. They will delay a project to get more buy-in or to gain more extensive coverage. Risk tolerant communities tend to use the flexible model of innovation, or one that gets more innovation out of the gate sooner (Kotelnikov 2006), involving more players in several subcommittees to launch a larger number of innovations in the shortest possible timeframe. These approaches assume that the community will win some and lose some, but at the end of the day, their chances of winning are increased with more innovations rather than fewer. One option is to promote risk-taking with pilot projects, motivating stakeholders toward a continuous flow of innovations. The thinking behind this is that synergy is created when there is increased innovation, which spurs more interest, which in turn launches more innovation. This positive feedback loop represents a synergistic and flexible model of innovation.

Key Concept: *A winning strategy will be difficult to implement unless the leaders of the transformation effort recognise resistance to change and are ready to address it. Roadblocks include cost, uncommitted leaders, misunderstanding the vision, objections to networking, exclusive silos, and risk aversion.*

Vander Veen (2006) noted that communities are not going to benefit from technology unless people start doing things differently. Certain people and groups do not want certain activities to occur, either because those activities will alter an existing state, require them to perform more work, change existing transactional patterns, or decrease their authority. The key here is leadership and a commitment to change. Communities need to identify leaders in organisations who will not back out of deals because some people are pushing against it or are not happy. The community network can help support its partners by reminding one another of the benefits of the vision and the need to stay the course.

Learning to deal with resistance will be key in developing a culture of innovation. If resistors win, it sends a message that new ideas are not welcome. On the other hand, if several innovative approaches are launched and communicated, it will signal others to step forward with more ideas. Think of the smart card system. Many of the regions that have tried to implement them were faced with concerns over security, privacy, recordkeeping systems and liability. These matters have been so efficiently addressed in the small Baltic country of Estonia that some 1.1 of its 1.7 million citizens have adopted the electronic ID card promoted by the government. The card was first developed as a data security system to support safe e-commerce. Now this document provides visual identification and a legally valid digital signature for both civic and commercial transactions. The card can be used as a ticket on public transport, as a bank card and as an authorization card for online voting (Profiles of the ICF, 2008).

Since the end of the Cold War, Estonia has developed an international reputation as a state with a transparent government. In answer to a question put to the City Manager of Tallinn, Estonia, at the 2008 ICF conference, "Why do Estonians trust all this personal information being available on the Internet?" his reply was "Some 80% of all commercial transactions are now done in our country on the public Internet. If people find that they can trust the Internet as a way for them to safely do their banking, they will worry less about everything else" (Sepp, 2008). At the end of the day, an innovative project can easily be dismissed because enough barriers were erected by stakeholders who resist any form of change, even when these resistors are in the minority.

Generating and implementing ideas and commercializing innovation may be hampered by unpopular, possibly unworkable, policies and practises. As a result, leaders must also take stock of the community environment for innovation and take steps to remove impediments. Policies on intellectual property rights are an example, as are the policies of organisations toward allowing employees to network with peers in other firms. Many universities, as an example, discourage innovation commercialization by financially penalizing inventors. The result is that a number of professors wait until they are out in private sector to advance their ideas.

Canada's University of Waterloo recognised the importance of changing processes to cultivate an innovation economy. Several years ago, it allowed its researchers to own and bear the fruits of their research. A number of entreprencurial firms were formed, among them Research in Motion (RIM), the producer of the BlackBerry. Today, RIM employs a large proportion of the Waterloo workforce directly and indirectly. Its leaders are also encouraging the development of complementary firms and have helped to establish a new economy on which Waterloo can build its future (Archives of the ICF, 2007c).

Organisations face myriad barriers to innovation when it comes to resources, of which the most important appear to be costs, risk and the availability of financing (DTI, 2006). Most organisations may not have enough people, skills and knowledge to find innovative solutions to problems; they may not have the financial resources to carry out innovative ideas; or they may not have the time to pursue innovative solutions. A lack of resources promotes risk aversion. The networked community environment may make it easier for members to share information and resources to minimize these problems.

In sum, success in innovation will depend on the degree of entrepreneurial drive, the availability of investment capital, the effectiveness of information networks, support from educational institutions, and regional strengths and assets. These success factors can be harvested on a community-wide basis, but they will continue to be challenges because there are always un-covered areas, and sectors that are more difficult to finance.

EVALUATION OF INNOVATION

According to Jungmittag and Welfens (2006), innovation can be measured in terms of the input of capital and labour into technology projects, patents, and real expenditures for licences. For evaluating networked communities, these traditional measures must be complemented by measures that recognise the importance of discussion groups and places where ideas can be generated, discussed, shared and acted upon since they are critical to the development of an innovation culture. Evaluations should look at opportunities for clustering, strategies for forming new clusters and involvement in encouraging innovation. Finally, evaluators must identify barriers to innovation and how to remove them. Table 1 outlines potential tools for measuring innovation. Some of these may have already been linked to economic development.

Table 1. Innovation evaluation

Indicators	Possible approaches to measurement
Promoting growth in innovation through idea generation	Listing of opportunities outlined through a strategic planning process
	Growth in the number of ideas for new products and services
	Actions toward improvement in existing processes of local firms and organisations
	Number and type of citizens participating in idea generation and implementation
	Open innovation examples
Promoting growth in innovation through entrepreneurial drive	Increases in the number of commercial businesses resulting from new innovation
	Increases in the number of home-based businesses assisted by innovation efforts or as a result of ICT growth
	Increases in the use of ICT-related products and services to drive new business growth
	Increases in revenues stemming from ICT products and services
	Increases in the number of ICT-related businesses
	Sector transformations as a result of ICT innovations
Promoting innovation commercialization	Linking idea generators with implementers in number of cases
Growth in R&D	College and university IT-related research and support systems
	Collaborations between researchers and private sector
	Number of patents and new licenses
Promoting a good policy environment by removing barriers to innovation	Reducing red-tape
	Evaluating time to completion
	One-stop-shops where innovators obtain a spectrum of services
	Granting ownership rights to creators of innovation

CONCLUSION

For each community, innovation and creativity will lead to different outcomes depending on available infrastructure, knowledge and talent of professionals and volunteers. Attention was given in this chapter to creating a more diverse environment so that collaborative activity can spur innovation. Old models of innovation have not worked for most communities—as they have either relinquished the responsibility for innovation to a handful of companies with the resources to innovate, or have done very little, believing it to be in the purview of the private sector. Opportunities in value-added, technological advantages, or even break-through innovations could be realised if the right players were allowed to work together in the right environment.

The recent attention given to clustering to develop economies of scale and strategic advantage for regions has yielded enough benefit to make us believe that a multi-sectoral and multi-organisational network of innovators could also develop synergy and create economic development opportunities for communities. These groups could assemble in clusters, focused on issues that are not necessarily within their current business activity, but are of benefit to their community. Stakeholders rallying around a challenge to co-build economic foundations will be a priority among most networked communities, and this will be achieved by building a learning community, one that has established a culture of innovation that yields continuous benefits. Also worth investigating are open innovation environments where firms and organisations are encouraged to seek new sources of knowledge and ideas.

The authors agree with Hicks and Nivin (2000) that IT and related capital are capable of transforming entire national and global urban systems. It is incumbent on community leaders working with interested stakeholders to devise the unique strategies that will enable them to take advantage of opportunities and innovate.

REFERENCES

Abraham, J. L., & Knight, D. J. (2001) Strategic innovation: Leveraging creative action for more profitable growth. *Strategy & Leadership, 29*(1), 21-26.

Agres, C., Edberg, D. & Igbaria, M. (1998). Transformation to virtual societies: Forces and issues. *The Information Society, 14*, 71-82.

Antonelli, C. (2000). Collective knowledge communication and innovation: The evidence of technological districts. *Regional Studies, 34*(6), 535-547.

Archives of the ICF – The Intelligent Communities Forum (2007a). Evora, Portugal – Nomination submitted for the Intelligent Community of the Year Award. New York.

Archives of the ICF – The Intelligent Communities Forum (2007b). Sunderland, UK – Nomination submitted for the Intelligent Community of the Year Award. New York.

Archives of the ICF – The Intelligent Communities Forum (2007c). Waterloo, Ontario, Canada – Nomination submitted for the Intelligent Community of the Year Award. New York.

Archives of the ICF – The Intelligent Communities Forum (2005). Melbourne, Australia – Nomination submitted for the Intelligent Community of the Year Award. New York.

Archives of the ICF – The Intelligent Communities Forum (2004). Spokane, Washington, USA – Nomination submitted for the Intelligent Community of the Year Award. New York.

Archives of the ICF – The Intelligent Communities Forum (2002). LaGrange, Georgia, USA – Nomination submitted for the Intelligent Community of the Year Award. New York.

Birkinshaw, J., Bessant, J. & Delbridge, R. (2007). Finding, forming, and performing: Creating networks for discontinuous innovation. *California Management Review, 49*(3), 67-84.

Boekema, F., Morgan, K., Bakkers, S. & Rutten, R. (2000). Introduction to learning regions: A new issue for analysis? In F. Boekema, K. Morgan, S. Bakkers and R. Rutten (Eds.), *Knowledge, innovation and economic growth: The theory and practise of learning regions.* Cheltenham UK: Edward Elgar.

Carty, A. J. (1997). NRC: A model for bottom-up approach to innovation. *Canadian Journal of Regional Science, 20*(1-2), 277-278.

Chesbrough, H. W. & Appleyard, M. M. (2007). Open innovation and strategy. *California Management Review, 50*(1), 57-76.

Chakravorti, B. (2004). The new rules for bringing innovations to market. *Harvard Business Review, March 2004,* 59-67.

deBono, E. (1988), *Letters to thinkers: Further thoughts on lateral thinking.* London UK: Penguin Books.

DTI. (2006). *Innovation in the UK: Indicators and insights.* (2006, July). DTI Occasional Paper No. 6. Retrieved April 15, 2008, from http://www.berr.gov.uk/files/file31569.pdf

Fuller, J., Bartl, M., Ernst, H. & Muhlbacher, H. (2006). Community based innovation: ow to integrate members of virtual communities into new product development. *Electron Commerce Res.,* 6, 57-73.

Eggers, W. D. (2005). *Overcoming obstacles to technology-enabled transformation.* Retrieved December 1, 2007, from the Harvard University Government Network Web site: http://www.innovations.harvard.edu/showdoc.html?id=2592

Gillis, W., & McLellan, S. (1998). In J. Marsh and A. E. Grant. (Eds.), *Blue sky: Dreams and imagination in creating 21st century communication technology.* Commack NY: Nova Science Publishers Inc.

Gurstein, M. (2004). ICTs and local economic development: What do we know and where do we go? Presentation given at the IDRC/UNCDF/UNECA Workshop on ICTs and Local Governance, Addis Ababa, Ethiopia. Retrieved September 6, 2004, from http://www.idrc.ca/uploads/user-S/10908787151ICTs_&_Local_Economic_Development_M._Gurstein.ppt#269,17,Slide 17

Hicks, D. A. & Nivin, S. R. (2000, April). Beyond globalization: Localized returns to IT infrastructure investment. *Regional Studies, 34*(2), 115-127.

ICF – The Intelligent Communities Forum (2008a). *Community profile of Taillin, Estonia.* Retrieved June 5, 2008 from www.intelligentcommunity.org (Click on Events/Awards).

ICF – The Intelligent Communities Forum (2008b). *Community profile of Dundee, UK.* Retrieved June 5, 2008 from www.intelligentcommunity.org (Click on Events/Awards).

ICF – The Intelligent Communities Forum (2008). *Community profile of Tallinn, Estonia.* Retrieved June 5, 2008 from www.intelligentcommunity.org (Click on Events/Awards).

ICF – The Intelligent Communities Forum (2008b). *Community profile of Winston-Salem, USA.* Retrieved June 5, 2008 from www.intelligentcommunity.org (Click on Events/Awards).

Igbaria, M., Shayo, C. & Olfman, L. (1999). On becoming virtual: The driving forces and arrangements. Paper presented at the meeting of *SIGCPR,* New Orleans, LA, USA, 27-41. Available online from http://portal.acm.org/citation.cfm?id=299513.299610

Isaksen, A. (2001). Building regional innovation systems: Is endogenous industrial development possible in the global economy? *Canadian Journal of Regional Science, 24*(1), 101-120.

Jacobs, J. (2001). *The nature of economies.* East Mississauga, Ontario, Canada: Vintage Canada.

Jungmittag, A., & Welfens, P. J. (2006). *Telecommunication dynamics, output, and employment.* Bonn, Germany: Institute for the Study of Labor.

King, R. T. (1994, September 9). High-tech edge gives U.S. firms global lead in computer networks. *Wall Street Journal*, A1.

Kodama, M. (2000). Business innovation through strategic community management. *Strategic Change, 9*, 177-196.

Kotelnikov, V. (2006). *Innovation process: Traditional and new approaches.* Retrieved August 15, 2006, from http://www.1000ventures.com/business_guide/im_process_main.html

Meha, M. (2006). Growth by design: How good design drives company growth. *Ivey Business Journal, 70*(3), pp. 1-10.

One laptop per child. (2007). Retrieved December 5, 2007, from http://laptop.media.mit.edu/

Pôr, G., & van Bekkum, E. (2003), *E. innovation and communities of practises.* Retrieved November 21, 2007, from the Community Intelligence Web site: http://www.CommunityIntelligence.co.uk

Rosenfeld, S. A. (1997). Bringing business clusters into the mainstream of economic development. *European Planning Studies, 5*(3), 23.

Swann, P. G. (2002). *Innovative businesses and the science and technology base.* Report for the Department of Trade and Industry. Manchester University Business School. Manchester UK.

Sepp, T. (2008), *Tallinn, Estonia City Manager response to a question,* at the Intelligent Community Forum Conference, New York.

Tapscott, D. & Williams, A. D. (2008). *Wikinomics: How mass collaboration changes everything.* New York: Penguin Books.

Vander Veen, C. (2006). *The cost of static.* Retrieved July 10, 2008, from the Government Technology Web site: http://govtech.public-cio.com/story.print.php?id=99808

Westley, F., Zimmerman, B. & Quinn-Patton, M. (2006). *Getting to maybe: How the world is changed.* East Mississauga, Ontario, Canada: Random House Canada.

Zhuang, L. (1995). Bridging the gap between technology and business strategy. *Management Decision 33*(8), 13-21.

Chapter VII
Strategies for
Community Development

"ICTs will certainly change the way in which we socially interact. But whether these changes are for the better or for the worse depends on the overall structured framework and societal strategy within which these changes are taking place." (Simon, 2004, p. 492)

Overview: The transformational changes brought about by the Internet stimulate the planning of social and economic development in networked communities. This chapter will cover the following topics:

- The community and its economic and social development;
- The importance of development strategies and theory:

- ° An introduction to types of strategies and theories
- ° The influence of ICTs on community development
- Strategic planning in a community:
  - ° An outline of strategic planning
  - ° The role of ICTs in the strategic planning process;
  - ° Examples of ICT community development opportunities;
- Key success factors in implementing a community development strategy;
- Evaluation and measurement of community development.

The strategic inclusion of information and communication technologies (ICTs) within community development plans can be compared to organisational re-engineering. They both require effort to become more efficient, and novel perspectives are needed to develop new economic values. Within the broad context of the human condition, they both involve understanding what people need and want, how inequities can be bridged, and how to minimise the negative impact of making changes. A lesser approach runs the risk of communities resolving one challenge only to see new problems spring up. As was aptly put by Matthiessen, Schwarz and Find (2006), "[Creation] of wealth in an economy of ideas is derived far less than we imagine from the technological hardware and infrastructure. Rather it is dependent upon the capacity to continually create content or new forms of widely distributed knowledge for which there is a need to invest in human capital throughout the economy" (p. 15).

Information technology has acted as an important trigger for the development of business process re-engineering in firms (Attaran, 2004), and ICTs have had a similar impact on communities—they expand the need to keep up with global changes. Innovative use of IT has led many firms to develop ways of more effectively coordinating their activities and at lower costs, thus giving them strategic advantages. Similarly, communities around the world are paying attention to the Internet economy, realising that it is a source of opportunity that also presents many challenges. Firms and communities are often linked; as more businesses participate in work that is network-intensive, local communities have the opportunity to learn how they too can grow and change as a result of being networked, or at least learn to be a supportive ally.

DEFINING COMMUNITY DEVELOPMENT

Key Concept: *The most sustainable forms of development are based on steps that members of local communities can take to solve their own problems.*

We live in an era of "locality-based development" or "self-development", phrases used by McGuire, Rubin, Agranoff and Richards (1994) to frame one of the basic elements of community capacity building. They define capacity in terms of the level of citizen participation and leadership, infrastructures and development instruments (the tools used to attract investment). Unfortunately, many communities still hope for major government intervention, or the appearance of a local saviour. The authors believe that economic and social development cannot be left solely to the private sector or government. The private sector does many things well, but pursuing a social mission isn't one of them (Surman, 2000). The successful networked communities of the 21st century will be those that rise to the challenge of "self-development". As "locality–based organizations" with the infrastructure for interconnecting all local players, networked communities are in an advantageous position to bring both profit and non-profit sectors to the table in search of a total solution that includes social mission as integral to economic development.

Many communities recognise the importance of community development and make it a planned activity. Staff members located in economic development offices often report to municipalities, regional governments or stand-alone corporations. These local structures become players in the regional and national development agendas that roll out top-down and bottom-up instruments intended to create wealth and improve the quality of life. The bottom-up approach lends itself most easily to local adaptation. The community can "invoke the positive features of daily activities as a starting point for setting objectives" (Cam, 2004). When invited to collaborate, multi-organisational and multi-sectoral partners can be included, and citizens from all walks of life can be drawn into the process of planning the future development of their communities. These locally initiated self-help processes will more often reflect the better practices for sustainable community development.

One must take care in any discussion of sustainability. Sustainability is often considered the main reason for undertaking a community development plan, yet Voinov and Farley (2007) caution that sustainability is the "maintenance of a certain level of activity into an indefinite future" and could inhibit future changes that should be made but could not have been anticipated (p. 104). For those communities looking for transformational change, growth and innovation, a dynamic version of sustainability is required that allows for change while preserving many of the value-adding activities that firms and organisations will be offering along the way.

The standard instruments of economic and social development are entrepreneurship, capital investment, growth of small and medium enterprises (SME), a good education system, and personal and professional development programs. Each helps to foster an environment where individuals can better themselves physically, spiritually and economically. These instruments can be complemented by the role of a facilitator, who promotes local economic development by engaging with the citizens, stakeholders and major organisations of the community. Through data collection, planning and marketing, along with support for an environment conducive to development, such facilitators can hope to attract those new businesses and investments that will serve the community's unique needs.

Some community residents may have an aversion to the idea of development. Having seen the problems experienced by other communities, they are committed to avoiding the kinds of growth that create social and environmental problems that make things worse rather than better. These individuals will not be that interested in seeing the shopping centers going up on the edge of town and the big box stores paving over the green space with parking lots. But those same people may be quite content to see the community join the online economy as a way to contribute locally produced knowledge-based goods, and to use telecommunications as a way to reduce traffic congestion and minimise the environmental impact of travel. The term "Smart Growth" is a catch phrase commonly used today. The following definition is provided by the city of San Diego (2003): "Smart growth is a compact, efficient and environmentally sensitive pattern of development that provides people with additional travel, housing, and employment choices by focusing future growth away from rural areas and closer to existing and planned job centres and public facilities." Many smart growth initiatives focus on ICTs because they provide the freedom to explore ways to reduce environmental impact and increase choices for users.

Successful communities will be those demonstrating both economic and social development. Economic development's goal is to create wealth by promoting an environment that stimulates job creation and the social benefits that result from high levels of productivity. At the same time, social and cultural programming is of vital importance. Success in economic development is most frequently measured by the size and prosperity of the local economy, and the evidence is jobs and wages. The number of jobs created by industry is based on spending within the community, the ability to replace imports through local provision and the ability to sell to the outside world, drawing in externally-based dollars (Scorsone, 2002). It is also clear, however, that a community's economic development is closely tied to its social development. Corporations look for more than economic or financial benefit; they must have a community where their employees want to live.

Chapter I on the Network Society emphasises that a viable community is based on local-global links that create synergies by sharing resources and ideas. This vision is achieved through a balance of economic and social development priorities. As in any organisation, a community's most valuable assets are its people, and the human dimension must be considered a vital part of the future planning process.

DEVELOPMENT STRATEGIES AND THEORIES

Key Concept: *Rarely are communities blessed with abundant natural resources from which economic growth and job creation flow automatically. More often, community leaders must take matters into their own hands to identify local assets and partnerships that capitalize on community strengths.*

Development strategy can either be emerging or planned. Silicon Valley is an example of an emerging, almost accidental, strategy of growth that followed the introduction of new manufacturing technologies and software in the age of the computer. This California region was among the few areas uniquely positioned to launch an entirely new high-growth industry. The region boasted an outstanding university, Stanford, that itself benefited from the research and development work of Fairchild Semiconductor mass producing integrated circuits, Intel Corporation producing DRAM chips, Apple computer building microcomputers, Sun Microsystems creating servers and graphic workstations, Cisco Systems producing network gear, Netscape Communications introducing a user-friendly browser, and Yahoo aggregating Web sites.

It was fortunate that the rise of Silicon Valley found readily available real estate. Stanford University leased to the growing high-tech industry a considerable portion of its 8,000 acres of former fruit orchards south of San Francisco. The Stanford Industrial Park in Palo Alto, California, is thought to be one of the most successful research and development complexes in the world. Bob Metcalfe's 1998 quote that "Silicon Valley is the only place on Earth not trying to figure out how to become Silicon Valley", is apt in this discussion (Metcalfe, 1998).

Although Palo Alto represents a classic "emerging" strategy, in that no amount of advance planning could have anticipated what actually happened, a great deal of thought was invested as Silicon Valley began to take on its mythic shape. Few communities or regions are as fortunate to inherit economic success from an emerging strategy, or a *laissez-faire* environment that can take care of itself; most will require a strategy based on collaborative efforts of local or regional stakeholders. Paul Romer, economics professor at Stanford University, and an expert on economic growth, stated: "The problem with the classical description of *laissez-faire* is its suggestion that the best of all possible arrangements for economic affairs has already been discovered and that it requires no collective action. The lesson from economic growth is that collective action is very important and that everything, including institutions, can always be improved" (Romer, 1993, p. 388).

Romer, an advocate of endogenous growth or new growth theory, believes that "technological advances come from things that people do" (Romer, 1994, p. 12). The idea is that economic growth is an endogenous outcome of an economic system, not the result of forces that impinge from the outside. Growth in any given community will be driven by local or regional change from players who share a vision and create a sense of urgency for change.

Romer's assertions are supported by Cortright's (2001) paper on New Growth Theory, which illustrates ways communities or regions have collaborated in building the knowledge economy. Cortright notes that the technology economies are characterised by increasing returns, and they drive growth because ideas can be infinitely shared, re-used and accumulated without limit (p. 2). Traditional economic models, on the other hand, are plagued by the laws of diminishing returns. Capital and raw resources are used with increasing efficiency, which diminishes the need for human resources. Eventually production decreases as needs are satisfied and technologies change.

New growth theory experts suggest that economic strategies need to focus on creating new knowledge in all segments of the economy and society. All workers need to participate in creating innovations, and a knowledge-based growth can give rise to a self-reinforcing cycle leading to more growth (Cortright, 2001, p. 25). The City of Sunderland, UK, is an example of a strategy of transformation becoming a critical success factor in achieving digital-age prosperity. As mentioned in Chapter VI, this community possessed few natural information technology resources. Yet, through public-private participation and a sense of urgency, it was able to turn its economy around. In the 1980s, the unemployment rate exceeded 30%, but by 2003, the unemployment rate was down to 4%, and the city was ranked as one of the top five most competitive business locations in the UK (Archives of the ICF, 2005).

New growth theory was demonstrated by Sunderland, whose citizens took matters into their own hands to turn their economy around. They employed new economy tools and worked with their assets to create new opportunities and attract new types of business activity into their region.

ICT AND ECONOMIC DEVELOPMENT

Key Concept: *The constraints of time and distance have been relaxed by the Internet and broadband communication applications that enable local and distant collaborators to connect at a moment's notice. This development has changed the mindset of citizens on the future of their local communities.*

Less than a decade ago, proponents of economic development were focused on physical assets. Communities in Canada and the U.S. were developing business parks and analyzing the cost of locating investment in localities as strategies for attracting new plants and creating new jobs. The advent of ICTs has changed that emphasis because the new multimedia technologies and related networks are allowing communities to think differently about development, to visualise and plan for transformational change or incremental change, depending on their circumstances. Having ICT capability allows communities to sell other types of resources—knowledge-based resources—and promotions and marketing can be built around services that transcend geographical boundaries. ICTs create the condition for communities thinking about themselves differently, not just as a place but where their rightful place is in an interconnected world where information services hold value equal to the production of material goods.

In the *Age of Unreason*, Charles Handy (1990) wrote about upside-down thinking—the ability that Einstein, Copernicus and Galileo exhibited in coming up with new ways of thinking about familiar things. The networked economy is providing opportunities for this same upside-down thinking that that community leaders are hoping will lead to important gains in both economic and social development.

Networked communities are the advance guard of a large-scale movement toward using knowledge for the betterment of peoples' lives. Communities are installing high-speed telecommunication facilities with the idea of stimulating economic development and improving quality of life, and there is evidence that such results are being achieved. Sunderland (UK) and Spokane (Washington, U.S.) are just two examples of many cited by the ICF and discussed by the authors in Chapter V on innovation. The authors believe there will be even greater opportunities and results with the advent of broadband; once ubiquitous networks are a practical reality and can be accessed at any time for any reason, people begin to see and experience their potential.

When taught how to use ICTs and provided with useful applications, ordinary citizens will invent innovative ways to meet the challenges of day-to-day life. They may come upon these opportunities by applying patterns tested elsewhere, or they may create new applications that they have tried out at home and, finding their efforts successful, will share their creations more broadly. By exploring either path, people will be self-creators of economic and social development using the technologies at hand.

As communities build networks of institutional and personal partnerships around an efficient infrastructure and functional applications, they also develop the kind of social cohesion and cooperation that becomes the basis for community re-engineering. It is easy to see how established sectors will be, and must be, overhauled and improved as process and product innovations appear locally. For example, new medical and scientific advancements present opportunities to stimulate local enterprises related to DNA research, wireless technologies, home-based tele-health and expert systems, among many others. These opportunities often reveal themselves when organisations and individuals come together to review what others are doing and to think about possibilities within the local community. This planning begins by researching what is possible, dreaming about new ways of doing things and setting out to make needed changes.

ICT DEVELOPMENT OPPORTUNITIES

Key Concept: *Access to broadband communication networks and tools of digital creation and distribution can help communities think differently about their approach to community development. Establishing common cause and an attitude of continuous learning is more easily formed in this context.*

Communities are historically self-defined and been defined by others in terms of their natural resources. For example, a mining town would attract mining workers and mining suppliers who would work hard physically and whose entertainment included extreme sports and adventure. Such communities could only offer the essentials to their citizens, but transport and trade were profitable ventures. In modern times, telecom technologies, the networked economy and global outsourcing have changed the pace, character and opportunities available within communities, and they define themselves differently. Towns that were solely focused on mining are more likely today to be more diversified, needing to develop strengths in other fields and offer a greater variety of jobs for local residents. Local antique shops, flea market sellers, artists and craftsmen can cluster their wares and sell online, or use the Internet to attract the public to their local shows. Adults as well as younger students can join universities located anywhere around the world, completing much of their formal education without leaving home. Such a situation can level the playing field for relatively disadvantaged communities by providing access to jobs and resources not previously available. However, it also signals the need to re-think social and economic structures.

Communities can sometimes meet citizens' needs in unconventional ways using ICTs. Places in Japan have for many years been offering skiing and golfing experiences through virtual reality (VR) centres. These types of off-line innovations are now being moved onto the Internet. The Japanese like communal experience, and the local VR centres address the people's need for exercise and recreation while accommodating to the country's premium on physical space. In the future, entirely new industries will emerge when programmes devised to meet local needs in a single market are extended to communities of other users around the world. Gaming is a good example of a form of local recreation—even education—that has been brought online to allow players in local, regional and international communities to participate.

Another example is auctioneering. eBay.com is so successful in the computer-mediated auction business that hardly anyone is sceptical when the company refers to itself as the "world's online marketplace". Local auctions seem to be popular the world over; thus, it is not surprising that someone would come up with the idea of putting auctions online. That person was Pierre Omidyar, a French-born Iranian computer programmer working in San Jose, California, who wrote the code for the Auction Web service that later became eBay (eBay, 2008).

As the transactional capabilities of telecommunication networks have become more facile, the computer–mediated communities of today, sometimes called online or virtual communities, have a lot more in common with physical communities. Renninger and Schumar (2002) explored these similarities, and some important differences, in their book *Building Virtual Communities: Learning and Change in Cyberspace*. They concluded that there were several defining elements that characterised computer-mediated communities. There was always a core group of members or users who participated actively and regularly over a period of time. The means for identifying areas of common interest were easily established and embellished. New members were given information, feedback, advice and support in ways that demonstrated their participation was appreciated. Even when participants' true identities could not always be revealed, an acceptable level of trust was present. And there was a physical infrastructure they shared in common that supported and sustained the purposes that held those communities together.

These online communities are all subsets and sub-subsets of physical communities, rather like communities within communities. For this reason, they are commonly referred to as "communities of practice". They consist of people from any place who share a concern, a set of problems or a passion about a topic who are using computers and the Internet as an additional medium of engagement. They form their own social structures and establish their own rules of discourse, while deepening their experience, knowledge and expertise as they participate (Wenger, et al., 2002). Individual members can and do participate in more than one of these online communities of practice at the same time. With familiarity and frequency of participation, the need to make a distinction between physical and virtual, between off-line and online, disappears.

While one would suppose that a new understanding of community is being created, a set definition continues to escape us as our understanding of ourselves within the context of community continues to evolve. In the act of digital capture, processing, storage, retrieval and distribution, using electronic/photonic networks for instant interconnection with others around the world, many of the age-old constants of time, speed, place, location, distance, language, and culture are fading as factors of constraint. Figuring all this out and accommodating to the reality of it can be quite a challenge in the one-industry towns that once had a set identity, and now don't. Suffering most will be the larger number of residents who have no idea what the knowledge economy is, and even less an idea about how to embrace it.

Communities undergoing change have no choice but to engage in re-education, to become communities of learning and of self-development. This change process extends over time, but both physical and electronic networks can help accelerate matters. Stewards of these communities can ease the transition by creating new social compacts between non-profit organisations and private and commercial sectors. Such collaborative networks permit a different kind of thinking about the larger purposes of the member organisations and the way they use their human resources. This upside-down thinking will stimulate opportunities for strengthening the economic as well as social fabric of communities.

The new economy requires radically different strategies for success, away from competition to co-opetition. "Today's firms have the ability to influence what that future will be like. Instead of accepting what is, they can ask 'What game would I like to play?'" (Nalebuff & Brandenburger, 1997, p. 29). According to Nalebuff and Brandenburger, we are in an era where collaborative competition is both needed and possible, where firms and organisations can view each other as "complementors" rather than competitors. In their role as complementary organisations, firms can seek to enlarge the pie, rather than find ways to subdivide the existing pie (Yoffie & Kwak, 2006). In the ongoing partnerships that must occur in a knowledge economy, communities have new opportunities to seek clusters of strength and gain economies of scope based on the local, regional and network relationships they have developed. And they will need to be in perpetual learning mode to be successful at it.

In service to their organisations and communities, chief information officers (CIOs) and other technology managers will continue to play the traditional roles of automating back office functions, supporting office routines, providing inventory control, training network users, and adding efficiencies and cost-savings through upgrades, purchases and acquisitions. But there are other ways IT can be a transition point for institutions. While supporting ongoing projects, these offices will be evolving into self-learning and teaching units for the whole organization. IT managers are the ones seeking faster, more efficient ways of doing things. There will now be a higher level of expectation for IT staff; they will not only be the outsourcers and integrators of products and services; they will suggest how organisations and communities might develop new products and services in collaboration with others, and they will be teaching those involved how to make it happen with the tools at hand.

Officials of the non-profit organisation OneCleveland, which installed a fiber network encircling much of the City of Cleveland and surrounding suburbs, argue convincingly that a shared community platform is the best way to cost effectively improve access to educational and workforce development in their region. OneCleveland and its partners have connected more than 1,500 sites in 18 counties, including schools, libraries, higher education institutions, hospitals, government offices, and arts and cultural organisations. Even though Cleveland was a "rust belt" remnant of once-thriving steel manufacturing and automobile assembly plants along the southern edge of Lake Erie, its proponents believe that continuous infrastructure improvements and multi-sector collaboration will lead to positive synergies. Information technologies have been introduced into almost every facet of community life in the region (Archives of the ICF, 2006a).

From a resource-based perspective, developing new virtual organisations creates strategic advantages. Communities can use these multi-sectoral networks to identify core competencies within the region and plan for the kinds of clustering that can create development opportunities. Existing economic players will hopefully be able to grow their current operations. External attraction programs will identify potential new projects from outside that might be brought in. These projects can bring new resources, including investors and franchises. The multiplier effect of a single cluster can be significant. An in-depth assessment of these opportunities is best achieved through community strategic planning.

STRATEGIC PLANNING

Key Concept: *Both internal and external factors will affect community strategic planning and development. Given the openness of modern communities, fresh perspectives from both inside and outside the community will promote adaptive decision-making.*

Strategic planning is integral to developing a successful collaborative model for a networked community. McGuire et al (1994) researched small, non-metropolitan communities and concluded that those communities who implemented a strategic planning process possessed higher levels of development capacity than those who did not.

Tianjin, China, for example, saw an increase of 36% in its high-technology industry output within one year following adoption of the "informatisation" plan. Electronics and information manufacturing industries saw an increase of 38% in 2004 over the previous year, and exports increased by 52% (Archives of the ICF, 2006f).

According to McGuire and his colleagues, who examined the ways smaller communities were building development capacity, the more successful communities had greater knowledge of their internal capacities and saw the opportunities stemming from the international environment. The following sections on external and internal analysis are meant to provide a bird's eye view of this process.

Outward (External) Analysis. Developing a strategic plan requires specific steps. To begin, community leaders normally consider various vision and mission statements based on their knowledge of existing community capabilities and local-global opportunities. This leads to an external environmental analysis, including a review of past and current events outside the community that could potentially affect the long-term health of the community. Global trends and strategies of competing communities and regions are reviewed. Outside expertise may be required to gain a better understanding of these issues, and to help in devising a plan. Ashley and Morrison (1997) recommend an exhaustive external analysis: a scan of the regional, national and global government policies, economic structures, technologies, social and cultural dimensions, and comparative studies of competing players. In an ICT-focused strategy, communities performing this analysis should attend to the following:

- Changes in the political environment, including new government policies that make investment easier or more difficult, such as regulations that could hamper the development of broadband or content. Some states in the U.S. have discouraged investment in broadband infrastructure by municipal governments, arguing that tax dollars should not be used to compete with private enterprise.
- Changes in the economic environment that could trigger changes in investment. For example, economic downsizing could motivate transformational changes, or it could demotivate change as people become entrenched and focused on protecting the community's wealth and jobs. Similarly, growth could encourage collaborators and stakeholders to seek online solutions, or it may distract them as they attend to the pressing negative consequences of growth such as rising housing prices and increasing pollution.
- Changes in the social and cultural fabric of society could have a large impact on the future of the community. Demographics are a good example. The average age of the population, immigration, changes in the productive activities

of residents based on technological breakthroughs and purchasing patterns may push the community to be more or less involved in developing ICT applications. An aging workforce may present problems of technology adoption, whereas a younger population may demand more ICT services.

- Changes in technology. Opportunities for bringing new devices to various segments of society, upgrading of telecommunication infrastructures, testing or piloting of new innovations and trends in robotics may offer competitive advantages. When some communities introduce cellular service, they force others around them to demand a similar service to meet resident needs. Technology is sometimes used as a way to draw in users.

- Changes in ecology and the environment. The reality of global warming and the energy crisis are pushing some communities to use ICTs to advise residents of dangerous situations and to enlist them into collecting relevant data for analysis (on water quality, storms, accidents, hazard areas, and so forth); or to decrease travel, through the adoption of tele-work.

- Changes in the activities of competitors including attraction campaigns that could encourage local residents and firms to leave the community. New organisational processes and the need for efficient decision-making in organisations may promote investment in ICT solutions. University campuses in North America are competing to attract students by wiring dorms with high speed networks. Communities around the world are advertising their high-speed capacities to attract new IT investments.

- Changes in the activities of suppliers, buyers or distributors—including moves to acquire or vertically integrate activities that could impact local firms, or product substitutions that erode markets away from goods produced locally. When the majority of the business community automated inventory systems many years ago, communities who were not digitally connected lost small businesses that were required by a large client or supplier to automate their systems. ICT availability became a location incentive. Devising collaborative strategies that minimise negative impacts and maximise opportunities is critical. Among these strategies are clustering and common purchasing/selling that can be accomplished through ICT solutions and networking.

Internal Analysis. Another step in the strategic plan is the internal analysis that includes a review of core capabilities and local resources that may be useful in developing a new online economy. The internal environment is not always evident to the citizens living in the community—knowledge can hinder discovery. Knoblick and Oellinger (2006) described this phenomenon as follows: "[E]xisting knowledge can prevent a person from creatively defining where the solution to a problem might lie" (p. 41). Residents may be focused and specialised in their work; they may ignore important infrastructures or inventories that could spur new industry development. Innovative thinking is often shelved or discouraged by the negative attitude of "we tried it in the past and failed". Upside-down thinking skills could help the community to identify new opportunities, and among those individuals useful in this exercise are government staff, researchers from other regions, specialised consultants and the IT/CIO offices from within the region (Albert, 2007).

This process should not fail to involve local citizens in decision-making as well. As mentioned by Cam (2004), "the development of built environment has conventionally been and should always be viewed as being initiated, developed, and occupied and used by people". When citizens play an active role at the early stages, the community is better able to bridge "any gaps that occur between lifestyle and sustainability" (p. 64). Internal analysis includes a review of infrastructure, capital and human resources available in the community. Networked community leaders need to consider:

- Land, buildings, natural resources and human resources. Only through collaborative activities and a thorough understanding of resources and their capabilities can communities find new opportunities that will lead to economic development. Preparing a comprehensive up-to-date inventory via a collaborative partnership among community stakeholders and making the information widely available online is one of the strategies available to networked communities. There are examples where communities have transformed old buildings into "smart" structures equipped with the latest technology, with the salutary effect of attracting technology firms into an incubator-style facility.
  In planning a new university in a Northern Ontario region, a skills inventory was performed. Residents were astounded by the number of Ph.D. graduates and highly experienced master's level graduates who were interested in teaching full- or part-time in the region. Smaller communities find pearls in their own backyard when they look for them. Individuals with skills outside the mainstream of the community's economy can help to spur entirely new industries. Skills inventories are not only useful for planning purposes, but can be advertised online to attract new investment.
- Clustering opportunities: the business world is increasingly using cooperative competition (co-opetition) and clustering as a way to improve value-chain activities and expand market potential. For example, individual blueberry producers in Quebec compete regionally but collaborate when marketing internationally. Italy is also the real expert in "clustering", with entire towns specialised around a product with the result of becoming the leading world provider for certain types of goods. Community developers can encourage clustering, and the online environment can foster networks for reaching

beyond the town and creating a shared environment for marketing and planning. Depending on the project or the product, communities may not be able
to develop economies of scale to compete in the global economy, or may lack
the support organisations to form a proper cluster. Collaboration with other
regions, using ICT technologies, may eliminate these problems.

Networks also allow firms to explore new relationships with customers, suppliers, substitutors and complementors (Brandenburger & Nalebuff, 1995).
These new relationship could be directly in the firm's backyard or anywhere
on the globe.

- Import replacement: communities purchase products internationally but seldom
  consider whether these products and services might be manufactured or made
  available locally through a subsidiary. Corporations have often brought the
  purchasing process far away from smaller and more remote communities, making it difficult for local players to compete for supply contracts. Collaboration
  among regional and/or local companies can allow firms in remote communities to strike strategic alliances and improve their capacity to sell through the
  use of ICTs. They can also track products that they purchase themselves and
  potential new sources of suppliers that may be attracted locally.

- Growth of firms: monitoring firm or sector growth can help economic development professionals find new opportunities for supporting industries, creating
  a collaborative environment within the community to promote clustering and
  new network development.

- Entrepreneurship: in encouraging an investment-friendly climate, community
  leaders are always on the lookout for entrepreneurs. The networked community working collaboratively will uncover numerous knowledge workers
  who will fit the description of innovators. Many of these people will be small
  scale entrepreneurs who have an "idea," but not the skills to prepare a plan or
  negotiate financing. Many are disadvantaged by the investment community,
  which tends to favour existing or proven firms. Risk capital is difficult to
  obtain, and the situation is worsened when the entrepreneur has few personal
  assets, which is often the case. The ICT network can provide training material for new entrepreneurs, access to online capital investor networks, online
  mentors and more.

Entrepreneurs need ample support. It may involve helping to reduce costs
(such as in incubator facilities, cooperative marketing, and collaborative
purchasing), concretizing plans (business planning, developing an Internet
presence), offering access to loaning circles or angel capital, support during
the first few years of business development, and providing training. Access
to high speed telecommunication and supportive computing and software can
bring about unimagined opportunities. The community should address how it

can encourage a more fertile entrepreneurial environment and how the needs of independent innovators can be met online.

- Tourism: every community has assets, whether physical, knowledge-based, cultural or historical that could be developed into a tourist attraction. An audit of the history of the community (significant events or key figures) reveals, for example, cultural differences that could be demonstrated through experiences and demonstrations; artistic communities that can perform or host craft shows and exhibitions; special environmental features that offer sightseeing, sports and recreation activities; and packaged tours, educational activities, and conferences and festivals. Each community must find ways to promote itself regionally, even internationally, and leverage its assets through collaborative activity. Using the Internet as a strong ally, local networks can embellish the appeal of local products and services, and ensure that the message is forwarded to the right consumers.

- Social development: growth in health, education and other social programs can bring long-term jobs to communities and help build an environment conducive to investment. Strategic planning exercises related to tele-health, e-learning, digital libraries and museums, and online recreation are all possibilities in the quest to reveal the strengths of communities. Included in this analysis will be the tools available to make these projects happen, an awareness of the resistance that may develop and ways of countering it.

A properly structured strategy takes into account organisational capabilities. These include infrastructure and hard assets, human skills and knowledge, and soft assets such as image, reputation and patents. However, the strategic plan is only one of the instruments available to promote ICT in communities. Jordana, Fernandez and Sancho (2005) identified other policy instruments utilised in Spain that included government planning, sector-focused programs, inter-sector programs, single action, organisational action, support to external actions, pilot projects, and coordinated action (pp. 341-351).

To amass the information discussed above at a community level requires a tremendous amount of knowledge about geography, natural resources (farming, mining, forestry, energy, bio-industries and value-added production), manufacturing capabilities, supply industries, retail, tourism, and real estate. Since a community is made up of a number of public and private sector organisations, the resources are normally present to identify opportunities in all sectors. Through collaboration, this mammoth task becomes manageable, supported by extensive use of the digital search, storage and distribution capability.

External and internal analyses allow the community to identify opportunities and devise a strategy based on its core competencies and differentiation (see Appendix to this chapter). The discussion that follows gives an overview of typical economic development functions in private and public sector development, and proposes activities that can spur economic and social development. ICTs can provide many value-added and complementary services to normal economic and social development activities.

TAKING ADVANTAGE OF PRIVATE AND PUBLIC SECTOR OPPORTUNITIES

The networked community planning effort should support initiatives in both the public and private sectors, and bring key players in both sectors to the table for discussions that could lead to synergistic activities.

Private Sector Development. Generating new opportunities for entrepreneurship is a task ready-made for the Internet. Examples include online support services to those who use the Internet—personal training, online sharing of expertise and resources, online mentor programs, online access to financial resources. Potential entrepreneurs can access think blogs, discussion groups, online sales, online support services, services in data management and security, software sharing, entertainment products, and publications. Ideas and initiatives flow when the users understand the technology and feel comfortable working in the new online environment. Young people tend to have a greater level of comfort in cyberspace, but other segments of the community can also function effectively. The adult community is where experience and capital will be found to increase the likelihood of sustainable innovations.

The basic skills needed to bring innovative ideas to commercial reality are already present in most communities. The most likely people to bring the entrepreneur's inventions to the marketplace can be found in retail, warehousing, brokerages, hospital management, food services, recreation centres, and architectural and design shops where they manage innovation. Private sector development can also come from clustering, and collaboration and competition—the so-called co-opetition. The community can encourage groups to come together to sell products online and access larger global markets.

Taipei, Taiwan, built three technology parks, and these were combined to form the "Taipei Technology Corridor" (their version of Silicon Valley). There are more than 2,203 companies located in the first two parks employing more than 85,400 knowledge workers. Taipei is creating a comparative and competitive advantage based on its knowledge workers as a result of that community's vision to aggregate knowledge workers into a broadband park. The third technology park still in process will include housing, culture, education and logistics, providing a clustering effect and a quality of life environment for workers and companies. This complex, called Neihu Technology Park, is a collaboration between government and the private sector. (Archives of the ICF, 2006e)

In certain communities, consultants, engineers, and architects have joined forces to bid on higher level projects around the world. Clustering can occur over a wide geographical region, involving diverse competencies and expertise and increasing the attractiveness of the resources found in local communities. Grouping these competitive capabilities can stimulate future activity and allow the participating firms to build networks that can often be used for other unforeseen purposes. Clusters encourage collaboration among firms in the same sector, especially in seeking markets outside the region.

Ichikawa, Japan, established an "intelligent building" in 2002, bringing together information-related enterprises, as well as the IT section of the city administration. Citizens, enterprises and universities draw on the resources of this plaza to participate in e-government programs and to patronize local businesses. The plaza is also a regional data centre for surrounding municipalities, non-profit organisations, resident's associations and SOHO (small office/home office) owners. It also hosts personal computers for public use (Archives of the ICF, 2006b).

An example of investment data, including resource accessibility, made available online can be found in the databases of the Government of Ontario, Canada. One of their ministries hosts digital collections of documents relating to land, buildings and human resources that are continually upgraded by local communities. This information resource allows international location experts to evaluate resources and contact the relevant communities to explore investment opportunities. Such a site allows municipalities to put their best foot forward in describing the assets and reasons why investors should choose to visit them. Some communities have chosen to pre-equip buildings as a way to attract investment. Increasingly, communities are also performing skills inventories to identify the knowledge base available. These skills inventories are allowing communities and regions to strategize around best use of resources, as portrayed in the following examples:

The Government of New Brunswick, Canada, realised more than a decade ago that they could use their remoteness as an asset. They sought to overcome problems of location with investments in broadband. Facing a depressed economy and loss of jobs, they tried some upside down thinking and began to sell their reasonably-priced and often bilingual human resources for call centre operations. Eventually, the little eastern-Canadian province built an industry around call centres. The increased skills and knowledge gained by residents enabled them to do other kinds of work online and offline. New Brunswick was able to diversify its economy while increasing skills (Larner, 2002).

Another interesting illustration of the value of a skills inventory is the Eastserve Project of Manchester, UK, where a report identified that more than 40% of businesses could not recruit locally. The economic development strategy of the EastServe Project challenged local residents to take advantage of an opportunity provided them to attend ICT-related courses at the local Higher Education College and nine local community online centres. Understanding industry needs and providing training can go a long way toward creating new opportunities. (Archives of the ICF, 2006c)

Cooperation in advertising and packaging can also serve community development goals. Private companies and non-profit organisations have collaborated on combined Web sites or portals. Sharing marketing costs and pooling finances for advertising campaigns can sometimes benefit the community as a whole. The City of Sudbury, Canada, encouraged tourist operators to work together to package their products into a series of "get-aways" that resulted in an increase in tourist business within the community.

Public Sector Development. Government and non-profit organisations have regular opportunities to demonstrate their capabilities to take on new projects. These projects often come with soft-funding, temporary staffing and limited operating budgets, a common situation in the territory of volunteer work and government service. These organisations are overloaded with everyday demands and it becomes difficult for them to respond to anything new. Knowing that there are ways to involve other community players in the work that needs to be done can sometimes give encouragement. Access to an online network of partners can lead to collaborative working arrangements that draw on other agencies and citizens as the need arises.

Government departments and programs are under continuous scrutiny, requiring evaluation and marketing to justify their existence. Again, collaborative networks can help to access the human resources and political power needed to measure viability of current programs and make appeals for continued support. Such networks can also help identify other programs of interest that could be attracted to the community. Just as with private sector attraction programs, government departments and non-profit organisations need sound business cases, a demonstration of local leadership and political will to attract new public investment.

In networked community environments, private and public organisations will begin to share the cost and management of broadband infrastructures, and collaboratively develop applications for those networks. Examples the authors have seen include the provision of "wireless hotspots" for Internet connectivity within buildings, and extending broadband wireless, such as WiMax high speed Internet, throughout urban areas. Because non-profits and government organisations, as well as private and commercial businesses, find instant communications a basic necessity, online services should be viewed as a basic utility that is financially supported by everyone. Web portals may be managed by one sector or the other, but in practice, the software and network gear is often provided by the private sector and managed by public and private sector organisations.

IMPLEMENTATION OF THE STRATEGIC PLAN

Key Concept: *An appropriate strategic plan is essential for community development, but the enabling complement is careful implementation.*

Implementation of an ICT strategy is not possible without an underlying ICT infrastructure. Accessibility to new telecommunication-related devices and software is often dependent upon population density, income, education, race, and innovative producers, factors that can leave smaller communities at a disadvantage. These are the conclusions of Lentz and Oden (2001), who studied digital divide and digital opportunities in the Mississippi Delta region of the U.S. They observed that since infrastructure is not as prevalent in smaller locales, a more extensive job must be done in creating a culture of use and innovation. Lack of access can affect economic development, and can potentially have a large social impact. The younger generation's ability to keep the pace with their counterparts in larger communities is a prime example. Lack of access can mean that potential users who most need information and training are denied the opportunity. Smaller communities may require a higher level of collaboration among stakeholders and a more personal commitment to securing the digital resources that help make them competitive.

Timmins, Iroquois Falls, Chapleau, and the Haliburton region, all in Ontario, Canada, had difficulty convincing the private sector to make the investment required to bring high-speed telecommunication lines to those remote communities and to make services affordable. They rallied support from their non-profit sector organisations and some larger private sector companies to study the feasibility of cooperative investment. The collaborators soon realised that by pooling their resources, they could obtain higher levels of service for the same budget. In many cases, the threat of a competing infrastructure was enough to get private sector providers to come to the table; in others, it was the only way to bring new economy tools to the region.

Economic development projects are often judged by the number of jobs they create. As a result, there is often a feeling that some central body within the community must be responsible for job creation. Our view is that development projects are more successful when they are managed by a network of local or regional stakeholders working cooperatively to accomplish agreed upon goals. Centralization in any organisation rarely encourages stewardship or innovation. It segregates people and focuses the decision-making power on fewer individuals, which further divides the community. A distributive-style of project management will likely be more effective, especially in advancing the networked community agenda.

Encouraging effective management in local or regional institutions has become a priority for communities to compete in the new knowledge economy. Romer (1994) advised that for public institutions to influence the effectiveness of an economy, they must be willing to collaborate and change along with changes in markets and technology. This adaptivity usually entails "the creative destruction of the existing economic and political order", which means that communities and regions, in their strategic planning efforts, will seek to re-invent themselves through a networked community agenda. As hard as it may be to rise to this challenge, communities have the ability to restructure or re-engineer programs and services to fit their needs. The key is to convince public and private sector institutions of the need for change. "The most important job for economic policy is to create an institutional environment that supports technological change." Re-engineering efforts often lead to greater efficiency, allowing communities to find new sources of funds for projects (Romer, 1994, p. 21).

Although the entire responsibility cannot rest with elected officials, local governments do play a role in creating an environment that provides incentives. Guided by the theory of endogenous growth, the best solutions will be those worked out within the community. These solutions include trying out different incentives and support mechanisms, such as tax subsidies for private research, government procurement, support for innovation, protection of intellectual property rights, and establishing links between private firms and universities (Romer, 1994).

In reviewing Intelligent Community Forum (ICF) archives, the authors observed that there are at least seven critical success factors when considering ICTs as components of the community development strategy. They are:

1.   **Learning about ICT at work.** The sophistication and speed with which people learn to use digital technologies closely correlates with those who first learn at work, and the most effective learning takes place in informal and mediated communities of practitioners (Allan and Lewis, 2006). Workers tend to have more time and greater opportunities to become familiar with the technologies, which facilitates the learning process. The workplace also accelerates propagation of knowledge; workers with good access to technologies can train others to use them at home and elsewhere. Policies to encourage telecommunication use among and within firms can therefore accelerate adoption and the development of a culture of use. New methods of learning online, where users are assisted by streamed video and multimedia, can also promote informal communities of practitioners. Communities can promote networking among learners by pointing them in the direction of these communities of practice.

2.   **Collaboration among non-profit organizations, government agencies and the private sector.** Networked communities typically have multiple activities involving many sectors and stakeholders. Brugmann and Prahalad (2007) identified four stages in the convergence between corporate sector and the civil society beginning with a competitive environment where competing entities reproach each other's conduct. During the second stage, NGOs and the private sector agree to co-exist, and some corporations are involved in projects with joint social responsibility. During stage three, companies and NGOs experiment on projects together and learn from each other. In this stage, networked community activists are working hard. During the final stage, companies develop models with NGOs to deliver value in each other's operations, allowing both partners to innovate and grow using each other's strengths. A fully networked community would have multiple public-private partnerships occurring at the same time with collaborators working on several projects at once.

3.   **Measurement**. Measurement is a means of informing the community, building confidence in the effort and encouraging stakeholder involvement. One of the first expectations imposed on networked community leaders is to provide proof of success. Too often, community projects do not plan for benchmarking and measurement of the impact of telecommunication infrastructure and the applications developed for it.

     According to Lowenberg (2007), who worked with a group of experts to quantify the results of the Eco/Info Project, "Measuring the success or failures of these initiatives is a difficult task…. [T]o date, there has been no appropriate means for accurate determination of the relationship between telecommunication systems and services, and geographically specific and dynamic education, economic or other demo-social trends. Without the ability to begin substantiating the impacts of these funding and subsidization programs, their effectiveness and continuing existence is in jeopardy, and many pioneering public networking initiatives will be left with a precariously uncertain future" (pp. 189-90).

There has been some advancement in this field, as demonstrated by Intelligent Community applicants who are beginning to provide benchmarks to showcase their accomplishments. Governments in Europe and Canada have been working on this challenge and have contributed possible solutions. Examples of benchmarking and measurement tools are discussed later in this chapter.

4. **Access to strong educational systems**. The most successful digital communities tend to base their competitive advantage on the rich intellectual and organisational resources of nearby colleges and universities. Education at all levels is a basic requirement for sustainable communities, but the spin-off technologies, commercialized inventions and patents, and expert guidance in science, management, telecommunications and engineering applied in local communities have given many universities the advantage to excel. Collaboration can accelerate innovation, generate new knowledge and give ready access to a knowledge workforce. One of the most prominent examples of a constructive "town-gown" relationship is that of the city of Palo Alto, California, and Stanford University that together helped to foster the Silicon Valley phenomenon.

5. **Access to knowledge workers**. Building skills is vital for community economic development that is increasingly changing from a greenfield to a holistic approach that seeks to develop opportunities in the knowledge economy. This methodology includes evaluating the skills of young and old, and matching them with industries worldwide, or using development programs for career enhancements. Gone are the days when economic development was principally building an industrial park to attract conventional industries.

    The City of Ottawa, Canada, has begun to inventory and use their knowledge workforce through a project entitled "TalentWorks" that seeks to integrate talent pool initiatives and assist employers to build the supply of qualified workers. Communities are realising that they must build on current competencies (Archives of the ICF, 2007b).

6. **Entrepreneurship**. As people are educated about opportunities, entrepreneurship will change, as well. Communities often suffer from the "me too" syndrome: one person opens a pizza restaurant and does quite well until five others do the same and all plunge into bankruptcy from a saturated market. As people are provided with a wider choice of business opportunities and their

markets are not necessarily restrained to a geographical area, a more balanced and healthy economy can be generated in all communities. The supportive infrastructure includes information analysis and sharing, and training on marketing, culture and digital delivery.

7.   **Managing data**. Networked communities will collect knowledge and communicate opportunities in the widest number of sectors so that its residents can make the right choices. We have already witnessed the difficulties in managing the tremendous quantity of information from the Internet and attempts to organise it into qualitative segments. Networked communities can help to bridge this gap and gather the necessary resources (knowledge and capital) to assist new entrepreneurs.

The role of community or regional portals could become increasingly important to search and release information likely to assist residents in a push-pull fashion. The City of Sudbury, Canada, developed a platform to encourage collaboration among tourist outfitters and was able to increase the number of packaged deals sold to tourists (Archives of the ICF, 2006d).

The City of Fredericton, Canada, showcasing a pull strategy, created the "Fred-e zone," a free network of 300 WiFi access points throughout the downtown and business corridors using libraries, rinks, parking structures, water towers, traffic signals, and streetlights owned by the City. The wireless network is encouraging economic development, including several private sector companies attracted by the highly innovative spirit of the city who wanted to test various applications on the network. Some research companies also decided to move to Fredericton. It is also pulling residents in, making broadband familiar and inexpensive. As people experiment and learn, they will become future innovators and entrepreneurs (Archives of the ICF, 2008).

OneCleveland adopted a three-prong strategy: (a) connect stakeholders to a shared digital ultra broadband network that continues to grow in speeds well beyond traditional broadband projects; (b) enable new products, applications and tools to be used by all local industries to expand market reach and improve service; and (c) transform the way people live by fostering expanded collaborations, increased resource use, innovation and economic development opportunities. The community intranet and VLANs have already attracted companies involved in security, disaster recovery and web hosting. The evolution allows the region to build greater capacity to address pressing social challenges with innovative technologies and associated support systems. Economic development is supported by a high visibility provided to each partner in the project. This visibility is attracting partnerships with such larger companies as Intel, Cisco, Sun Microsystems, and IBM, where all partners continually discuss new ways of innovating and partnering on projects.

The high visibility is also attracting investments worldwide, including some from Asian countries. OneCleveland is working on Web servers, blogs, Wikis and other services to advance community priorities, including grid computing (Archives of the ICF, 2006a).

Table 1. Economic development evaluation

Indicators	Possible approaches to measurement
Promoting economic development through job creation	Percent of job growth in community and % attributable to ICT or online efforts
	Percent of online workers
	Quality of online work
Promoting economic development through business development	Number of new ICT-related businesses
	Number of new home-based businesses
	Percent of growth in IT-related sales
Promoting economic development through tourism development	Growth in number of tourists visiting
	Number of online visitations
	Growth in number of products available online
	Quality of products and services being advertised
	Shared online packaging from local suppliers
	Number of packaged deals offered to tourists
	Growth in tourism as a result of better online packaging
Promoting social development programs	Number of services available online
	Percent of eligible population using online services
	User satisfaction with online services
	Improvements in educational standards attributed to e-learning efforts
	Changes in student achievement with new online programming
	Number of online users of educational programs and services
Promoting quality of life	Surveys of user satisfaction and needs
	New value-added programming available online
	Avoided costs, avoided personal disruptions

EVALUATION AND MEASUREMENT

Table 1 provides an overview of possible ways to measure community development. Although not comprehensive, these examples may begin the discussion of possible evaluation systems to support the development of a networked community and more specifically, for the development of a community development agenda. Possible approaches include the measurement of job creation, new clusters developed and their outputs, increases in tourism, increases in investment, and expansion of social capital or programs geared to improvements in quality of life in the community. The intent of Table 1 is to provide a starting point from which communities can tailor their own evaluation and measurement system based on the community development activities they will choose to undertake.

CONCLUSION

In the corporate world, access to advanced telecommunication products and services has become a major factor in firm location and economic success. However, a robust telecommunication infrastructure is not sufficient when few know how use it, demand is low, and traffic is stagnant. The continuous improvement of technologies requires ongoing community investment in a culture of use. Barr and Riis (2000), writing in *Information Society*, noted a strong correlation between the development of a culture of use and innovation. Growth in innovation allows communities and regions to prosper. As users become more literate, they are able to stimulate innovation. The consequence is that there are strong ties between economic development, innovation and culture of use. Each of the chapters in this book builds upon these ties and attempts to explain how a networked community can develop and succeed.

Leaders and stakeholders of networked communities need to understand that community economic and social development is a planned process requiring ongoing attention and collaboration. It will have a substantial impact on a community's quality of life. The planners, elected officials, and business owners and CEOs need to innovate around a common vision to attract new economic and social development using telecommunication infrastructure as a facilitating agent. Economic and social development projects will be affected by the global environment, but their success will be contingent on internal capabilities. As a result, community leaders wishing to undertake a networked community agenda need to understand the current resources available in the community, differentiate or focus efforts based on the external environment, and comprehend the opportunities available to create jobs and improve quality of life. These exercises, addressed through strategic planning, uncover a wide range of challenges that will require a collaborative approach to solve. The rate of change has become almost overwhelming, especially as it relates to ICTs. Solutions include dividing the work among community stakeholders and making more efficient use of existing resources.

Adopting ICTs and using digital networks have encouraged communities to mobilise knowledge and use existing human resources as a new focus for growth. In addition, ICTs are creating new opportunities for improving the internal environment of communities through different types and forms of re-engineering. Opportunities exist for promoting clusters or creating economies of scope to produce certain types of knowledge and services. There are also opportunities for upgrading existing infrastructures to better take advantage of new technologies and applications.

Community development—both social and economic—requires excellent communication and a commitment to continuous learning, which can be tremendously helped by an extensive telecommunication infrastructure. Communities engaged in "self development" will need to think outside the box in terms of their own ability to compete on a world scale and how they can take advantage of new opportunities. To do so, these communities must understand their particular strengths and weaknesses and be prepared to leverage strengths to seek new opportunities in previously uncharted territory.

REFERENCES

Albert, S. (2007). Transition to a forest bio-economy: A community development strategy discussion. *Journal of Rural and Community Development, 2*, 65-84.

Allan, B. & Lewis, D. (2006). Virtual learning communities as a vehicle for workforce development: A case study. *The Journal of Workplace Learning, 18*(6), 367-383.

Archives of the ICF – The Intelligent Communities Forum. (2008). *Fredericton, New Brunswick, Canada – Nomination submitted for the Intelligent Community of the Year Award.* New York.

Archives of the ICF – The Intelligent Communities Forum. (2007a). *Gangnam-Gu, Seoul, Korea – Nomination submitted for the Intelligent Community of the Year Award.* New York.

Archives of the ICF – The Intelligent Communities Forum. (2007b). *Ottawa, Ontario, Canada – Nomination submitted for the Intelligent Community of the Year Award.* New York.

Archives of the ICF – The Intelligent Communities Forum. (2006a). *Cleveland, Ohio, U.S. – Nomination submitted for the Intelligent Community of the Year Award*. New York.

Archives of the ICF – The Intelligent Communities Forum. (2006b). *Ichikawa, Japan – Nomination submitted for the Intelligent Community of the Year Award*. New York.

Archives of the ICF – The Intelligent Communities Forum. (2006c). *Manchester, UK – Nomination submitted for the Intelligent Community of the Year Award*. New York.

Archives of the ICF – The Intelligent Communities Forum (2006d). *Sudbury, Ontario, Canada – Nomination submitted for the Intelligent Community of the Year Award*. New York.

Archives of the ICF – The Intelligent Communities Forum. (2006e). *Taipei, Taiwan – Nomination submitted for the Intelligent Community of the Year Award*. New York.

Archives of the ICF – The Intelligent Communities Forum. (2006f). *Tianjin, China – Nomination submitted for the Intelligent Community of the Year Award*. New York.

Archives of the ICF – The Intelligent Communities Forum. (2005). *Sunderland, UK – Nomination submitted for the Intelligent Community of the Year Award*. New York.

Ashley, W. C., & Morrison, J. L. (1997). Anticipatory management: Tools for better decision making. *Futurist, 31*(5), 47-51.

Attaran, M. (2004). Exploring the relationship between information technology and business process reengineering. *Information & Management, 41*(5), 585-596.

Barnes, T. J., & Hayter, R. (2005). No "Greek-letter writing": Local models of resource economies. *Growth and Change, 36*(4), 453-470.

Barr, F. & Riis, A. M. (2000). Tapping user driven innovation: A new rationale for universal service. *Information Society, 16*, 99-108.

Brandenburger, A. M. & Nalebuff, B. J. (1995). The right game: Use game theory to shape strategy. *Harvard Business Review, July-August*, 51-71.

Brugmann, J. & Prahalad, C. K. (2007). Co-creating businesses' new social compact. *Harvard Business Review, February*, 80-91.

Cam, C. N. (2004). A conceptual framework for socio-techno-centric approach to sustainable development. *International Journal of Technology Management and Sustainable Development, 3*(1), 59-66.

Cortright, J. (2001). New growth theory, technology and learning: A practitioner's guide. *U.S. Economic Development Administration*, 4, 35.

eBay. (2008). *Marketplace fast facts.* Retrieved June 10, 2008, from http://news.ebay.com/fastfacts_ebay_marketplace.cfm.

Eger, J. (2007). *Smart growth and the urban future.* World Foundation for Smart Communities, retrieved November 5, 2007, from http://www.smartcommunities.org/library_cities.htm

Friedman, T. (2006). *The world is flat.* New York: Farrar Straus & Giroux.

Handy, C. (1991). *The age of unreason: New thinking for a new world.* Boston: Harvard Business School.

Innis, H. A. (1956). The teaching of economic history in Canada. In M. Q. Innis (ed.), *Essays in Canadian economic history.* Toronto, Ontario, Canada: University of Toronto Press.

Jordana, J., Fernandez, X. & Sancho, D. (2005). Which Internet policy? Assessing regional initiatives in Spain. *The Information Society, 21*, 341-351.

Knoblich, G. & Oellinger, M. (2006). The eureka moment. *Scientific American Mind, October/November*, 38-43.

Larner, W. (2002). Calling capital: Call centre strategies in New Brunswick and New Zealand. *Global Networks: A Journal of Transnational Affairs, 2*(2), 133-152.

Lentz, R. G. & Oden, M. D. (2001). Digital divide or digital opportunity in the Mississippi Delta region of the U.S. *Telecommunications Policy, 25*(5), 291-313.

Lowenberg, R. (2007). *Digital cities.* New York: Springer.

Matthiessen, C. W., Schwarz, A. W. & Find, S. (2006). World cities of knowledge: Research strength, networks and nodality. *Journal of Knowledge Management, 10*(5), 14-25.

McGuire, M., Rubin, B., Agranoff, R. & Richards, C. (1994). Building development capacity in nonmetropolitan communities. *Public Administration Review, 54*(5), 426-433.

Metcalfe, R. (1998). *Asian tour provides useful insight on Silicon Valley's worldwide Internet edge.* Retrieved November 5, 2007, from IDG.net, www.infoworld.com

Nalebuff, B. J., & Brandenburger, A. M. (1997). Co-opetition: Competitive and cooperative business strategies for the digital economy. *Strategy & Leadership, 25*(6), 28-35.

Renninger, K. & Shumar, W. (Eds.). (2002). *Building virtual communities: Learning and change in cyberspace*. New York: Cambridge University Press.

Romer, P. (1993). Implementing a national technology strategy with self-organising industry investment boards. *Brookings Papers on Economic Activity: Microeconomics, 2*, 345.

Romer, P. (1994). The origins of endogenous growth. *Journal of Economic Perspectives, 8*(1), 3-22.

Roth, B. N. & Washburn S. A. (1999). Developing strategy. *Journal of Management Consulting, 10*(3), 50-54.

San Diego Smart Growth Initiative. (2003*). Smart growth definition, principles and designations*. Retrieved May 2, 2008, from http://www.lisc.org/san_diego/assets/asset_upload_file873_6802.pdf

Scorsone, E. (2002). *Strategies for community economic development*. Department of Agricultural Economics, University of Kentucky. Retrieved March 22, 2007, from http://econ.iastate.edu

Senge, P. M., Carstedt, G. & Porter, P. L. (2001). Innovating our way to the next Industrial Revolution. *MIT Sloan Management Review, 42*(2), 24-38.

Simon, S. (2004). Systemic evaluation methodology: The emergence of social learning from environmental ICT prototypes. *Systemic Practice and Action Research, 17*(5), 471-496.

Surman, M. (2000). *Community informatics: Enabling communities with information and communications technologies*. Hershey PA: Idea Group Publishing.

Voinoiv, A. & Farley, J. (2007). Reconciling sustainability, systems theory, and discounting. *Ecological Economics, 63*(1), 104-113.

Wenger, E., McDermott, R. & Snyder, W. (2002). *Cultivating communities of practice*. Boston: Harvard Business School.

Yoffie, D. B. & Kwak, M. (2006). With friends like these: The art of managing complementors. *Harvard Business Review, September,* 88-103.

APPENDIX: ECONOMIC DEVELOPMENT ACTIVITIES

Activities	Typical Economic Development Strategies and Tactics	Where ICT Can Fit
Private Sector Development	■ Entrepreneurship development ■ Promoting innovation ■ Investor attraction ■ Cluster development ■ Investment data (land, buildings, capital, human, technology, new markets), & market intelligence, ■ Property improvement programs ■ Product development ■ Co-op advertising, networking & group packaging ■ "Shop Local" campaigns ■ Local business growth promotion ■ Immigration ■ Import replacement ■ Event organisation ■ Tourism marketing	■ Entrepreneurship online help ■ Collaborative frameworks for innovation ■ Investor attraction ■ Cluster development online ■ Investment data (land, buildings, capital, human, technology, new markets) & market intelligence ■ IT Service development (call centres, data management) ■ Co-op advertising, networking & group packaging ■ "Shop Local" campaigns using portal technologies ■ E-commerce promotion with local businesses ■ E-entertainment ■ Tele-work ■ New online applications and devices ■ Immigration promotion ■ Event promotion ■ Tourism marketing
Public Sector, Non-Profit Development & Social Development	■ New program development (government administration, health, education, social organisations) ■ Public-private partnerships (new project development, purchasing) ■ New public infrastructure ■ Quality of life projects (sports & recreation, transportation, telecommunication, affordable housing, arts & culture, & professional services) ■ Festival & event organisation ■ Youth attraction & attraction of specialised skills	■ New program development online in any sector ■ Public-private partnerships online extending beyond the region ■ E-health ■ E-learning ■ E-government ■ E-entertainment ■ Online libraries & museums ■ Portals ■ Citizen participation ■ Information exchanges ■ Skills inventories ■ Communication ■ Tracking (youth, migrant workers)

Chapter VIII
Citizen Empowerment and Participation

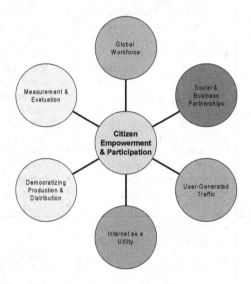

"Now we have armies of amateurs, happy to work for free. Call it the Age of Peer Production. From Amazon.com to MySpace to craigslist, the most successful Web companies are building business models based on user-generated content. This is perhaps the most dramatic manifestation of the second-generation Web. The tools of production, from blogging to video-sharing, are fully democratized, and the engine for growth is the spare cycles, talent and capacity of regular folks." (Anderson, 2006a, 132)

Overview: This chapter on citizen empowerment and public participation explores the following ideas and assumptions:

- Internet collaboration and creation make possible global workforces and marketplaces that reach into every nation and community;
- Community members fortunate enough to have broadband access and the skills to use them can form social and business partnerships that assure their needs are met faster and more effectively;
- Democratizing production and distribution, and connecting supply and demand are the forté of the broadband Internet;
- Even though a severe access gap keeps many citizens of the world from fully participating, user-generated traffic will continue to grow exponentially as two-way telecommunication networks become a basic utility at the community level;
- Strategies are needed for benchmarking, measurement and evaluation of citizen empowerment and participation that demonstrate the extent to which communities benefit.

A NEW GLOBAL ORDER

Key Concept: *The first decade of the 21st century will be the pivotal period for the New World Information and Communication Order, when ordinary citizens in communities of all sizes will begin to realise that they have the means to shape their future.*

Judging from what is happening in networked countries and their communities, a new world information and communication order is forming. The visible consequence of this new order is that communities with access to advanced information and communication (ICT) technologies will have a much greater chance of shaping their own destinies by aggressively pursuing what they need.

Under the best of conditions, the emerging Network Society will stimulate economic development, improve organisational performance, and greatly enhance those factors relating to living the good life. It can make this promise because communities will for the first time in history have a framework for working together both locally and globally. It makes possible more active and informed development, as defined by citizens themselves. This unique scenario has local people with a voice in deciding what they want their future to look like, and the means to articulate and work with others over time to turn that vision into a reality.

The empowering development can be linked to a run-away technology called the global Internet. This telecommunication entity was created by government for its own purposes, and later taken over by corporations for their purposes. In the 21st century, the Internet has been appropriated by the public for its own (not yet well-defined) purposes. The government funded it, the corporations built it and the public has embraced it in many mutually beneficial ways, but now neither governments nor corporations can control it.

The new digital networks are self-reproducing and perpetuating because they have unleashed expectations that no one imagined would be realised. These networks are highly valued because of the mutually beneficial relationships they establish between consumers and producers. Providers of communication, entertainment media, public services and consumer goods are now scrambling to find new ways to keep their customers happy, and their customers are willingly rewarding them for the effort.

In his 2008 article entitled "Millennials: The future is now", John Giere of the global telecom firm Alcatel-Lucent wrote:

> To understand what the future holds for telecommunications service providers around the world, look no further than teenagers with iPod earbuds in their ears, cell phones in their pockets and laptops under their arms. While previous generations of consumers would be happy for content and applications to stay in their discreet environments (songs on iPods, voice on the phone and data on laptops) the new "Millennial" generation—generally speaking those after 1980—is insisting on two critical requirements to satisfy their hunger for new technology and their willingness to pay for it: interoperability and integration.

> Unlike previous generations, Millenials do not take a passive approach to technology. They want to be able to add, subtract and change key elements of technology offerings and find new ways of using their tools to advance their personal and professional objectives. As a result, they expect their phones, music players and notebook PCs to share data and applications (interoperability), and they will reward any player in the market who helps them organise and manage their different technological investments from a centralised platform (integration).

> This is a generation of natural-born technologists. They are willing to create their own mash-ups of services, and as a result are simply looking for someone to provide a venue or platform over which they can support their lifestyle. As a group, they are specifically interested in service providers that let them harness technology in a way that allows them to get their work completed quickly and access their entertainment in short segments. . . Because of this, Millennials are a very different type of consumer (Giere, 2008, p. 9).

Gere's message about Millennials was not written for a consumer audience; it was targeted at service providers who are attempting to understand the rapid changes surrounding the Internet. He wrote:

> At Alcatel-Lucent, we believe this "mash-up environment" of devices, communications capabilities and delivery options is giving rise to a rapidly growing market for what we are calling "blended lifestyle services". These services seamlessly combine elements of existing offerings with completely new, user-centric services. In short, we believe that it is imperative for service providers to rapidly create new business models that offer businesses and consumers highly personalised offerings in a highly profitable manner (p. 9).

Giere concluded by advising the telecommunications industry that to "not pay attention to the new demand patterns presented by Millennials" is to do so at their peril. He reminded them that "because of both their large numbers and the nature of the new service that they are demanding", the Millennials are a force to be reckoned with. These new customers will be redefining what it means to be a service provider, and what information and communications technology will be called upon to meet their wants and needs. "This generation of consumers (and future workers) expects service providers to adapt technology and services to their needs, not the other way around", he says (p. 12).

Giere is describing an unexpected turn of events, where the consumer finds him or herself in the position of decision-maker and corporations in the position of figuring out what the next generation of users might need or want. This reversal of roles doesn't stop there. A further unanticipated, and possibly quite negative, consequence for the provider industry is that consumers will be expecting to assert their new-found independence. They will be weaning themselves wherever possible from established retailers, music labels, video production houses and journalistic gatekeepers, and by giving preference to products and services that they have created (mashed-ups), over which they have some ownership and control, and which they are quite capable of distributing—for profit or not—entirely on their own initiative. For the telecommunications providers, this undesirable scenario envisions them as common carriers of commodity products and services over which they have little or no control.

The principal vehicles by which such behavioural changes take form are via the new digital networks, the most widely known form of which is the broadband Internet. Access to the Internet has become a symbol of empowerment for our times, for the small retailer, the corporate executive, the social activist, the creative artist, the school child, the parent, the senior citizen, and the person who is disabled.

Broadband is a technological term indicating the quantity and quality of information that can be exchanged over a distance using telecommunication channels. However, broadband has taken on more than just a technical meaning. It is "a business and social goal yet to be achieved, a way of expressing corporate and public aspirations for a more perfect society based on people's ability to get more of what they want, faster" (Flournoy, 2004, p. 1).

The older crowd among today's consumers learned to use electronic media to enjoy programming produced by select groups of very creative people: The Beatles and Bob Dylan, "Sesame Street" and "ABC Sports", the "CBS News" and the *New York Times*. Today, the broadband generation has many more choices in where to go for, and how to make use of, the media, including new opportunities to create and distribute its own content. "Future media fare will be richer, more diverse and interactive, produced by people of all ages and of all levels of training and income, no matter where they are located. Available live or on demand will be real events, fictional stories in audio and video, music, computer creations, multiplayer games, or any products and services people will wish to offer for sale or to freely share" (Flournoy, 2004, pp. 1-2).

Campus radio programmes of the broadband generation can be enjoyed on the Internet by millions as well by a few students in the dorms. In addition to personal messaging and e-mail, students' own Web creations—think FaceBook and MySpace—can be viewed by family and friends or by anyone in the world who wants to connect and take a look. Visitors to student pages can share photos of themselves or music they have created, and point out other Web sites of interest. "Broadcast quality" animations created on home workstations can be streamed out to viewers directly, or simply uploaded to a distant professional studio for further editing and enhancements, so that same work can be turned into a movie, concert promotional or commercial advertisement, sometimes the equal of Hollywood or Madison Avenue.

As a result of the extraordinary new technologies and software being made available, personal communication has taken on the form of public billboards and shared radio and television creations. The art of storytelling has returned, with the capability to reach widely dispersed audiences. Increasingly, personal media that originates locally is being consumed globally. Entertainment products are reaching large numbers but being enjoyed according to schedules that suits individual listeners, viewers and players. Marketing and retailing continue in physical space, but also online through such outlets as Yahoo, Amazon, eBay and iTunes. The global Internet helps entertainers, retailers and marketers to reach geographically and culturally diverse publics. Yet, the two-way capabilities of the Internet enable these same populations to alternately be the audience and the performer, to be at one moment a consumer and at another a seller.

LAST AND FIRST MILE

To use the parlance of telecommunications, consumers are able, at their discretion, to participate as first-mile producers and distributors and as last-mile consumers and receivers. The "last mile" describes the interconnections between target customers and the local telephone switching offices and cable headends originating the service. The telephone companies call this configuration the local loop. In cable, they refer to the area of penetration. Broadcasters call it the area of coverage. The term also surfaces in the trade literature of terrestrial wireless and satellite communications and in reference to Internet service provider (ISP) networks, almost always when addressing the means by which suppliers of information products and services gain access to local customers. For all of these media—telephone, cable, wireless, satellite, broadcast, and Internet—the last mile represents their principal market, thus its importance.

The "first mile" phrase has rarely been used for the simple reason that industry players never had need for such language. Given the historic customer-based business model, it was unthinkable that local people in their homes, schools and businesses would require a broadband communications infrastructure whose outbound path was as robust as the path coming in. What would the public do with such a voluminous capability? Now it is clear that the carrying capacity for traffic on the network that originates from users must be at least as fast as that needed for downloads, and in some places in the world it has surpassed 100 Mbps.

The dramatic increase in upstream traffic has profound implications for traditional business models in the media industry, notes the *Economist* magazine. These models tend "to be based on aggregating large passive audiences and holding them captive during advertising interruptions. In the new media era, audiences will occasionally be large, but often small, and usually tiny. Instead of a few large capital-rich media giants competing with one another for these audiences, it will be small firms and individuals competing or, more often, collaborating. Some will be making money from the content they create; others will not and will not mind, because they have other motives" (Kluth, 2006, p. 4).

Inbound signals via broadcast, cable and satellite are technologically much easier to deliver and not as expensive; comparable outbound signals are more difficult and expensive to provision. Until now, the idea that content network and service providers might make money empowering local customers was far-fetched. Enabling these customers to initiate their own entertainment, multimedia communications, file sharing, person-to-person commerce, and community-enhancing services was considered costly and lacking demand. Now, every provider acknowledges this shift and takes it seriously with the hope of competing profitably in niche markets.

LOCAL AND GLOBAL MEDIA

A good before-and-after illustration of the impact of user-generated content is the news programme "CNN World Report". In 1987, Cable News Network founder Ted Turner introduced a new international newscast and global news exchange that became a distinctively original approach to newsgathering. It was on that date that CNN asked private and public television stations around the world to submit to Atlanta weekly news items from their own perspective. CNN upset the established news world when it agreed to air "local perspective" news on its globally distributed satellite networks without editing.

"CNN World Report" was an early attempt at participatory journalism on a global scale. As the first planetary newscast in which any country in any part of the globe was free to contribute news, it was also the first global news exchange in which any station could, without charge or copyright restriction, make free use of any contributed news from any other station. According to Turner, "[T]he idea was to create within the context of CNN an international newscast open for wide participation, and make it a news exchange so that everybody could use everybody else's material. It would be a barter arrangement so that stations contributing would get something back. Everyone would benefit" (Flournoy, 1992, pp. 9-10).

Turner was a strong proponent of the New World Information and Communication Order initiatives of UNESCO that sought to give greater voice to nations less often heard from, and make it possible for them to air stories from their point of view. Turner's strategy of inviting local and television news organisations to submit stories to "CNN World Report", and his pledge to transmit these stories unedited and uncensored, was a way of addressing some of the criticism aimed at the big news agencies, who tended to have a narrow self-centred news agenda that, in the case of international news, focused heavily on the negative.

On the 10th anniversary of "CNN World Report", former U.S. President Jimmy Carter wrote, "One of Ted's goals is to bring the peoples of the world closer together, and there is no better example than the founding of Cable News Network in 1980. CNN, the world's first live, round-the-clock all news TV network, broke all molds of television journalism. Now seen in more than 200 countries, CNN has done more to close the gaps of misunderstanding between the world's people than any enterprise in recent memory. Ted gave life to Marshall McLuhan's prediction that television would create a global village" (Flournoy & Stewart, 1997, p. vii).

Flournoy and Stewart (1997) concluded in their book *CNN: Making News in the Global Market* that while "CNN World Report" began as a kind of "public service gesture", over time it came to be seen as a smart business strategy, a way for CNN to change staff mind-set internally and build its reputation as a serious news player abroad. The news company said publicly that one of the reasons it aired "unedited and uncensored news and perspectives", and worked hard to see that these stories were properly framed and as close to production quality as possible to its own product, was recognition that a world of news existed that no one else was covering, and that in the very nature of news resides the possibility of more than one point of view (pp. 205-206).

Reminiscent of that CNN innovation, both CNN and its global competitor the BBC today call on viewers to submit content in breaking news stories. The CurrentTV cable channel, founded by former U.S. Vice President Al Gore, uses 30% viewer-created content in its programme mix. "ABC News Now", the digital news service of the U.S. commercial TV network, looks for viewers' help in covering "stories that matter". "This is about freedom and democracy in action", ABC News Digital Executive Producer Michael Clemente said. "It's one thing to shout on talk radio and post something on a message board, but if you can talk back to people making decisions, that will be very powerful" (Kaminski, 2006, p. 205).

Whether the sources of content are the professional news organisations or individual citizens, the fact that user-generated data traffic continues to grow demonstrates the extent to which the "first mile" of broadband telecommunication is now in place. Both providers and consumers are in the mix. Two-way flow, with a big pipe up as well as a big pipe down, is now one of the basic necessities of modern societies, whether for personal exchanges, for business transactions or for community collaboration and sharing.

BROADBAND EMPOWERMENT

Key Concept: *For broadband bi-directional telecommunication and the empowerment of citizens, the Internet is the big pipe that matters most.*

Today's Internet is conveying some 60 billion e-mails each day. In the United Kingdom alone, mobile phone users are sending as many as 126 million text messages per day and some one million of these are multimedia picture messages that use Internet Protocol (IP) as the common standard (Georgescu, 2007). The same IP network that serves as a platform for e-mailing and messaging is also evolving into the most uniquely personalised medium for mass marketing and selling the world has yet experienced. The Internet has surprised everyone with the extent to which it has become a favourite source of information, education and entertainment.

Internet shopping was expected to hit 15% of retail sales in the United Kingdom by the end of year 2007 and was predicted by InternetRetailing.net to account for nearly 40% of all retail sales in the UK by 2020 (Herrod, 2007). This network is not only for shopping, however. Mother is using the Internet from home to do office work, the kids are doing research for school, father is listening to international radio stations, and every member of the household is watching videos and playing games whenever they want by way of streaming media.

The Internet is more than just an application, more than just a way to send and receive mail, purchase and sell products or download movies for on-demand viewing. It is now unique, a telecommunications medium with its own applications. In some ways, the Internet has taken on the broadcast functions of radio, television and satellite networks. In other ways, it is an interactive medium more closely related to the telephone and data networks on which it is based. The identity of this evolving technology is distinctive, and its dimensions are multiplying.

We now understand that the Internet is a highly flexible electronic distribution system that can be used for either one-way or two-way communication. In the new era of "always on/available everywhere" broadband digital telecommunications, Internet users can be customers at one moment and creators, producers, marketers and distributors of content at another. The act of consuming and the act of creating can be done by the same people using the same medium.

As a medium, the Internet is not particular whether the user logs on at home or at the office or at some remote site. Users can access the Internet by way of a personal computer or a television set or some special communication device, such as an advanced cellular telephone or personal digital assistant. Information exchanged can consist of brief messages of a few bits or massive data files of one gigabit or larger. Transmission can be symmetric or asymmetric, with lots of information flowing one way and less flowing the other; it can be synchronous or asynchronous, in real time or not.

The Internet is a versatile network of receiving/contributing devices that can support very user-centric activities. Users can correspond, make secure telephone calls, hold business conferences, upload corporate files, exchange songs, view movies, play games, or engage in electronic commerce all from a single location, or from multiple locations, interacting as easily with machines as with humans. In fact, the time has already arrived when the Internet is being accessed daily by more machines than people, hosting highly automated computer-like sensors and other devices communicating with each other, both giving to and taking from the Internet.

It can be said that the Internet is "platform agnostic" in that the service is not wedded to a single transmission medium. Internet traffic can travel over telephone, cable, wireless, broadcast, satellite, or power lines, which means that almost everybody in the world is going to have more than one way to be connected. How and at what cost they will be connected will depend on factors affected by economics, regulation and culture, both local and global.

Finally, the Internet is a mass medium with a difference. Among the things it does best are very personal, such as enabling an individual user to read a daily newspaper from a distant city, fax a tax form to a child away at college, order a pair of shoes, gather statistics and related images to be used in a business presentation, view a real estate offering, receive periodic updates on a stock portfolio, and participate in a recreational virtual community. All this can be done at times that are convenient for the user. The difference is that this most personal of all media has massive reach and influence (Flournoy, 2004, p. 322-323).

The new digital networks will not be everywhere, but for the communities fortunate enough to be connected, they promise two-way, always-on, on-demand broadband communications available to anyone who know how to use them. For those most privileged of communities, businesses and individuals, the network promises that working and communicating across oceans and continents will be just about as easy as working and communicating across town. No sooner will the constraints of time and distance have been relaxed than the veil of darkness will be lifted from the human imagination, or so it seems.

At present, the best—and that means cheapest and most readily available—means for allowing common people to collaborate with others at a distance is the broadband Internet. No prior technology or set of technologies has allowed for the free exchange of information in such volume and diversity. Implementing IP broadband as a shared global network is bringing humankind into closer daily contact and making it possible for people working together to be more creative in problem solving. The ready accessibility of the Internet in our communities and its many applications changes not only what we can do as citizens; it changes what we can now think about doing. Such infrastructures and software have prompted dramatic shifts in how the public today is getting its needs met.

The community is integral to social interaction not only locally but globally. The broadband community is one that can more easily reach out and engage citizens in other locations, achieving their group and individual goals faster and more efficiently. As a result, borders, politics and ideologies hold less power to constrain cooperation and innovation. The wealthier countries have the advantage, for they tend to be more wired and have leapt ahead with social acceptance and training. With cost reductions for the technology and related telecom services, and better understanding of what is at stake, however, the rest of the world is paying attention and catching on, if not catching up.

From their vantage point, world citizens have observed the unprecedented opportunities for "on demand access", the ways to know about and participate both virtually and actually in an infinite marketplace of ideas, goods and services. Access when one needs it has been made more compelling with the incremental advancement of such delivery and access technologies as the coaxial cable, fiber optic and DSL lines, the IP satellite, wireless WiFi/WiMax, cell phones, and such peer-to-peer devices as the portable Sony Playstation. Each of these distribution systems has its own particular usefulness, but each transmits and receives data quicker and more flexibly than the dial-up services of the old phone companies. Users can get real time news updates via a television receiver, a computer monitor, a video gaming platform, a cell-phone or PDA, or even a wrist watch, and citizen journalists as well as the professionals have a much better chance of reporting the news "live and on location" wherever they are.

With advances in retail consumer electronics, such as those with the brand names of Apple Computer, Sony and Samsung, the everyday user has the chance to become the creator of content of potential interest to others. Through connection via the Internet, this content can be directed to a single designated person online or uploaded and streamed around the world by any interested party. Content creation technologies linked to high-speed networks have enabled common citizens to become recording artists, filmmakers and journalists. With a US$2,000 investment in equipment, someone with no formal training can strive to be the next pop star of YouTube, the Steven Spielberg of film and animation or the Walter Cronkite of the blogging universe.

COMMUNITY EMPOWERMENT

Key Concept: *Community networks are popping up because they are giving people more ways to get more of what they want.*

Just as attendance at big media and mass entertainment events now compete with personal media and participatory recreation, user involvement in commercial transactions and the conduct of societal business has taken a radical turn from passive consumption to active search based on individual needs and wants. However, one-size-fits-all consumption is not at risk of disappearing; because active participation proves to be complementary.

It is human nature to want to participate. The human genetic code makes us to want to be engaged in what we are doing at work, and exercise more control over how we are engaged. We want more—not just more things, but to be able to do more—not later but right now. Not somewhere else but wherever we happen to be at the moment. People want to share what they know and what they do with others. Media consumers are also media producers these days because there is also a willing audience for consumers who talk back. The opportunities are numerous: becoming an online photographer and chronicler of the neighbourhood, writing political blogs, posting podcasts of local sports events, sharing home produced videos, correcting content on user-created encyclopedias, testing and ranking products that provide feedback to other consumers on shopping sites.

The variety of consumer electronics devices that can be connected to the Internet has made it possible for more consumers to think about assembling and distributing products and services from their location. Whether via wire or wireless, last-mile capacity around the world is under enormous pressure to offer equal service as the first-mile broadband path out of homes, offices, cafes, hotels, automobiles, airplanes and remote locations in the field. Why this drive for pervasiveness? The moment consumers realise something they have dreamed about might be done, they will want to try it (Flournoy, 2005, p. 57).

Lee Rainie, director of the Pew Internet & American Life Project, gave a presentation to the 2008 Intelligent Community Forum Conference in New York, in which he reported that:

- 55% of young American adult Internet users (33% of all adults) use video-sharing sites;
- 15% of young adult Internet users (8% of all adults) have uploaded videos to the web;
- 20% of online young adults (11% of online adults) say they remix content they find online into their own artistic creations;
- 19% of online young adults (6% of all adult Internet users) have created an avatar that interacts with others online;
- 58% of online teens (33% of online adults) have created their own profile on a social network site like MySpace or Facebook;
- 37% of young adult Internet users (32% of all adults) have rated a person, product or service online;
- 40% of younger Internet users customize news and other information pages (half are on specialty listservs); and
- 14% of young Internet users (12% of all adults) download podcasts (Rainie, 2008).

From the telecommunication provider's point of view, having numerous homes feeding the Internet looks promising, but it is also worrisome. It is positive because it generates a lot of new traffic to bill. However, it creates special challenges because providing connectivity quickly becomes a commodity business for which there is never enough capacity and for which infrastructure investments have to be made repeatedly.

From the users' perspective, bi-directional communication is about adding value to the telecommunications asset. In this case, value added can mean having faster, more efficient ways to go onto the Internet to find products to buy. An even more important value will be having the capability to do whatever else one wants to do, on demand. Keeping the "producing consumer" satisfied places an extra burden on providers because it means provisioning two-way voice, data and video networks that allow customers to go online at any time for transactions as modest as sending an instant message or as demanding as a long session of multiplayer 3D gaming.

What are the requirements of all-digital access when consumers are given free rein to do what they want? They are not trivial. Ideally, such services will include: 1) anywhere broadband access via fixed and wireless networks, 2) seamless interconnectivity with hand-off between home, office, and field locations, and 3) integration of network management to keep up with users and devices so they can accomplish what they want, and the provider can charge for services rendered (Boggaert & Tournassoud, 2005, pp. 26-31).

In 2006, Alcatel of France, provider of broadband communications technologies, merged with its U.S. competitor Lucent Technologies, the former AT&T Bell Labs spin-off, to create one of the largest and most respected "innovation and technology solutions" companies in the world. With a history of telecommunications R&D, Alcatel-Lucent is in the forefront of ideas about how service providers, enterprises and governments can more effectively deliver voice, data and video communication services to end-users, and provide for end-users to talk back.

Alcatel-Lucent researchers foresee that all voice, video and data will eventually travel over the same connections, and that those connections will be the High Speed Internet. These researchers, and their colleagues at other advanced technology think labs, are predicting that the High Speed Internet of the future will be a more open environment enabling multiple services from different locations with seamless hand-off. Ultimately, the new High Speed Internet will be all optical and all digital using MPLS/transport, a means of prioritizing services over the Internet using a multitude of networking protocols in traffic engineering.

An open transport environment will be required because the network must be able to respond to a broadband hierarchy of needs that can only be met with differentiated services using a diversity of devices and connectivity. This means the first- and last-mile networks, the ones that travel into and out of homes and offices, must be extensible and easily modified. The Internet is a useful platform because it provides ubiquitous end-to-end connectivity and access (Cerra & Kan, 2005, pp. 6-10).

The broadband Internet is not everywhere, however, and to ask a "best effort" narrowband network to support real time applications with quality service requirements is unrealistic. As IP-based services evolve to include video communication and personal content sharing, equivalent bandwidth will be required in the upstream. Also, latency must be reduced and security added. These are not trivial problems.

In the future, where the edge of the network is defined as "wherever the user is", the meaning of first-mile and last-mile telecommunications will need to be redefined. Users will carry their access authorisations and devices with them. In this scenario, the active users are always in the spotlight, since the space around them lights up to receive and transport communications in response to their presence. The idea of user-centric networks implies that users can be connected virtually wherever they go. To the extent possible, such networks will be robust and scalable, capable of asymmetric and symmetric, synchronous and non-synchronous delivery. They also will be sufficiently intelligent to figure out what the user needs at that moment and to carry out the transaction on command (Flournoy, 2005, p. 58).

NETWORKING ACROSS COMMUNITIES

Key Concept: *Connecting community networks into communities of networks will create the greatest single workforce and the most profitable marketplace on earth.*

In 1973, sociologist Mark Granovetter wrote a now-classic paper entitled "The Strength of Weak Ties". He argued that "our acquaintances (weak ties) are less likely to be socially involved with one another than are our close friends (strong ties). Thus the set of people made up of any individual and his or her acquaintances comprises a low-density network (one in which many of the possible relational lines are absent) whereas the set consisting of the same individual and his or her close friends will be densely knit (many of the possible lines are present)" (Granovetter, 1983, pp. 201-233).

This theory of social networks gives a useful perspective from which to view the online networks that operate in both virtual and real communities. Granovetter observed that we tend to have a collection of close friends, most of whom are in touch with one another "in a densely knit clump of social structure". At the same time "we have a collection of acquaintances, few of whom know one another". These acquaintances, however, are likely to have close friends of their own. Thus, the weak ties between us and our acquaintances become "a crucial bridge" between the two densely knit clumps of close friends. Granovetter says "these clumps would not, in fact, be connected to one another at all were it not for the existence of weak ties" (1983).

Decades ago it would not have been possible for Granovetter to have imagined Facebook.com, a Web site that gives individual users a space for keeping in touch with close friends online, yet also permits contact with distant others. According to its Internet description, "Facebook is a social utility that connects you with the people around you. Facebook is made up of many networks, each based around a

workplace, region, high school or college. You can use Facebook to: share information with people you know, see what's going on with your friend, look up people
around you" (www.Facebook.com).

Via telecommunications, local community networks may be interconnected
either formally or informally, intermittently or over time with any other community
network. Depending on the circumstances, some distant network acquaintances
become even more valuable for the online users than the network of friends close
at hand. The Internet now permits users to "search" for those who will become
acquaintances for a particular reason or purpose, people of common interest, people
with special knowledge or experience to share.

In recent years, *Wired* magazine editor Chris Anderson has spent time on the
lecture circuit presenting new ways of looking at "buying and selling" on the
Internet. He advocates the idea that the future mega sales in online retailing will
be made in the least popular products, the products that nobody knew were there
(Anderson, 2006b). The Internet retailers Amazon.com, eBay.com, Netflix.com
and iTunes.com have made available items that people want but have been unable
to locate. The noteworthy contribution of these online providers is to gather the
multiplicity of "niche" products and services (books, movies, music, tools, and flea
market wares) that have been out of reach and then help consumers who have the
digital connections find and acquire those items. These dotcom companies have
also positioned themselves to help the owners and producers of specialty items who
want to be in touch with potentially interested customers.

Anderson's idea is expounded in his popular book *The Long Tail: Why the
Future of Business Is Selling More of Less*. He illustrates with a graph showing
a head consisting of popular products that are "hits" and the professionally made
items that are "best sellers", and a long and increasingly thin tail extending across
the page, consisting of used books, old movies, missed TV shows, garage band
music, antique cars, period pottery, and other such items that are either out-of-date
or are of lesser professional quality. The short head and the long tail need not be
in competition, he says, because both are needed. All such items are valuable and
can be profitable since they are part of a continuum appealing to the generic and
specialty interests of consumers.

We are all part of mass culture, Anderson says, yet we each have very specific
interests to satisfy. In the past, most of us have tended to be content satisfying our
popular culture interests by sitting in front of the TV, watching the primetime fare
designed by the commercial networks to attract large audiences, or by reading the
popular *Life* or *Look* magazines. Sometimes we went downtown to see a cult movie
or browsed the big bookshops to find a specialty magazine that satisfied an interest that was uniquely ours. Nowadays it is much easier to spend more time on our
individual specialty interests. Whereas the number of movies and TV shows and

magazines have multiplied by the hundreds, the number of Web sites that cater to niche interests on the Internet has grown by the thousands and millions (Anderson, 2006a).

Anderson uses blogging as an illustration: a single commentator addressing a specialty topic via the Web can draw more than a million viewers a day, which is beyond what most mainstream magazines and newspapers would dream possible.

The online merchant uses digital networks to connect to buyers and potential clients outside the reach of the physical retail facilities and service-provider agencies. According to Anderson, such networks are a way to connect unlimited supply with unmet demand, making scarce items readily accessible at modest conversion cost and distribution effort (Anderson, 2006a).

How are these developments possible? The answer lies in the convergence of digital processing, digital storage and telecommunications—linking PCs into digital networks backed by smart servers capable of tracking user interests and making recommendations for products and services that ordinary but unaware people might want. The Internet has the unique ability to overcome many of the constraints of scarce time, scarce space and great distances, converting text and voice and video into bits and bytes of data storage, processing this information and making it available for acquisition at the convenience of those who might conceivably be interested in it.

"The Internet has made possible a new world in which the combined value of modest sellers and quirky titles equals the sales of the top hits", says Anderson. He suggests there are three "forces" that are operable in the added value present in the Long Tail of modern markets: the democratization of the tools of production, the democratization of the tools of distribution and connecting supply with demand (Anderson, 2006a, pp. 54-56).

COLLABORATION NETWORKS

Key Concept: *Spaces have been created on the Internet that deliver the tools of collaboration and creation into the hands of anyone who has modest equipment and skills, and a broadband connection.*

Time magazine's pick for "Person of the Year" for 2006 was a surprise, for the annual choice was not a single person or even a team of people. Rather, the decision was to appoint "you" and "me", the creatively engaged public, for that singular honor. In perspective, the editors said that historically they looked to pick for the cover "the person or persons who most affected the news and our lives, for good or ill".

Time's choice in picking the public, they said, arose from their observations and conviction that the public was "seizing the reins of the global media", creating "an explosion of productivity and innovation", and helping to frame a new digital democracy. The editors wrote, "It's a story about community and collaboration on a scale never seen before. It's about the cosmic compendium of knowledge Wikipedia and the million channel people's network YouTube and online metropolis MySpace. It's about the many wresting power from the few and helping one another for nothing and how that will not only change the world, but also change the way the world changes" (Grossman, 2006).

Wikipedia, a Web-based, free and open encyclopedia whose content is written collaboratively by volunteers around the world, has editions in multiple languages and contains entries both on traditional encyclopedic topics, current events and other items of general or specific interest. Anybody can edit and add to one of its articles. According to the *New York Times*, Wikipedia is "the biggest encyclopedia in the history of the world". In 2005, "it was receiving 2.5 billion page views a month, and offering at least 1,000 articles in 82 languages. The number of articles, already close to two million, is growing by 7% a month". Traffic to the site was doubling every four months" (Seelye, 2005). By 2007, it had accumulated some 6.4 million articles, and there were thought to be more than 5 million volunteers contributing to or editing its content. Palo Alto HP Labs researchers who studied the site found "a crucial correlation between article quality and number of edits, which validates Wikipedia as a successful collaborative effort" (Wilkinson & Huberman, 2007).

YouTube and MySpace are popular social networking Web sites through which users can share a variety of information. With YouTube, users rate movie clips, TV shows and music videos, as well as amateur content that has been uploaded, based on the number of times a video has been watched. The company was acquired by Google Inc. and named *Time* magazine's "Invention of the Year" in 2006. MySpace is a highly flexible and participant-friendly site for interactive networking, forming of interest groups, posting of personal profiles, blogging, and sharing of photos, music and videos. Owned by News Corp., MySpace was judged in 2007 to be the world's fifth most popular Web site in any language.

Technology is especially useful when it helps us do and learn things that were previously beyond our reach. The organisational and retention capabilities of networked computers and software have given us new ways to think about attaining the unattainable. Expectations of what one can do on the Internet have escalated as computers and broadband access have become basic consumer utilities.

The tools needed for online collaboration are still being refined, and their successes are yet to be fully demonstrated, but trends can be noted in such societal events as file sharing among peers, IP voice and IPTV, news and information blogging, user-created encyclopedias, and search engine advertising.

Peer-to-peer (P2P) file-sharing, or exchanges of files stored on the hard drives of personal computers, became a popular pastime of young people sharing MP3 music in the late 1990s. Although Napster, Gnutella, Freenet, Kazaa, and others experienced copyright infringement troubles with the Recording Industry Association of America for providing the computer servers and software that made sharing music files easy, the technology has persisted and proved to be useful in a host of applications that could not have been planned or even imagined in advance.

Some of these P2P file-sharing systems have evolved into information distribution networks of a vast scale characterised by decentralised control. Such sharing of digital resources has caught on as a useful tool among corporations and universities as well as within the general public. Their services, sometimes called "mesh networks" or "grid computing", can be simple applications aiming for mass usage, such as the MIT-based Roofnet project giving low-income residents access to the wireless Internet using a series of radio transmitters and receivers randomly dispersed over an area (Savage, 2006). They can also be complex science and engineering projects with a long-term ambitious goal, such as the SETI@home project that employs distributed computers to process data collected from outer space in search of evidence of intelligent life.

VoIP, Voice-over Internet Protocol, is defined by the U.S. Federal Communications Commission as "a technology that allows you to make voice calls using a broadband Internet connection instead of a regular (analog) phone line. Some VoIP services may only allow you to call other people using the same service, but others may allow you to call anyone who has a telephone number—including local, long distance, mobile and international numbers. Also, while some VoIP services only work over your computer or a special VoIP phone, other services allow you to use a traditional phone connected to a VoIP adapter" (IP-Enabled, 2007).

Skype is a popular VoIP computer-to-computer system that provides free phone calling to any other Skype users world-wide. Skype functions as a person-to-person file transfer programme and an Instant Messenger client. Recent hardware upgrades make possible Skype-to-home telephone set connections, with a monthly fee for connection to the local telephone network. Because of the high cost of long distance calling, many international migrant workers use Skype to keep in touch with their families back home. On a more advanced scale requiring broadband Internet connection on each end, instructors at Ohio University in the U.S. and the National University of Kyiv, Ukraine, are using the Skype service to teach courses requiring real time interaction with audio, video and PowerPoint slide presentations projected on classroom screens in both locations.

IPTV, television distributed over Internet Protocol, was something dreamed by the newly deregulated phone companies who wanted to get into the cable TV business. As cable companies have upgraded their networks with fiber optic lines and reconditioned their coaxial cable lines from one-way broadcast to two-way interactive systems that allow for more symmetric communication, they too are finding Internet Protocol a suitable vehicle for managing voice, video and data traffic delivered into and out of homes. Given the new high-speed infrastructures in place, whether via telephone, cable lines, wireless, satellite, or broadband power lines, it is inevitable that home users will take advantage of these installations to add television, even HDTV, to their upstream communication. In other words, more than one home consumer will seize the opportunity to be a production unit in distributed ventures, and the broadband Internet will be the platform.

MAKING MONEY VIRTUALLY

Key Concept: *Business collaborations in cyberspace are not new, but the expanding variety of new businesses and commercial opportunities based on the newly developed ICTs of the Internet could not have been predicted.*

On-demand streaming of video content over the Internet is something the average user could not have done a decade ago. Now, uninterrupted viewing-while-downloading of movies, real-time videoconferences and video sharing events, and participating in virtual communities as an active visual presence are quite common. Such applications are readily available on the free video sharing site YouTube, the videoblog site Blip, the video portal Metacafe, the search service Google, and the online community Second Life. With the arrival of broadband and some greater sophistication in compression technologies and software, doing business online has become easier.

The collaborative features of the Internet make it possible to make money in virtual space. Blogs are real businesses, with real revenue streams and real advertisers, assert Paul Sloan and colleagues writing in *Business 2.0*. The writers say that blogs have gone from self-indulgent hobbies to flourishing businesses. "Blogs today benefit from what might be termed uneconomies of scale: they are so cheap to create and operate that a lone blogger or a small team can, with the ever-expanding reach of the Internet, amass vast audiences and generate levels of profit on a per-employee basis that traditional media companies can only fantasize about" (Sloan and Kaihla, 2006, pp. 65-74).

"Mash-ups" are a new niche in online communication. Maps have been available on the Internet for some years, but the introduction of Google Earth added a widely adopted localizing dimension to the cartography market, called Mash-up Maps. On the same day Google added "address search" and "geocoding" support to its maps, Australia's leading provider of classifieds Fairfax Digital made it possible for online users to view commercial real estate on Domain.com.au, its online property search site. The site advises users to plug in any Australian postcode or suburb name. In the search results page, there is a link called "View properties on a Map". The link says "Click that link and you're there! Tiny little house map icons showing you your next castle! :)" (Australian, 2006).

CNN news anchors can now point to the exact location of events described in video footage and commentary using Google-provided perspectives from space. Home viewers are often given an overview of a region in the news, the picture zooming down to a city-wide view and then to the event itself, with actual footage playing in the foreground. In blending several visual applications, mash-ups are thought to be important as user-participation innovations. Google's applications allow users to build their own personalised maps that plot the locations of everything from cheap gas locally to the latest earthquakes worldwide (CNNMoney, 2007).

Cyworld is a Korean virtual community project founded in 1999. Operated by SK Communications, a subsidiary of Korean wireless provider SK Telecommunications, the company posted sales of $160 million and a profit of $25 million in 2005. According to *Business 2.0*, half of that revenue and a majority of the profit came from Cyworld. In 2006, Cyworld was expected to contribute $140 million in sales, with virtual products accounting for 70%. Cyworld was said to be the largest social network in Asia.

Korean customers were paying more than $100 million for the 400,000 items of virtual inventory on the site, with Cyworld splitting its revenue with the small graphic design shops and licence holders that created the items (Schonfeld, 2006, pp. 86-87). A third of that revenue was for copyright-negotiated music that visitors could stream onto their homepages for about 50 cents each, with the site selling six million songs a month (Schonfeld, p. 87).

Cyworld apparently takes advantage of the unique characteristics of Korean society that motivate young people to congregate on the Web. Once inside the site, users can choose from among thousands of digital items with which they can construct unique spaces of their own. The thought is that young people, in Korea at least, like playing with their identities, and participate in these social communities as a way to explore themselves.

LEVERAGING DIGITAL NETWORKS

Key Concept: *Democratizing production and distribution, and connecting supply and demand, are among the essential strategies of networked communities for digital creativity and collaboration.*

E-government networks are being established on the Internet with the goal of fostering more transparent and effective government and as a stimulus for increasing citizen participation. A study of e-participation projects in emerging democracies by the Estonian e-Governance Academy examined ways the Internet is strengthening citizens' capacity for collective action and political influence. In looking at the ways political corruption can be exposed, the study concluded that an open and accessible public Internet can "discourage corrupt officials from seeking powerful political offices", as well as "support law enforcement efforts through easier access to information for prosecutors". The Internet can empower citizens by providing them "with specific rules and reduce, if not eliminate, much of the discretionary power and uncertainty related to the process of obtaining a government service or permit" (Coleman & Kaposi, 2006, p. 11).

Civic web sites can bring the knowledge and voices of stakeholders closer to the centre of accountable governance, provide for horizontal communications and interactions between citizens and their government agencies, and enable constructive collaboration. The Estonian report concluded that the emerging information and communication technologies (ICTs) such as the multimedia Internet added a new dimension to the public sphere by creating more direct channels of engagement, consultation and discursive interaction. Power within such networks "tends to be decentralised, resulting in qualitative changes in the distribution of politically useful knowledge". Users need not rely exclusively on mass media channels for information (p. 11).

E-business networks do much the same thing. The world's most innovative companies, according to Jean McGregor writing in *Business Week*, are effectively using networks to speed up decision-making by making it easy to collaborate. "Today, innovation is about much more than new products. It is about reinventing business processes and building entirely new markets that meet untapped customer needs. Most important, as the Internet and globalization widen the pool of new ideas, it's about selecting and executing the right ideas and bringing them to market in record time" (McGregor, 2006, pp. 63-74).

McGregor described how Apple Computer Inc. launched the iPod using levels of innovativeness including: (1) cross-business networking, earning an agreement among music companies to sell their songs online, (2) creating a new business model, selling individual songs online for one dollar each, (3) using design and branding as a differentiator, and (4) simplifying the iTunes software platform that turned an MP3 player into a big source of revenue.

Slow development time represents a significant obstacle to business. "Fast changing consumer demands, global outsourcing and open-source software make speed to market paramount today" (p. 64). The best innovators reroute reporting lines and create physical spaces for collaboration, teaming up people from across the organisational chart.

E-medicine is an additional example. Innovative hospitals have made it possible for a single physician and a nurse to support bedside caregivers managing more than 100 patients at a time. Patients are monitored remotely using Web cams for visual checking, with personal communication only as needed. This innovation is now in place in selected intensive care units that seek to improve the efficiency of care. They combine video feeds with specially designed computer software and real-time patient information to enable frequent bed checks and faster decisions.

E-education and training networks allow students, researchers and citizens to access databases and learn things that were not previously available to them. Greater quantities and varieties of information can now be accessed via the Internet than can be found in any print-based library. Many public schools, community colleges and universities, as well as proprietary educational institutions, now offer classes that can be completed within a timeframe set by the student. Easy access and schedule flexibility are enabling professionals to further their education at their own pace.

iTunesU, an application of the Apple iTunes technology offered in conjunction with McGraw-Hill and Pearson Publishing, permits college professors to record their lectures as audio and/or video files and post them on Web sites for students to download. Lectures downloaded to a student's own iPod can be played back, for example, as that student drives to class.

Colleges can now think more creatively about how to best deliver education. Stanford University and the Massachusetts Institute of Technology (MIT) have made the contents of many of their courses available for public viewing online. Such an offer is a great boon to students around the world who want or need the content but who could never expect to attend Stanford or MIT classes in person. It also gives those who are looking to enroll in college a way to compare classes and test their self-preparedness. Finally, colleges can think about ways to help students prepare for futures in which international employment in virtual space is a growing likelihood.

"In the near future, it will be possible to think that operating in a virtual space and/or video game will be a major part of one's job. Video game technology is evolving quicker than any technology in the history of mankind", says John Bowditch, director of the GRID (Game Research and Immersive Design) Lab at Ohio University. "Fantasies are lived, fortunes are earned or lost, and laws are broken or obeyed virtually in games without any real world consequences. Despite the popular negative connotations associated with video games, gamers are developing skills today that will be utilized in their future careers. Video games teach multi-tasking, collaboration, perseverance, and borderless tolerance" (Bowditch, personal communication, April 15, 2007).

Bowditch described a 2006 job posting for a manager of a new software division at Yahoo. The description listed the usual requirements of strong leadership and good organisational and communication skills. The description also noted that applicants must not only have experience with a multiplayer online game (MMOG), but must also be a Guild Master—someone who has sufficient experience in these virtual worlds to be treated as an "elder"—in an MMOG fantasy world. Playing and mastering video games was understood by Yahoo as the learning vehicle for the skills needed by the staff person who must manage the new division as a successful business.

Yahoo's rationale was that this new division would be creating a global gaming venture with players from many countries and cultures. The company wanted someone who could work easily between the virtual world and the real world as a creative leader and learner. In this case, age, education, ethnicity and country of origin were less defining as criteria, because a different set of requirements was active in the new virtual workplaces.

THE DIGITAL ACCESS GAP

Key Concept: *The digital divide that separates those who have access to the riches of the Internet and those who do not is real and troubling for community stewards.*

Some think that the critical issue that detracts from the widespread benefits of computers and the Internet is the "digital divide", the term for the gap between those who have access and those who do not. What happens to those citizens who are not empowered by all this development? Do they end up as "welfare cases", contributing little and becoming a drain on community resources, or are they thriving outside the virtual world? Currently, there is no clarity on the impact of the digital divide.

Jan van Dijk of the University of Twente, the Netherlands, examined the achievements and shortcomings of digital divide research during 2000-2005, concluding that those at the wrong end of the digital divide tend to become second-class and third-class citizens or not citizens at all. Exclusion is classified under four types of access: motivational, physical, skills and usage. Van Dijk reports that progress is being made in terms of physical access. As for digital skills and the use of Internet applications, the divide persists and perhaps is widening (van Dijk, 2005). We know something about what is happening and why, but the effects are not well understood.

A report from the Centre for Democracy and Technology entitled "Bridging the Digital Divide: Internet Access in Central and Eastern Europe" noted that "in every region, progress is being made as governments, commercial entities, non-profits and grant-making bodies strive to expand Internet connectivity. However, the Internet is far from achieving its potential reach and impact, and there are concerns that the 'digital divide' is growing". Some of the conclusions drawn include:

- A major barrier to Internet usage is the poor state of the underlying tele-communications infrastructure. Most people, particularly residential users and NGOs, currently are dependent on telephone dial-up connections to the Internet, and will remain so in the near future.
- Governments in the region have an ambivalent attitude toward the Internet. While the overall trend is positive, several governments maintain regulations that hamper Internet development. Government policies regarding privacy and censorship could also chill the use of the medium.
- Privatisation of the former state-owned telecommunications monopolies attracts the foreign investment needed for infrastructure improvement. However, in recent years, there appears to be in some countries a shift to more lucrative business services at the expense of universal service objectives (Bridging the, 2007).

In 2004, the BBC carried a news story on the Alliance for Digital Inclusion, a coalition of businesses and charities that had joined forces to address the approximately one-half of the adult population of Britain described as being "digitally disengaged". This group had been charged "with finding ways of persuading the 48% of refuseniks to use the net and other new technologies". The alliance was led by the public advocacy group Citizens Online, and founders included British Telecom, AOL, Microsoft and Intel. A government report entitled "Enabling a Digitally United Kingdom" identified the groups most at risk of becoming further excluded as older people, those from lower socio-economic groups, the unemployed and the disabled (Push, 2004).

Speaking at the launch of the initiative, spokeswoman Ruth Kelly said, "We need to develop a much better understanding of context—how people live their lives and how people can use technologies to improve their lives". She explained that "for people from lower social-economic groups, education, housing and em-ployment" may represent critical barriers, or these factors could serve as potential solutions. "For older people, the integration of electronic and traditional health and social services may be a driver for digital take-up". John Fisher, a representative of Citizens Online, was quoted as saying, "The solution is not getting everyone a PC. The starting point has to be to get people motivated" (Push, 2004).

In 2006, a pan-European drive to use information and communication technolo-gies to help people overcome economic, social, educational, territorial, or disability-related disadvantages was endorsed by ministers of 34 European countries. The "e-Inclusion" goals included halving the gap in Internet usage by groups at risk of exclusion, including older people, people with disabilities and unemployed persons. Within the European Union, only 10% of people over the age of 65 were found to be using the Internet. An EU press release, "A Barrier-Free Information Society", noted that "a huge percentage of the population in the EU cannot participate in and contribute to economic and social life" (Internet, 2006).

In brief, it appears that almost every community and every nation is aware that some citizens are being excluded and that the reasons have to do with more than simple access to computers, high speed infrastructure and training. There is an older generation and there are disabled persons who cannot or will not participate; there are also people who are unemployed, displaced, homeless and poor. Such individuals will be reached more slowly—if at all—by efforts at digital-inclusion.

MEASUREMENT AND EVALUATION OF CITIZEN EMPOWERMENT

Key Concept: *Although measuring citizen empowerment and participation can be difficult in the context of local communities, systems of assessment should be devised to report the changes on multiple measures.*

Winston-Salem, North Carolina USA was a Top Seven Intelligent Community finalist in the ICF awards in 2008. Winston-Salem served as a clear model of a community working with some success in ensuring equal access to the broadband Internet and achieving broader public participation:

> How does Winston-Salem measure the results of its many investments and partnerships? There have certainly been economic successes. Winston-Salem and Forsyth County now count 37,000 biotech employees as residents, and biotech companies contribute an estimated $10 billion in annual revenue to the area. Dell Computer opened a manufacturing facility in Forsyth County in 2005 that will create another 1,500 jobs and contribute at least $100 million in new investment.

> But Winston-Salem also measures progress in human terms. WinstonNet is now in discussions with the school district and community leaders on development of a programme to place computers in the homes of low-income students. The programme proposal covers funding, curriculum integration, teacher training, technical staffing, hardware and broadband

connections. If WinstonNet is successful in attracting funding, as it expects, the programme will start in 2008/09 with 550 students in middle schools with high percentages of low-income students. Success, then, is measured not only in today's jobs. It is also measured by the community's ability to build a more prosperous and inclusive Broadband Economy for tomorrow's citizens. (Archives of the ICF, 2008)

Table 1 provides an overview of potential indicators having to do with the empowerment of citizens. Some of them are not easy to track because the actions and decisions of many individuals and organizations are at play. The approaches outlined are modest and doable.

Table 1. Citizen empowerment

Empowerment issues to be evaluated	Possible approaches to measurement
New local and global markets are formed	Percent of businesses participating in key markets
Responsive local and global workforces are made available	Number of degree-completion programs available online
Production and distribution are democratized	Number of degree-completion programs available online
Supply and demand are more synchronous and rationalized	Efficiencies and cost savings
User-generated traffic increases over broadband	Percent of citizens participating
Internet-based collaboration leads to creative solutions for communities	Products and services generated
Citizens are more able to participate in the processes of government	Sharing of best practises
Users form social and business partnerships online	Number of online partnerships
The digital divide leaves some segments of the community unconnected and underserved	Access for the elderly & poor

CONCLUSION

The digital networks are serving as the foundation for a new information and communication order in which greater quantities of information, products and services are globally available. These same networks are making it possible for individuals, communities and nations to be active contributors to that store of knowledge, content and opportunity.

User-generated traffic will double repeatedly as broadband bi-directional telecommunication becomes a basic community utility for homes, schools and businesses. There are many examples in which the connective infrastructure of community networks, the democratization of the tools of production and access to the devices for open sharing of content have resulted in accelerated digital innovation, created new marketplaces and opened up the possibilities of virtual as well as location-specific employment. As a result of the personalization of computing and the opening of the once-tightly controlled telecommunication networks, the tools of collaborative creation are for the first time in human history in the hands of the people, and they like the feel of it.

The challenge ahead is to realise the vision of a global, decentralised, user-controlled and affordable infrastructure for content creation and sharing that is accessible to all people. There are still too many homes, schools, businesses and communities that do not have the equipment, the skills and the broadband connections for citizens of all ages and economic means to be full participants.

Community leaders and their stakeholders should stop thinking of themselves as peripheral. The world is now upside down. What was the periphery is now the centre. The edges of the network are now at its core. The digital divide aside, everyone in every community now has a voice and a means to articulate it. It is up to communities and their leaders to decide what they want to say, what they aspire to be. The illustrations in every chapter of this book demonstrate the truth of these remarkable assertions. All societies are on the move—in transition to a new world information and communications order that will bring with it with major social and economic adjustments. Those persons interested in helping shape the future of their communities have the opportune moment to become involved.

REFERENCES

Anderson, C. (2006a). *The long tail: Why the future of business is selling less of more.* New York: Hyperion.

Anderson, C. (2006b, July). People power: Blogs, user reviews, photo-sharing: The peer production era has arrived. *Wired*, 132.

Australian real estate Google Maps mash-up boom. (2006). Retrieved Setpember 7, 2006, from http://googlemapsmania.blogspot.com/2006/09/australian-real-estate-google-maps.html

Bogaert, J. V., & Tournassoud, P. (2005). User-centric broadband networks. *Alcatel Telecommunications Review, First Quarter*, 26-31.

Bridging the digital divide: Internet access in Central and Eastern Europe. (2007). Retrieved April 26, 2007, from the Centre for Democracy and Technology Web site: http://www.cdt.org/international/ceeaccess/report.shtml

Cerra, A., & Kan, D. (2005). User-centric broadband services: Demand drivers and market opportunities. *Alcatel Telecommunications Review, First Quarter*, 6-10.

CNNMoney: Google Maps get personal (2007). Retrieved September 12, 2007 from http://www.thegooglenews.info/GoogleEarth/GoogleMapsgetpersonal_11492.html

Coleman, S. & Kaposi, I. (2006). *New democracies, new media, what's new?: A study of e-participation projects in third-wave democracies.* Retrieved January 20, 2008, from Estonian e-Governance Academy Web site: http://www.ega.ee/handbook

Flournoy, D. M. (1992). *CNN World Report: Ted Turner's international news coup.* London UK: John Libbey and Company Ltd.

Flournoy, D. M. (2004). *The broadband millennium: Communication technologies and markets.* Chicago: International Engineering Consortium.

Flournoy, D. M., & Stewart, Robert K. (1997). *CNN: Making news in the global market.* Chesham UK: University of Luton Press.

Flournoy, D. M. (2005). Triple play: It's human nature. In *Achieving the triple play: Technologies and business models for success.* Chicago: International Engineering Consortium.

Giere, J. (2008). Millennials: the future is now. *Alcatel-Lucent Enriching Communications*, 2(1), 9-12.

Georgescu, I. (2007). *1 million picture messages sent each day in the UK.* Retrieved April 12, 2007, from Softpedia Web site: http://news.softpedia.com/news/1-Million-Picture-Messages-Sent-Each-Day-in-the-UK-43331.shtml

Granovetter, M. (1983). The strength of weak ties: A network theory revisited. *Sociological Theory, 1*, 201-233.

Grossman, L. (2006). *Time's Person of the Year: you.* Retrieved September 15, 2007, from the *Time* Web site: http://www.time.com/time/magazine/0,9263,1101061225,00. html

Herrod, E. (2007). *Internet retailing to hit 15% of retail sales at year end.* Retrieved April 10, 2007, from the InternetRetailing Web site: http://www.internetretailing. net/news/internet-retailing-to-hit-15-of-retail-sales-at-year-end

Internet for all: EU ministers commit to an inclusive and barrier-free Information Society (2006). Retrieved June 12, 2006, from Europa Web site: http://europa.eu/rapid/pressReleasesAction.do?reference=IP/06/ 769&type=HTML&aged=0&language=EN&guiLanguage=en

IP-enabled services (2007). Retrieved April 10, 2007, from the Federal Communications Commission, Consumer & Governmental Affairs Bureau Web site: www. fcc.gov/voip

Kaminski, P. (2006). *Technology boosts power of citizen journalism.* Retrieved May 24, 2006, from TV Technology.com Web site: http://tvtech.com/dailynews/one. php?id=3891

Kluth, A. (2006). Among the audience. *The Economist,* p. 4.

McGregor, J. (2006). The world's most innovative companies. *Business Week,* pp. 63-74."

Push to win over net "refuseniks" (2004, October 13). Retrieved October 13, 2004, from the BBC Web site: http://news.bbc.co.uk/2/hi/technology/3737614.stm

Rainie, L. (2008). *Director of the Pew Internet and American Life Project,* in a presentation to the Intelligent Community Forum conference in New York City.

Savage, N. (2006). *Municipal Mesh Network.* Retrieved February 27, 2006, from MIT's *Technology Review* Web site: http://www.technologyreview.com/InfoTech/ wtr_16427,258,p1.html?a=f

Schonfeld, E. (2006). Cyworld attacks. *Business 2.0,* pp. 86-87.

Seelye, K. O. (2005). *Snared in the web of a Wikipedia liar.* Retrieved December 4, 2005, from the *New York Times* Web site: http://www.nytimes.com/2005/12/04/ weekinreview/04seelye.html?ex=1291352400&en=fd6ae777b9a365c9&ei=5088& partner=rssnyt&emc=rss

Sloan, P. & Kaihila, P. (2006). Blogging for dollars. *Business 2.0,* pp. 65-74.

Van Dijk, J. A. G. M. (2005). *The deepening divide: Inequality in the information society.* Thousand Oaks CA: Sage.

Wilkinson, D. M., & Huberman, B. A. (2007). *Assessing the value of cooperation in Wikipedia.* Retrieved February 22, 2007, from the *First Monday* Web site: *http://www.firstmonday.org/issues/issue12_4/wilkinson*

Chapter IX
Leadership and Collaboration

"While leadership is essential, the creation of an Intelligent Community is never a solo performance. Every successful one has been the result of a cross-fertilization among business, academia and government, usually beginning with informal partnerships that evolved into specific projects, programs or organisations. There is a clear opportunity for government to start and foster this cross-fertilization through persistent and consistent effort." (ICF, 2007)

Overview: This chapter discusses several basic elements of leadership and collaboration in building networked communities. It includes:

•   The context for collaborating, that is, the new economy imperative of digital competition;

- The continuum of goals in networked communities—from simple communication objectives to more complex economic development objectives;
- The structures needed to encourage the widest community collaboration;
- The leaders that are needed within organisations and across industries;
- The leadership style adapted to the formation and performance phases of networks;
- The recruitment and retention of leaders;
- Evaluation of the leadership and collaborative environment of the networked community.

ECONOMIC IMPERATIVE FOR COLLABORATIVE LEADERSHIP

The transformational change that networked communities envision employs the Internet to create innovations, and attract social and economic development. The idea is to make digital usage and Internet connectivity so pervasive that the constant development of products and services will become the normal state of affairs.

Leadership, project management and collaboration were found to be critical by Industry Canada (2003) and by ICF (2007) in the development of intelligent communities. To develop the broadband infrastructure and the complementary innovations and applications, the collaboration of many individuals and organisations takes place in support of a common vision.

Because communities and regions are aware of the competitive advantage of connecting to broadband telecommunications, they generate demand for faster high-speed digital networks. At this early phase, strong leadership is needed to recognise internal and external trends that will affect the future of the community, and to build the collaborative environment needed to ensure a sustainable infrastructure. The networked community is a top-down and bottom-up approach that starts with a commitment to use ICT in each organisation, business and home within the community, and expands by building ICT networks that will promote growth, efficiency and quality of life. Leaders must come from many sectors within the community to create both supply and demand of broadband capability. Each sector will have its unique challenges best resolved by leaders who understand its environment, and each organisation will have its own political setting that calls for individuals with the power to convince stakeholders to take action. Each community will have opinion leaders, transformational leaders, charismatic leaders and influential individuals who can help make or break a project.

Communities that come together open the door to improved resource management, creating an environment of trust and collaboration that allows local organisations and all citizens to explore the advantages of the new networks and to create projects that increase quality of life.

Key Concept: *Collaboration can help projects to progress and innovate. The leadership style and structure adopted must establish a non-threatening environment in which several organisations and players can share decision-making powers.*

Today, society must engage in collaborative problem-solving across several sectors, including business, government and communities (Gillis & McLellan, 1998). Interdependence is best achieved through two or more stakeholders pooling resources to resolve common problems, and partnerships—often called clusters by private business—are often formed to jointly solve problems that are too large and complex for a single organisation. Multi-organisational partnerships are the foundation of networked communities because the online environment and ICTs create common challenges and opportunities that promote sharing as a coping strategy. These multi-organisational partnerships involve teamwork and collaboration to deal with the knowledge explosion. According to Wheelan (1999), teamwork occurs when it is no longer possible for individual contributors to function alone to achieve their respective organisational goals.

Modern communities address the challenges of technology and resolve a variety of user-related problems, infrastructure problems and financing issues (Tapscott, 1998). Building sustainable networks for digital collaboration requires a certain degree of technological literacy and ready access to high-speed communication lines, computing devices and software. Individual organisations are limited in their knowledge, control and resources to meet their own needs and those of the community. For example, a school board may have the resources to connect and deliver to a number of their own schools, but some sites may be too far away to service, and certainly, they would not be able to build the infrastructure or applications necessary for students, parents and teachers at home.

Communities updating their infrastructure may need partnerships to share the cost and risks of construction and to update their technology. Organisations wanting to offer innovative applications using the new digital networks may benefit from brainstorming with like-minded partners. Businesses may need partnerships to deliver and market new services on such community networks. Many players—including those in health, education, government, entertainment, tourism, manufacturing, and retailing—should be sought out to create a networked community.

TRANSFORMING THE COMMUNITY

Leaders need to consider the impact of each type of change on people, processes and structure (Jurow, 2007), regardless of its size and frequency. Leadership plays a key role in developing a proper vision for change, and the impact will be different in each organisation and sector. Consequently, many leaders need to commit to the vision. In a free market economy, the networked community becomes another organisation with its own behavioural challenges, which may be complex because there is no central authority. Volunteer engagement by numerous stakeholders may choose to cooperatively build economic foundations, and the networked community is usually started by a committed champion from a municipal council or an economic development body. However, this individual does not possess enough power to effect a lasting change, especially one that transforms every sector into an integral part of a networked community. Transformational and visionary leaders are needed to introduce and guide the change process in each participating organisation. In most cases, the visionary leader will work to create trust and engage others, and establish acceptable structures that will attract other powerful leaders to join the networked community effort.

According to Jan Tucker (2007), communities will go through a developmental, transitional or transformational change brought about by the new knowledge economy and globalization. She asserts that developmental change is an incremental and low risk improvement over existing systems. An example is Laurentian University in Canada, which introduced an online MBA to meet the needs of the Certified General Accountants of Canada. The MBA programme was amended to meet the requirements of a dispersed client group, shortened to meet the busy schedules of these part-time students, and continues to be amended to meet changing requirements as a result of technology. The methods used to stimulate discussion, handle conflicts, encourage participation and collect and monitor exams are different from those of a standard university programme. As a result, the MBA Programme has undergone a developmental change led by visionary leaders.

Tucker's transitional change is more disruptive in that it replaces one or more systems and includes the introduction of new technology. The fax machine and conventional mailings were largely displaced by e-mails in the Laurentian online MBA. Online learning may one day replace much of the capital-intensive classroom modes of delivery. These types of transitional change affect communities that host the companies producing these goods, and all businesses that sell and service these technologies within communities around the world. Although there is an effect, the change takes place over long periods of time, allowing affected individuals and organisations to adapt with tolerable pain.

Finally, transformational change, according to Tucker, adds another layer of disruption and usually happens in dire circumstances. The changing demand and supply of wood resources have left many communities in Northern Ontario in distress, calling for radical change to regain some level of stability to wood producing communities. Towns and regions in distress are more apt to embrace transformational change to resolve their economic problems. However, some communities are wise enough to not to wait until they are seriously affected by such dire circumstances, and begin a transformation process to diversify their economy before the situation is critical.

Change can also be described as gradual, continuous or discontinuous, as discussed in Chapter VI on innovation. The ICT economy and globalization tend to escalate the rate of change over time, and more communities come to experience discontinuous change. This concept is closely linked to transformation change in that there is a rupture with the status quo. According to Weick and Quinn, (1999), transformational change requires transformational leaders who can develop intellectually stimulating projects and inspire followers to transcend their own self-interests for a higher collective purpose, mission or vision. At an organisational level, this collective commitment is likely rooted in the various steering committees and within each of the stakeholder organisations participating in the networked community's development.

COMMUNITY GOALS AND COLLABORATION

Waits (2000) describes collaborative networks in terms of their pursuits or goals. Examples of such purposes include:

- Co-inform: actions to identify members and impacts, promote a heightened awareness of the issues and improve communication among the members;
- Co-learn: educational and training programmes sponsored by the network;
- Co-market: collective activities that promote member products or services domestically or abroad;
- Co-purchase: activities to strengthen buyer supplier links or to jointly buy expensive equipment;
- Co-produce: alliances to make a product together or conduct R&D together; and
- Co-build economic foundations: activities to build stronger educational, financial and governmental institutions that enable the community to better compete.

Key Concept: *Collaborative networks can be formed to serve the simple purpose of informing citizens, or the more extensive goal of rebuilding a community's economic foundation to create efficiencies, new opportunities and quality of life for all citizens. The higher level goals require higher levels of trust among collaborators.*

Some of these goals, such as to co-inform and co-learn, are easier to realise and only require a modicum of trust. They are more likely to give quick "small wins". Others, like co-market, co-purchase, and co-produce, may be challenging and require resilient trust; their success will require more time but will be more highly valued. Co-building economic foundations appeals less to self-interest and more to a communal effort, and depends on a broad vision that will lead to a series of concrete actions and sustained effort (Waits, 2000). These objectives are compatible with one another, but they require different timeframes and commitments.

The community must establish agreed-upon common and individual goals. Not all collaborators will be ready at the onset to jump into a social agenda; many still operate in situations that represent their own specialised interests and will be looking at the networking project to find something from which they can benefit. Therefore, the process of working together must slowly build trust and lead to a change in each partner's perception so that higher level goals can be achieved. The following are some best practices that the authors have found in our research on networked communities:

a.   As a general rule, trust is key. The leadership style adopted in forming the network will influence all of the stakeholders' commitment in the subsequent performance phase of the network. For example, a strong collaborative environment built on trust will encourage participants to be more patient in their expectations and willing to invest time and resources to achieve long term goals. As a result, such a network may easily proceed to a higher level goal, such as co-building economic foundations.

The networked community must balance the individual needs of collaborators with the higher level need of transforming the community. If goals are too nebulous and collaborators cannot clearly see a benefit for themselves and their organisation, they will more easily detach or shift their resources to targets that are perceived to deliver a larger payback. Trust is such a large component of building an effective collaboration that network leaders need to create an environment where participating organisations share in the decision-making structure and therefore are comfortable sharing resources within the network.

b.   The networked communities can involve business clusters of private enterprises, such as networks of producers who conduct purchasing in common or form marketing bodies to strengthen their local, national or international position. Private sector involvement tends to become long term, and succeeds when there is trust and commitment (Das & Teng, 1999), and when there is organisational compatibility and equal power (Bucklin & Sengupta, 1993). Leadership is needed to gather the group of private sector interests and to keep it running.

c.   Non-profit organisations tend to look for ways to minimize duplication and make more effective use of scarce resources. Those agencies backing digital collaboration within public sectors can often provide the impetus for change and improvement in service. Their actions will draw in those who resist when a measure of success can be demonstrated.

d.   Collaboration between profit and non-profit organisations may start with objectives that are quite dissimilar at the onset, but a common ground can be achieved through negotiation. According to J. E. Austin, who examined marketing's role in cross-sector collaboration, a better understanding of mutual goals can evolve into a long-term relationship (2003). Such collaborations can strengthen the long-term sustainability of networked community projects. The non-profit organisation may be interested in reaching a broader population, hoping to increase awareness, while businesses may be more interested in enhancing their visibility and public relations or in practicing socially responsibility (Whymer & Samu, 2003). The business interest may also start as philanthropic; however, the networked community can work toward the higher level goals that require long-term commitment and collaboration.

Austin (2003) and Brugmann and Prahalad (2007) identified three stages in a continuum of relationships between private and public sectors. In the philanthropic stage, the levels of engagement and resources are relatively low, and perhaps infrequent and non-strategic. At the transaction stage, there is a significant two-way value exchange, and the partners become more important to one another. In the mature integrative stage, the strategic alliance between public and private sector organisations is built on a merger of values and compatibilities. At this stage, "People begin to interact with greater frequency and many different kinds of joint activities are undertaken" (Austin, 2003, p. 24). Clearly, the integrative stage of public-private collaboration would be more likely to encourage synergy and innovation of the kind that characterises the networked community.

e.   A number of collaborative activities can and should happen to involve the consumer. Each of the three possible collaborative networks discussed above (public, private and public-private) must consider the impact and the involvement of consumers and other stakeholders in these processes. Several studies described by Kavanaugh et al. (2001, 2005) have pointed to improved success when users were involved in planning and implementing telecommunication networks and were engaged in building social capital.

For example, the state of Michigan was able to refine and increase task completions while reducing the time needed to complete online tasks through a re-design effort based on user involvement (Brinck, 2005). Designers of the state portal were surprised to learn how well users understood content and made their way through the various pages and levels in the portal. User involvement allowed them to perfect a system where users would have a minimum of clicks to get to the needed information or service. These kinds of improvements can go a long way toward promoting a culture of use.

Touching for a moment on how and why stakeholders get involved in inter-organisational networks, Ebers (2002) notes that "effective collaborations need to operate at different and sometimes contradictory levels" (p. 13). To illustrate, Hock (2000) mentions that collaboration may be both significant in some respects and insignificant in others; centralised in some respects and decentralised in others; local in its appeal and decisions, but national or even global in its scope; maximizing independence while providing a necessary interdependence; encouraging differences but within limits; and leading from the centre while allowing management by the parts. These apparent contradictions are part of an environment in which it is difficult to lead and manage change. Though there is no "one-size-fits-all" to bring people to the table, Gray (1985) has found that the determinants of collaborative efforts to include:

- Cost/benefit;
- Level of participation in decision-making;
- Member inclusion and exclusion;
- Power sharing;
- Network leadership; and
- Team effectiveness.

More effective collaborations are characterized by clear purpose, congruency, high and mutually balanced value creation, effective communication, and deep reciprocal commitment (Austin, 2003). The organisational culture of a community-based network partnership places a high value on (a) championing common community vision, (b) respect for participants' roles and mandates, (c) achieving goals through collaboration, (d) contributing each organisation's unique assets and expertise to the partnership, and (e) pursuing cost-efficiency and organisational effectiveness. To implement the networked community strategy and business plan, the partners share authority, jointly invest resources, obtain mutual benefits and share risk, responsibility, and accountability. The partners must find value in the partnership; therefore, network goals must be congruent with personal goals. People are more likely to make sacrifices for something in which they believe, and when team members feel they can accomplish the task at hand (Bass & Avolio, 2000).

LEADERSHIP AND GOVERNANCE STRUCTURES

Leadership is more than just appointing a leader who is responsible for the change process. The leader or champion needed in networked communities must have access to resources through alliances with partners to build social capital (Kavanaugh, Reese, Carroll & Rosson, 2005). Distributing leadership and extending communication to a larger circle of stakeholders and players appear to be more effective, based on a review of successful networked communities. Whymer and Samu (2003) argue that a distributed leadership system allows the networked community to:

- Work toward equalizing power among organisations;
- Improve communication among organisations that may feel threatened by the strengths or size of participating organisations;
- Increase trust among partners; and
- Encourage the development of innovation.

In some political environments, leadership may be more centralised, and a single powerful leader will make a tremendous difference. In this context, the higher the status of the leader, the more impact he or she will have. The mayor will possess the power to influence a larger number of organisations and their functions, and will have the clout to change rules and regulations, sometimes at high government levels. In these societies, a high-ranking official within the municipality, the region, or even the country may initiate the project. He or she will engage a multidisciplinary team to ensure that a number of partners are brought to the table to ensure a wide audience. Together, they promote sustainability, cross-fertilization and synergy in the development of applications and innovations—in essence, they develop a culture of use and innovation. Though heavily top-down in decision-making, the networked community projects attract many players, who see benefits from its implementation.

Taipei, Taiwan is an example. Under the mayor's leadership, the Taipei City Government is collaborating with private enterprises and NGOs to improve public services, build a broadband infrastructure and foster a competitive and convenient environment for all residents. In the first phase, 34 projects were successfully carried out and 20 projects were part of phase 2. Their plans included five critical strategies:

(1) Content is the key to delivering citizen-pertinent services through broadband infrastructure;
(2) Collaboration between academics and professionals will shorten the time to transform students into knowledge workers;
(3) The platform and environment must allow innovation;
(4) Services will be provided to ensure digital equality; and
(5) Taipei's efforts and advantages will be marketed to sustain business development.

Taipei reported that there are more than 16 representatives of key organisations working to develop the initiatives representing the public sector, private sector and NGOs, including academia, a foundation and a computer association and trade council (Archives of the ICF, 2006d).

In more democratic societies where power is less centralised, other structures can be considered. Under a conventional leadership system, the network would be led by a single leader making many of the decisions and relegating other powerful community leaders to a secondary position. This is often unacceptable to organisational leaders who need to be convinced to relinquish power to make the project work. A distributed leadership system (Pôr & van Bekkum, 2003) may be more effective as it would divide the power according to projects and/or sectors and would also rotate leadership to allow an opportunity to share power among leaders.

Key Concept: *Since organisations and their visionary leaders tend to resist central decision making when it affects their operations, distributed leadership, whose activities encourage participation via shared power, offers an excellent alternative.*

In a traditional system, there are high risks to the community network when leaders are lost through job change, illness, or death. Leaders also may lose credibility with or threaten the power of other vital collaborators through attempts to control other organisations' resources under the guise of efficiency. Collaborators must feel comfortable that they are sharing—not donating or losing—power.

A culture of change requires synergy and some measure of accelerated development. Is it possible to encourage this synergistic and sustainable model of innovation within a tightly controlled traditional leadership system in Western society? Will people agree to share power? The traditional leadership systems operate in an environment where committees and organisations are ultimately responsible

Figure 1. Traditional leadership system

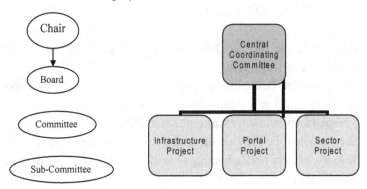

to a central body in the form of the board, chair or coordinating committee. The traditional system is represented in Figure 1.

The authors observe that networked communities are often nonhierarchical in their approach—organic, dynamic and informal rather than bureaucratic and static. This observation supports the research of Lawless and Moore (1989), who suggest that dynamic networks include several key characteristics: vertical dis-aggregations of agencies performing specialised functions; a more flexible governance structure with virtually no hierarchy; single strategy makers acting in the role of brokers who coordinate the strategic decisions for members; and full information sharing and disclosure to members.

Lawless and Moore's research helped develop the system of distributed leadership represented in Figure 2. Although a cross-functional approach is depicted, these types of systems can also be organised along sectoral lines, so that each node or cluster could represent an industry; cross- fertilization between sectors can occur as a result of the rich linkages.

Leaders of networked communities encourage inter-organisational collaboration. They gather the owners and decision-makers of various resources in the community or region into a web of interconnected transformational leaders who manage the multitude of projects, with each transformational leader becoming responsible for his/her node. The networked community as a whole allows new nodes to form and grow organically and independently. The effectiveness of the whole is measured by the ability to manage the interaction between nodes. In a highly productive community, the number of nodes may be large and extremely varied. When the number of projects increases, along with the complexity of the knowledge involved, there is an inevitable shift away from the traditional forms of leadership toward a distributed leadership system.

Figure 2. Distributed leadership system

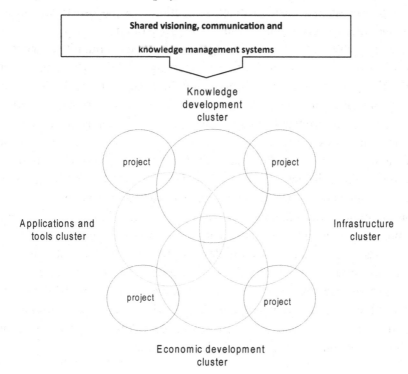

An example is Waterloo, Ontario, Canada. In 2000, the Mayor of Waterloo launched a significant, city-wide public consultation process to discern the best possible future for Waterloo. "Imagine! Waterloo" culminated into the city's Intelligent Community Strategy where the quality of life, business growth and ever-expanding knowledge workforce will benefit from the entrepreneurial spirit, interest and investment that have been made in the community. Three of the highest officials at the municipality are members of the Intelligent Community Steering Committee, as are a half dozen key private sector officials and more than a dozen non-profit organisations—including school boards, libraries, universities, technology associations, and members of the general public (Archives of the ICF, 2007).

Community networks that encourage inter-agency cooperation can become dynamic open systems that encourage evolutionary approaches within a group or team. Over time, closed systems are maladaptive and therefore perishable. To foster open systems, community networks must encourage multi-level partnerships (among managers and staff in organisations) and multi-agency (several organisations within the same sector), multi-industry (several sectors such as partnerships between health and private sector), and multi-tiered networks (network-to-network, including national and international organisations). The group of multiple agencies becomes the team responsible for further advancing the networked community concept. Each node has its own set of responsibilities in effecting the transformation. Dynamic networks also provide both specialisation and flexibility, with each partner in the network responsible for a particular expertise. To be successful, the network must create a network culture that transcends ownership and organisational borders.

As shown in Figure 2, the network provides some measure of centrality brought about by a high level organisation that helps to provide an overall vision, but does not control or direct the activities of each node or cluster. The model allows each node to negotiate and undertake its own project(s) and additional nodes to emerge to resolve common issues that may be short or long term in nature. However, the central body may challenge each node with ideas about technology and processes, and encourage interaction between nodes toward synergy. The optimal medium between control and guidelines will make it easier for users to understand the products and services being offered and minimize duplication or wasted effort, while also allowing a flexible and decentralised environment where individuals and organisations can thrive. One of the better examples of distributed and widespread leadership can be found in Philadelphia, Pennsylvania, U.S.

In 2004, Philadelphia's mayor appointed a 17-member Wireless Philadelphia Executive Committee to serve as an advisory and advocacy group for wireless community networking through community outreach programmes, communications with the press, and participation in meetings and conferences. Membership included leaders from business, education, the municipality and interested citizens. The committee was charged to develop partnerships with the goal of providing wireless access throughout the city to increase economic development in neighbourhoods, to help overcome the digital divide and to improve quality of life for all Philadelphians.

To achieve these goals, the Committee engaged in detailed study and discussion, with assistance from the universities and private-sector companies, on issues ranging from stakeholder analysis, requirements definition, business model scenarios, funding options, investment potential, and technical architectures. The committee also identified stakeholders and invited them to participate in 13 focus group discussions charged with developing nodes equipped with their own leaders. Each focus group meeting was organised by one of Philadelphia's business, cultural and social organisations. Examples of such sponsors included the Chamber of Commerce, tourism bodies, healthcare groups and innovation-oriented groups. To ensure inclusiveness, the municipality organised a Town Hall meeting.

Wireless Philadelphia was not without its hurdles. The passage of House Bill 30 (OrangePolitics.com, 2004) by the legislature of the Commonwealth of Pennsylvania threatened to derail the project. Although in 2004, the governor signed House Bill 30, called the "Verizon Bill", the city negotiated a compromise with the incumbent telephone provider Verizon allowing the Wireless Philadelphia project to proceed. Strong leadership within City Council kept the project on track by creating an environment where teams could continue their work. (Archives of the ICF, 2006c)

The Philadelphia initiative illustrates the effectiveness of a distributed leadership system. Its wide acceptance in the community encouraged development of several levels of activity within which project leadership emerged. Like a snowball, Wireless Philadelphia gained speed and breadth as it progressed and became a national model for grassroots community action, even though its Wireless Philadelphia project failed to meet its objective with the 2008 withdrawal of its wireless ISP partner EarthLink (Kerkstra, 2008).

LEADERSHIP THROUGH THE VARIOUS NETWORK PHASES

Albert and LeBrasseur (2006) proposed that network development takes place in two interactive phases that, over time, create a culture of use and a sustainable network (see Figure 3). In Phase 1, the formation of the community network is marked by the emergence of a leader and/or a board of directors to respond to environmental pressures. These pressures may occur as a result of globalization and the need to remain competitive with other communities or regions, or as a result of downsizing or social development pressures resulting in a lack of medical practitioners or loss of youth, for example.

Phase 2, network performance, involves the concrete objectives and steps that the board takes to achieve the community goals that were agreed upon. Larger communities tend to have less pressure in developing infrastructure but need to resolve economic and social pressures. Smaller communities need collaborators to solve a wider variety of challenges that include infrastructure and resource problems. In this second phase, the network can develop a culture and structure that gives meaning and coherence to a variety of projects. Some communities adopt a "Field of Dreams" approach and are more liberal and hands-off, allowing the private sector and citizens to develop content and opportunity. Others intentionally plan a

Figure 3. Model of phases of development of community networks

vision around community transformation based on an improved telecommunication infrastructure, which means more direct involvement in developing applications, pushing for innovation and planning economic development.

Phase 1 relies heavily on leadership dynamics whereas Phase 2 is closer to managerial dynamics—but with a distinctive collaborative flavor. These two phases are inter-dependent over time, where formation sets the stage for performance, and performance influences board and leadership dynamics. Positive outcomes at the performance phase consolidate the dynamics of the formation phase; negative outcomes challenge the board and leadership and initiate a re-formation phase. This iterative process was demonstrated in the feedback loop (Figure 3) by Arino and de la Torre (1998). The third and last phase—outcomes—is where evaluation and measurement will solidify or question collaborations in the network. A culture of use must be planned at the onset to strengthen sustainability but many other good team management techniques will also help to ensure that the outcomes meet the requirements of all participating members of the network. More on measurement and evaluation will be discussed near the end of this chapter.

The first step in the formation phase is to have a key individual (or group of individuals) form a coalition of people who are enthusiastic about the potential of technology to help their community and who are prepared to explore their mutual interests. A formal committee that includes champions or leaders and members from various public and private sector stakeholders is assigned the responsibility of developing a vision and a strategy for the networked community. As identified by Heemstra and Kusters (2004), "a group of individuals with a sufficient diversity in disciplinary backgrounds, position, roles and tasks, will counterbalance the perceptual one-sidedness of individuals... we can use the group to create superior knowledge through interaction of specialised individuals who share their knowledge, by turning private knowledge into public knowledge and tacit knowledge into explicit knowledge" (p. 261). The team must be able to work together toward common goals, using the best skills of its members in an efficient manner. The team's effectiveness in tackling problems throughout the community and in their respective organisations will directly affect the achievement of the objectives. A high-performance team is one that can develop a stronger commitment to the team and its goals, which will translate into a greater probability of success (Wheelan, 1999).

Carroll and Rosson (2001) explained that a community groups often share a high level vision or sense of purpose, but rarely coordinate their agendas at the operational level. Efficient networked communities attempt to improve this level of coordination among agencies. If they cannot develop well articulated dependencies, it is more difficult to realise a high performance team environment. The partnership becomes solid once the community strategy and business plan are developed. While members of networked community committees or boards are striving toward a common vision or purpose, their actions may require approval by a regional or municipal government, funding agency, independent community board, their own agency, or a combination of these authorities. The ability of the organisational representatives to effect change, to convince and negotiate within their own organisation and with other community stakeholders, is critical. These network explorers must have the power (whether legal or persuasive) to negotiate and effect the change required within their respective organisations and in collaboration with other community partners.

OneCleveland did not feel it was enough to just build a next generation network. The community leaders in this U.S. community in Ohio wanted a platform for mobilising and aligning the region's resources and talents into a cohesive offensive strategy that would propel them into a strong globally competitive economy. In the 2006 Intelligent Community of the Year competition's nomination process, the authors learned that the organisation faced a number of challenges, from a need to improve public safety to the need to eliminate a culture of poverty. The ICF staff wrote the following:

> In order to re-invent itself, the organisation established working groups to attract and maintain passionate engagement and interest within the community. They tapped public and non-profit organisations to become providers of services and collaborators on projects as a means of penetrating a larger market within Cleveland. Their objective is to out-work, out-collaborate and out-innovate other regional economies by leveraging existing tools and resources and sparking the imagination of the entire community. They are reaching Cleveland residents at home and abroad. The strategy is simple... Connect, Enable, and Transform. (ICF, 2006).

Leaders of networked communities must therefore pay attention to the specific leaders required by each project and the network as a whole based on the situation—whether it is going through the formation or performance phases. Transformation leadership is needed during the formation phase, with structured leadership believed to be more effective during the performance phase.

Partners must share a common vision throughout the network construction. During the performance phase, a different kind of leadership may be needed—a transactional leader that is capable of transforming ideas into projects and establishing evaluation mechanisms to measure outcomes. Without this transition, the network will have difficulty continuing the cycle of innovation, and stakeholders may eventually abandon the team when they can no longer see a benefit, whether they are individuals or organisations. Bouwen and Taillieu (2004) researched the dual requirements of leadership and management that deal with the interdependence of network members, the development of a shared purpose and coordination of actions at both the operational and strategic levels. Though leadership and management are both necessary throughout the life of an organisation, their relative importance and interaction vary at different phases of the network's development. The level of success that the network achieves depends upon the balancing and integration of these roles.

FINDING LEADERS

Three basic types of leadership are found within networked communities: individual, organisational, and team. They are distinct but can be mutually reinforcing.

Individual leadership. The network needs individuals who are super-leaders: visionary leaders, emergent leaders, or transformation leaders. There can be several of these remarkable individuals within the network, and each will bring specific skills and knowledge to it. They are likely to flourish within a network node or cluster. They will be able to share their own networks and resources with other members, encourage innovation and participation at all levels and deal with resistors. Even if these leaders are not at the helm of their own organisation, they can be influential people within the organisation and perhaps the community. They will not necessarily have technical knowledge but will understand the opportunities.

A conscious effort to develop and champion breakthrough applications of ICT can help to empower citizens and improve personal income even in the poorest of communities. An interesting example of transformational leadership and collaboration is found in the work of Professor Muhammad Unus, founder of the Grameen Bank and 2006 Nobel Peace Prize Winner who said "an individual poor person is an isolated island by himself and herself. IT can end that isolation overnight"(Grameen, 2008, p. 1).

Bangladesh, a poor country with a population of 140 million, had a wireless telephony penetration rate of less than two phones for 1,000 people in 2001. Bangladesh was the site of the Grameen Village Phone experiment of that era that began putting cellular phones in the hands of women who used them to create small local business ventures. The strategy was to enable poor and often illiterate women to secure a loan to purchase a phone with which small producers could check market prices and therefore better negotiate with middlemen a fair market price for their goods.

By 2008, according to the Grameen Foundation Web site, Grameen Telecom was the largest cellular phone company in all of South Asia with some 8.5 million subscribers. More than 220,000 "micro entrepreneurs" using small loans from the Grameen Bank were "bringing phone service to at least that many rural villages in Bangladesh" (Grameen, 2008, p. 1). The result was a breakthrough in cross-community collaboration. This innovation put money into circulation within the community, helped new business activity and made easier public access to the tools of distance communication for calling, messaging and e-mailing. Lower interest rates to borrowers and new loan programs that attracted additional clients became available. The borrowers became more self-sufficient and initiative-taking. "We are transforming the microfinance sector through innovations and collaborations that improve the delivery of financial services to the poor and integrate microfinance with the global financial system" (Grameen, 2008, p. 1).

Individual leaders can make a real difference within communities or regions. Although formal leaders, such as those found in political office, are and continue to be an important source of networked community leaders, individuals capable of instigating visionary and transformational change can be found almost anywhere. Successful networked communities strive to harness their energies on a continual basis.

Organizational leadership. Organisations in the community need to be innovative and supportive of the networked community effort through direct representation by their leaders or by officially supporting the individuals who represent their interests and their ideas for change. Organisations must be willing to change and entertain new ideas, eliminate silos, encourage innovations and collaborate in the transformation effort. Supportive leadership at the higher levels is needed, especially when the organisation only sends a representative on its behalf. Organisational leaders must provide sufficient power to these individuals to engage in negotiation. Organisation leaders also need to motivate employees when they are called upon to implement the network's goals. Organisational leadership can be encouraged through conferences, individual meetings and written communication of the opportunities. Christensen, Marx and Stevenson (2006) in the *Harvard Business Review* present a useful review of the tools for encouraging cooperation and change within organisations including using leadership, power, culture and management tools.

Team leadership. A team has more information and knowledge than an individual (Heemstra & Kusters, 2004) and can process and manage more complex and larger projects. To realise a networked community, several community leaders must share a common vision, and they must be willing to lead through teamwork in a decentralised environment. This critical team must be willing to take on responsibility for projects, build its own competency, seek advice and tools, monitor and evaluate progress, and create a culture of change. The team's environment should harness the power, skills and knowledge of all stakeholders involved in the network strategy.

Champions of community networks are most likely sophisticated leaders who view the future of their communities in an entirely new light. These champions must come to a common vision, and the team must be managed effectively to maximize the chances for success. Leading change requires the conscious nudging of individuals and groups away from one state of affairs toward another (Reeves, Duncan & Ginter, 2000). Networked communities are more likely to be developed by community champions who are aware of international trends and foresee an opportunity for their own community or region (Bass & Avolio, 2000).

Leaders with vision may get involved for personal satisfaction, to realise economic development opportunities for the community or to generate cost savings for one's own organisation. In a survey of Canadian Smart Communities by Albert and LeBrasseur (2005), economic development, cost savings, the need for the infrastructure and personal vision were all significant factors in the decision to get involved in a community network initiative. These managers were often the kinds of leaders needed for new and emerging projects because they brought a broader perspective to the task. The study showed that many of these leaders wanted to see high bandwidth services provided to their own organisations, as well as to the community. Therefore, initiators of individual projects may find they must provide opportunities to a wider section of the community to attract the right champion to lead their broadband telecommunications initiative. Partners with high infrastructure needs include school boards, hospitals, municipalities, large and small business employers, and telecommunication service providers.

Avolio, Bass and Jung (1999) suggest that networked communities should be led by teams of individuals coming from various sectors, backgrounds, and organisations; otherwise, their objectives will tend to be restrictive in scope (p. 441). The diversity of their personalities, backgrounds and experience is thought to be a key determinant of a project's success, driving people to excel beyond the standard limits and self-interests to realise community-wide objectives. Similar studies have shown that these teams also tend to be associated with higher project quality, inspiring a sense of mission, encouraging members to transcend personal interests and addressing technical issues where several disciplines are needed. The following illustration from Ichikawa, Japan, was taken from the ICF nomination for the 2006 ICF Intelligent Community of the Year.

The core of Ichikawa's strategy was the establishment of a business plaza to promote the growth of businesses and provide e-government programs to citizens. The plaza is a highly innovative atmosphere, allowing public use and hosting a data centre for surrounding municipalities, non-profit organisations, resident's associations and SOHO owners. This pool of talent has spurred innovation and creativity and continues to create new opportunities for Ichikawa. The city also became involved in a collaborative project with six other municipalities to establish a common GIS system for regional planning and administration. The city then extended its collaboration to Seoul, South Korea, in order to share knowledge in technology applications and begin a staff exchange with Gangnam-gu, considered the most advanced ICT region in Seoul. They have developed a highly productive team environment that continues to innovate (Archives of the ICF, 2006b).

Collaboration and teamwork, aided by distributed leadership may not be easy to realise in the pursuit of a networked community. Some resistance to change can be expected, even when negative economic conditions are causing hardships for people. Network members must be patient and keep broadcasting the vision and its promise of better times ahead. A distributed leadership provides the flexibility for different rates of learning and participation, and can even find a place and role for the late adopters.

MEASUREMENT AND EVALUATION

Among the most difficult dimensions to measure is that of leadership. Communities must find indicators to mark their progress in ensuring a system of leadership that can survive changing economic times, that can encourage inclusiveness and

Table 1. Leadership and collaboration evaluation

Indicators	Possible approaches to measurement
Multi-organisational shared leadership	Ability to grow the project even if a key leader is no longer available
Strength of leading structure	Extent of multi-nodal system
	Reporting and information sharing system
Transformational leadership with a change management plan	Common vision of partners
	Understanding of actionable items and their impact
	Ability to effect change
Visioning and achievement oriented	Events & symbols
	Evaluation system
	Benchmarking
Increased collaboration as demonstrated by the range of public & non-profit organisations involved	Number of partners from different health organisations
	Number of partners from different educational organisations
	Number of partners from different governmental organisations
	Shared decision-making power
Range of private sector organisations	Number of partners from IT-related firms
	Number of partners from different industrial groups
	Level of representation of industrial fabric of community or region
	Shared decision-making power
Sustainability as demonstrated by the extent of collaboration	Number of public organisations participating in governing structure
	Number of private organisations participating in governing structure
Sustainability as demonstrated by strategic planning effort	Agreeing upon plan that includes short and long term action items with deliverables and assignment of responsibilities
	Broad participation in the development of the plan
	Regular monitoring and amendments to the plan in response to the internal and external environment

innovation, and that can promote community-wide collaboration so that a wide range of sectors will be involved in the effort. The history of relationships among local organisations becomes important, as does the ability to agree on a vision and take pride in accomplishments.

Leadership is often demonstrated through events and symbols. For example, an inclusive strategic planning effort that includes citizens, as well as private and public organisations, is a visible demonstration of leadership. The extent to which collaboration plays a part in planning, in infrastructure development, in content creation and in recruiting business development are measurable factors. Partnerships, joint ventures, shared risk, revenue production and long-term commitments to projects are other ways to measure qualities of leadership.

Eger (1997) recommended looking at the possible effects on the way people govern themselves and the impact of collaborative activity such as voter participation levels, civic participation in local issues and decision-making, and citizen-government contacts by type and number. Table 1 is a useful guide for tracking leadership effectiveness.

CONCLUSION

Four important leadership concepts were proposed in this chapter:

- Leadership of networks must be transformational to develop innovative approaches that will allow communities to compete regionally and internationally;
- Distributed leadership in societies in which organisations are concerned about sharing power can encourage collaboration among a greater number of agencies and lead to synergistic activity;
- Leadership and the development of nodes should be developed throughout the community in a variety of sectors to encourage participation and commitment to the project's objectives; and
- Different types of leaders may be required at the formation and performance phases of the network's development.

Any number of leadership systems and structures can exist among networked communities around the world, depending on political systems and the power structure of communities and regions. Yet, the networked communities will be those planning for transformation, rather than reacting to change or having it emerge on its own. Whether by way of a centralised or decentralised decision-making structure, successful projects will involve a variety of supporting organisations that have been called upon to help implement the vision.

In Western society, the decentralised approach is proposed as offering a higher level of synergistic activity and sustainability; it allows a greater number of community leaders and innovators to be involved and maintains, to an extent, greater control within existing organisations. The sharing of power is always difficult and is at the root of our organisational and institutional silos. Finding solutions to minimize disruptions and reducing the threat that organisations feel are important steps in sustaining collaboration efforts. The decentralised approach relies heavily on a common vision and excellent communication systems to counteract the tendency for isolation.

Identification of transformational (yes, even charismatic) leaders is proposed for the formation phase of the network. These leaders are best able to focus people's attention and sell them on the vision. Once the network is operational, projects will need transactional leaders, those individuals who can manage details and measure output in a decentralised or distributed governance environment.

This chapter has attempted to rally community leaders around the higher level goal of co-building economic foundations, challenging them to build complex nodes of relationships with a distributed leadership system. This is not an easy task, but it is one that can promote greater stewardship and buy-in from stakeholders. The theme of webs of relationships was presented in preceding chapters. In the innovation chapter, we referred to building a learning community—not simply a number of clusters, but a culture of innovation by assembling dissimilar organisations for cross-fertilization. A similar approach was offered in the chapter on applications, where multi-organisational, multi-sectoral partnerships were proposed as a way to initiate cross-fertilization, develop economies of scale and make projects more sustainable. These threads have come together in this chapter in that collaborative leadership, in one form or another, is proposed as the key to managing change.

REFERENCES

Albert, S. & LeBrasseur, R. (2005). Implementation challenges for networks. *International Journal of Technology, Knowledge & Society, 2*(1), 1-10.

Albert, S. & LeBrasseur, R. (2006), Collaboration challenges in community telecommunication networks. *International Journal of Technology & Human Interaction, 3*(2), 13-33.

Archives of the ICF – The Intelligent Communities Forum. (2007). Waterloo, Ontario, Canada – *Nomination submitted for the Intelligent Community of the Year Award*. New York.

Archives of the ICF – The Intelligent Communities Forum. (2006a). Cleveland, Ohio, U.S. – *Nomination submitted for the Intelligent Community of the Year Award.* New York.

Archives of the ICF – The Intelligent Communities Forum. (2006b). Ichikawa, Japan – *Nomination submitted for the Intelligent Community of the Year Award.* New York.

Archives of the ICF – The Intelligent Communities Forum. (2006c). Philadelphia, PA, U.S. – *Nomination submitted for the Intelligent Community of the Year Award.* New York.

Archives of the ICF – The Intelligent Communities Forum. (2006d). Taipei, Taiwan – *Nomination submitted for the Intelligent Community of the Year Award.* New York.

Arino, A. & de la Torre, J. (1998). Learning from failure: Towards an evolutionary model of collaborative ventures. *Organisational Science, 9*(3), 306-325.

Austin, J. E. (2003). Marketing's role in cross-sector collaboration. *Journal of Nonprofit & Public Sector Marketing, 11*(1), 23-39.

Avolio, B. J., Bass, B. M. & Jung, D. I. (1999). Re-examining the components of transformation and transactional leadership using the multifactor leadership question-naire. *Journal of Occupational and Organisational Leadership, 72*(4), 441-462.

Bass, B. & Avolio, B. (2000). *MLQ: Multifactor leadership questionnaire for teams.* Redwood City CA: Mindgarden.

Bouwen, R. & Taillieu, T. (2004). Multiparty collaboration as social learning for interdependence: Developing relational knowing for sustainable natural resources management. *Journal of Community & Applied Social Psychology, 14*(3), 137-153.

Brinck, T. (2005). Constructing a state Web portal through design alternatives, measurement and iterative refinement. *Bulletin of the American Society for Information Science and Technology, 31*(2), 14-17.

Brugmann, J. & Prahalad, C. K. (2007). Co-creating business's new social compact. *Harvard Business Review, February,* 80-91.

Bucklin, L. P. & Sengupta, S. (1993). Organising successful co-marketing alliances. *Journal of Marketing, 57*(2), 32-46.

Caroll, J. M. & Rosson M. B. (2001). Better home shopping or new democracy? Evaluating community network outcomes. *CHI 3*(1), 372-377.

Christensen, C. J. Marx, M. & Stevenson, H. H. (2006). The tools of cooperation and change. *Harvard Business Review, October*, 72-81.

Das, T. K. & Bing-Sheng, T. (1999). Managing risks in strategic alliances. *Academy of Management Executives, 13*(4), 50-62.

Ebers, M. (2002). *The formation of inter-organisational networks.* Oxford UK: Oxford University Press.

Gillis, W. & McLellan, S. (1998). In J. Marsh and A. E. Grant. (Eds.), *Blue sky: Dreams and imagination in creating 21st century communication technology.* Commack NY: Nova Science Publishers Inc.

Grameen Foundation (2008). *Our Heritage: Grameen Village Phone in Bangladesh.* Retrieved May 5, 2008, from www.grameenfoundation.org, 1.

Gray, B. (1985). Conditions facilitating interorganisational collaboration. *Human Relations, 38*(10), 911-936.

Heemstra, F. & Kusters, R. (2004). Defining ICT proposals. *Journal of Enterprise Information Management, 17*(4), 258-268.

Hock, D. (2000). *The chaordic organisation.* San Francisco: Behrett-Koehler Publishers.

ICF – Intelligent Communities Forum. (2007), *Leadership is key to a successful intelligent community.* (2007). Retrieved April 29, 2007, from http://www.intelligentcommunity.org

Industry Canada. (2003). *Smart communities broadband.* Retrieved May 25, 2008, from http://198.103.246.211/documents/governance_e.asp

Jones, C., Hesterly, W. S. & Borgatti, S. P. (1997). A general theory of network governance: Exchange conditions and social mechanisms. *Academy of Management Review, 22*(4), 911-946.

Jurow, S. (2007). *Change: The importance of the process.* Retrieved October 18, 2007, from http://www.clir.org/PUBS/reports/pub85/change.html

Kavanaugh, A. & Patterson, S. (2001). The impact of community computer networks on social capital and community involvement. *American Behavioural Scientist, 45*(3). 496-509.

Kavanaugh, A., Reese, D. D., Carroll, J. M. & Rosson, M. B. (2005). Weak ties in networked communities. *The Information Society, 21*(2), 119-131.

Kerkstra, P. (2008). EarthLink to pull the plug on its Wi-Fi project in Philadelphia. *Philadelphia Enquirer.* Retrieved June 11, 2008, from www.philly.com.

Miles, R. E. & Snow, C. C. (1986). Organisations: New concepts for new forms. *California Management Review, 28*(3), 62-73.

OrangePolitics.com. (2004). *The future of public wireless.* Retrieved October 24, 2007, from http://orangepolitics.org/2004/11/the-future-of-public-wireless/

Pôr, G. & van Bekkum, E. (2003). *Innovation and communities of practices.* Retrieved November 21, 2007, from the Community Intelligence Web site: http://www.CommunityIntelligence.co.uk

Reeves, T., Duncan, J. W. & Ginter, P. M. (2000). Leading change by managing paradoxes. *Journal of Leadership Studies, 7*(1), 13-30.

Tapscott, D. (1998) *Growing up digital: The rise of the net generation.* New York: McGraw-Hill.

Tucker, J. (2007). *Types of change: Developmental, transitional and transformational.* Retrieved October 18, 2007 from the Suite 101.com Web site: http://businessman-agement.suite101.com/article.cfm/types_of_change.

Waits, M. (2000). The added value of the industry cluster approach to economic analysis, strategy development and service delivery. *Economic Development Quarterly, 14*(1), 35-50.

Weick, K.E. & Quinn, R. E. (1999). Organisational change and development. *Annual Review of Psychology, 50*, 361-386.

Wheelan, S. A. (1999). *Creating effective teams: A guide for members and leaders.* Thousand Oaks CA: Sage Publications.

Whymer, W. W. & Samu, S. (2003). Dimensions of business and non-profit collaborative relationships. *Journal of Nonprofit & Public Sector Marketing, 11*(1), 3-22.

Chapter X
Promotion and Relationship Marketing

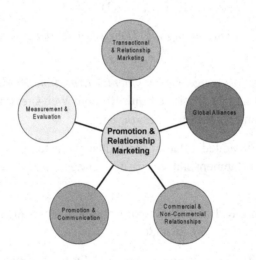

"A stakeholder should have an interest in the decisions and actions of all the organisations that affect the stakeholder's life and well being, a claim to the rights of consultation, access to all relevant information, and most importantly, participation in decision making." (Thomas, 2000, p. 528)

Overview: This chapter introduces the concept of marketing and explores its relevance for networked communities. The specific topics include:

- An introduction to relationship marketing;
- A review of transactional marketing;
- Transactional versus relationship marketing, with Ottawa, Canada, as an example;

- Commercial relationships, giving the example of the Digital Harbour, Australia;
- Non-commercial relationships such as the Education Development Center;
- Global alliances using the examples of the Intelligent Community Forum (ICF) and Global Cities Dialogue (GCD);
- Measurement and evaluation of marketing efforts.

RELATIONSHIP MARKETING

Key Concept: *There are internal and external relationships that networked communities consider critical for realising their sustainability goals and that fit their situation. Investing in these relationships allows communities to position themselves to succeed in the Network Society.*

Many community leaders and agencies have identified broadband capability and its many potential applications as essential ingredients in their vision of community. To support the implementation and development of ICTs in their communities, they have given marketing a growing role, with a focus on relationship marketing, as opposed to the more traditional transactional marketing. For our purpose, relationship marketing is defined as the effort a community makes to foster and communicate a common vision among community stakeholders around broadband development and community sustainability.

Relationship marketing has two spheres of activity in the networked community: building and enhancing relationships within the community, and between the community and communities around the world. The goal is to become fully connected electronically both locally and globally so that community members, whether individuals or organisations, will continue to satisfy their needs and pursue their aspirations. In this manner, communities can position themselves within the larger Network Society.

In a simple market economy, buyers and sellers meet and transact a sale, an exchange of money for a product or service. Traditional marketing, commonly known as transaction marketing, tries to influence buyers through such tactics as publicity and promotions. In contrast, relationship marketing focuses on more complex exchanges over longer periods of time; the exchanges are multiple and both direct and indirect in nature. Michael Thomas (2000), a marketing researcher, compares transaction marketing to relationship marketing, which is closer to community development in that it involves active participation, loyalty and social cohesion. In transactional marketing, building a relationship with the customer takes place after the initial sale, and focuses on customer service and repeat sales. In relationship marketing, establishing and enhancing the relationship between the supplier and "customer" is a concern even before the first "sale" or transaction and will continue possibly for a lifetime.

George Brenkert (2002) has emphasized the importance of transparent effort in the pursuit of social ends. Community leaders must explain, justify and rationally defend why those ends are the right ones. Marketing plans that are manipulative—that aim to persuade potential buyers by any legal means—undercut public discourse that involves conversation, debate and dialogue. The usual approach in social marketing, he says, is to extend "the logic of persuasion with regard to commercial products to the adoption of social goals" (p. 24). Brenkert protests that the dictum of "let the buyer beware" is inappropriate for community marketing. Since community members constitute the most important stakeholder group helping to define these social goals and are the ones deciding the means by which they will be achieved, manipulative marketing is unlikely to be effective. A marketing strategy in tune with the human condition would seem more appropriate and effective. Radio, television, newspapers and the Internet are all media that relationship marketers can use to elicit the views of the affected public, build consensus and promote acceptance of goals.

Table 1 summarizes the characteristics of relationship marketing and the advantages for the community and its members. Based in the Stockholm University School of Business, Evert Gummesson (2002) has championed relationship marketing as a paradigm shift appropriate for the 21st century. Relationship marketing builds on traditional and modern marketing views and practises, but goes beyond it by focusing on relationships. From this perspective, the Network Society involves a shift from impersonal market forces to human and collective forces that operate through networks. This idea is developed further in this chapter, which relies heavily on the ideas of Gummesson.

A community that practises relationship marketing is keenly aware of who its stakeholders are, who represents it, and how best to communicate with them. In the Network Society, stakeholders are both local (e.g., citizens, associations and organisations) and global (e.g., markets, partners and associations) in nature. As community stakeholders collaborate over time, they co-develop and offer new products and services that make the local community more efficient and more interesting for its members.

Table 1. Characteristics of relationship marketing (RM) in the networked community

Definition of relationship marketing (RM)	RM is marketing based on interaction and exchanges in networks of relationships. It is composed of thirty types of relationships.
Values	Trust and mutual assistance are key values. The parties in a network are co-producers of value; they seek more win–win and less win–lose situations. All parties carry responsibility in these long-term relationships.
Implications for management and administration	RM represents an aspect of the total management of the organisation and community—and is not limited to marketing or sales departments; the marketing plan becomes part of the strategic plan of the community.
Advantages to the community	Increased participant retention and duration. RM adds collaboration to competition and regulation; the synergy of these three approaches contributes to a dynamic marketing equilibrium and achievement of community goals.
Advantages to citizens and customers	Increased focus on co-development of products and services; increased customized production and marketing to the individual; and reduced focus on standardized mass production and mass marketing.

Adapted from Gummesson (2002), Table 9.1, p. 310.

TRANSACTIONAL MARKETING

Relationship marketing expands the scope of transactional marketing, but also builds upon it. Transactional marketing makes use of the 4 Ps framework developed by McCarthy (1978). Egan (2004, p. 11) describes the 4 Ps as follows:

- Product: new product development, brand management, features, benefits, packaging and after-sales service
- Price: costs, profits, liquidity, competitiveness, value and incentives
- Place: channel management, retail location and image, and logistics

- Promotion: marketing communications mix and integrated communications.

The judicious mix of product, price, place and promotion ensures that the firm is responding effectively to market forces (threats and opportunities). The success of the marketing mix can be measured in terms of product profitability and market share. Gummesson (2002) discusses the marketing mix in terms of key relationships among suppliers, customers, and competitors within the context of distribution channels and legal contracts.

The classic dyad—the relationship between the supplier and the customer. This is the parent relationship of marketing, the ultimate exchange of value that constitutes the basis of business and exchange. For example, a telecommunication network supplies broadband capability to an Internet provider; an Internet provider offers connectivity to individuals; a government portal offers a variety of administrative services to citizens.

The classic triad—the drama of the customer–supplier–competitor triangle. Competition is a central ingredient of the market economy. In competition there are relationships between three parties: between the customer and the current supplier, between the customer and the supplier's competitors, and between competitors. For example, a community has several Internet access providers that compete on the basis of price, bps (bits per second) and reliability of service. Competitors monitor one another to set competitive offerings and seek an advantage. When a town has only one Internet access provider, users become a captive market. Similarly when only one broadband provider is available, content providers become a captive market. This dependency leads to relatively low innovation and poor service.

The classic network—distribution channels. The traditional physical distribution and modern channel management, including goods, services, people and information, consists of a network of relationships. A community's digital network is composed of a variety of relationships among connectivity providers, content providers, regulators and assemblers who bundle these products and services. The channel starts with the basic products and ends with the customer. The profit motive typically drives the creation and use of these distribution channels.

The legal contract. The customer-supplier relationship is legally defined with recourse for both parties. A legal framework is essential to community life for protecting the rights of individuals and organisations. However, the Internet has proven to be difficult to control, and requires both formal and informal control mechanisms. Self-monitoring by interest groups can be effective in establishing norms.

Transaction marketing continues to be relevant to exchanges that are simple, short-term and standardized, such as obtaining Internet access. Customers, whether local or global, will make a decision based on the traditional criteria of price and value. To influence these customers, a marketing mix composed of the 4 Ps (price, product, promotion and place) makes sense. Transaction marketing is alive and well, but insufficient for networked communities who operate within the Network Society. The world is covered by the Internet and the applications that ride upon it. Relationships, and networks of relationships, use the communication channels for their mutual benefit. Thus, building and sustaining relationships becomes more important in capturing these benefits for the local community.

FROM TRANSACTIONAL MARKETING TO RELATIONSHIP MARKETING

Key Concept: *Relationship marketing allows local communities to obtain public support for developing and improving telecommunication networks to better connect individuals and organisations within those communities.*

Gummesson (2002, p. 28) has rearranged the 4 Ps of marketing (product, place, price and promotion) into thirty relationships that he thinks would best be managed under the umbrella of relationship marketing. He then sorts these relationships into four categories:

- Classic market relationships that include customers, suppliers and competitors, plus the distribution channel;
- Special market relationships that include interactions between customers and service providers, between customers as members and electronic relationships;
- Mega relationships that include local and global alliances tied to knowledge acquisition; and
- Nano relationships including internal customers, owners and funding agencies.

Both transactional and relationship marketing can be applied to the local and global context. However, they differ in their time horizon, complexity of products and services, and underlying goals, for example sales goals and market share vs. sustainability.

When two-party exchanges are complex, long-term and individualized, transactional marketing is relatively ineffective when compared with relationship marketing.

If a person is looking for online training and education leading to a diploma, building a relationship between this person and representatives of an educational institution is more appropriate than focusing on the 4 Ps. In all communities, special interest groups of professionals, youth, educators and IT enthusiasts display loyalty to their common goals and activities. Membership is both local and global, and strong ties exist across groups. The 4 Ps take on a supportive role to relationship building and enhancement instead of playing the leading role (Gummesson, 2002, p. 312). The relationship mix, the portfolio of relationships, networks and interactions, is promoted by understanding how the 4 Ps support these relationships.

Community marketing spans the local population and touches the decision-makers in their various organisations. These decision-makers are likely to appreciate both the local and global connectivity provided by communication networks. These communication systems will help in building relationships locally and globally. Broadband telecommunications networks will be used not just as a means to grow the local economy but to focus on building awareness and acceptance of ICTs, promoting collaboration across sectors, meeting public needs and encouraging broad participation. All stakeholder groups with a local presence will want to be involved in community development. This process is ongoing and is aided by both transactional exchanges and relationship marketing.

Some communities have a marketing and promotion department embedded in an economic development corporation. Some may also have a promotion programme headed by a director of telecommunications. All municipal staff who have contact with the public will play a role in customer service and will be expected to adopt a service orientation. Relationships in the community are typically robust but demanding. Handling complaints and adjusting service offerings is a daily event. Dissatisfied Internet users are likely to seek alternatives elsewhere when local providers do not satisfy their needs and wants. Some individuals and most groups will want to be active players on the Internet. Giving them an outlet and opportunities for expression allows them to obtain satisfaction in the local community.

Internal marketing can be seen as a part of relationship marketing in that it gives indirect and necessary support to the customer relationships that municipalities, agencies and firms value. Customer service is an attitude. How well communities treat their local citizens is a good indication of how they will treat external relationships. Attitudes and values are thought to be pillars of communities, just as they are with individuals. Integrated management assures quality products and services. Organisational innovation is just as important as technological innovation and applies as equally to the community as it does to profit and non-profit institutions.

Ottawa, Canada, has been very active on the marketing front. The Ottawa region, with a population of 1.1 million, including Gatineau, is a global technology centre with more than 1,841 high tech companies employing more than 78,000 employees in the growth sectors of telecommunications, photonics, semiconductors, software, defense and security, and life sciences. Supported by a strong professional services cluster, Ottawa's economy is also complemented by a vibrant tourism sector and the presence of more than 90,000 federal government employees.

After extensive consultation with Ottawa residents and businesses, the city of Ottawa devised the 20/20 Plan—the city's blueprint for where it wants to be in 20 years, and how to get there. Its vision of the ubiquitous Information Society guides its plan and strategic priorities, one of which is to promote Ottawa domestically and internationally as an ideal location for people, companies, tourism and investment.

Beginning in 2001, a multi-year strategy was adopted based on two research studies: the Ottawa Economic Generators Report and the Ottawa Marketing and Branding Study. Ottawa's Global Marketing division had gained international recognition as a key source of information about business, investment and career opportunities in Canada's capital city and the region. The division was given the mandate to implement strategies to:

• Establish Ottawa as a global technology centre;
• Increase the awareness of Ottawa's major attributes among targeted decision makers;
• Provide a coherent brand image of the city to internal and external audiences; and
• Foster economic prosperity in the region by attracting investments, people and companies; and increase the investment from private and public-sector partners.

Ottawa Global Marketing is realising its social and business objectives by focusing its efforts on responding to requests for information and strategic support from internal and external stakeholders; taking the lead in developing and promoting a consistent message that positions Ottawa and Ottawa-based businesses for success; and working in partnership with key decision makers at home and around the world.

Ottawa Global Marketing has successfully promoted partnerships with major U.S. cities and regions to develop business and attract investment. It has also established connections with such European states as the UK, Germany, France and Italy and reached into the emerging markets of Asia and Latin America.

Dell Computer is an example of a success story in job creation and development of new marketing strategies. Dell opened a 500-person technical support centre in Ottawa in 2006. At the opening, Dell announced that staff responsibilities and skill requirements would be upgraded. Expansion to 1,500 staff members was also under consideration. Other multinational companies attracted to Ottawa include Cienna Networks, Harman Inc. and Abbott Point of Care with an expanded presence for IBM, Adobe and Microsoft.

On the marketing front, Ontario's ICT centres in Ottawa, Toronto and Waterloo have integrated their efforts under the Ontario Technology Corridors banner. A 2006 visit to China by the Ottawa Global Marketing team resulted in new plans to reach out to Chinese companies who would like to have presence in Ottawa and to market Ottawa in China. An Ottawa Web site in the Chinese language has been constructed (Archives of the ICF, 2006).

The Ottawa example demonstrates how relationship marketing focuses on both internal and external stakeholders, and builds long-term relationships to meet local economic development objectives. Because of its ample resources, Ottawa established a specialised division (Ottawa Global Marketing) for reaching out to global corporations and distant communities. Smaller communities are more likely to undertake relationship marketing under the auspices of the mayor's office or that of the economic development officer.

COMMERCIAL RELATIONSHIPS

Key Concept: *Commercial relationships that develop broadband applications are important for the networked communities. They are often intertwined with non-commercial relationships. Improved quality of life is the goal that unites them.*

Elected officials and staff of municipalities are likely to have close working relationships with the local providers of broadband capability. These relationships will be stronger when these two organisations are partners in creating and developing the broadband network. Similarly, broadband networks require good working relationships with content providers to keep the network attractive to Internet users. Unlike the broadband provider, content providers have a short-term horizon because of low-cost competitors and users who are loyal only to their own interests. These commercial relationships are embedded in personal and social networks. In most communities, who you know is just as important as what you know. Relationships are often based on common values, perceived benefits and activities of mutual interest; these commonalities work to sustain communication networks. Once the broadband network is operational, commercial development can be pursued.

A notable example is that of the Digital Harbour. This facility is located at Melbourne's Docklands, Australia, and covers 4.4 hectares. Planned in the late 1990s, this urban renewal project has transformed a port railway yard into a technology park integrated with a fully serviced community with cafes, a small theatre for exhibitions and seminars seating up to 180 people, and retail outlets. Funded by public and private money, Digital Harbour offers fast and affordable communication services through its i-Port facility. Space in the Innovation Building is leased to technology-based companies with a mix of education and training groups, and research and development arms of major corporations. Current tenants include Business Strategies International, Telstra Innovation Centre, Telstra Wireless Mobility Group, Wompro (digital marketing firm) and the Australian Film Television and Radio School (Digital Harbour, 2007).

NON-COMMERCIAL RELATIONSHIPS

Key Concept: *Non-commercial relationships that extend the culture of use of broadband applications are also important in networked communities. These partnerships ensure that the applications are meaningful for the entire community and improve the local quality of life.*

Relationships among the public sector, citizens and customers include voluntary organisations and their activities that operate outside the monetary economy. Personal relationships complement commercial ones. Community is about both kinds of relationships and how they contribute to quality of life and sustainability. The non-commercial relationship encourages Internet access for all, diminishing the digital divide.

A prime example is the Education Development Center, a not-for-profit corporation operating from Newton, Massachusetts, New York, and Washington, D.C., that, as of 2008, manages some 325 education, health, technology, human rights and related projects in 35 countries around the world. EDC is guided by the principle, quoted on its Web site, that "learning is the liberating force in human development.... We are committed to education that builds knowledge and skill, makes possible a deeper understanding of the world, and engages learners as active, problem-solving participants" (Education Development Center, 2008). The EDC has built an extensive network of civic collaborators who are tackling the challenge of the digital divide.

The Education Development Center is composed of multiple divisions. For example, the Applied Research and Innovation Division addresses the need to develop, implement and evaluate innovative education approaches that take advantage of the potential of information and communications technologies. Another division, the Education, Employment and Community Programmes Division, is focused on the social and economic development of communities. This division tackles IT literacy, user-centred and technology-based education, building skills for work. The EDU also hosts several centres and programmes, among them:

- **The Centre for Media & Community:** Initiated by the Benton Foundation, this centre "works in partnerships to develop policies and model practices that strengthen underserved communities globally in their educational and economic development." The CMC "creates and facilitates virtual communities of practice to promote initiatives focused on the digital divide, education technology, and ICT literacy" (Centre for Media, 2008).
- **Health and Human Development Programmes:** EDC works with communities to assess and strengthen their infrastructure to address school health issues. EDC creates tools, offers training, and builds partnerships to draw on the best practises in the field of health promotion. For example, EDC and the World Health Organisation worked with Education International (the world's largest teacher trade union) to develop training programmes on HIV prevention for African teachers (Health, 2008).
- **Centre for Children & Families:** The CC&F works to improve the lives of children by supporting the organisations and institutions that serve them and their families. Its projects combine research and practice, promote professional development and systemic change, forge community links, and influence policies that affect the lives of children. The centre's partners include state agencies, non-profit organisations, schools, local child care and Head Start programmes, universities, and national associations (Centre for Children, 2008).
- **Digital Divide Network:** This is an interactive online Web site that features interactive collaboration tools to help digital divide activists around the world to work together. This network claims to be "the Internet's largest community for educators, activists, policy makers and concerned citizens working to bridge the digital divide." The Web site includes free blogging, news and articles on the digital divide, event announcements and discussion boards serving more than 10,000 users in 70 countries (Digital, 2008).

MEGA RELATIONSHIPS

Key Concept: *Alliances among communities elevate the playing field in the Network Society. Through alliances, communities can learn more quickly about best practise and accelerate their own development.*

Quality of life in a community depends on an integrated approach to commercial and non-commercial relationships. Communication systems that allow local players to cooperate and ally with external players support the attainment of sustainability. When two organisations develop a close relationship and collaborate on some common agenda, they have formed an alliance. Thus, competition is partly curbed, while collaboration is given a higher priority to make the market economy work. Both collaboration and competition happen when communication networks are developed and used for commercial and non-commercial purposes. Both are inevitable because the community is composed of a diverse population where power is shared, and because networks are embedded in value-added chains.

Knowledge can be the most strategic and critical resource and "knowledge acquisition" is often the rationale for alliances. Knowledge can be acquired from another organisation, but using it effectively typically requires a long-term relationship between the two organisations. Knowledge evolves through learning, which requires extensive communication among knowledge workers.

Building and enhancing relationships across communities allow the participants to exchange experiences and learn from one another. Examples include such twinned cities as Ichikawa and Gangnam-gu, and larger networks such as the Intelligent Community Forum (ICF), Global Digital Cities Network, and Global Cities Dialogue.

Twinning of Cities. Ichikawa, Japan, is a small city (population of 467,000) east of Tokyo noted for its proximity to Tokyo and surrounding airports. This ICT-sophisticated city has entered into a number of twinning relationships with other progressive cities. In 2005, Ichikawa began an exchange programme with Gangnam-gu, a suburb of Seoul, Korea, and a leader of advanced ICT use. The programme allowed both municipalities to exchange and implement each other's technologies and measures. On a broader front, Ichikawa entered into "sister" relationships with the city of Gardena in California, Leshan in China, Medan in Indonesia and Rosenheim in Germany. Ichikawa also joined the Healthy City Programme of the WHO (World Health Organisation) in which more than a thousand cities employ a variety of measures to ensure the healthy lifestyles of their residents. Ichikawa was a founding member of the Japan chapter of the West Pacific Region Alliance for Healthy Cities. Participation in this rich network of cities allowed Ichikawa to learn best practises, promote itself, and offer improved services to its citizens (Archives of the ICF, 2005).

Intelligent Community Forum. As mentioned in the Preface of this book, ICF is a non-profit think tank and promoter of the broadband economy in the local community. Through its activities and award programmes, ICF creates a network of leaders in broadband applications at the community level. The annual conference and awards are produced in association with Polytechnic University in New York and its Institute for Technology & Enterprise. These *"Building the Broadband Economy"* conferences attract a wide array of participants including local government officials and their private-sector partners in telecom, IT, finance, real estate and consulting. "It offers a global perspective on the best ways to create broadband infrastructure, attract knowledge workers, foster innovation and implement e-government programmes that contribute to economic growth and bridge the digital divide" (ICF, 2007).

The ICF Awards categories have created a wealth of examples of best practises to inspire community leaders:

The Intelligent Community of the Year. Documentation for this award provides the foundation for this book.

Intelligent Facility of the Year. Awarded to a building, facility, campus or office park that has been occupied by tenants for at least six months and has used broadband and information technology to add demonstrable value to the property as well as to contribute to the formation or growth of an intelligent community. Generally, technology parks or related strategic initiatives fit this category.

Intelligent Community Visionary. Awarded to either an individual or an organisation in the public sector, private sector, academia or nonprofit sector who has taken a leadership role in promoting broadband technology as an essential utility in the Digital Age. This individual or organisation must have a proven track record in bringing about effective cooperation between the public and private sectors in economic development.

Broadband Application of the Year. This award is granted in two categories:

The **Commercial Award** goes to the provider of one or more computer-based applications delivered over broadband that have the potential to expand industries or service categories, or to create sustainable new industries or service categories, and lead to employment growth.

The **Nonprofit Award** is given to the provider of a computer-based application using broadband to deliver services that make a positive contribution to human welfare by increasing efficiency, reducing costs, creating new capabilities or extending existing capabilities to people previously unable to access them due to geography, cost or other barriers.

In 2007, the ICF introduced an Immersion Lab: an "action learning" experience that allows participants to see first-hand the world's leading intelligent communities, Each Immersion Lab provides a 7-9 day tour of ICF's Intelligent Communities of the Year and Top Seven Intelligent Communities, featuring:

- Meetings with senior government officials and business executives who are local "champions" for Intelligent Community development;
- Visits to public-sector and private-sector technology sites to see first hand the investment, training and collaboration that are producing results;
- Classroom-style briefings and lectures on key success factors; and
- Social events that encourage one-to-one networking in a relaxed setting.

ICF's 2007 Immersion Lab was an eight-day visit to Intelligent Communities in three of Asia's most dynamic economies, and its 2008 Lab focused principally on visits to cities and regions in North America. This initiative allows community leaders to meet face-to-face and discuss the challenges and opportunities in the local context.

Global Cities Dialogue (GCD). In contrast to the ICF, Global Cities Dialogue (GCD) is a political network. Founded in 1999, the mission of the GCD is to provide an open framework for policy debate and action among cities addressing concerns of the emerging Information Society. GCD is a worldwide network of cities interested in ° creating an Information Society free of digital divide and based on sustainable development (GCD, 2007):

[GCD] is an initiative proposing an open framework for action for all cities interested in working together to realise the potential of an information society free from social exclusion and based on sustainable development. It builds on the premise that cities have a key role to play in the information society. They are the geographical, political, socio-economic and cultural entities where millions live, work and directly exercise their rights as citizens and consumers. They are close to grassroots processes and directly face a number of information-society issues, changes and opportunities from local democracy to more cost-effective services.

The preamble of the constitution of GCD summarizes its perspective on the Information Society and the central role played by communities:

- "We, Mayors signatories of the Declaration of Helsinki 'Mayors of the World for a Global Cities Dialogue on the information society',
- Aware that the information society is a massive challenge and presents cities with a wide range of issues, changes and opportunities, from democracy to more cost effective services, including electronic commerce and others;
- Believing that the development of the information society should be for the benefit of all citizens, communities and peoples of the world, regardless of race, social position, creed, gender, disability or age;
- Recognising the role of local authorities in global areas of governance such as the divide between the "information rich" and the "information poor", low technological literacy, poor public access and shortage of skilled people,
- Recognising the major role of cities in the development of electronic government and democracy, in the introduction of evolutionary innovation in public services, in creating a favourable business environment and in stimulating the wide uptake of electronic commerce and of the new economy;
- Believing that global dialogues are essential for the achievement of mutual understanding, information exchange, and the emergence of best practises in the making of a global, inclusive, peaceful and multi-cultural society;
- Considering the strong pioneering experience of cities and local and regional organisations in the implementation of information society technologies, in order to improve access and services for the citizens, consumer communities and business; and that a growing number of cities and local administrations have obtained very good and practical results, but that most cities are only in the beginning of a learning process" (GCD, 2007).

Membership for this organisation has two requirements: community goals that support the mission of GCD, and strong endorsement and participation by a high-ranking official, such as a mayor. Currently, there are more than 150 community members from all over the globe. Some of these communities endorse the organisation on their own Web sites. A municipality can join GCD by signing the Helsinki Declaration, and this is free of charge (the Declaration should be signed by the Mayor). Personal participation in the General Assembly Meeting is required, and concrete actions should be undertaken to realise an "Information Society for all", a crucial step for the competitiveness of cities and regions in the next decade.

The main focus of this organisation is to assist one another in developing ideas and structures for an improved Information Society. The GCD also helps to extend the networks of the associated members, done through semi-annual meetings held in various places. It also encourages local meetings within a country or continent. Topics of interest to GCD include, but are not limited to, the following:

- The development of e-Democracy at local level
- The use of ICT in the education field
- E-Security & risk management
- Promoting the access to Internet for all and reducing the digital divide
- E-Public Services
- Co-operation to be developed with the private sector
- Co-operation to be developed with other networks operating in the IT field
- Promoting the GCD-philosophy and favouring the participation of new member cities (dissemination)
- Improving the quality of the GCD Web site

GCD is very structured with a general assembly and a steering structure of committees. Member cities sitting on the steering structure will have to demonstrate a clear commitment to offer and implement specific actions that will help build the dialogue into a relevant and exciting enterprise. The main steering committee develops and adopts an Annual Action Plan, comprising individual initiatives and events, common specific tasks related to the most relevant issues and the information and communication strategy, with particular attention to the use of the Internet as a communication and participation tool.

MEASUREMENT AND EVALUATION OF MARKETING

The Intelligent Community Forum places a high value on community promotion, communication and marketing: "Intelligent Communities market themselves effectively, based on knowledge of the competitive offerings of other cities and regions, clear understanding of what leading-edge businesses require, and a determination to deliver it" (ICF, 2007). Both local and regional marketing are keys to the success of future-oriented communities. Locally, information campaigns are mounted to encourage effective use of broadband communications infrastructures and devices. Public relations efforts, advertising, conferences and progress reports make local citizens and businesses aware of the purposes and progress of community projects

Table 2. Measurement and evaluation of marketing

Indicators		Possible Approaches to Evaluation
Promotion	Local dissemination	Number of press releases and articles in media
		Online public advisories or broadcasts
		Public television broadcasts
		Information sessions or public meetings
	International dissemination	Conferences organised
		Positioning of portal on Internet
		International conference presentations
Relationships	Local exchanges	Boards with mixed compositions Volunteer work of salaried executives and professionals
	International exchanges	Twinning with cities of similar size and/or focus Membership in alliances Participating community in projects

and encourage them to contribute in some manner. Regionally, information is disseminated to attract investment and collaborative partners. Internationally, the exchange of information and expertise allows communities to articulate their best practices and benchmark their progress against other leaders.

Equally important is the tracking of key local and global relationships that the community is trying to maintain, establish or enhance. While it is relatively easy to identify and count these relationships, measurement of their effectiveness is difficult because many of the benefits are intangible. Table 2 outlines possible evaluation approaches to cover both transactional and relationship marketing efforts.

CONCLUSION

Many local communities promote themselves as part of their economic development programmes, which is the practise of transactional marketing. Fewer communities have made the transition to relationship marketing, which situates promotion as one of several ways of establishing and enhancing relationships with individuals, organisations and other communities. Relationship marketing is concerned about the entire community and its network of relationships. Local community success in the digital society depends upon the influences, initiatives and opportunities that are flowing through the worldwide communication networks. The local and global exchanges are complex, but much depends upon the trust and goals that the participants share. For these reasons, it is important that local leaders connect to such global networks as the Intelligent Community Forum (ICF), the Global Cities Dialogue (GCD), and the Education Development Center (EDC). These networks give local leaders exposure to best practise and an opportunity to connect with individuals who share their concerns. The world is composed of diverse local communities and can offer solutions for a particular community through replication, when the social economic and political contexts are similar, and through adaptation when the contexts are somewhat dissimilar. Close relationships are needed for one community to learn from another, hence the importance of practicing relationship marketing.

REFERENCES

Brenkert, G. (2002). Ethical challenges of social marketing. *Journal of Public Policy & Marketing, 21*(1), 14-25.

Archives of the ICF – The Intelligent Communities Forum. (2005). *Ichikawa, Japan – Nomination submitted for the Intelligent Community of the Year Award.* New York.

Archives of the ICF – The Intelligent Community Forum. (2006). *Ottawa, Canada – Nomination submitted for the Intelligent Community of the Year Award.* New York.

Centre for Children & Families. (2008). Retrieved June 12, 2008, from http://ccf.edc.org

Centre for Media & Community. (2008). Retrieved, June 12, 2008, from http://main.edc.org

Digital Divide Network. (2008). Retrieved June 11, 2008, from www.digitaldivide.net

Digital Harbour. (2007). Retrieved November 25, 2007, from www.digitalharbour.com.

Education Development Center. (2008). Retrieved June 12, 2008 from www.edc.org.

Egan, J. (2004). *Relationship marketing* (2nd ed.). Harlow, England: FT Prentice Hall.

GCD. (2007, April). *Global cities dialogue.* Retrieved November 15, 2007, from www.globalcitiesdialogue.org

Gummesson, E. (2002). *Total relationship marketing: Marketing management, relationship strategy and CRM approaches for the network economy* (2nd ed.). Amsterdam: Butterworth Heinemann.

Health and Human Development Programmes. (2008). Retrieved June 12, 2008, from http://main.edc.org/theme/health.asp

ICF. (2007, April). *Intelligent Community Forum.* Retrieved November 12, 2007, from the Intelligent Community Forum Web site: www.intelligentcommunity.org

McCarthy, E. (1978). *Basic marketing: A managerial approach* (6th ed.). Homewood IL: Richard D. Irwin.

Thomas, M. (2000). Princely thoughts on Machiavelli, marketing and management. *European Journal of Marketing, 34*(5/6), 524-537.

Chapter XI
Conclusion

COMMUNITIES OF THE NEW WORLD ORDER

A new set of conditions for healthy growth and adaptation is emerging for 21st century communities. This book has sought to explain what some of these conditions are, and to advise forward-thinking community leaders and stakeholders about how to take advantage of broadband bi-directional telecommunications to assure a better future for all.

The high-speed Internet has given individuals, institutions and businesses ways to more efficiently connect and collaborate with one another, locally and globally. With pervasive digital networks in place, the economics of access, innovation and distribution have undergone radical transformation. The costs continue to drop throughout the value chain of products and services.

The instruments of digital product, service and content creation that only a century ago were in the hands of governments, and only a decade ago were in the hands of big business, are now in the hands of local entrepreneurs and citizens as well. Anyone with a personal computer can now be a publisher, and anyone with an Internet connection can be a producer, marketer and distributor. Ordinary citizens who once thought of themselves only as consumers of other people's products can now create their own content and build applications that can be—and are being—sold and adopted globally as well as locally. The democratization of the tools of content and service production and the collaborative networks that make information exchange more efficient and productive allow for more prosperous communities.

The reality of the Network Society and its effects are rooted in the past. The vision of a New World Information and Communication Order (NWICO) was initially articulated in the United Nations in the 1980s. A similar vision again surfaced in the 1990s with the World Summit on the Information Society (WSIS) sponsored by the International Telecommunications Union. Perceiving that information services were a new and important form of trade that excluded them, less economically advanced nations wanted access to the technological infrastructure needed to assure their future participation. These international debates focused on policy and structural solutions for democratizing communication and correcting imbalances in information flow between and among countries.

In the first decade of the 21st century, variations on the New Order and the Information Society debates continue, but with a surprising new focus on policy and structural solutions for local communities. The emphasis has shifted from national and international players to local stakeholders and players. The strategies are those of self-help and collaborative partnerships that democratize down to the citizen level. With the advent of the broadband Internet, the Network Society has taken on a different materiality in that it has no physical boundaries and is global in scope, yet its management takes place at local and regional levels with a very different set of dynamics than was ever anticipated.

The authors admit that ubiquitous connectivity and local empowerment are not the reality of the first decade of the 21st century. However, the new digital infrastructure and the means to access are sufficiently widespread to act as a force for community-initiated change. Thus, wherever they exist, they provide a context for hope.

Since 2003, the Intelligent Community Forum (ICF) has helped community leaders and stakeholders to understand the promise of the Network Society. The ICF is a New York-based think tank focusing on job creation and economic development in what it calls "the broadband economy". In giving Intelligent Community of the Year awards to towns, cities and regions, the ICF has drawn international attention to the unprecedented confluence of technological, economic and social conditions that make it possible for communities to think collaboratively about repositioning themselves for a better future.

The authors, serving as advisors to the ICF and working in our own communities, have come to view "networked communities" as the front line of a global transformation that will shape the future of all humankind for decades to come. Towns, cities and regions are where people live and work, and reach out to the world.

Connected to the broadband Internet, they can locally and globally innovate and deliver goods and services on the digital highways. The networking of communities will ultimately affect the economy, politics and culture.

As scholars, we have shared our views of the Network Society and the best community practices from around the world in writing *Networked Communities: Strategies for Digital Collaboration.* Throughout the book, we present our insights on networked communities and the strategies that support successful digital collaboration. The sections that follow present a summary.

THE NETWORK SOCIETY

The Network Society involves a global transformation that creates an impact on local communities. In responding to the unprecedented opportunities for connectivity and collaboration, local communities become a potent force for societal change. As nodes on the global network, local stakeholders play role at both the local and global levels.

- The effects on communities of the rapidly changing global landscape of the digital era is a matter of urgent concern for local leaders and shareholders focused on empowering their citizens and institutions;
- With today's Internet, everyone is potentially connected to everyone else. The infrastructure for global connectivity now allows citizens and their communities to reap multiple social and economic benefits;
- Information and communications technologies and software have proven to be unparallel transformational tools in the hands of social entrepreneurs;
- Transforming communities are likely to thrive only when they adopt a stewardship approach in which the tools of digital creation exist to serve everybody;
- Effective change at the collective level requires everyone's consent and everyone's participation; and
- Respect for the goals, choices and freedom of expression of all individuals, groups and organisations can act as a lever that taps into the dynamism and creativity of the community as a whole.

TECHNOLOGY, COLLABORATION AND REGULATION

Communities with deep Internet penetration, user-friendly applications and ubiquitous use become possible when community leaders champion the principles and practices of open access.

- In the Network Society, the channels of inter-communication and exchange are the telecom networks, and the vehicles of greatest influence are the applications that these networks make possible;
- Acceptance and use tend to go up as the technologies of communication and influence become more accessible, capable and affordable;
- When the tools of digital collaboration are more widely available, citizens become more involved in decisions about how to best use local resources;
- Community leaders and stakeholders, working together to move in directions the community has itself defined, will energize the places where they live and work;
- Good public policy will spawn strategies for bringing all people online;
- Open access (sometimes called net neutrality) is related to the idea that access to broadband communications has become a basic right similar to clean air, pure water and nutritious food; and
- Leaders will want to lobby controlling authorities to ensure that regulations favour service and application initiatives that embody community ownership and control.

KNOWLEDGE WORKFORCE

While the digital networks are open to all, some segments of the population predominate. Referred to as knowledge workers, they are the key to the health and expansion of networked community.

- Managing community networks and their myriad applications requires a workforce with special training and skills;
- Knowledge workers are the people who can be expected to drive ICT use and digital creation because they are the principal keepers of the telecommunication networks and the innovators who use them;
- A local market for knowledge workers will often be developed through partnerships with local education and IT-using sectors;
- Community leaders will be expected devise long-range plans for meeting the ongoing demand for knowledge workers in an environment of competitive digital recruitment;
- Public and private sector leaders are encouraged to craft strategies for integrating digital learning into the full range of community activities to create a culture of use.

CREATING APPLICATIONS AND A CULTURE OF USE

Local communities can develop their economies by participating in the rapidly expanding Internet markets of products and services. The opportunities are numerous in both the private and public sectors, but they are realised only when and where local conditions are favorable.

- A timeframe of five to ten years is appropriate for realising the economic development opportunities inherent in the Network Society;
- Applications and services that emerge depend on multiple factors, such as good institutions, capital investment, public policy and regulation, infrastructure, knowledge and skills, and the creative talent of the local population;
- Applications being developed through partnerships with local and distant stakeholders include the areas of tele-work, tele-health, e-learning and e-government. E-commerce and related business applications can open unforeseen online opportunities for economic development;
- Involving users—both citizens and organisations—in planning and learning about technology adoption patterns ensures that local community needs and aspirations are addressed; and
- Leaders will need to assess the impact of created applications on the local telecom infrastructure and make plans for its modification.

INNOVATION: CREATING IDEAS

Innovation is the foundation for wealth creation. Innovation at the individual and collective levels can be fostered with a local environment of broadband technology and a culture of collaboration.

- Strong ties tend to exist between economic development, innovation and a local culture of computer and Internet use;
- Networked communities look to attract or grow their own innovative businesses to ensure long-term employment and a solid tax base;
- In some cases, entirely new businesses and markets are introduced thanks to the inventions and applications created by local users;
- Even though each community will express its creative potential in its own way, the creation of new content, services and products is more likely to flow from a supportive and collegial environment;
- Break-through innovations will be realised when the right environment is created for players to work together, online and off;

- Clustering is recommended as a way to gain strategic advantage for corporations and small businesses;
- Leaders should consider promoting multi-organisational, multi-sectoral networks, linking organisations in like-minded communities and regions; and
- The success of clusters will depend upon both technical (broadband technology) and social support (culture of collaboration) to nurture innovation and applications development.

STRATEGIES FOR COMMUNITY DEVELOPMENT

Local community development is an ongoing exercise in collaboration, one that is focused on a vision of what the town, city or region can become as an engaged member of the Network Society.

- Community development can take place via the broadband infrastructures that feed the development of a knowledge workforce, which in turn contributes to a rising level of innovation;
- To advance a networked community agenda, local leaders will need to have a good understanding of the current resources and deficiencies within the community (a community audit);
- Effective leaders will find ways to differentiate and focus on projects that have the best chances for success within the local environment;
- The success of any strategic planning process requires a common vision, a persuasive message to the community and a collaborative approach to problem solving;
- Community development requires close working relationships among local citizens, institutions and investors to create synergies;
- The community needs to be confident in its ability to compete on a larger scale and to take advantage of a few chosen opportunities;
- Participating members must understand their own strengths and limitations and be prepared to address weaknesses and leverage strengths in uncharted territory; and
- Stakeholders are challenged to accept change as a normal condition of life, transforming their communities through openness to ideas, searching for new solutions and learning from what they see happening both within the community and beyond it.

CITIZEN EMPOWERMENT AND PARTICIPATION

At the local level, quality of life depends in great measure upon the actions and contributions of many individuals. The broadband Internet can support these individuals by giving them tools to express themselves and allowing them to network with others locally and globally.

- User-generated traffic will double again and again as broadband bi-directional telecommunication becomes a basic community utility for homes, schools and businesses;
- The connective infrastructure of community networks, the democratization of the tools of production and access to the devices for open sharing of content are ideal conditions for accelerated digital innovation;
- Such innovations can create new marketplaces and open up the possibilities of virtual as well as location-specific employment;
- The challenge is to realise the vision of a global, decentralised, user-controlled and affordable infrastructure for content creation and sharing that is accessible to local people;
- There are still too many homes, schools, businesses and communities that do not have the equipment, the skills and the broadband connections that make it possible for the average citizen to be a full participant;
- The successful projects tend to be those that involve a variety of supporting organisations that have helped in identifying and implementing the local vision; and
- Decentralised approaches tend to offer a higher level of sustainability and synergistic activity because they allow for a greater number of community leaders and innovators to be involved.

LEADERSHIP AND RELATIONSHIP MARKETING

The transformation to a "networked community" binds and enables the local stakeholders and players. Attaining the benefits of joining the Network Society is the goal that drives them to take on leadership roles. Together with the help of digital networks and the applications they spawn, they shape their communities over time.

- Leadership can emerge from among elected officials, government employees, business executives, colleges and universities, nonprofit organisations or the interested citizenry;

- Charismatic leaders appear to be key at the formation stage of most digital networking initiatives;
- Once the network is operational, however, such projects will need transactional leaders with the ability to manage details and measure output;
- Effective leaders are those who can identify challenges and set priorities, use their influence to communicate a compelling vision and foster a sense of urgency;
- Among the more obvious ways to transform communities is to work collaboratively, promoting citizen empowerment and participation;
- Collaborative leadership is a management style that works well in situations where ownership must be taken within the community;
- Relationship marketing is an effective technique for building and enhancing partnerships with individuals and organisations, and with other communities;
- Local leaders should consider connecting to such global networks as the Intelligent Community Forum (ICF), the Global Cities Dialogue (GCD) and the Education Development Center (EDC);

MEASUREMENT AND EVALUATION

Transforming a town, city or region into a "networked community" requires attention to detail and the application of corrective measures in the many ongoing interventions and broadband projects. To effect the desired community change, digital vision and collaboration must be complemented by a system of measurement and evaluation.

- Effective leaders will incorporate measurement and evaluation into their change agendas;
- Projects in which the community invests should demonstrate sustainability over time;
- Measurement must be planned at the onset of each project, establishing a baseline from which future assessments can be carried out;
- Understanding outcomes is important for the long-term health and growth of any intervention in the community; and
- Benchmarking against networks in other communities can provide valuable information for local improvement.

The authors have sought to share their understanding of the nature of networked communities through a combination of stories, illustrations and literature review. It falls to local community leaders themselves to decide on the steps they must take to transform their local institutions into fully connected and active participants of the Network Society. We hope that this book will serve as a useful resource for thinking about managing change for the 21st century at the community level.

Glossary

Baseline: An established line from which to measure the next state. In change management, baseline is the marking of the significant points in a series of changes over time. Baseline is used in combination with benchmarking, where communities establish the current state in order to properly evaluate progress over time.

Benchmark: A standard used in measuring quality or value as a comparison against other communities. In organisational management, benchmark is a point of reference in evaluating best practise.

Broadband: The quantity and quality of information that can be exchanged over distance using one or more telecommunications channels. The International Telecommunications Union (ITU) sets the differentiation point between narrowband and digitally transmitted broadband data at speeds of 1.5 Mbps (mega bits per second) or greater.

Broadband Community: A community that uses computer processing and telecommunications connectivity to accelerate its economic and social development. Synonyms include intelligent, smart, wired, digital and networked communities.

Cable TV Network: The transport infrastructure of local community cable television systems. In broadband communities, cable TV networks will be upgraded from uni-directional to bi-directional delivery systems for voice and data communications, as well as video.

Change Management: A systematic effort to influence and shape the direction of change. In the context of networked communities, the change management framework consists of three inter-related components: the context (both local and global), the content (broadband applications, community objectives and programmes), and the process (acts of collaboration among individuals and organisations).

Chaos Theory: A construct from physics that portrays dynamic states in nature that are far from equilibrium. In organisational behaviour, the theory is sometimes used to describe complex systems that are observed to be unpredictable yet seem to follow an ordered pattern. Organised chaos (chaordic approach) is used in this book as a metaphor for depicting the rate of accelerating change and the response from networked communities.

Citizen Empowerment: Applications offered by the new digital networks that enable local citizens, including K-12 students, senior citizens, the disabled and the unemployed, to be more productively and creatively engaged in solutions to community problems.

Clusters: A number of similar things grouped together. In the business world, firms of similar intent group together to realise economies of scale or to gain a competitive or a comparative advantage over other firms or groups of firms. In networked community development, examples of clusters include sector-specific groups, but also multi-sectoral groups that include commercial firms, government agencies and academic institutions using telecommunications to support working together, sometimes on a global basis.

Collaboration: The pooling of resources (experience, expertise, money, labour) by two or more stakeholders or partners to solve a set of problems that neither can solve individually.

Collaborative Learning: The process by which information, knowledge and opinions are shared within a peer group. An example in community networks is the use of computer communications to promote collaborative learning among geographically dispersed individuals and organisations of common interest.

Communities of Practice: In networked communities, these are dispersed groups of people with a passion and proficiency for something who regularly interact to share experience and increase learning.

Core Competencies: Those talents and tasks for which individuals and groups are best suited. Within communities, core competencies can take the form of unique products and services of high quality, an enterprising culture or an attractive natural environment.

Culture of Innovation: A defining characteristic and mindset of communities that invest in education, research and development with the aim of framing their unique position within the Network Society.

Culture of Use: A defining characteristic and mindset in which citizens of all ages and status within communities have committed themselves to the mastery and application of information and communication technologies for their own and others' benefit.

Digital: A communications protocol in which information is transformed by computers into a near-universally adopted language. Communities, employing information and communication technologies (ICTs) for economic and social development, are often referred to as digitally networked communities.

Digital Culture: A society or group of societies embracing ICTs as the basis for information exchange.

Digital Economy: Those parts of the local and global economy that make use of information technology (IT) hardware, software, applications and digital telecommunications as the principal basis for transactions between business, government, non-profit organisations and individuals.

Economic Development: Steps taken by actors at all levels of a community or society to improve their economic well being and environmental health by investing capital, creating businesses and jobs, and working with others to grow the local tax base.

Economic Indicators: Business measures or statistics that provide a baseline from which communities can evaluate progress. Network community leaders use economic indicators as a basis for economic analysis and as a predictor of future performance.

Electronic Network: A system of interconnected electronic components or circuits over which digital information flows in the form of voice, video and data. An electronic network is often called a data network, the most common form of which is the public Internet.

Entrepreneurial Spirit: The willingness to take risks and invest in new business development, growth or innovation. Entrepreneurial spirit is often associated with the creation of new firms, but can also refer to the willingness to innovate in non-profit organisations.

Equal Access: A social justice issue having to do with opportunities to share and participate in the benefits of society. In networked communities, the phrase is often used interchangeably with "open access" and "net neutrality", meaning that all people should have equal access to the Internet.

Fiber Optic Network: A telecommunication transmission line consisting of highly transparent glass fibers capable of relaying vast quantities of information quickly in the form of encoded laser light pulses.

First and Last Mile: The last mile is a historic reference to the interconnections between the local telecom providers originating service and their target customers. The first mile is a symbolic reference to a change of circumstance in which consumers have become such active producers of content and information services that equal or greater network capacity is needed on the outbound path.

FLOSS: An acronym for Free/Libre/Open Source Software.

GIS/GPS: The acronyms for satellite-based geographic information systems and global positioning systems whose applications are widely used by communities for land use planning and management of transportation flows.

Governance: The process by which decisions are made and implemented, whether at corporate, national or local levels. In the context of community, "good governance" is characterised as participatory, consensus oriented, accountable, transparent, responsive, effective and efficient, equitable and inclusive, and following the rule of law.

Hard and Soft Skills: Hard skills refer primarily to such technical proficiencies as network systems management, computer programming and design of Web sites. Soft skills tend to be observational, intuitive and interpersonal in nature, and include a high level of verbal and written communication, artistic expression and persuasiveness.

Human Condition: Those elements that make individuals and their societies uniquely human—or work against their humanity. In networked societies, "the human condition" refers to the inevitable tension that exists between the current state of the community and what it would like to become, expressing the ongoing struggle between satisfying basic human needs and satisfying higher level human expectations and aspirations.

ICT: An acronym for information and communication technologies, which includes computer and telecommunications components, products and services that make up the building blocks of "electronic" and "digital" community networks.

Information: The raw data or facts on which knowledge is based.

Information Society: Individual communities or an aggregation of communities in which information development, storage, management and distribution are deemed a priority.

Information Workers: People who have the training and skills to carry out the social and economic work of information societies.

Innofusion: A hybridization of the words innovation and diffusion, used in organisational change as the process by which goods, services and guiding principles come into being and are diffused within an organisation or community.

Intelligent Community: Those communities that demonstrate a commitment to using computer processing and telecommunications connectivity to accelerate their economic and social development, sometimes called smart, wired, digital, broadband and networked communities.

Internet: A globally interconnected computer network that uses a common language or protocol (TCP/IP), sometimes called the World Wide Web, the Web or the IP-Net.

Internet Protocol: The TCP/IP standard for adding address information to the packets of data that travel over the Internet.

Key Concept: A theory, general principle or strategy of significance, in this case related to the design, implementation or evaluation of networked communities.

Kbps/Mbps/Gbps: Units of measurement for telecommunications signal speed or capacity. One kilobit/kilobyte per second represents one thousand bits/bytes; one megabit/megabyte per second represents one million bits/bytes; one gigabit/gigabyte per second represents one billion bits/bytes.

Knowledge: The shaping of raw data (information) into forms that are more usable and sharable in the process of learning about and gaining mastery over the natural and social environment.

Knowledge Economy: The creation of wealth based on the intelligent exploitation of information to increase the productive capacity of capital goods, labor and natural resource inputs. The knowledge economy is present in advanced stages of the information society, namely the Network Society.

Knowledge Management: The process of systematically and actively gathering, analysing, organising, managing, sharing and otherwise leveraging the stores of knowledge that might be of use within a community or enterprise.

Knowledge Workers: Employees and self-employed individuals who create and manipulate knowledge to help themselves and their organisations achieve goals. Knowledge workers are often using ICTs to create, process, manipulate, store, retrieve and distribute information.

Labour Markets: Pools of individuals seeking employment. In the case of networked communities, the key labour markets include those individuals who have the relevant skills that organisations need to be productive.

Learning Community: A community culture in which groups of people are engaged in ongoing self-education and provide mutual support for learning that improves performance. In learning communities, innovation occurs naturally, almost as a by-product of how conscientiously people attend to their work and society.

Long Tail: The many niches of old and new products, described by author Chris Anderson, that are being turned into mass markets of near limitless choice by people connected to the Internet.

Measurement Systems: A process for the systematic determination of merit, worth and significance of something or someone. In the context of communities, these processes are of value to measure steps taken toward a goal and to assess opportunities.

MPLS: Multiprotocol Label Switching is a technological innovation allowing Internet Service Providers to treat different kinds of data streams differently so as to give priority to certain information, diverting and routing traffic around link failures, congestion and bottlenecks.

Networked Community: The virtual and physical arrangements in which people live and work using computer processing and telecommunications (ICT) connectivity to improve the quality of their lives. Similar concepts include the "wired community", "broadband community", "smart community", "digital community" and "intelligent community".

Network-Connected Devices: A reference to the thousands of content originating or content receiving terminals used to interface with the Internet and its applications.

Network Society: A theoretical construct describing individuals, groups and organisations relying on information and communication technologies (ICTs) for exchanging such products and services of the knowledge economy as know-how, expertise and intellectual property. The Network Society is an advanced state of the information society.

Net Neutrality: A principle relating to the concept of "open access" stating that the broadband Internet should be implemented everywhere as a public utility, and that users should be in control of what content they view and what applications they use.

Open Source: This concept refers most commonly to the source code of digital software that has been made publicly available with little or no intellectual property restrictions.

Partner: A community partner is any person or organisation that makes a financial or in-kind contribution to the success of the community.

Process Re-Engineering: A management approach that seeks to restructure to improve efficiency and effectiveness. For communities, such an approach will require looking at operations from a "clean slate" perspective to determine how they might be improved.

Project Communities: Groups of people sharing a common interest in a project and who decide to collaborate in creating and developing it.

Relationship Marketing: A marketing framework, based on the quality of interaction and exchanges in networks of relationships, that encourages long-term relationships for the pursuit of common goals. Relationship marketing is contrasted with transaction marketing, which is based primarily on a sales relationship.

Reliability: Measuring something consistently. Reliability is usually contrasted with validity, which is concerned with the value or importance of what is being measured.

ROI/SROI: Return on investment refers to the financial gains resulting from an investment. Social return on investment is an attempt to measure the social as well as the financial value created by an investment.

Satellite Network: Space-based communications systems that provide global coverage for the two-way delivery of voice, video and data communications on land, sea and sky.

Silos: A term frequently used to describe organisations or business units that are incapable or unwilling to engage in collaboration or sharing with others.

Skills Supply Strategy: A formal plan to ensure that organisations or clusters of organisations within a community have an adequate supply of the right kinds of knowledge workers for the near and medium term.

SMEs: An acronym for small to medium size enterprises and businesses. The description of what constitutes a small business in terms of size fluctuates depending on the agency or country using the term.

Social Capital: That which promotes individual or collective action. In networked communities, social capital normally will originate within networks of relationships based on reciprocity, trust and commitment to the values of stewardship.

Social Development: Steps taken to improve the social well being and environmental quality of citizens within a community or region.

SOHO: An acronym for small office/home office, referring to the small enterprises that often emerge in family residential environments based on the availability of broadband Internet connectivity.

Stakeholder: A community stakeholder is defined as an individual, group or organisation that has a stake in the success and failure of community programmes and services.

Stewardship: A term frequently used in the context of communities in which personal responsibility and commitment of time and resources go beyond the contractual requirements of a job.

Strategy: A plan of action designed to achieve a particular goal.

Strategic Planning: A process to determine appropriate strategy. It includes an analysis of the internal and external environment of the firm, organisation, community or region as well as a determination of the alternatives and the actions needed to properly implement a plan.

Sustainability: A process or state that can be maintained at a certain level indefinitely. In the context of community sustainability, it is the process of learning, innovation and renewal embedded in the local culture that successfully accommodates a changing environment.

Synergy: When two or more actions create an effect greater than what is possible by individual actors or than predicted by knowing only the separate effects of the individual agents.

Tacit Knowledge: The difficult-to-access kinds of knowledge that people carry in their minds and hearts. Although difficult to access, tacit knowledge is needed to advance community development when a collaborative environment is created.

Transformational Leader: One of the roles of leadership is to raise others to higher levels of motivation, performance and morality. Transformational leaders in communities tend to be those capable of motivating staff, volunteers and investors to reach beyond expectations and sometimes go in entirely new directions.

Universal Technical Standards: In reference to telecom networks and devices, the goal of engineers is to create information processing and distribution formats that will facilitate adoption and diffusion among all users.

User-Centric: In reference to community networks, the emphasis on the convenience, specific needs and desires of the end users rather than of providers.

Virtual Community: A community of people who share common interests, pursue common goals, and work and learn collaboratively in an electronically facilitated environment.

Virtual Private Network: Using the public-switched Internet to exchange secure data between government, corporate, community and other local area networks, while giving direct and priority access to selected others without expecting them to bear all of the leased line and dial-in costs of remote access connectivity.

Wireless Network: Home, office or community networks, such as 4G cellular, Wi-Fi and WiMax, that provide on-demand access to the Internet, often at broadband speeds.

Wi-Fi Network: A limited range but high capacity wireless technology that allows users to transmit and receive voice, video and data over distances of a few hundred feet.

WiMax Network: A high-capacity wireless communication system offering voice, video and data connectivity over distances up to 30 miles for fixed stations and up to 10 miles for mobile applications.

About the Authors

Sylvie Albert, doctorate in business administration, certified economic developer and human resource manager, is assistant-professor of strategy in the Faculty of Management at Laurentian University since 2004, and president of the management consulting firm Planned Approach Inc. since 1997. This is her second book dealing with online communities. Dr. Albert is a researcher and evaluator for selection of the Top 7 International Intelligent Community Awards, a member of the Council of Ontario Universities, and a former director of two Ontario (Canada) provincial boards on community development dealing with telecommunication innovation. Dr. Albert has acted as project manager and advisor on many telecommunication networks across Canada and has been called upon to assist government in drawing policy and planning for regional telecommunication project development and evaluation. She was also a municipal director of economic development (1992-1997), and a human resource consultant (1986-1992).

Don M. Flournoy, PhD, is a professor of telecommunications in the School of Telecommunications, Ohio University, Athens. His research interests lie in the application of information and communication technologies (ICTs) to the solution of human problems. He is the author of seven books, including *The Broadband Millennium: Communication Technologies and Markets*, Chicago: International Engineering Consortium, 2004, and hundreds of scholarly articles and papers. From 1990-2007, Dr. Flournoy was director of the Ohio University Institute for Telecommunications Studies. He is the founding editor, *Online Journal of Space*

Communication (www.spacejournal.org), and serves as education VP on the board of the Society of Satellite Professionals International (www.sspi.org), the professional development association of the satellite and space industry. Prof. Flournoy holds an undergraduate degree from Southern Methodist University (1959), and graduate degrees from the University of London-UK (1961) and the University of Texas (1965). He was assistant dean, Case Institute of Technology, Cleveland (1965-1969); associate dean, State University of New York/Buffalo (1969-71); dean of the University College at Ohio University (1971-81).

Rolland LeBrasseur, PhD, is a professor of organizational behaviour and director of the School of Commerce & Administration in the Faculty of Management at Laurentian University. He has published extensively in academic journals on a range of management topics. Winner of several Canadian research awards in small business, he is a member of the editorial review board of the *Journal of Small Business & Entrepreneurship* and a judge for the selection of the top 7 for Intelligent Community Forum annual award. His current interests focus on the development taking place in small businesses, organizations, and communities.

Index